THE
ENGLISH HOUSE

THE
ENGLISH HOUSE

THE ENGLISH HOUSE

BY HERMANN MUTHESIUS

Edited with an introduction by Dennis Sharp

and a preface by Julius Posener

translated by Janet Seligman

RIZZOLI
NEW YORK

Published in the United States of America in 1979 by
Rizzoli International Publications, Inc.

First paperback edition published in the United States
of America in 1987 by
Rizzoli International Publications, Inc.
597 Fifth Avenue, New York, NY 10017

Library of Congress Cataloging-in-Publication Data

Muthesius, Hermann, 1861–1927.
  The English house.

  Translation of: Das englische Haus.
  Includes index.
  1. Architecture, Domestic—England.
2. Architecture, Modern—19th century—England.
3. Dwellings—England.   I. Sharp, Dennis.
II. Title.
NA7328.M8713   1987   728'.0942   86–31594
ISBN 0–8478–0826–2 (pbk.)

Das englische Haus was originally published by
Wasmuth, Berlin in 1904, 1905 (3 volumes).
Second edition, Berlin 1908–11 (3 volumes).
The English-language edition is a slightly abridged version of
the second edition consolidated into one volume.
It was created, designed and produced by
Lund Humphries Publishers Limited, London
for Crosby Lockwood Staples, 1979.
Paperback reissue published by
BSP Professional Books 1987

Printed in Great Britain by
Butler & Tanner Ltd, Frome and London

Contents

Preface

by Julius Posener

Das englische Haus was published in Berlin in 1904/05. Seventy-five years later, the book is published for the first time in England. This long delay is not due to the fact that Muthesius's subject, the English house between 1860 and 1900, had already been adequately covered by English writers. As a matter of fact, the period receives but scant attention in those books on English domestic building that do exist. This neglect has, in part, historical reasons. Richard Lethaby stated them as early as 1915, when he wrote:

'. . . about 1900, the German Government attached to its embassy in London an expert architect, Herr Muthesius, who was to become the historian – in the German language – of English free architecture. All architects, who about this time have built anything were studied, classified, registered and, I must say, understood. Then, just as our English building became real, or at least very, very nearly real, a pusillanimous reaction set in, and again the old styles emerged out of the catalogue of styles.'

This puts it in a nutshell: while English free architecture – or, as Lethaby more often calls it, building – was producing results, English critics did not very much care for it. And at the very moment somebody did care, someone from abroad, the cognoscenti dismissed this new architecture (or building), which was the architecture of Philip Webb, Norman Shaw, of Lethaby himself and of Voysey. Ten years later, Geoffrey Scott's book *The Architecture of Humanism* disposed of the remains. Country-houses were built in 'Bankers' Georgian', while Voysey, in protest, reverted to neo-Gothic. By 1930, the International Style reached England from the Continent; after World War II, the 'New Brutalism' emerged; but the efforts of two generations of English architects, to free building from Architecture (with a capital 'A'), had been almost forgotten.

These architects considered the plan of the house more than its elevations; they were concerned with aspect, circulation and above all with the distinctive shape and character of each single room, its position in the house, its relation to the garden. Yet none of these English architects, not even Lethaby, has given a concise analysis of this new English house, still less did they bother to trace its roots back into the history of mediaeval and Tudor building. Muthesius, coming from abroad, did just this. He, so to speak, discovered the English house. For him, and for Germany at that moment, the discovery was of vital importance.

It is true that the immediate effect of his book, though very strong, was short-lived. The war put an end to the country-house movement in Germany. But the functional – or organic – principle Muthesius's book embodies was taken up in the twenties by Hugo Häring and Hans Scharoun. Like Lethaby, they spoke of building, not of Architecture (with a capital 'A'). They called their programme the new way of building – '*Das neue Bauen*'. It is probably more than a coincidence that the English edition of *Das englische Haus* should appear in England at the same time as Peter Blundell Jones's book on Hans Scharoun. England is ready for both. Architects and lovers of architecture wish at last to close the gap in English architectural history, because the domestic architecture of the last third of the nineteenth century is once again coming to prominence. The Victorian Revival had not filled the gap. It was concerned with the vigorous, the picturesque, the quaint. It hardly considered the late Victorian house as an organism closely adapted to a way of life. This is Muthesius's subject. His book is a very thorough historical study, knowledgeable, careful, critical, detached. At the same time, however, it is a pamphlet; and every page of its three volumes is alive with a kind of pedagogic zeal. For both reasons, the book is immensely readable. I confess that quite often I revert to it, though I read it for the first time when I was twenty; and every time I read it, I feel informed, enlightened – and refreshed.

In condensing Muthesius's three volumes into one, the English editor had to make a difficult choice. Part of Muthesius's historical introduction had to be omitted, and those parts dealing with some of the more specialised aspects of the construction of the country-house had to be shortened. This, and other omissions, one may regret. Perhaps no contemporary reader would be found willing to plough through three solid volumes of a study covering only forty years, but in condensing Muthesius's extensive study, the editor has saved its substance. This substance, I am sure, will come to many an English reader as a surprise. Muthesius had discovered for his countrymen the great domestic architecture England produced before 1900. Now, at long last, it will be discovered for the people in England.

Foreword and Acknowledgments

by Dennis Sharp

A new formula for the re-publication of Muthesius's *Das englische Haus* had to be found, as the production of three separate volumes would have made the whole exercise unviable. The first English-language version, which comes out incidentally on the 75th anniversary of its original publication, has been under discussion for many years. In consultation with Professor Sir Nikolaus Pevsner and myself, the publishers agreed to its publication on the basis that it would be a single volume and the text shortened to make it a more manageable – and marketable – proposition. In agreeing to this conclusion and hoping that with the book produced as one volume it would meet a much wider public, I was, as editor, faced with the problem of what to leave out. Although Muthesius's original text is complex, well-linked and tight, there were two obvious areas for pruning. The two most drastic cuts to the original text were in those sequences where Muthesius was dealing with the history of the English house and its interiors. Muthesius's use of historical examples was of course interesting and pointed, but his general historical analysis is well known to anyone acquainted with the architectural literature on the English house, cf. Gotch and Brown, Eastlake, Statham, Fergusson, Rickman, Gwilt, Kerr and others. Clearly he drew on material from these and other sources, such as Robert Dohme's book *Das englische Haus* published in Berlin in 1889. What is interesting about his histories is his display of preferences. For example, he disliked the neo-Palladians because they were plagiarists who did not 'represent cultural achievements' but only provided imitations. Cultural achievement, for Muthesius, was the *sine qua non* of architecture which, in his words: 'comes through an independent artistic achievement'.

He greatly admired the work of Vanbrugh and Kent and the 'true Gothicism of Pugin'. (He shared the belief of Ruskin and Morris that 'salvation must come from the middle ages'.) The love of medievalism shown in the work of William Morris and in the writings of John Ruskin seems to Muthesius to preface the new free architecture of his champion Shaw and his followers. This admiration is clearly expressed in the sections retained for this new version of *Das englische Haus*. Where other omissions have been made it is to cut out a few superficialities and to tighten the meaning of the text itself. I trust that these cuts will not appear too drastic for those who have always wished Muthesius to be read in full, but history has indicated that if we wait for that opportunity, then time will take us and Muthesius over.

The books themselves have had a long and honourable publishing history in Germany. The first two volumes were published by Wasmuth, the Berlin architectural publisher later associated with Frank Lloyd Wright's *magnum opus*, in 1904 and the last volume in the trilogy issued in 1905, also by Wasmuth. A second edition, on which this single volume is based, was revised and brought up to date and published between 1908–11. Muthesius himself explains the reasons for this in his introduction to the second edition and also reproduces the original introduction, outlining the structure of the book. There is little point in repeating that information here. However for those readers who wish to refer to the earlier German books it is probably sufficient to record that the following sections from the original versions have been omitted, viz., pp. 11–94 and pp. 210–18 from Volume I; pp. 165–235 from Volume II and pp. 1–66 from Volume III.

All the illustrations have been retained that accompanied those parts of the original German text which are included in this English edition – photographs, drawings and plans. The plans have had their extremely detailed legends converted into English.

In laying out this new single-volume edition, the designer has attempted, as have the translator and editor, to respect the original, yet to give it a breath of new life. Julius Posener, who has graced this new edition with an elegant preface, has probably done more for Muthesius and his ideas than any other writer in the English language, yet his accounts have been limited. It would be most appropriate in this new edition also to acknowledge what he has done in Berlin in persuading the Akademie der Künste to create a full exhibition of Muthesius's work, and of course his own personal efforts in conserving many of Muthesius's villas in Berlin itself. He has kindly supported the whole formidable task of converting Muthesius into English, and although not party to any of the necessary editorial cuts, has given encouragement at all times to the making of this book.

I would also gratefully acknowledge the information, advice and help of Herr Eckart Muthesius, Hermann Muthesius's third son; Herr Wolfgang Muthesius; Dr Stefan Muthesius of the University of East Anglia; Herr Eckhard Siepmann of the Werkbund Archive, Berlin; Dr Hans-J. Hubrich, Münster-Wolbeck, who has recently completed a thesis on Muthesius; Dr Friedenthal, London; Mrs W. Dernbach, London and various English friends and colleagues who have specialised over the years in the history of the Arts and Crafts movement, the Werkbund, and what is still loosely called the architecture of the English free school. I am greatly indebted to Mr John Taylor and Miss Charlotte Burri of Lund Humphries Publishers Ltd for the great care they have taken over the whole production of this book, for their patience and fastidious attention to detail, and of course to Professor Sir Nikolaus Pevsner, for his initial and continuing encouragement of the idea to have the work published in English.

Dennis Sharp
Epping Green, Hertford
January 1979

Preface to the Paperback Edition

by Dennis Sharp

Nearly a decade has elapsed since the first English edition of Muthesius's famous three-part work *Das englische Haus*. It was welcomed at the time like a long awaited relative who had not exactly got lost, but whose renewed presence brought assurance and inspiration. Indeed, the book, in its English form, obviously brought profound enjoyment to many readers. 'Muthesius' was always spoken of as if an English translation had always existed. Of course it had not, although it is surprising how many people possess a translated version of various parts of the text. A paperback version of this important work is now welcome because it will, hopefully, open up a whole new and much younger readership.

Although there were many difficulties in attempting to get the book published in the first place I am very pleased to record that the publisher's judgement in attempting an English language version has been wholly justified. The sumptuous first edition has now sold out and this original version won for Janet Seligman the Schlegel-Tieck Prize for the translation from German into English. While I would like to have seen some of the edited parts of the original work put back into this edition, this has not proved viable from a publishing point of view so, for the time being at least, English readers will have to accept this shortened version of the original three-volume edition.

The new paperback follows the same form as the original which has been wonderfully rendered into an English that reflects the precision, enthusiasm and conciseness of Hermann Muthesius's original German text yet resonates with its proud, grand and eloquent Edwardian phrases.

In all of this it should be remembered that Hermann Muthesius was the transmitter of the English tradition, particularly that of the English Arts and Crafts movement, to Germany and *not* the reverse. A good many years later this influence, and the profound regard that it generated for the English tradition in design, were in fact put into effect. It is probably worth remembering that in the same year that the first volume of *Das englische Haus* appeared in Berlin, Muthesius had been appointed to an important post in the Prussian Ministry of Education. It was a position, as Pevsner has pointed out, in which he was instrumental in securing the appointment of Peter Behrens at the Düsseldorf Academy, Hans Poelzig at the Breslau Academy and possibly Bruno Paul at the School of Applied Arts in Berlin. Before the second and third volumes of the book appeared Muthesius had also resumed his architectural practice, designing English style villas and interiors for wealthy and fashionable clients in the suburbs of Berlin. This absorption with Anglo-Germanic connections, therefore, can be seen as a cornerstone in the new practical and political debate encouraged by Muthesius on artistic reform. In 1907, the year in which he was also instrumental in the inauguration of the *Werkbund*, he was appointed to a newly created chair in applied art at the Handelshochschule, Berlin, where his inaugural address proved so controversial that it led to his opponents appealing to the Kaiser for his immediate dismissal. It was a move that played into

Muthesius's hand, to such an extent that it eventually helped to bring about the multi-discipline nature of the *Werkbund*, an acceptance of a programme of progressive ideas and industrial and commercial reforms which was clearly based on a desire for the kind of 'good designs' that he had observed in Britain over many years. In a sense one can see the formation of the *Werkbund* as a natural outcome of the educational, social and technical reforms that had occurred in Britain in the 1890s.

Dennis Sharp
Epping Green, Hertford
February 1987

Introduction

by Dennis Sharp

'The house is a mirror of the personal culture of those who live in it.'
Hermann Muthesius, in *Das Jahr 1913*.

'The genuinely and decisively valuable feature of the English house', Hermann Muthesius states in the third part of *Das englische Haus*, 'is its absolute practicality.' In his view this reflected 'the unassuming naturalness' of the English character which he so admired. The practicality of architectural ideas as well as the characteristics, fads, foibles, manners and modes of the English in their 'castles' (whether town or rural ones) are the main themes running through Muthesius's study of the English house. He displays in his book a genuine love for the English people and their houses. As in all well-run affairs his regard for the English allowed him to praise that which he admired, and to criticize, unmercifully at times, those features that appeared to be both out of keeping with progress and culturally insensitive or even negative in housing. On the one hand he praised the innovative work carried out by the 'progressive' architects of the day but on the other hand ridiculed the buffoonery and 'uncharacteristic idiocy' of English housing speculators, describing those who laid out many of the inner parts of the large cities as possessing the lowest order of intelligence. He was also shocked at the lack of artistic appreciation to be found among the general public.

Muthesius admired the habits of the middle classes and applauded the combination of town and country living. The weekend in the country he saw as the ideal way of spending leisure time and commended it as an 'economic' activity. It provided, he maintained, a sharp contrast to the habits of continental city dwellers who found in the city – with its dinner parties, 'at homes', theatres and races, etc. – an adequate expression of life. The English had wider horizons. The hunting, shooting, fishing and 'outdoor' activities of the English middle class would appear, in Muthesius's estimation, to be an ideal way of life. He also observes that, on the whole, English country-houses are of more importance architecturally than the town houses, although he has little sympathy with 'the dreariness of the English suburbs'.

At the turn of the century interest in English cultural achievements reached a high peak; it originated with the Crown Princess Victoria, the daughter of the Queen. It was the princess who introduced special bathrooms into the Berlin palace. Of particular interest to the Germans were aspects of British '*Wohnkultur*', technical and industrial developments, fashion and the aesthetics and writings of Carlyle, Morris and Ruskin (Hermann Muthesius devoted a magazine article (see Bibliography) to a discussion of Ruskin in German). *The Studio* magazine was widely read and some German art journals copied its format. According to Friedenthal even the Emperor William II who was not noted for progressive views in matters of taste or choice of architects 'was not unaffected by this [English] trend'. Indeed, he goes on, 'Muthesius was one of the few modern architects who enjoyed his favour to some degree'. Friedenthal continued: 'It should not be overlooked that at the beginning of the century there was even politically an – unfortunately not lasting – movement of closer relations to Great Britain'.[1]

Muthesius's own interest in English things continued up to the time of his death

[1] In a letter to the writer, January 1979.

in a tram accident in 1927, although his later architectural work is by no means so overtly influenced as his earlier villas set in their 'garden estates'.

The English Garden City Association was of particular interest to German architects and planners after its foundation by Ebenezer Howard and his colleagues in 1899 as was the growth and development of Letchworth Garden City (founded 1903) as an exemplar of this approach. Walter Crane, a friend of Muthesius's during his London years, was closely connected with the Association. The reciprocation of ideas between the German and English Garden City fathers was of great significance to the Garden City movement: the English pioneers admired the Prussian Government's efforts in acquiring land for 'growth and expansion, and housing reform'; the Germans, according to Bernhart Kampffmeyer, Secretary of the German Garden City Association, writing in the British *Garden City* journal in 1905 considered 'the Garden City movement as something real and important'.[2]

Earlier, in 1889 Robert Dohme had published his book *Das englische Haus*, thus establishing – in historical terms at least – a special interest in the aesthetics of English domestic architecture and its social context. Muthesius was to further this interest, using the same title for his own monumental study. His *Das englische Haus* is without doubt the most important contemporary survey of domestic architecture available. In it Muthesius clarifies the aspirations and practical and theoretical ideas of the architects and designers of the period between 1870–1903 with remarkable perception. He sets the work of the innovators of domestic architecture in Britain (it covers far more than the merely 'English' scene) into an historical context and delineates the fresh currents of influence at work at the time as well as the old streams of tradition and eclecticism. He was a thoroughly 'modern' man looking forward constantly in the light of present references yet consciously glancing backwards to validate the pedigree of an idea or a particular precedent. The book is objective in its appraisal of the observable new trends and forcibly polemical too through the author's insistence on an architecture appropriate to its age and culture.

Throughout his book one can sense Muthesius's rational mind at work. He relentlessly pursued a search for ideal housing 'types' and meticulously endeavoured to record and classify his examples into a Linnaean-like system. Few commentators at the time had Muthesius's flair for accurate observation and clear reasoning; few, I imagine, travelled as far as he did over a short period of time to experience, photograph and catalogue examples of so many houses. The problems facing such a commentator in classifying trends and styles were extremely difficult. Hardly anyone in Britain knew what to make of the general confusion that existed in the British architectural scene at the turn of the century. J. M. Brydon, writing in the *Architectural Association Notes* for January 1901 suggests something of the confusion prevalent at the time: the 'feature of the [nineteenth] century', he wrote, 'has been the eclecticism of many of the architects. Not only has a man worked in several styles – sometimes simultaneously – but he has done so in different phases of the same style, ringing the changes, as it were, in the search after novelty. This has become so marked towards the close of the century that we find hardly two men working in the same phase of any one style . . .'

[2] A note on p. 24 in *The Garden City*, Vol. 1, No. 2, Feb. 1905.

However, Brydon (himself a popular and perceptive architectural critic at the time) located the 'one great achievement of the nineteenth century' in the 'artistic regeneration of the English home'. He wrote: 'If there is any one thing in which English architects of the latter half of the nineteenth century excelled it is in their domestic work. The advance has been enormous, and progressive in the highest sense. There are no more beautiful . . . comfortable and well planned modern homes in the world, than are to be found in this England of ours, and none so characteristic of the country in which they are built – an artistic result . . . which we owe, in the main, to the genius and influence of Mr Norman Shaw.'[3] Although these words were written a few years before the publication of *Das englische Haus* Muthesius clearly concurred. His hero architect was Shaw, his theoreticians Morris, Ruskin and Lethaby and the prize to the most promising young star on the horizon was awarded to his close friend Charles Rennie Mackintosh.[4] But not all British architects saw the regenerative aspects of domestic architecture in the same light. Halsey Ricardo, reviewing Muthesius's earlier book on English contemporary architecture (*Die englische Baukunst der Gegenwart* 1900) in the *Architectural Review* in 1901 wrote: 'Mr Muthesius congratulates us on our national architecture. He takes the house as the most essential sign of the times. We would prefer to be judged by our schools, hospitals, asylums and public buildings.'[5] Ricardo of course probably misunderstood Muthesius's mission. He was not a casual scholar engaged on summarising architectural developments in England for the delectation of practising architects but a diplomat reporting on many aspects of technical endeavour in Britain for the Prussian Board of Trade and an architect who wished to learn from the English. What he saw and admired became ingrained in his consciousness and seriously affected his roles as architect, educational advisor and pioneer of a modern attitude to architecture after his mission was completed and his sojourn in London was over. While this may all sound rather dramatic I would hasten to add that there appears to be little truth in the often quoted assertion that Hermann Muthesius was merely some sort of 'cultural spy'. His appointment to the German Embassy in London began in October 1896 and ended in 1903. Initially he was appointed technical attaché to the Ambassador but combined this role later with that of cultural attaché.[6] His research work for the Embassy included preparing reports about railways, gasworks and other industrial installations. However, his real passion was for the English house as the main content of a letter written from London in 1897 to the Grand Duke Carl Alexander of Saxe-Weimar indicates:

'. . . I am hoping in the near future to find time for a project that is dear to my heart, namely, a thorough investigation and exposition of the English House. Literature on this topic offers little; the only German contribution being a short article by Dohme which deserves to be fully expanded into a wide-ranging and expert study. There is nothing as unique and outstanding in English architecture as the development of the house. In England, the house has already been subject to much attention. Indeed, no nation is more committed to its development, because no nation has identified itself more with the house.' On 19 April the Grand Duke replied giving his enthusiastic support to the research which was eventually to form the basis of *Das englische Haus*:

' I hope with all my heart that you may soon succeed in fulfilling your project. Such a publication would be of great value, especially here in Germany. Because of history, the notion of homeliness and home comforts is less developed here, in our less fortunate Fatherland, than in England.'[7]

Muthesius's training as an architect, writer and editor provided him with the

[3] J. M. Brydon, *AA Notes*, Vol. XVI., No. 167 1901 in an article entitled 'The Nineteenth Century', pp. 1–5.
[4] Muthesius wrote extensively on Mackintosh and the 'Glasgow Four' in German journals (see select bibliography). He also provided the introduction to the volume of *Meister der Innenkunst*, Darmstadt, 1903 devoted to Mackintosh's 'Das Haus eines Kunstfreundes'.
[5] Halsey Ricardo in *The Architectural Review*, Vol. 9, 1901, p. 143.
[6] The role of 'technischer attaché' was instituted by the Prussian government in 1882. The duties and scope of the new appointment were outlined in the *Zentralblatt der Bauverwaltung* in 1882 and 1884. When Muthesius came to London the post of cultural attaché did not exist in the German Embassy.
[7] The original letters are now in the Werkbund Archive, Berlin.

necessary background to carry out his ambitious programme of research and writing.

In 1900 he summarised his work load, which mentioned the books either published, or proposed, on new Protestant churches, the title on English contemporary architecture referred to earlier, the teaching of art in London schools, and Arts and Crafts 'Dilettantismus' in England.[8]

At the same time he mentioned his background: he was born in Gross-Neuhausen in Thuringia on 20 April 1861, the son of a master mason. During his preliminary education at the village school his talents were noticed by a local pastor who sent him to high school in Weimar and recommended him for higher education to the Grand Duke of Saxe-Weimar. Between elementary school and high school he learned masonry for two and a half years under his father. From 1881–3 he studied philosophy at the King Friedrich-Wilhelms University, commencing his architectural studies in the latter year at the famous Technical High School, Berlin-Charlottenberg. During this period he also worked with the architect Paul Wallot – the 'Reichstag' architect – in Berlin. From 1887–91 he went to Tokyo, working as an architect for the German firm of Ende & Böckmann; he built an Evangelical church for the German community there. He returned to Germany via China, Thailand, India and Egypt in April 1891 to work in public architecture. In 1893–4 he was employed in the architectural offices of the Prussian government and then became editor of the *Zentralblatt der Bauverwaltung*. This was followed by a study tour of Italy (1895–6). On his return to Berlin he married Anna Trippenbach; in the autumn of that year Muthesius and his new wife moved to London.

Muthesius was in many ways an extraordinary man; from family accounts he is remembered as conscientious and hardworking, outspoken yet modest, somewhat shy and retiring. He was by no means the line-toeing patriot nor the conventional diplomat that some reports from people – who either did not know him or disagreed with his ideas – have intimated. During his period in London, when he enjoyed the privileges of high office in the diplomatic service, he chose to live among his artist and architect friends in 'The Priory', Hammersmith, and not in a district of London reserved for government officials. His many friends included Walter Crane, the McNairs, Charles and Margaret Mackintosh and the Newberys from Glasgow who later became the godparents of his third son Eckart. Eckart recalls that his mother Anna's role in his father's life was of the utmost importance: originally a professional singer she gave up her career after marriage and devoted her time outside the family to painting and the arts and crafts. Hermann Muthesius consulted her, it is said by Eckart, on matters relating to the decorative arts. Her close friends Margaret Mackintosh and Jessie Newbery influenced the writing of her own book *Das Eigenkleid der Frau* (published in Krefeld in 1903) whose cover was designed by Frances McNair, the sister of Margaret Mackintosh. Frances McNair probably designed the title piece for the covers of the second edition of *Das englische Haus*[9] (which incidentally has been retained for the binding and jacket of this edition).

On his return to Berlin, Muthesius's first project of 1904 was the design of a house for Hermann von Seefeld, his former employer at the Ministry, in the Berlin suburb of Zehlendorf. It was a first attempt, although perhaps not a very

[8] For fuller biographical details see the Akademie der Künste's catalogue *Hermann Muthesius, 1861–1927*, Berlin, 1977, pp. 52–3.
[9] Information kindly supplied by Herr Eckart Muthesius, Berlin.

brilliant one, to combine German and English ideas in the planning and elevational treatment of a 'villa'. The plan, with its Voyseyesque bays and special rooms, as well as the smooth clay-tile finish roofs, indicate a type of architecture that was later – and not always kindly – referred to as Muthesius's '*Englischer Landhausstil*'. However, he was not fanatical over mere 'Englishness' in design, and a house for E. Bernhard, built in Berlin-Grunewald in the same year, has much closer affinities to Olbrich and the Viennese Secession than to the English free movement. Such a contrast is well worth mentioning at this point, as Muthesius understood well the currents of continental *Art Nouveau* and the work of the Secessionists and the *Jugendstil*. He wrote extensively, for example, on the Paris Exposition of 1900 for the *Zentralblatt der Bauverwaltung*. However, if he sought for correspondences to these ideas in Britain, he makes little of them in *Das englische Haus*. He saw his Glasgow friends as having a marginal contact with the main continental trends and indeed seems to imply that the British contribution provided a much firmer base for a genuine modern attitude to architecture than the continental developments. Muthesius's own aims were to build up, together with his many colleagues and friends, cultural enlightenment and awareness in Germany. He was personally interested in literature, theatre and fashion, the press and art education in order to modernise them and direct them towards what we would now describe as the Modern Movement (a term not unfamiliar to Muthesius in the early years of the century). This movement had as its centre after 1907 the German Werkbund which successfully brought together architects, artists, craftsmen, industrialists and manufacturers. This 'craft association' set out to 'ennoble industrial labour through the cooperation of art, industry and handicraft, by means of education, propaganda and united action on relevant questions'. Its main concern was with the establishment of design standards, '*gute Form*', the revival of craftsmanship, in the William Morris sense, and the destruction of outmoded design styles.

Muthesius's position as one of the main leaders of this reforming movement is undisputed. At the time, however, he did not receive the credit that was due to him for his zealous efforts to change and modernise German artistic values. He met opposition from many quarters. Indeed he was so strongly cricitised in 1907, when the question of 'Der Fall Muthesius' was hotly debated in Berlin, that he did not attend the inaugural meeting of the Werkbund later that year in Munich; his paper setting out his position was read by his friend Fritz Schumacher. But such bad feelings were soon overtaken by events and Muthesius's importance to modern developments in Germany were recognised as was the gift he had in attracting the goodwill of officials and institutions. By 1911, when he gave the main address to the Werkbund Congress 'Wo stehen Wir?'[10], his position as the leader of modern ideas was clinched. In 1914 he was battling, at the Cologne Werkbund Exhibition of that year, on the more detailed aspects of his philosophy, with Henri van der Velde.[11] In approximately a decade he had graduated from being the commentator on and analyst of the burgeoning modernism to champion of the cause.

[10] For a full text see *Jahrbuch des Deutschen Werkbundes*, Jena 1912
[11] For a detailed study of the foundation and growth of the Werkbund see Eckstein, H. (Ed.) *50 Jahre Deutscher Werkbund*, Frankfurt am Main and Berlin, 1958. For a summary of this, and other information in English see Taylor, G. *The Arts and Crafts Movement*, London 1971 pp. 184–90 and Banham, R. *Theory and Design in the First Machine Age*, London, 1960, pp. 68–78.

Contemporary photographs of Hermann Muthesius
and his wife Anna

Photographs on pp. xviii and xix © Eckart Muthesius

Hermann and Anna Muthesius taking tea at
'The Priory', Hammersmith 1896

Select Bibliography

Hermann Muthesius's output as a writer was enormous and a virtually complete bibliography is given in the catalogue prepared for the exhibition on his work held in Berlin at the Akademie der Künste during December 1977–January 1978: *Hermann Muthesius 1861–1927*, pp. 141–6. A list of references to Muthesius and his work by other writers is also included in the catalogue on pp. 138–9.

References to Muthesius in English are rare or, as in more recent books mainly parenthetical, with the exception of references in Nikolaus Pevsner's *Pioneers of Modern Design* (Harmondsworth, 1949), Reyner Banham's *Theory and Design in the First Machine Age*, (London 1960) and the essays of Julius Posener on 'Hermann Muthesius' in the *Architect's Year Book 10*, (London 1962) and in *From Schinkel to the Bauhaus* (London 1972).

The purpose of this selected bibliography is simply to isolate the titles of those books and magazine articles which directly relate to Muthesius's period and his interest in housing in Britain: the abbreviation ZB refers to the *Zentralblatt der Bauverwaltung* in which most of his articles on English architecture, art, design and education were published.

1894 'Das "Imperial Institute" in London'. In: ZB, XIV.

1895 'Das Volkshaus in Bishopsgate in London'. In: ZB XV

1897 'William Morris und die fünfte Ausstellung des Kunstgewerbe-Austellungs-Vereins in London'. In: ZB XVII
   'Die Ausbildung des englischen Architekten'. In: ZB XVII

1898 'The Architectural Review for the Artist and Craftsman'. In: ZB XVIII
   'Das Gerichtsgebäude in Birmingham und die neuere Terracotta-Bauweise in England'. In: ZB XVIII
   Die neuzeitliche Ziegelbauweise in England. In: ZB XVIII

1899 'Das Fabrikdorf Port Sunlight in England'. In: ZB XIX
   (Note: a further article published in the same year appeared in *Dekorative Kunst* on the workers' houses at Port Sunlight, II, 1899. p. 43f.)

1900 Three articles appeared in *Dekorative Kunst* III, 1900 on British architects by Muthesius: M. H. Baillie Scott, George Walton and Ernest Newton.
   Der kunstgewerbliche Dilettantismus in England . . ., Berlin 1900
   Die englische Baukunst der Gegenwart, Beispiele neuer englischer Profanbauten, Leipzig and Berlin.

1901 'Ruskin in deutscher Übersetzung'. In: ZB XXI
   'Die Arbeiterwohnungs-Politik des Londoner Grafschaftsrathes'. In: ZB XXI

1902 'Die Glasgower Kunstbewegung. Charles Rennie Mackintosh und Margaret Macdonald-Mackintosh'. In: *Dekorative Kunst* V
   Stilarchitektur und Baukunst, Mülheim/Ruhr

1903   'Kunst and Leben in England'. In: *Zeitschrift für bildende Kunst*, XIV. An important article which discusses at length the work of British architects, painters and sculptors.
        'Das englische Haus und die nationale Bedeutung des Einzelhauses'. In: *Deutsche Monatsschrift für das gesamte Leben der Gegenwart* III

1904   *Das englische Haus*, Berlin. Volumes 1 (2nd edition 1908) and 2 (2nd edition 1910)
        Das Moderne Landhaus und seine innere Ausstattung, Munich (Foreword by H.M.; 2nd edition 1905)

1905   'Das englische Haus der Gegenwart'. In: *Die Baumeister* III
        Das englische Haus, Berlin. Volume 3 (2nd edition 1911)

        [DS]

Part I: Development

Preface to the first edition

Credit for having been the first observer in Germany to draw attention to the cultural importance of the English house must go to R. Dohme. Dohme's treatment in his excellent little book, *Das englische Haus* (Brunswick 1888), although aphoristic and rather untechnical, provides a clear picture and an acute characterisation of the nature of the English house. Among English books, that of Robert Kerr, *The English gentleman's house* (1861) at least gives an exhaustive account of what English opinion of the 1860s expected of the large country-house. But quite apart from their piecemeal treatment of the material, both books are already out of date, since their authors had not witnessed the enormous increase in house-building in England during the past ten or twenty years. Nor has there been a new book on the subject in England. It is true that a mass of illustrative material in English periodicals dealing with English domestic architecture has reached Germany recently, but since it is scattered and lacks explanatory text, the non-English reader can gain no idea of the subject. Furthermore the illustrations have usually been reproduced from drawings instead of from photographs, which alone provide a true picture. My longer book, *Die englische Baukunst der Gegenwart* (Leipzig and Berlin 1902), of course, contained many large illustrations of houses from photographs taken specially, but they only appeared with other, mainly public, buildings to form a survey of English architecture as a whole.

The idea of writing a book on the English house thrust itself upon me almost from the moment when I began my tour of duty at the Germany Embassy in London seven years ago. It has only been the magnitude of the undertaking that has delayed by years the conclusion of the work I began at that time. My original intention was to deal only with the modern house, that is to say, the type that has developed since about 1860. But because the modern house has simply reverted to historical traditions, without a knowledge of which it would be unintelligible, it became necessary to summarise its whole historical development. Besides, the history of the house is also the history of a culture, and the modern English house engages our attention largely because of the high level of culture it expresses. But only in history can we trace the steps by which the domestic culture that is so highly evolved today has developed.

This has meant that instead of the two parts originally planned, the material has had to be divided into three, the first dealing with the development of the house, the second with the conditions governing it, its planning and building, the third with its interior.

Volume 1 contains the actual historical section*, which occupies the first half of the volume, in condensed form. But it seemed desirable to describe the development of the present-day form of the English house that began around 1860 in greater detail, not only because it proves to be one of the most pleasing manifestations of contemporary culture but also because its successive phases permit us to draw many parallels with the movement now beginning on the continent; indeed, it more or less points the way to this movement.

The first main section of Volume 2 contains an account of the geographical, social and all the other conditions governing the English house that are rooted in the life-style of its occupants, and thus seeks to illuminate the connection – so often overlooked – between form and character; I also discuss the extremely important laws of land-tenure and the building laws. A second main section contains a detailed consideration of the layout and all the individual rooms of the larger country-house and its outbuildings as the most highly evolved form of the English house. Similar consideration is given to the small country-house; special chapters are devoted to the town and the suburban house. A long chapter describes the garden, which is so extraordinarily important and highly developed in England, together with all its associated terraces, summer-houses, gateways and ornamental beds.* The third main section of the volume deals with the building of the house in both the constructional and aesthetic sense and discusses technical and sanitary arrangements.*

Volume 3 is entirely devoted to interiors. It contains a historical section† dealing with rooms and furniture from Elizabethan times to the present day, but the main section is devoted to contemporary interiors. Walls, ceilings, floors, windows and doors, fire-places (a detailed section), also furnishing fabrics, wallpapers and modern furniture are all discussed fully; the final section includes a discussion of the special fixtures and furniture of the individual rooms of the English house.

Each of the three volumes contains a wealth of illustrative material specially commissioned for the book; there was in fact so much that I had to select the best and most typical. Despite the number of illustrations, the book is not intended to be a picture-book like the pattern-books that currently dominate the book-trade or the series in which, according to one publisher, the text only exists to facilitate the making-up of the plates. The immensely greater ease with which illustrations can now be produced brings its own hazards as does the projector at lectures: it may lure one into superficiality. Before all else this book is intended to be read.

Today especially, when so many people are beginning to feel the need to retreat from the ever-increasing turmoil of life into the quiet of a home of their own, the conditions of English domestic life become more interesting than ever. Englishmen have a vision of the peacefulness of life, they live as their natural philosophy dictates, governed by no minor considerations, restricted by no social trammels. The Englishman lives only as he does because he believes that it is for the good of his inner self and of his family that he shall make the most of his life and develop his

---

* Much of this section has been omitted from this new edition both for the sake of economy and because Muthesius's record of English architectural history can be found in the writings of his British contemporaries, e.g. Fergusson, Statham, Rickman and the various authors of specialised studies on the English house mentioned in the text. [DS]

* See my introduction for other small omissions. [DS]
† This historical section has also been omitted. [DS]

individuality. If we are to give an illuminating account of conditions in England we must widen our scope beyond a bare description of the house; we must describe the conditions that govern it, i.e. English domestic life, its *mores* and, indeed, the Englishman's whole philosophy of life. This means discussing everything from the English attitude towards nature down to table-manners.

The proverbial German hankering after things foreign has today in the case of England generated a reaction which, however welcome it may be from the point of view of national self-awareness, is once again beginning to blunt our perception of what is really good there so that we are failing to make good use of it. For some years now German opinion of England has lurched back and forth between over-estimation and its opposite. Similar vacillations occur in our appraisal of English art. Soon after the new movement in art which originated in England had focussed the attention of the whole world on that country, word went round that England had been overtaken by the new continental movement: a rash judgment that must astonish all who know the circumstances. As though our artistic development were a matter of rivalry and sensation-seeking stunts! For the past forty years events in England have been quietly pursuing their course and continue to do so without quickening their pace. The reflection of this silent development is to be found in the English house. A sound and unostentatious but finely developed taste is so firmly rooted therein that it has now produced an up-to-date national art – a cultural achievement for which England is certainly to be envied. Admittedly there are no startling exhibition-pieces and there is, thank heaven, no trace of *art nouveau*. Everything breathes simplicity, homeliness and rural freshness, occasionally, indeed, verging on the vernacular. But a fresh breath of naturalness wafts through the house and a sound down-to-earth quality is combined with a sure feeling for suitability. What we principally find here is a practical, indigenous and pre-eminently friendly house; and instead of a sham modernity expressing itself extravagantly in whimsical artificiality we find purely functional, unaffected design that many may already regard as more modern than all the fantastic excesses of a so-called modern style.

However, to avoid misunderstandings, let it be said at the outset that the type of house that is considered here is still not entirely general, even in England. England has its full quota of tasteless speculative housing, in the cities whole acres are covered with wretched, absolutely uniform small houses and the urban terrace-houses of the well-to-do often hide behind trivial façades designed without understanding. Indeed, even in the interiors of houses there are still tasteless elements in England as elsewhere. However, it has not been my concern to discover the bad examples but to present the good features of English housing in the proper light. My remarks therefore cover such houses as are valuable as models, having been built by artists for highly cultivated clients. Though they may appear superfluous in themselves, these explanations have been necessitated mainly by the failure to understand on the part of persons of a certain type who have hastened to counter my occasional remarks with their experiences in low cultural classes in England. Moreover, it must be stressed, first, that the number of modern houses in England that are artistically eligible for consideration is very large, perhaps many hundred times larger than in Germany, so that even twenty years ago they could prompt R. Dohme to write the general survey of architecture that we have mentioned; and second, that the spread of a new artistic culture has after all embraced far wider circles in England than has so far been the case with us.

As I have worked on the subject I have tried to present the material in such a way that the book shall also appeal to a wider public, for I believe that in this sphere more can be learnt from the general than the particular. My concern has been less to recommend imitation of the English house or any part of it than to make the thinking behind it accessible to the German reader. If something of its freedom and naturalness should put down deeper roots in Germany, if the numbers of those who are already attempting something similar at home should be increased, I should consider my labours to have been richly rewarded.

Sincere thanks are due to my English colleagues for the exceptionally courteous way in which they have helped in the preparation of this book, especially in procuring illustrative material, sometimes at the cost of considerable trouble to themselves. I must also thank all the owners who have allowed me to look over their houses and to photograph them. I cannot omit to mention specially the extraordinary kindness and hospitality that has been shown me and has enabled me to do everything that I wished to do.

Especially I owe most heartfelt thanks to my appointed superiors, whose moral support alone enabled me to undertake work on such extensive material. The book forms as it were the summing up of my long years of study in England, for which my official position afforded me such a good opportunity and to which I look back as work that was not only instructive but also pleasurable and enjoyable with the hope that it will not fade away and leave things quite unchanged.

Hermann Muthesius
Nikolassee near Berlin, March 1904

Introduction

Individuality of the English a result of the country being an island

A deeper insight into English life confirms what one has heard, that in all its ideas and feelings, in its *mores*, its philosophies and in its whole outlook on life, England stands apart from the countries of the continent of Europe, that it is a world of its own displaying an individuality of a quite special character in every aspect of culture. Examples of island kingdoms that lie close to the mainland and yet possess a fundamentally different style from it are not uncommon in themselves: one has only to think of Japan and China, Ceylon and India, Venice and Italy. At one and the same time the sea separates the island from its nearest neighbour and links it with the remotest. Separation from its nearest neighbour gives the island its independent development; links with the remotest bring influences from afar which are bound to intensify its individuality. Islanders are formed by the sea, those who live in large continents by the land. Thus England too is something special, different from anything on the mainland of Europe. Even the differences between the Germanic and Latin peoples of the continent, striking though they are, are as nothing compared with the rugged English individuality. The traveller from Germany to France and even to Italy finds basically the same customs and practices, the same political institutions, social and philosophical ideas. But in England at every turn he comes up against differences in every field.

Living in private houses

On the purely superficial level this difference is nowhere more striking than in the style of living. England is the only advanced country in which the majority of the population still live in houses, a custom that has survived all the political, social and economic changes that European civilisation has undergone in the past hundred and fifty years. Whereas on the continent these changes caused mass migration into the cities, where people became imprisoned in giant multi-storeyed barrack-like blocks, in England, where, indeed, industrial development had started so much earlier, they barely touched the inborn love of country life; on the contrary, the necessity of working in the city appeared to strengthen it. The riches that poured into the country as a result of the new order of things, from commerce, wholesale trade and from the opening-up of vast territories by colonisation, created no spectacular urban developments like those of the continental countries; instead, they streamed into the rural areas, creating dwelling-places for individuals, making them into little separate worlds and concentrating and incorporating all the comforts of life in them. Except for Edinburgh, therefore, which is favoured with a magnificent position, the British Isles have produced no real metropolis in the continental sense; and London itself is no more than an immense village, a vast unplanned and haphazard congeries of houses, with no streets, squares or public buildings of note. To judge by the situation in England, one would be justified in asserting that the Anglo-Saxon race has been denied the gift of building cities; and this demonstrates another well-known element in its character: the inability of the individual to subordinate himself and his belongings to the whole. But this failure is largely a result of the uncommonly highly developed independence of the individual, which means that, as is so often

the case, it is simply the outcome of virtues that have been cultivated too one-sidedly.

Preference for living in the country

The great store that the English still set by owning their home is part of this powerful sense of the individual personality. The Englishman sees the whole of life embodied in his house. Here, in the heart of his family, self-sufficient and feeling no great urge for sociability, pursuing his own interests in virtual isolation, he finds his happiness and his real spiritual comfort. Outside pleasures, the hubhub of the metropolitan streets, a visit to a *Bierkeller* or a café, are almost hateful to him. This, incidentally, is the reason for the desolate monotony of English cities that every continental has felt, for the hurried and purely commercial dealings in the city streets, for the absence of inviting places where a drink and a rest may be had and which are so highly evolved on the continent. The Englishman hurries up to town for the sole purpose of doing business. In the evening he hastens back to the heart of his family and makes no bones about travelling for up to an hour by railway in order to spend his few hours of leisure as far away as possible from the bustle of the metropolis. In England one does not 'live' in the city, one merely stays there. England differs from all the other countries in the world in that even the royal residence is not in the capital, but far away in the country and the town palace is now used only for overnight stays. All the aristocracy and every well-to-do commoner lives in the country in his well-appointed country-seat, some of them of royal dimensions and most in splendid, though remote and isolated, natural surroundings. These men possess smaller town houses where they stay on visits to the capital and for a brief period during the so-called season, that is, during the spring months. Those whose daily work takes them to the city seek their place of residence as far out as possible in a suburb that has retained its rural appearance and they do not begrudge the sacrifices that this entails. Others who are obliged to live in the city at least rent a country-house in some pleasantly situated village, either for the summer months or for the whole year, where they regularly spend the time between Saturday and Monday and where they leave their family throughout the warm season. All this indicates a flight from the metropolis and an instinctive urge on the part of each individual to preserve his direct link with nature and to seek his life's contentment nowhere but in his own house.

Proverbial love of home. Names of houses

The Englishman's love of his home has become proverbial. Many common expressions describing it[1] have also passed into the language of the continental peoples and we universally use the English word for the quality that the Englishman looks for specially in his house, namely 'comfort', in its English form – for it is as difficult to translate its precise meaning into a foreign language as is that of our German word '*Gemütlichkeit*'. Another purely external reflection of the Englishman's love of his house strikes one immediately. This is his habit of giving it a name, which is so general that very few house-owners use the number alone. In itself the number is shorter and more practical

---

[1] E.g. 'Home, sweet home', lines from a well known popular song, 'My house is my castle', 'East and West, home is best', and many others.

but it does suggest a measure of indifference to the house, whereas a name springs from a special affection.

The Englishman's sense of independence one of the reasons for living in a house

As all national characteristics can be explained in terms of two basic causes — inherited qualities and climatic influences — it would not be difficult to discover a connection between the Anglo-Saxon fondness for living in houses and these two formative forces. But it is certainly not easy to establish which of the present characteristics are inherited and which have simply been acquired through the habitation and its special conditions. Very generally it is probably true to say that throughout the course of its development in England, the Anglo-Saxon race has displayed one fundamental characteristic: this is its pronounced sense of self-sufficiency and its attendant powerful urge to independence. Both are closely connected with the custom of living in houses, which, moreover, is restricted to England proper, that is, the part of the country that is largely inhabited by Anglo-Saxons, for in Scotland and Ireland most people live in multi-storeyed buildings. The English sense of self-sufficiency has been the cause, for example, of the extraordinarily early political independence for which England is outstanding and the reason for the proliferation of religious sects; it is the key to many striking qualities, such as the Englishman's self-confidence (which, alas, all too often becomes self-satisfaction), his assurance in outward demeanour, the determination and imperturbability with which he pursues his plans, his common-sense and the dislike of abstract brain-work and purely scientific research that goes with it. But it also explains his instinctive urge to be master in his own house, to be able to live a full life there, and there to enjoy the highest degree of personal freedom that our social order permits. This urge is suitably reinforced by the decidedly conservative sense of the Anglo-Saxon, who seems scarcely to recognise the charm of change and finds any alteration in his way of life – such as we experience automatically and all too frequently in our life in multi-storeyed buildings – doubly disturbing. These people ask relatively little of external life, a circumstance which has enabled them to preserve a certain countrified quality in the midst of their great prosperity and helps to make rural life acceptable; and the pronounced lack of sociability which makes the Englishman so different from the continental prevents him from finding anything objectionable in the seclusion of his lonely abode.

Climatic influences

The damp English air and perpetually overcast sky are surely important among the purely climatic influences likely to foster the Englishman's love of his house. Though the climate is temperate and free of extremes it is still unfriendly and the constantly damp-laden air oppresses the spirit. Gathered round the fire in the seclusion of the room, the family seeks refuge and comfort. For there is not the temptation to spend time out of doors that there is in southern countries; nature does not seduce them into idleness in the open air. But oppression of the spirit prompts a definite reaction that anyone who has lived in England will have felt: a desire for physical exercise. Physical exercise is the only lasting antidote to the depressing influence of the English climate. Games have been played in the open air since time immemorial but have recently become a veritable passion and there are the further pleasures of hunting, fishing, walking and cycling, all of which can well be explained as consequences of climatic conditions. The climate forbids a leisurely pause by the wayside even in the streets of the city and precludes those long hours spent idly in the piazza beloved of the southerner and the

Parisian's stroll down the boulevard — even supposing the English character were disposed to such enjoyments. Thus the need for physical exercise in the open air itself makes it desirable to live in the country.

The beauty of nature in England

Yet another element that contributes to the English preference for life in the country is the beauty of the English countryside. The extreme moisture of the atmosphere combined with a temperature made mild by the Gulf Stream and even by the fact that the country is an island has produced a luxuriant plant-life unrivalled by any continental country. The damp atmosphere preserves the green in all its lushness until late autumn and prevents dust settling and leaves withering prematurely as they do by high summer on the continent. This is why every English hedgerow, every patch of garden fronting a labourer's cottage looks so uncommonly fresh and clean. Although climatic conditions must always have made nature powerfully attractive, this has been much increased at the present time by the progressive dwindling of agriculture until almost the whole of the countryside has been transformed into a vast green field. Summer and winter alike the meadows lie resplendent in the same fresh green and the trees stand singly or in groups with their magnificent dark green crowns so that the whole countryside is in fact one great park. Anyone who sets foot in this countryside, or even traverses these fields in a train, must be enchanted by it – so how much more so those who walk or cycle through it! This English meadow landscape with its lush groups of trees is one of the most unusual and most beautiful that any traveller can hope to see, and this despite the lack of sunshine, which rarely breaks through the cloud cover: in its way it can stand comparison with the finest mountain landscape of more favoured lands. In view of its great beauty it is hardly surprising that a man-made feature, the country-house, has been added to the meadows and trees, the two natural elements of the English landscape as proof of man's love of nature. Country-houses large and small are scattered over the whole landscape; some are surrounded by parks that extend far into the fields, other more modest dwelling-houses sufficing for the needs of the middle-classes are clustered together in estates. They lie fresh and trim amid the natural greenery. And together with this garden-like landscape they reflect the wellbeing of the country, the comfortable life-style of a people that has remained close to nature, for whom a fresh breath of country air blowing across the fields is worth more than the refinements of an artificial city life. One glance at an Ordnance Survey map can teach us something about the remarkable character of the country, for in certain counties, such as Surrey, Kent, Somerset, Cheshire and Derbyshire, the countryside is simply one great succession of estates, the parks and fields of which abut closely on one another.

Urban living

The house is also the rule in English cities and every house has its garden, however small. In certain parts of London the houses are built round a garden for the communal use of the inhabitants; it lies sometimes behind, sometimes in front of the house, when it becomes the characteristic garden-like London square. The inhabitants have, of course, to cross the street to reach the garden. On the whole these gardens are of more use to the general public than to the inhabitants. London's first blocks of leasehold flats have been built only quite recently. But this trend is not of any great consequence, on the whole it appears to be a temporary phenomenon or a product of special circumstances. Should the custom become more widespread, however — which at the moment seems unlikely — this could only be a sign of economic recession and, even worse, would spell the demise of one of the best aspects of the English heritage.

The advantage of living in a private house

For there can be no doubt that to live in a private house is in every way a higher form of life. Its most important qualities are ethical and are virtually incalculable. Just as a higher force determines that a man shall found a family, so he certainly has an inborn instinct to create a permanent dwelling-place for himself and his family, his own little kingdom in which he may rule, spread himself and blossom. This natural urge moves men at every level of culture, it is the root of every human order of society, the basis of every culture and every higher moral development of mankind. To a man, even a man of modest circumstances, it has always been a matter of course that he should live in his own house and it was only with the advent of the metropolis with all its artificiality that the situation changed. Thus if the individual of today with his allegedly numerous cultural achievements were no longer to be in a position to build a house for himself, if current economic circumstances were to cease to allow it, this would be an indictment of a period which prides itself on the most unheard-of progress and yet is unable to honour the simplest human rights. For one cannot expect the present-day urban flat to replace all the moral and ethical values that are inherent in the private house, the family home. Accommodation from which we can be given notice at the next quarter-day is hardly likely seriously to engage our domestic interest. We accept it with the same indifference that we show towards an hotel room. The calm certainty of having 'our own four walls', the feeling of contentment, the development of our personality and the fostering of all our natural talents that derive from it and must be regarded as our mission in life, can hardly find a place in the nomadic life of metropolitan removals. Like the metropolis itself, so in the narrower sense, metropolitan living conditions make for instability, dissipation and shallowness in human society.

Flat-dwelling can only be regarded as an emergency substitute for living in a private house and every time a country's economy takes a turn for the better, the number of those who wish to return to live in their own house is bound to increase, a process that is beginning in the present rapid economic upswing in Germany too. Every thoughtful person must groan under the pressure of the barrack-like life of the city. Those who have had the good fortune to grow up in their parents' own house, in whom all the memories, all the poetical impressions stored in their hearts as children in the old type of family house are still alive, cannot begin to imagine the gaping emptiness that must strike the soul of the city child who has been dragged round five or six lots of rented accommodation during the same period. The economic and commercial changes to which the present-day world is subject, together with the tempting pleasures of the metropolis drive innumerable men daily into the arms of the city's prostitutes. Yet the value of what they exchange against their own more modest, but nobler qualities of life is more than questionable from the point of view of the higher political economy. The imponderable reservoir of national strength that has been built up through generations of the contented tranquility of a fortifying country life is all too soon squandered in the maelstrom of city life. It takes but a single generation for sturdy country-dwellers to become the characterless population of the metropolis. The results of urban inbreeding are no better at higher social levels. It is a well-known phenomenon that the great majority of men who are active promoters of culture come from country or small-town families and that the metropolis

could not survive spiritually without continual fresh influxes from this source. 'We must look upon our people', said Goethe, 'as a storehouse from which the energies of failing humanity are continually replenished and refreshed'. If the influence of the metropolis is dulling in itself, to allow children to grow up in urban multi-storeyed dwellings can only intensify the influence, for it cuts people off from their rightful world as unnaturally as a cage does an animal from its home in the wild.

The most valuable gain from living in a private house is this closer contact with nature and the greater bodily and spiritual health which it brings. Even the house in the city has this great advantage over the multi-storeyed dwelling. It has some connection with the ground at least and it is easier to breathe fresh air. If it also has a garden, contact with nature is already assured, for the owner, and especially the growing generation, cannot help taking some interest in it and so has a means of escape from the sad fate of the city-dweller whom Bismarck described as having to grow up among houses, paving-stones and paper. And this is quite apart from the greater elbow-room enjoyed by the dweller in a house by virtue of his closeness to the outer world, no matter if his rooms are smaller than those of the ostentatious urban flat.

Living in private houses necessary to an artistic culture

And not least, there is another drawback that is indissolubly linked with it and is of the greatest importance, especially now when there is so much talk about the re-awakening of an artistic culture – and indeed, if this were achieved, a foundation for human happiness that had been submerged in the whirlpool of modern times would have been built afresh. Where should art for the individual start but in his house? Could one imagine such a thing happening in the present-day urban flat, tainted as it is with the taste of the parvenu speculator? It is inexplicable, but significant of the nadir at which contemporary culture stands, that people with even a rudimentary artistic sensibility can survive in this flashy but mean environment at all. Yet not only do they do so, they also feel at ease in it. There must be something in the concept of culture in disorder, for the aesthetic sensibility that is lacking today has always been part of this concept. The occupants of the showy flats would all indignantly reject any attempt to doubt their culture on this account.

We must be clear about one thing: for all our efforts on behalf of art, an artistic culture can only begin with the individual and the individual can only exercise his artistic sense by shaping his immediate surroundings, his living-rooms and his house – assuming that he has any interest in those general questions of art that lie close to our heart. We shall not achieve our aim by studying the history of art, learning about styles, visiting museums or other newly discovered substitutes for the practice of art. If the individuals that make up our society do not begin to think in an artistic way, all its artistic knowledge will be useless, it will remain as inartistic as, for example, an un-musical person who seeks to make himself musical by studying musical history.

Artistic education is loudly advocated today but obviously its only basis can be the privately owned house. A man's house – he may even have built it himself – is bound to need furnishing and so he is directly faced with involvement in the practice of art. This should give everyone the key to the art of others and at least provide a foundation for an understanding of the work of the artists of the day. For the house-owner is now something of an artist himself, as were we all in our natural state, until the relevant part of the brain was allowed to atrophy. Nothing is more significant of the atrophied artistic sense of contemporary society than its total inability to establish any kind of attitude towards architecture. People are interested in the anecdotic element, at least, in painting and sculpture, but architecture remains entirely unintelligible. Should not the torn threads of understanding of architecture be used to develop a link with the lost feeling for the family house? If domestic architecture were to regain acceptance this would certainly build a bridge by which general questions of art could be brought closer to the people. But a revival of interest in the dwelling-house is absolutely essential if the applied arts are to persist in their renewed activity and to thrive. The house is their only possible home; the sole aim of any arts and crafts movement must be to furnish the dwelling-place and the house.

Influence of its way of life on English culture

Looking back at England, which, as we have said, has retained a close interest in the house and an appreciation of the private house to this day, we are bound to ask whether there is any evidence in the character of the present-day English of the advantages we have extolled of living in private houses. While I do not underestimate the hazards that the observer may encounter in formulating consequences that rest on more or less fluctuating values, I can say for certain, following on from the point about the recent revival of the applied arts, that this could never have become as widespread as it is without the practice of living in houses. The work of William Morris, the revival of arts and crafts in England, began quite specifically in the house and only began to appear in periodicals and exhibitions after ten years or more of silent development had produced tangible results. How different from the stir the new movement is causing with us at home! But there are other characteristics that may be observed in England today which originate in the practice of living in houses; these include the sedulous reading of books and the associated widespread interest in fine literature; the relatively high degree of religious observance that is found in England today; the highly developed family life that is expressed in good domestic practice, the striking harmony between all the occupants of the house and the excellent upbringing of children. The connection between living in a house and the upbringing of children is particularly enlightening; the English upbringing based on independence, good manners and moral rectitude is quite inseparable from the English habit of living in houses. For as a country's good upbringing of its children is quite certainly a proof that its family life is good, both must unquestionably be regarded as the results of living-conditions.

Restricted access to diverting amusements

Yet there is no mistaking the fact that the two-fold advantages of living in a house – one on the side of health and ethics, the other on that of the emotional life – also demand certain sacrifices, which might appear to favour urban flat-dwelling. The most serious of these are the quite long journeys that those who live in houses in the country have to face. They make social life difficult, complicate visits to the theatre and to concerts and the physical effort that such journeys entail effectively restricts all visits to the inner city. But it must be said that our transport systems are constantly improving and are doing much to reduce these difficulties, so that the restriction of life outside the house is perhaps not as great a disadvantage as at first appears. This immense increase in the excitements offered by the modern city tends to make city-dwellers indifferent. Nobody can digest and assimilate the intensive intellectual pleasure offered to a receptive mind by plays rightly enjoyed or good concerts in such swift succession as the modern theatre- or concert-going city-dweller is apparently able to do. An evening of music-making at home, an evening's reading *en famille* is more rewarding to thoughtful natures than three visits a week to the concert-hall or opera-house. Such performances should be regarded as red-letter days in the round of home-produced art and not every-day fare. It is noteworthy that it is in fact those who are indifferent who cannot do without these constant intellectual diversions, whereas more thoughtful people taste them sparingly. Thus, while life in the more isolated house entails restrictions, these must if anything be regarded as salutory.

Economic questions

However, the economic side of life in the private house is another story and if dimensions are to be similar to those of rented accommodation (as is usually the case in Germany since the owner wishes it so) it becomes decidedly unfavourable. The English house offers useful pointers on this question as to how the private house can also meet more modest needs; indeed, this might have been expected, since in England people of every level of income live in private houses. The chief reason for the greater number of such houses, lies, of course, in the English conditions of land-tenure, which have not been established in Germany because of the speculation in building-sites that goes on. But a powerful contributory reason is the Englishman's more modest requirements as to the size of rooms. The cubic capacity of the English house is always much smaller than that of the small flat in Germany. But this is no hardship and is, indeed, justified by the fact that in areas where there are country-houses the air is better than it is in cities and therefore the space for air in the rooms can be smaller; and also by the circumstance that the occupant of a private house is in touch with nature on all sides, whereas the flat-dweller is more or less isolated on his own floor and therefore finds more difficulty in resolving to go out into the fresh air.

Exemplary qualities in the English house

English houses, as we can see, are wisely reduced to essentials and adapted to given circumstances; the point, therefore, that is worth copying from them is the emphasis that is laid on purely objective requirements. The Englishman builds his house for himself alone. He feels no urge to impress, has no thought of festive occasions or banquets and the idea of shining in the eyes of the world through lavishness in and of his house simply does not occur to him. Indeed, he even avoids attracting attention to his house by means of striking design or architectonic extravagance, just as he would be loth to appear personally eccentric by wearing a fantastic suit. In particular, the architectonic ostentation, the creation of 'architecture' and 'style' to which we in Germany are still so prone, is no longer to be found in England. It is most instructive to note at this point that a movement opposing the imitation of styles and seeking closer ties with simple rural buildings, which began over forty years ago, has had the most gratifying results. This same down-to-earth quality which we see in the design of the house is apparent too in its siting and in the way in which it relates to the country round it. The aim is to adapt the house closely to its surroundings and to attempt to make house and garden into a unified, closely-knit whole. A fairly recent movement in garden design has revolutionised the surroundings of the house and in particular has removed from the scene the erroneous views of impersonal landscape gardening. Like the changes to the exterior, changes to the interior of the house have simplicity, objectivity, plainness and unobtrusive comfort as their aim. At the same time a very highly developed recognition of sanitary requirements has much of interest to teach us. Thus in many respects the English house gives us food for thought and much of it will provide pointers for our own development.

The English house a product of English conditions

On the whole, however, it will probably be as well to note at the outset that the greatest merit of the English house as it stands completed before us is that it is *English*, that is, it conforms totally to English conditions, embodies totally English ways of life, is totally suited to local climatic and geographical conditions and in its artistic design it must be considered totally a product of a native artistic development. Its exemplary qualities for us are therefore limited. And as we have also to develop the German house to conform to German conditions, the prime purpose of a study like the present one must be to show how closely all the external forms of the English house meet the natural conditions obtaining in England, rather than to pick out fine examples that would be worth copying in our situation. But the great instructive value of such an investigation must lie in the discovery of the manner in which this adaptation has taken place. To face our own conditions squarely and as honestly as the English face theirs today, to adhere to our own artistic tradition as faithfully, to embody our customs and habits in the German house as lovingly – these are the lessons we can learn from the English house.

The development of the modern English house

A. The earlier architects

England's pioneering work. The Pre-Raphaelites

The end of the nineteenth century saw the remarkable spectacle of a new departure in the tectonic arts that had originated in England and spread across the whole field of our European culture. England, the country without art, the country that until recently had, so to speak, lived on the art of the continent was pointing the way to the world and the world was following – admittedly after some consideration, but all the more decisively and enthusiastically for that. Given this opportunity for the first time to look more closely at English art, one saw that indeed by keeping strictly to her own paths she had repeatedly discovered new artistic ground. England had possessed a native school of painting since William Hogarth (1776–1837). Reynolds and Gainsborough, her first painters to attain the status of master, immediately distinguished themselves for their firm independence and by the turn of the eighteenth century England already had her Turner (1775–1851), who looked at nature as it had never been looked at before. Constable (1776–1837) developed the principles of modern landscape painting which were then consolidated by the French Romantics. And about the middle of the nineteenth century in the work of the Pre-Raphaelites English painting again underwent a revolution which subsequently spread to the farthest limits of our cultural area and the effects of which are still felt in the artistic situation of today. This movement not only represented the first, and ultimately extremely successful, break with the academic art that dominated everything at the time, but it also pointed the way to the cultivation of entirely new values: the study of nature in the minutest detail and a mood of spirituality invoking a profounder world of ideas. A true child of Romanticism, Pre-Raphaelite art went straight to the heart of what we may describe as the Germanic view of art in contrast to the classical as embodied in academic art.

The foreshadowing movement in literature. Carlyle and Ruskin

Clearly this movement was bound to merge with that of the Gothic Revival, for its range of ideas was similar. But it interpreted them much more widely and generally and differed from the Gothic Revival in being progressive rather than archaising; it also had at its head men who did not merely continue to reproduce the external forms of earlier art as did the Gothicists, but devoted themselves heart and soul to the new ideas in all their aspects, like walking personifications of a growing new understanding of the arts as a whole. The changes which began to occupy the minds of the best men at this time were profound. Carlyle in his own rugged way had already turned a beam of light on the vague classicising ideas of the time – they were still uppermost, despite all the enthusiasm of Sir Walter Scott – explaining and illuminating them from the standpoint of a Germanic and native interpretation. He recognised three supreme obligations for modern man: 'work, silence and sincerity'. He criticised the industrial products of the time, which he called 'cheap and nasty', a criticism that was later echoed in Germany. The mid-1840s saw the emergence of a writer whose rousing eloquence and burning zeal for art was to carry wide sections of the public with him and open their eyes to this new idea. The writer was John Ruskin (1819–1900), a man to whom England owes measureless gratitude in matters of art. Perhaps it is no longer possible to understand this fully. His importance is of his own time and can only be measured against the background of his age. The translations into German now being prepared will reveal to us some of the pearls of his writings, but will on the whole paint a picture of a markedly personal, somewhat unusual, thinker, rather than that of a prophet of the enormous importance to art that Ruskin was. To the England of his day he was the prophet of a new artistic culture. He was not only the first to point to the importance of Turner, the first to accept the Pre-Raphaelites, despite the scorn and ridicule that attended their first efforts, he was also the first to champion the ideals that later became the guiding principles of the new Arts and Crafts movement: simplicity and naturalness in art, honesty in tectonic design, the conditions for which must be sought in the purpose, material and construction, emphasis on the workmanlike, the characteristic, the indigenous, a synthesis of artistic creation and observation of nature. But he looked for one thing above all others in tectonic creation: good, decent, solid workmanship like that practised so splendidly in the hand-made objects of old. This desire was bound to emerge earlier in England than on the continent, for the old culture based on craft guilds disappeared there some fifty years earlier and by the mid-century the machine had completely destroyed the old tradition of handicrafts. The demand for good work always automatically brings up the question of the conditions out of which it must come: the social position of the worker. Thus Ruskin was the first to reach the point of calling in question machine civilisation as a whole. He maintained that it made man himself a machine, since it forced him to spend his whole life performing a single mechanical operation and was thus literally death to the worker's spiritual and material wellbeing. The worker, he believed, must once again become a thinking being, able to enjoy the independent creation of his hand; this, he thought, was the prerequisite for human existence. To restore every worker's enjoyment of his work became the core of Ruskin's social aims.

It mattered nothing at first that these aims were to some extent backward-looking and that the prospect of their being realised could scarcely be close; basically they had been formulated on the medieval conditions which Ruskin loved and admired beyond all else. Ruskin preached hatred of railways, factories and the creations of recent civilisation, from which he shied away throughout his life. But he achieved one thing: he brought an inner composure into the midst of a period of rising industrialism, which was in many ways reckless and destructive of all ideals, and into the rush for money at any price, which dominated English life as it did life everywhere in the nineteenth century.

William Morris

The Pre-Raphaelites and Ruskin kindled the flame of enthusiasm in many young men who were then on the threshold of active life and were to form the basis of the generation in which the new artistic ideals reached a wider public. Among them were two friends, both Oxford undergraduates at the time, William Morris (1832–1896) and Edward Burne-Jones (1833–1898).

Burne-Jones was later to make Pre-Raphaelite painting widely popular in England, while Morris took the important step of trying to realise the ideals preached by Ruskin in practical craftsmanship. He initiated a new movement in art. He began his career in the studio of the Gothic Revivalist architect George Street, but, finding nothing but dry formalism there, he soon turned his back on architecture. Instinct told him that what he had seen there were not the proper inferences from the achievements of our old civilisation; his creative urge sought something more lively, fresher, and he saw that he could achieve this only by going personally to the real roots of craftsmanship and making things himself. Morris spent most of the rest of his life learning one craft after another. Not restricting himself to the mechanical sort of handwork but working with the intelligence of the discoverer and pathfinder. His foundation was always the practice of the medieval craftsman. But as a modern man he could not help building on this foundation in a modern way, a way appropriate to the cultural conditions of today. In this it was far from his mind to search for 'new forms', but because he always returned to nature to use her in the way that medieval artists had done, as a modern man, automatically and without wishing to, he discovered something new. As an Englishman to whom business and tackling the practicalities of a case came naturally, he immediately founded an interior decorating business (Morris, Marshall, Faulkner & Co., established in 1861), the firm's aim being itself to produce everything that it offered for sale. He designed furniture, made stained glass, embroidery, weaving, printed wall-paper, wove tapestries and later practised each of the arts of the book. Thus the first modern workshop for artistic handicraft was established exactly thirty-five years earlier than similar foundations on the continent. The continent was following a movement that had become general: the idea was in the air everywhere, but with Morris's workshops it was a case of an individual with the strength of genius swimming against the tide of his age with nothing to follow but his artistic instinct. For at first he was not understood at all and it was only the fact that he had already made a respected name for himself as a poet – as such he soon became a national figure of the first consequence – and that as an Oxford graduate he belonged anyway to the highest ranks of English society, that saved him from utter failure.

Development through and after Morris

Morris was a pioneer in every field of his activity, he prepared the ground for the development which each of the branches of the new movement underwent subsequently. As personal friends and partners, Rossetti and Ford Maddox Brown were close to the workshops and unconsciously influenced their spirit even when they were not personally involved. Burne-Jones, Morris's closest friend, was genuinely and most actively involved from the beginning, producing designs for glass, tapestries, book illustrations and everything connected with figural composition. From the 1870s onwards there existed a body of artists who were all moving towards the same goal. At the beginning of the 1880s (1882) a group of artists, the Century Guild – which later issued a very interesting journal, *The Hobby Horse* (1884–1891) – and their driving force, the architect Arthur H. Mackmurdo, began in a wider sense to work along the same lines as those laid down by Morris. At the same time Walter Crane was drawing his illustrations for childrens' books, with which he not only reached the remotest sections of the population but also became the first channel to convey the ideas matured in England to the non-English world. The inspiration for his truly innovatory coloured illustrations came mainly from the Japanese colour prints with which Europe had recently become acquainted, for Japan, in the

artistic sense a discovery of this period, was altogether the most powerful stimulus to visual art of every kind. Other artists who emerged at this time and carried the movement forward included Selwyn Image, Henry Holiday and Lewis F. Day. By the first half of the 1880s the group was sufficiently numerous to join together to form an association, the Art Workers' Guild (founded 1883), from which, from 1888 onwards, came the celebrated series of Arts and Crafts Exhibitions at the New Gallery in Regent Street, London. These exhibitions gave a wider public the first historical evidence of the new art which had been maturing quietly and now became public as a finished product. From the year 1893 onwards the journal *The Studio*, founded by Gleeson White – a writer and artist of unusual merit – and devoted to the new movement, disseminated the new ideas throughout the world; and it was doubtless thanks to it that a strong desire now emerged on the continent to abandon the old practice of reproducing historical styles and to seek new ways in art.

The South Kensington schools

For the art that the English Arts and Crafts Exhibitions in Regent Street were showing the world was indeed something new. A new generation had now climbed upon Morris's shoulders and, entirely abandoning historical echoes, had created a tradition of its own. C. F. A. Voysey, Nelson Dawson, R. Rathbone, Alexander Fisher, H. Wilson, G. J. Frampton, C. R. Ashbee, Charles Ricketts and Lucien Pissarro are some of the names that now appeared beside the members of Morris's circle. They were the representatives of a genuine new style of artistic handicraft that had evolved in the twenty-five years during which Morris had been at work. Nor were they the sole prerogative of the leaders but already had a broad basis among working artists who had passed out of the many schools of artistic handicrafts.

These schools had been established energetically and in pursuance of a concerted plan in every town of any size all over the country by a central authority set up for the purpose and associated with the South Kensington Museum. It is a remarkable fact that it was actually England, the organisation of whose schools was backward in every respect and where, until 1870, all schools had been left entirely in the hands of private enterprise, that carried through this unified plan organising schools of artistic handicrafts. The plan was drawn up after the Great Exhibition in London in 1851, at which it had been observed that English crafts were in serious decline, and was essentially the work of Albert, the Prince Consort, in consultation with Gottfried Semper, the German architect who was at the time a political refugee in England. For a long time these schools were naturally conducted on the same lines as ours in Germany, i.e. art was studied on the basis of traditional art forms. But as new, modern forms based on a zealous study of nature were gradually evolved in Morris's circle and its growing following and as, in particular, an entirely new style of surface pattern found its way thence into industry, these successes were also eagerly taken up by the schools. They had already begun some two decades previously to represent the modern tradition. It had ceased to be an article of faith that historical art forms were the ones to imitate, instruction no longer began with copying old forms but with a sedulous study of nature, and design no longer derived from the forms of earlier art but from those of nature. For many years now, hundreds of draughtsmen, modellers, architects, teachers of drawing and artistic craftsmen of all kinds have been pouring from these schools and working and creating in the new tradition, which has thus maintained an entirely unified image in England and is no longer questioned in any quarter.

Domestic architecture and its three reformers

The architecture, especially the domestic architecture, of the time stood in as great need of reorganisation as the artistic crafts. As we have seen, the house was still in the cold grip of classicism, especially the ordinary small house. It was built to an axial and symmetrical plan, like a box, in the form known as the 'Italian villa' and was plastered and painted with oil paint. The form had spread across England with the trend in taste introduced by John Nash, replacing the old Puritan guild tradition. These houses were as cheerless inside as out. Rectangular rooms, unthinkingly planned on the axes of the windows, elaborate but extremely small doors, painted in oil-paint to look like marble walls, soulless siting of doors, fire-places and windows, the kitchen in a dark basement buried up to half its height in the ground – these were the features of the small house of the period. St John's Wood in north London is a good example of this style of building as practised in the 1850s. The large house had long had an open ground-plan with generously proportioned domestic offices which always extended to one side and were usually built round a working courtyard, but architecturally it fluctuated between a vague mixture of every possible style derived from Antiquity and the Renaissance and a Gothic that was false because it was adapted from ecclesiastical forms. It was becoming ever more obvious that a healthy development was as little to be expected of the Gothic Revival movement as of the pretentious form of the Italian palazzo. The Gothic Revival seemed as hopeless as the classical. Formalism reigned on either hand, both were pastiches.

The change was effected during the 1860s by three architects who took the bold step of abandoning mere pastiche in architecture. Their method was to look for their forms not only, as hitherto, in great works of architecture, such as castles, palaces and cathedrals, but to design more freely, paying attention to utility, material and other purely practical considerations. At the same time they looked towards the simpler country buildings, in particular houses in villages and small towns built in the tradition of the old masons' guilds. The three men were Philip Webb, Eden Nesfield and Norman Shaw.

Fine architecture and vernacular building

The step taken at this time was important in more ways than one. When we consider the architecture of the past we too often forget that side by side with fine architecture – the architecture practised since the Renaissance by cultivated architects usually on buildings of some pretention – there was always a great deal of ordinary building with which architects had nothing to do. The work was the responsibility of master-masons who belonged to guilds and represented local traditions in that autonomous way in which the old guilds handed on their craftsmanship from generation to generation. The great waves of stylistic change and fashions in architecture broke on the reef of the guild-members' restricted horizon; for they remained untouched by any literary or archaeological desire for change and were moreover faced daily with commissions in which economy and the traditional outlook of their patrons called for restraint. Nevertheless the changing styles of fine architecture did eventually penetrate to these areas, though always in a form from which all extravagances had been pared away. It has already been observed that by the eighteenth century Renaissance moulding and classical columns and cornices had entirely replaced all lingering Gothic memories and had become familiar currency to every craftsman.

This continued to be so until far into the nineteenth century, but the training in the use of these forms given by the guilds had ceased when the guilds disappeared. The nineteenth century saw the master-mason who had been trained in his guild replaced by the developer over the whole area of everyday practice. His disappearance marked the beginning of the gradual loss of accumulated tradition as a whole and its replacement by the debased standards that we have observed throughout the whole of the lower end of the building trade during the nineteenth century.

As a result of the growth of a class of educated architects on the one hand and the swift rise of the middle classes on the other, the architect was more and more often called in for these small commissions. He was at first too highly educated for them. He brought with him an architectonic ambition that made him attempt monumental architecture on these ordinary little commissions – this was the architect's fundamental failure in the last century. The essential characteristic of today's small-scale architecture is that the master-mason of the guild – who has died out, together with his consolidated tradition – has been replaced at best by the over-trained architect, but more often by the entirely untrained, or at least unsuitably trained, developer.

Vernacular building as the starting-point for modern domestic building

It was England's achievement – and it cannot be rated highly enough – to have been the first to find an escape from this dilemma and to have done so at a time when nothing of the kind was yet stirring on the continent. The escape consisted in the architects recovering the traditions of the old master-mason, abandoning any suggestion of fine architecture and beginning to build simply and rationally like the old guild masons. The idea seems very simple today, but was then so infinitely remote that its application amounted to an artistic revolution. For in order to conceive it, a two-fold recognition was required: first, that previous practice had been wrong, and second, that the old buildings of the guild-masons had been honester and nobler works of art than the abstractions from fine architecture which the new architects produced in similar situations. In short, the beauty of the old guild-masons' buildings, so long despised by architects, had to be rediscovered. Turning to Germany, we see that a general revival of awareness of the beauty of the small, unpretentious house – such as the farmhouse or the small-town house – is of extremely recent date. Only of very recent years have our eyes been opened to the charm of a village street or a group of buildings in a small town. Only quite recently have such buildings found their way into print and they have only just begun to influence living architecture, which in Germany is still largely governed by the great styles of architecture. Architects are only just beginning to recognise that their handling of these small commissions has been a failure in the past.

England had made the same discovery as early as the 1860s and it must be said at once that this formed the foundation of the brilliant development in domestic architecture that has since taken place in England. In England too vernacular architecture had been disregarded and scorned, just as Gothic churches had been dismissed during the period of Italian domination. But the inherent artistic charm of these buildings was now recognised and with it the qualities they had to offer as prototypes for the smaller modern house. They possessed everything that had been sought and desired: simplicity of feeling, structural suitability, natural forms instead of adaptations from the architecture of the past, rational and practical design, rooms of agreeable shape,

1   Old tile-hung farmhouse, Tenterden, Kent

3   Fire-place projecting from the outside wall of an old farmhouse, Tillington, Sussex

colour and the harmonious effect that had in former times resulted spontaneously from an organic development based on local conditions. Recognition of these values came first from these three men whose work based on it puts them at the top of the tree of modern English architecture.

'Queen Anne'

At first, however, as is almost invariably the case, architects worked more or less unconsciously, obeying an instinct rather than a premeditated plan. This is obvious from the fact that even for the leaders the central aims of the movement took time to clarify and they too had to extricate themselves from the imitative attitudes that had applied to varying extents in the works of their youth. Nor were they themselves entirely clear as

2   Old farmhouse, Hollingbourne, Kent

to which points they should pick up in reviving a more honest style of building. It was thought at first that the houses built in the reign of Queen Anne (1702–1714) would have most to offer in this connection. So the catchword 'Queen Anne' came into being to describe the new movement, which retained this label for decades. What was in fact being described was the smaller house of the seventeenth and eighteenth centuries, large numbers of which had survived all over the country and had only been overlooked because of their plain appearance.

Character of the vernacular houses

Round London, where the movement started, these houses were mostly simple brick buildings (Fig. 4) plainly constructed in the technique introduced into England by the Dutch, with red tiled roofs, leaded or wood-framed windows, the windows themselves small and low and in strips or simply extended from the wall-surface in bays, with great chimney-stacks, often as conspicuous as towers, and white painted woodwork. Half-timbered and plastered houses were also common (Fig. 2), tile-hung gable walls were almost typical, while sometimes the whole upper storey was hung on all sides with tiles (Fig. 1).[2] The interior was extremely simple, though it nearly always had a comfortable fire-place that projected from the wall on the outside (Fig. 3). It was shaped like a small bay, the long side of which formed the hearth, while at either side were two little windows bringing direct light to the seats that flanked the hearth. The fire-place, known as an ingle-nook, became the favourite motif of domestic architecture during the following decades. It cannot be denied that there was

[2] A selection of one hundred photographs of houses of this type has recently been issued by W. G. Davie under the title *Old cottages and farmhouses in Kent and Sussex*, London 1900. My Figs. 1–3 are reproduced by kind permission of the publisher, B. T. Batsford.

4 Old farmhouse on the east coast of England, Walberswick, Suffolk

nothing particularly striking about these English lower middle-class and labourers' houses, the discovery of which had so great an influence on English art; nor was there anything to set them apart from traditional vernacular buildings in other countries. On the contrary, our country buildings in Germany are perhaps more imaginative, more poetical and fuller of atmosphere, and a renaissance of our everyday architecture from this source would promise wonders, if only steps were taken to bring them to light.

Gothic, Renaissance and liberation from historical styles

It is a remarkable coincidence that in England both movements, the Arts and Crafts movement instigated by Morris and the movement associated with the discovery of the country buildings, came into being simultaneously without having anything much to do with one another. Indeed, they seemed almost to be opposites, for Morris and all his followers were resolutely medieval, while the Queen Anne school deliberately opposed the Gothic and looked back to domestic Baroque. Certainly the number of architectonic forms used in these country-dwellings was extremely small, yet mouldings, cornices, brackets, supports, etc. were Renaissance in style, although their character as a whole, their plainness and their down-to-earth quality and their general feeling could probably equally well have been called Gothic. But the Queen Anne school were certain that the notion of reintroducing specifically Gothic forms into modern art held no promise of success. The Gothic was dead and its revival in the nineteenth century was an artificial one. Moreover, although architects could acquire some facility in the use of their means of expression, rather as Latin can be learnt, the long decades of Gothic influence had had little effect on the craftsmen. Despite all attempts to influence them, they had retained something of the old Renaissance schooling, to which

they reverted when left alone. It was therefore considered that by fostering what remained of the Renaissance tradition there would be a more living sensibility to fall back upon. But there was little hope of converting Morris to this view. For him Renaissance meant unqualified sin and decay while Gothic was the golden age. So at first the two movements which were later to merge to form modern English domestic architecture proceeded side by side independently. Moreover, few had yet grasped the concept of the artistic unity of the house and its contents, so that architect and 'decorator' were different people who had little to do with one another. But mutual understanding was helped from the outset by the fact that the new architectonic movement did not attach overmuch weight to specific forms of any kind. Its adherents were, however, fighting the proliferation of forms, the parade and superficial understanding of historical styles which had been the lot of architecture at the hands of architects. War was waged not from the standpoint of one historical style against another but against style as such. The aim was freedom from the trammels of style, but not to the extent of scorning tradition.

Thus this period saw a break with the styles of fine architecture, a step of the greatest importance in the history of art. These architects changed their attitudes towards the styles of the past, the rules of which had previously been considered unassailable, though they did not achieve anything like artistic freedom.

Philip Webb and William Morris's house at Bexley Heath

Of the three men we have mentioned, Philip Webb (b. 1830) worked in close friendship and complete harmony with William Morris; he built a variety of houses with him, Webb acting as architect and Morris responsible for the decoration and furnishing of the interior. The first of these was the house that Morris built for himself in 1859 at Bexley Heath in Kent (Figs. 5–9) and called The Red House. It was Webb's first building and Morris was only twenty-five years old at the time and had not decided upon a career. Building this house was immensely important to him for through it he discovered his true mission in life. As he set about furnishing the interior according to his ideas, he found that in the then state of so-called decorative art he had to create every element afresh and he began to see ever more clearly that his life's work must be to re-organise the domestic interior. With Webb he created wall-hangings, furniture and stained glass for The Red House; his friend Burne-Jones began a decorative frieze for the drawing-room, of which three sections were executed (one can be seen in Fig. 9) and other friends assisted him in painting panels on the pieces of furniture. He himself painted the ceiling with its curious patterning in yellow and white. This was the first of Morris's houses (he left it a mere six years later to move to London) and is highly important in the history of art. It is the first private house of the new artistic culture, the first house to be conceived and built as a unified whole inside and out, the very first example in the history of the modern house. Not only was the interior revolutionary but in its external design too it was unique in its time. Built entirely of red brick, it was the first example of the use of this material for a dwelling-house, although William Butterfield had frequently used brick for churches and larger buildings. It has tall tiled roofs and gigantic red chimney-stacks. The name The Red House itself shows that Morris was consciously thinking of colour. It set a pattern and is still much favoured today, sometimes in one or other of many versions, such as Red Court, Red Roofs and so on. The over-all feeling of the house is Gothic, but in addition to openings with pointed arches, it has the tall, rectangular sash-windows of the domestic Baroque with their small panes and white-painted frames; the half-hipped roofs too are quite free

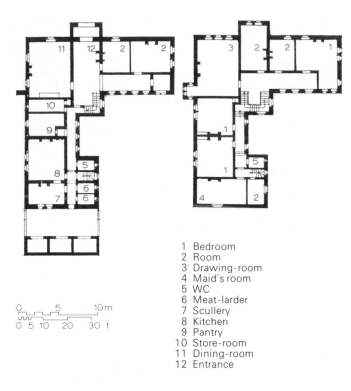

1 Bedroom
2 Room
3 Drawing-room
4 Maid's room
5 WC
6 Meat-larder
7 Scullery
8 Kitchen
9 Pantry
10 Store-room
11 Dining-room
12 Entrance

0 5 10m
0 5 10 20 30 f

5, 6 The Red House, Bexley Heath, nr London. By Philip Webb, for William Morris, 1859. Plans of ground floor and first floor

7, 8 The Red House. Front view and rear view

9 The Red House. Drawing-room (on the right, near the bookcase, part of the frieze by Burne-Jones)

and un-Gothic in treatment. In much of the interior, such as the fire-places (Fig. 9) and passages, the brickwork has been left unplastered. Everywhere there is entire independence and originality which contrasts with the reigning fashion of the plastered 'Italian villa'. So this house stands in every respect as a distinguished example at the threshold of the development of the modern English house.

Other buildings by Philip Webb

Philip Webb remained a close friend of Morris until the latter's death. There can be no doubt that he occupies a position of the first importance in the history of English architecture. The fact is freely acknowledged by everyone with a knowledge of architecture in England, though the less expert might not recognise the fact without a special effort. Almost a solitary by nature and fundamentally inimical to any publicity for his buildings and without any trace of desire to be what is known as a good business man, he has built comparatively little and that little is known only to initiates. His most celebrated house was built in 1868–69 for the Earl of Carlisle at 1, Palace Green in Kensington, London. Here again he worked in partnership with his friends Morris and Burne-Jones, who were together responsible for the splendid figural frieze that decorates the dining-room (Figs. 10, 11). The frieze, designed by Burne-Jones but executed by Walter Crane, represents scenes from Morris's epic *The earthly paradise*, an edition of which, illustrated by Burne-Jones, was just then being planned. Burne-Jones was not entirely satisfied with the execution of the frieze and later he partly repainted it and partly reworked it to produce a better colour effect. Below the frieze lines from the epic are written in fine roman majuscules. The decoration in the panels between text and frieze, together with the ceiling, are the work of William Morris. As the first attempt at a new kind of decoration and because of the personalities involved, the room is a document in the history of interior decoration. This remarkable house has a plain brick exterior with a minimum of actual art forms, though its size

10, 11 The Earl of Carlisle's house in London. By Philip Webb, 1868–69. Dining-room, designed by Morris, showing frieze by Burne-Jones and Walter Crane and dining-room, side wall

12, 13 Clouds, nr Salisbury, Hampshire. By Philip Webb. Hall and garden front

makes it imposing. Similar London houses, unostentatious but outstanding in their independent originality, are those of the Royal Academician Val Prinsep and Alexander Ionides, the well-known art-lover. Most famous of Webb's houses outside London is his country-house Clouds in Hampshire (Figs. 12, 13). The exterior is again plain and unostentatious; among the interiors, the hall is admirable for its spaciousness, monumentality and entirely original design. Another very attractive work by Webb is the extension he built on to the Elizabethan Tangley Manor, of which the library is illustrated in Figs. 14, 15.

Philip Webb was from the first distinguished by great restraint in the use of forms, combined with a thoroughly independent – an independence amounting almost to genius – but almost puritanically simple design. His effects are achieved through material, colour and mass, entirely without affectation. He is the embodiment of maximum honesty, seeking to appear less rather than more than he is. Most people might easily pass his buildings by without understanding them, for they shun ostentation, just as the true aristocrat of today neither is nor seeks to be ostentatious in appearance. So from the first Philip Webb has embodied the best elements of English artistic sensibility in their purest form. He is thus a classic representative of English good taste and this accounts for the respect with which every English art-lover looks up to the master who now lives in modest retirement in the country.

Norman Shaw and Eden Nesfield

The work of the two other pioneers was more accessible to a wider public. Nesfield, the younger of the two, was born in 1835 and died in his prime in 1888, while Norman Shaw, now aged seventy-eight, still plays an active part in the artistic life of the day. The two architects had been friends from youth and from 1862 until 1876 they shared a studio, although, except for one or

14 Tangley Manor, extension by Philip Webb, 1893. Library designed by William Morris

15 Tangley Manor. Library, grand piano decorated by Burne-Jones

two occasions, they never actually collaborated. The course of their training and development was curiously similar; both began their studies with a classicist, were dissatisfied and moved on to a Gothicist (Nesfield to Anthony Salvin, Norman Shaw to George Edmund Street). As young men both espoused the Gothic cause in the battle of styles that was then raging. Both went on study tours to the continent and published masterly sketches of Gothic buildings in large works that created a great sensation in their day and may still be considered masterpieces of the first rank in the field of architectonic drawing. Both later abandoned Gothic and took to domestic Baroque. And with fewer and fewer exceptions, the careers of both were devoted to domestic architecture, in which they cleared the field entirely of existing aberrations and misunderstandings of the truth and created what may be called the English house. If one looks more closely into their two careers it becomes clear that Norman Shaw was the leader and Nesfield the follower. Norman Shaw moved with easy brilliance along his glittering path of progress, but Nesfield was always close at his heels. If this relegates Nesfield somewhat to the background by comparison with Norman Shaw, it must be said that Nesfield was the only architect of his day who was capable of following Shaw so closely, was intellectually so well equipped to rise to the master's heights and almost to equal his great technical and artistic ability. As regards their influence on their period, they probably started out level and, indeed, of the two, Nesfield may possibly have been the more influential, at least during the 1860s.

Nesfield's work and influence

The main reason for this was probably that he had the opportunity to build on what might be called the beaten track, whereas Norman Shaw's first buildings were rather remote. In 1864 in Regent's Park in London and in 1866 at Kew Gardens, near London, Nesfield built a few small lodges that became very famous and immediately and quite specifically showed the younger generation the path they would have to follow in the future. The little building in Regent's Park (Fig. 18) was an adaptation of labourers' houses in Surrey, while that in Kew Gardens was modelled on the architecture of the early eighteenth century with its strong Dutch influence. These little houses were found not only to be well worth imitating but they also opened

the eyes of larger numbers of architects to their prototypes, the original buildings in these styles, many of which still existed in the country. There was now general eagerness to study them, and the fate of the so-called 'Italian villa' in English domestic architecture was sealed. It is revealing to note that since then the term 'villa' has become debased in linguistic usage, for until that time it had denoted something rather exalted and distinctive (roughly the meaning that it still has in Germany); today the term is used only to describe the class of poor, jerry-built speculative housing that is provided for an ignorant public and, indeed, in every-day parlance the term possesses comic and contemptuous overtones. The Englishman is proud to be able once more to call his dwelling-place his 'house', which – though it is, of course, simply a superficial view – one can regard as a triumph over Italian taste and foreign influence.

Besides these little park lodges which made Nesfield's name, several of his larger country-estates had a stimulating effect, their impressiveness resting largely upon Nesfield's masterly solution of the ground-plan, while at the same time, where external design was concerned, he was still picking his way through the labyrinth of styles. His first work, the enlargement of the country-house Combe Abbey, was done in 1859 in the French Gothic style. Cloverley Hall in Shropshire (1864), which we shall consider later, is Gothic too, but rather of the English variety, and displays a full, mature, almost exemplary solution of the ground-plan. His second large country-house complex was built in 1866 in late Renaissance forms – though these are of the plainer kind suited to domestic requirements, which were thenceforth referred to as a whole in a narrower sense as 'Queen Anne'. The house in question was Kinmel Park in Abergele. In returning to the plain, native, domestic Baroque in a house of this distinction Nesfield made the first considerable advance in the acceptance of this style. However, in other buildings he occasionally borrowed from other styles; thus in the house illustrated here, Plas Dinam in Montgomery (1872; Figs. 16, 17), he paid tribute to the forms of the half-timbered house with tile-hung walls. The market-place of the little town of Saffron Walden is surrounded by several buildings by Nesfield, including a Gothic bank and an inn in the so-called Queen Anne style and is a good illustration of his versatility. In all his country-houses he showed a particular fondness for small lodges,

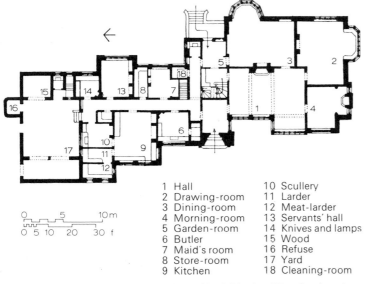

1 Hall	10 Scullery
2 Drawing-room	11 Larder
3 Dining-room	12 Meat-larder
4 Morning-room	13 Servants' hall
5 Garden-room	14 Knives and lamps
6 Butler	15 Wood
7 Maid's room	16 Refuse
8 Store-room	17 Yard
9 Kitchen	18 Cleaning-room

0   5   10m
0 5 10   20   30 f

16, 17   Plas Dinam, Montgomery. By Eden Nesfield, 1872. View from south-east and plan of ground floor

18   Park keeper's lodge, Regent's Park, London. By Eden Nesfield, 1864

which almost became his speciality. They were always modelled on the motifs of the earlier labourers' cottages of the various counties of England and the unusually pleasing design of the little buildings gave the strongest stimulus to the later pleasant flowering of the small private house on the same principle.

As regards interiors, his favourite motif was a fire-place of monumental proportions, especially the type known as an ingle-nook. For the rest he liked to return to the repertoire of the pre-Inigo Jones period, but in general he broke the space up too much and used too much ornament, so that nowadays his rooms appear out-of-date and almost oppressive. He borrowed other favourite motifs from heraldry, enthusiastically using heraldic decoration on fire-places, chimneys, gate-posts, etc.; on exteriors he usually had them executed in cut brickwork, an old technique which he revived and about which we shall have more to say. Occasionally also he used Japanese motifs, for he was one of the first to go in for the new craze for Japanese art.

There can be no doubt that Nesfield's work was far above the level of his time. If he lacks the powerful artistic conviction that we admire in Webb and if he does not approach the astonishing mastery of Norman Shaw, his many buildings always make a refreshing change from the other works of the period; moreover they are so sure and firm in detail and show such mastery of the ground-plan that their historical value is beyond question.

Richard Norman Shaw

By comparison with his two fellow architects, Philip Webb and Eden Nesfield, the life-work of Richard Norman Shaw (b. 1831) appears almost overwhelming, especially in its range. His was a sunny, successful and long life, accompanied by rare physical and mental health. But his endeavours were worthy of such a life. He put so much into it, so many works of such importance, that he carried the contemporary world with him; more specifically, he cogently showed the way forward for the architectonic development of his country. The development of his own work is the development of his period; the phases through which he passed are the phases through which English architecture of the past forty years as a whole has passed.[3]

Early works. Leyes Wood

It is not easy to give an account of Norman Shaw's early work, for it was not until the 1870s that more and better illustrations of buildings began to appear in periodicals as a result of mechanical methods of reproduction. But from that time on, the volumes of the journal *Building News* contained whole series of splendid illustrations of Shaw's work reproduced from the drawings exhibited annually at the Royal Academy. Even from the purely technical point of view these drawings are so important that they outstrip any others produced at the time; and they are so lucid, down-to-earth and free from any bravura or mannerism that we may call them classical. The first sheets to have been published in this way concern Leyes Wood, a house in Sussex built in 1868, of

---

[3] The career of Norman Shaw deserves detailed consideration. Several English publishers have hoped to devote a monograph to his work, but difficulties over personal matters have repeatedly prevented their doing so. For the moment the best source for a rough outline of his career is still the present writer's *Die englische Baukunst der Gegenwart*, Leipzig and Berlin, 1902, in which many of the collotype plates illustrate Norman Shaw's buildings.*

*See Muthesius's note. This gap (temporarily plugged by Blomfield's short biography of 1940) has at last been filled by Andrew Saint's book *Richard Norman Shaw*, New Haven and London: Yale University Press, 1976. Muthesius also included references to Shaw's churches in *Die neuere kirchliche Baukunst in England*, Berlin, 1901. [DS]

which we also reproduce ground-plans and a plan of the estate (Figs. 19–23). The house is a good example of the style in which Norman Shaw was building at the time and is typical of his ideas up to the beginning of the 1870s. The plan is extremely interesting in itself, for it is an excellent realisation of the notion of a courtyard surrounded by ranges of buildings. Entry is by a straight drive through geometrical gardens and here Shaw deals an early blow to the landscape garden (Fig. 19). The bird's-eye view (Fig. 22) shows the house with the fourth wing still unfinished. In its extensive use of brick surfaces, the tile-hung walls and the immense chimney-stacks, the architecture reflects a strong dependence on vernacular building styles. As in early architecture, the chimney-stacks have almost become the *pièces de résistance* of the building as they deliberately and resolutely raise their heads aloft. They are articulated in a style that is still Gothic and the windows with their stone mullions and the doorways with their pointed arches are Gothic in feeling. In his more important buildings Norman Shaw had still not entirely abandoned Gothic forms, a step which Nesfield had taken at Kinmel Park as early as 1866. But the building as a whole is already fundamentally different from those of Nesfield in one respect: the design is powerfully individual, whereas, for all his eclecticism, Nesfield did not rise above the academic. The individuality of design which is manifest here in the gate-house as well as in the whole disposition of the buildings distinguishes each of Norman Shaw's works afresh. He always produces something that is his alone, something original and surprising to the spectator. He invariably uses traditional forms, though he is no longer bound by them: he takes liberties with them and uses them only as instruments for his own ideas. Norman Shaw is the first in the history of nineteenth-century architecture to show this freedom from the trammels of style. It is true that in England Butterfield had already worked with greater freedom and that the brilliant John D. Sedding shared Shaw's aspirations in this respect. But taking it all in all, Shaw was indeed the first to learn all the lessons of the great school of styles at which the architects of the century studied and to feel himself strong enough to do what he wanted to do. To this extent he was the first of the modern architects.

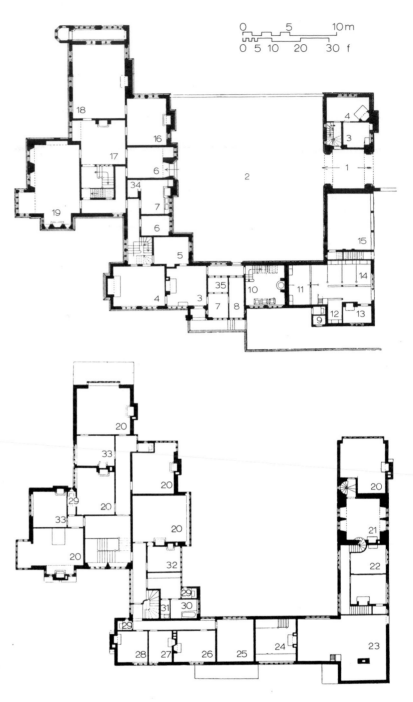

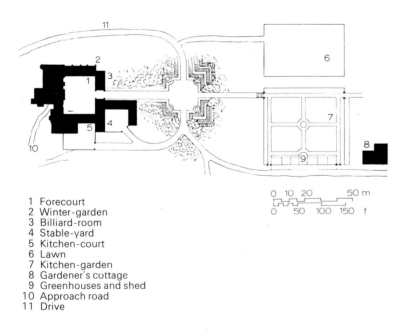

1 Forecourt
2 Winter-garden
3 Billiard-room
4 Stable-yard
5 Kitchen-court
6 Lawn
7 Kitchen-garden
8 Gardener's cottage
9 Greenhouses and shed
10 Approach road
11 Drive

1 Carriage-entrance	19 Dining-room
2 Courtyard	20 Bedroom
3 Scullery	21 Tower-room
4 Kitchen	22 Coachman's quarters
5 Servants	23 Store-room
6 Store-room	24 Ironing-room
7 Butler	25 Store-room
8 Meat-larder	26 Maid's room
9 Manure	27 Spare room
10 Laundry	28 Cook
11 Loose-boxes	29 WC
12 Stall	30 Bath
13 Harness-room	31 Brooms
14 Stables	32 Wardrobe
15 Coach-house	33 Dressing-room
16 Library	34 Silver
17 Hall	35 Larder
18 Drawing-room	

19   Leyes Wood, Sussex. By R. Norman Shaw, 1868. Site plan
(Note: Plan includes later additions to main building)

20, 21   Leyes Wood. Plans of ground floor and first floor
(Note: Original state, later altered)

22, 23 Leyes Wood. Bird's eye view and another view
(after drawings by the architect)

Other houses. Cragside

Among the larger houses of the 1860s mention must be made of Preen Manor near the half-timbered town of Shrewsbury, where formal design joins hands with the local black-and-white style – and of the house and studio Shaw built for the painter Frederick Goodall in Pinner, near London (Fig. 28). In the latter Norman Shaw introduced a feature that he was often to repeat: he broke up the flat façade into obtuse angles to ensure that as many rooms as possible should catch some sunlight. The large mansion known as Cragside in Northumberland begun in 1870 and built for Lord Armstrong, the armaments king (Figs. 24–26), takes us into the 1870s. It lies amid wild, romantic scenery of rocks and hills isolated from the inhabited world and accessible only by means of a bridge over the torrent Coquet. In certain respects the house marks a crisis in the master's development. Due no doubt to the jagged rocks on which it stands, the building masses are rather more strongly broken up, so that they appear to grow out of the ground as though they were continuations of the fissures of the subsoil. The exclusive use of stone, the local material, however, brought out the Gothic character of the building even more clearly than the earlier brick buildings had done. Thus a building went up here that had a markedly Gothic flavour and the overstated, artificial grouping to which the public were accustomed from the other Gothicists of the period. The house did not find the unqualified favour with Norman Shaw's followers that his previous works had done, nor did it entirely satisfy the master. Perhaps this partly accounts for a sharp change of direction in Norman Shaw's art that occurred as he now went over to domestic Baroque or what, in a narrower sense, was understood by 'Queen Anne'.

Swing to 'Queen Anne'. Lowther Lodge

It was not as though Norman Shaw had not already used the native domestic Baroque forms. He had indeed used them at the time when Nesfield was building his epoch-making lodges, or earlier still – as, for instance, in a house in Bromley of 1863, at Hawkhurst in Kent in 1864 and elsewhere. But this was rather in the manner of Nesfield's eclecticism. The move from Gothic to English Renaissance forms was now a matter of conviction. In 1872 Norman Shaw built his seminal building, New Zealand Chambers in Leadenhall Street, London, a building that contained as it were in a nutshell the programme for his subsequent work and that of his period, a building which had an important influence on the whole history of modern architecture.[4] Two years later he built Lowther Lodge (Fig. 27) in Kensington, London, on an urban site that was at the time still almost wholly undeveloped. Gothic was abandoned at a stroke. The forms that articulate the plain brick building are those of the Renaissance, the gables are low and some have curved contours, the windows have white-painted, cross-shaped wooden glazing bars that stand out gaily against the dark brick walls, chimney-stacks are articulated in a manner that has ceased to have anything to do with Gothic. Instead of a country-house of the usual Gothic or pretentious Italian type, this was a country-house of simple, domestic forms, the plain dress of which, especially its undecorated brick walls, seemed at the time to go almost too far, to be exaggerated in its simplicity. So strange did naturalness appear in a vitiated culture that it was at first taken for artificiality. Like New Zealand Chambers, Lowther Lodge, lying on a great London thoroughfare, became a popular topic for discussion. At first dumbfounding the public and provoking their scorn, it imperceptibly influenced the younger generation

[4] Presented and its importance assessed in my book *Die englische Baukunst der Gegenwart*.

24 Cragside, Northumberland. By R. Norman Shaw, for Lord Armstrong, 1870

25, 26 Cragside. Picture-gallery and dining-room

24

27 Lowther Lodge, Kensington, London. By R. Norman Shaw, 1874

superfluous elements being stripped away one by one until the point has been reached when the work of the best architects now building houses has become wholly puritanical in appearance.

Norman Shaw's ground-plans

The idea that emerges from this development is that the character of the house rests in its layout rather than in its forms. Norman Shaw used sometimes to say that the exteriors of his houses held little or no interest for him. The pleasure that he took in designing ended with the plan. And it is, indeed, his plans that form the kernel of Norman Shaw's art. They are the most striking reflection of his brilliance. They are models of utility and convenience yet at the same time, to the eye accustomed to plans, they promise comfort in the highest degree. But their interest does not end there. They always have an extra charm which springs from a certain poetical element that is quite independent of the qualities mentioned. He devises individual arrangements that make life more comfortable, sometimes creating long rooms with fine effects of perspective, sometimes ranging the whole house round a small central courtyard surrounded by walks; there are always staircases of surprising brilliance; and he breaks the height of the storeys at suitable points in order not only to save walled-in space but also to create another poetical motif, such as a view through a window or a bay in a deeper room. One cannot repeat often enough that each of Norman Shaw's ground-plans awakens the most intense interest in this respect. But at the same time his mastery is such that everything seems entirely natural; his plans are by no means primarily romantic, first and foremost they are practical. But while amply and even ingeniously satisfying all practical demands, the master still has the resources to meet the higher claims of purely emotional expectations with ease and brilliance. He is ready to draw upon the repertoire of ancient motifs, especially those preserved in the Elizabethan plan, but this does not in the least tempt him to make sacrifices. He is fond of using the medieval hall in his larger

of artists. This is the usual way of things; while the older generation is either amused at every new turn in art or bitterly opposed to it, the seed of novelty is implanted in young minds, the existence of which barely enters the consciousness of the old. The fruit then begins to ripen quietly, to mature later in the rising generation. With Lowther Lodge, Norman Shaw gave the really effective stimulus to the use of undecorated brick in architecture, which has since been followed in English house-building in contrast to the pretentious historicism of earlier years. Philip Webb had been quietly working in this manner and even more simply for ten years now, but it was left to Norman Shaw, who worked and brought his influence to bear far more publicly, to popularise these principles. They have since come to predominate and subsequent development has been logical, all

28   House at Pinner, nr London. By R. Norman Shaw, for the painter
Frederick Goodall, 1872 (after a drawing by the architect)

29 Town house, 185 Queen's Gate, London. By R. Norman Shaw, 1896

30 Town house, 180 Queen's Gate, London. By R. Norman Shaw, c.1895

country-mansions, introducing it in all its grandeur and romantic magic. Elsewhere he even takes fruitful suggestions from the Palladian plan: for example in the central domed hall that parades in chilly brilliance as the *salone* in houses of the eighteenth century, but which he transforms into areas of great charm. But he is never dominated by historical motifs, he is quite unhampered in his use of the hints he obtains from them. Of all the architects, it is perhaps Norman Shaw's work that shows the greatest variety. He found an entirely new solution for every commission he undertook. Like all great masters, he has always remained a learner, approaching each new commission with the strange feeling of a beginner who is bound to work without a store of experience to draw upon. He has never felt, as petty minds and superficial routine workers do, that he now knows his ground and has only to toss off the solutions. So in the course of his long career he accumulated limitless assets on which future generations can and will draw.

Town houses. London

Norman Shaw's great triumphal career began in the first half of the 1870s, commissions poured in and the overwhelming majority were for dwelling-houses. In addition to many large and medium-sized country-mansions, he built numerous town houses in London, together with many churches, but, alas, only one public building, New Scotland Yard in London. Except for a few large country-mansions, he adhered to the simple, domestic Baroque style that he had first used for New Zealand Chambers

and Lowther Lodge. Most of his town houses were built for artist friends in London, who approached the new movement with open minds; they included Heseltine (196 Queen's Gate) and Flowers (Old Swan House, Chelsea; Fig. 31). He also built many houses with studios for well-known painters (two different houses in Hampstead for Edwin Long; Three Gables, also in Hampstead, for Frank Holl; houses in Melbury Road, Kensington for Luke Fildes and Marcus Stone). One of his most delightful buildings is his own house in Hampstead, a masterpiece of spatial layout and furnished in a distinctive and comfortable style that was unique for its time (1875).[5] The most interesting of his houses in the centre of London are probably 185 (Fig. 29) and 180 (Fig. 30) Queen's Gate, which represent Shaw's design for domestic exteriors at its most mature. In these houses he achieves an ideal union between the practical and the monumental. Inconspicuous but genuine distinction could not be better expressed than it is here. These houses embody the spirit of the best type of rich Englishman: he has nothing of the parvenu about him and in his bearing he is the most modest and reticent of men. And at the same time these houses are the foundation-stones of a new architecture that disregards the now conventional idioms of past cultures fundamentally different from our own and no longer seeks its identity in aristocratic embellishments but in unadorned simplicity.

[5] All the houses named, together with other London houses by Norman Shaw, have been published in my *Die englische Baukunst der Gegenwart.*

Shaw's large country-mansions

In his country-houses, however, Shaw was unable entirely to break away from the romantic magic that the old English manor-houses hold for modern man and that can so easily influence working architects. In certain respects the large houses Adcote in Shropshire, Pierrepoint and Merrist Wood in Surrey, Whispers in Sussex and the charming smaller house for W. Quilter at Sunninghill, still belong to the Gothic tradition. All were built during the 1870s. Except for Adcote, all are half-timbered, a style that the master abandoned in his later years. Adcote is built of stone with brick walls and looks quite Gothic again. This house has become famous, mainly due to Shaw's fine autograph drawing (Fig. 32) prepared for the Academy and presented on the occasion of his election. A masterpiece of architectonic drawing, it now adorns the Diploma Gallery in London. The ground-plan of the house (Fig. 33) is no less interesting than the very original treatment of the architecture of the exterior. The vast hall, a tall, impressive room roofed with stone arches, provides the basic motif for both. The back of the house which lies obliquely to the rest, is old and was extended as a kitchen wing.

The large mansions form the core of Shaw's work. Not only did he enjoy the entire confidence of his clients in this field but these commissions were best suited to his talents. Himself a man of authority with an expansive personality, he found it easy to imagine himself in the most exalted walks of life and was socially and personally the equal of any client. He has been responsible for the best of the English country-houses built during the past thirty years and they stand as the classic embodiment of the concept of the English country-house of the last third of the nineteenth century.

At the beginning of the 1880s he built the mansion which he himself considered to be his best work. This was Dawpool, near Birkenhead, built for the Liverpool shipowner, Thomas Henry Ismay. It lies in virgin heathland, from which fine gardens and a park have been wrested and rises majestically in sombre dark red sandstone masses from the gently rolling country; a profound solemnity broods over the whole building. One look at the ground-plan (Fig. 35) tells us that the owner was a collector of paintings. The space normally allotted to the old English hall is in this instance a picture gallery. The appointments of the interior are extremely dignified and carefully thought out (Fig. 34) and the house is a jewel among English country-mansions.

Return to historicism

The 1880s, beginning with Dawpool, probably represent the peak of Norman Shaw's career. He was now in his fifties and in full possession of his artistic powers. This period saw the creation of works such as the charming Three Gables in Hampstead, the imposing premises of the Alliance Assurance Company in Pall Mall and New Scotland Yard, both in London.[6] It is therefore all the more surprising that towards the end of this decade his work took a remarkable change of direction. To put it bluntly, he returned to historicism. The pleasing feature of his buildings up to this date had been their free, individual design, making him in this respect almost a prophet in his time, the first architect to have broken away from historicism; but now he suddenly embarked on a number of buildings in a specific historical style, eighteenth-century English Neo-Classicism. His first house in this style was 170 Queen's Gate, begun in 1887, which, although heavily de-

[6] All three are illustrated in my *Die englische Baukunst der Gegenwart*.

31   Old Swan House, Chelsea, London. By R. Norman Shaw, 1877

pendent on this style, still showed certain individual characteristics. With the large country-mansion known as Chesters, begun in 1890, he carried Neo-Classical formalism a stage further. But he probably reached his peak in the mansion of Bryanston in Dorset (Fig. 36) begun a few years later. Here not only does the exterior exactly resemble a building by Sir Christopher Wren, but the plan is pure Palladian, with its square block communicating by galleries with four long lateral buildings. These three buildings no longer speak with Norman Shaw's voice, they deliberately use the language of the eighteenth century. In doing so, they are, of course, far and away more interesting than anything produced by his fellow architects in imitation of historical styles. They are extremely refined down to the smallest detail and do not belie Shaw's sovereign mastery of his architectonic experience. But their sole aim is to enter in the most intimate way into the feelings of the eighteenth-century masters; above all they seek to reflect the spirit of that time as faithfully as possible. What conceivable reason could have made the apostle of freedom, the first modern architect to have been produced by the present day, return to the fetters of historicism? What could have made the master return from the soaring flights of his imagination to the captivity of imitative design? It is a difficult question to answer and one to which different people would give

27

32 Adcote, Shropshire. By R. Norman Shaw, 1875 (drawing by the architect for the Diploma Gallery)

1 WC
2 Washing-place
3 Vault
4 Business-room
5 Front hall
6 Billiard-room
7 Great hall
8 Drawing-room
9 Conservatory
10 Library
11 Small hall
12 Light-well
13 Dining-room
14 Steward
15 Butler
16 Luggage-entrance
17 Silver
18 Cupboard
19 Side entrance
20 Rebuilding of old house
21 Servants' hall
22 Store-room
23 Pantry
24 Meat-larder
25 Milk-larder
26 Scullery
27 Kitchen
28 Ancillary kitchen
29 Drying-room
30 Skylight
31 Store-room

33 Adcote. Plan of ground floor

34 Dawpool, Cheshire. By R. Norman Shaw, c.1880. Gallery

nineteenth century we can see attitudes of mind changing and conservatism growing stronger at the expense of liberalism. The process was most marked in England, the leader during the past century, and can be seen in every intellectual sphere: in politics, religion and the social movement. Retrogression in art may be only a part of the great general movement. But we may at least hope that it is only the swing of the pendulum, a sort of passing reaction against a rather too highly charged freedom movement, which in the long run will only delay and not finally halt the real progress of the world.

Consequences

Whatever the outcome, in returning to the rigid restrictions of eighteenth-century classicism, Norman Shaw gave the signal to English architects to follow suit. The movement spread during the 1890s. In 1890–93 John Belcher built the premises of the Institute of Chartered Accountants in Moorgate Place, London, which may be regarded as a landmark in the switch of public architecture to the rigours of classicism. Since then the movement has slowly but surely gathered momentum and nowadays one sees practically nothing but these forms entered for competitions for public buildings. The architectural literature of the 1890s repeatedly added fuel to the flames. Reginald Blomfield's *History of Renaissance architecture in England 1500–1800* is so violently tendentious in this respect that despite all the author's literary talent one can hardly regard it as a genuine contribution to the literature of the history of art. Just imagine: he ends an abridged edition of the book that appeared in 1900 with an elementary illustration of the classical orders by way of fresh instruction in the correct use of columns! A book containing many illustrations of buildings of the seventeenth and eighteenth centuries edited by Belcher and Macartney that appeared some years ago gave the architect all the information that he could possibly need for building in the style of that period. Thus after a few decades of comparative freedom and independence England has swung right back to 'historicism'. Indeed, as at the time of the controversies between Gothicism and Neo-Classicism, spokesmen now began to use all their persuasive powers on behalf of the architecture of Inigo Jones against the freer style of previous decades. This, of course, meant the strict, obstinately Italianate architecture of the

very different replies. Those who have always remained captive would naturally say that the master had been re-converted to the truth, others would suggest that the wings of his inventiveness were wearying after having borne him up during the best years when he was in full command of his powers.

But such changes in people can never be explained by the event alone. True though it may be that personalities make a period, especially the art of a period, it is equally true that the period makes personalities. It is a situation in which it may well be difficult, if not impossible, to draw the line between effect and counter-effect. On all hands during the second half of the

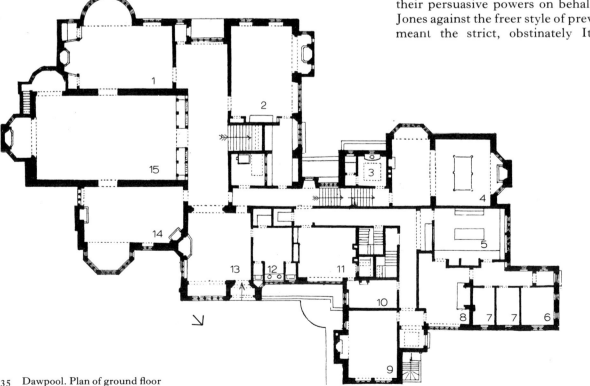

1 Drawing-room
2 Dining-room
3 Washing-place and WC
4 Billiard-room
5 Kitchen
6 Store-room
7 Meat-larder
8 Scullery
9 Servants' hall
10 Bedroom
11 Butler
12 Cloak-room
13 Front hall
14 Library
15 Picture-gallery

35 Dawpool. Plan of ground floor

36　Bryanston, Dorset. By R. Norman Shaw, 1895

classical orders and applied both to the building and its plan. Herein lies its difference from the Queen Anne style, which eschewed this very proliferation of forms and obsession with symmetry and fled from such exalted architectural idioms to the health-giving sources of popular art.

Architectural historicism in the dwelling-house

But the significant point about the present state of affairs is that however much ground the movement may already have gained in public architecture, it has so far been unable on the whole to exert much influence on domestic architecture. It is true that dwelling-houses are already being built again in the style of the eighteenth century, in particular medium-sized and large country-mansions – for which, indeed, Norman Shaw himself gave the signal. But the smaller house – and it is herein that England's real importance lies today – has remained fresh and untouched by the blight of historicism and architecture based on symmetry; here the development initiated over forty years ago has continued virtually unimpeded until quite recently and will richly repay examination. The leaders here are not the historical stylists but a quite different group that pursues the traditions of the 1870s and 1880s and sometimes considerably improves upon them. The buildings of the stylists, symmetrical houses with columns and pilasters, containing pillared halls and drawing-rooms with coffered ceilings are like everything of the kind in England, so extraordinarily uninteresting that they would have gone unnoticed here even had they occurred in greater numbers. Since, as we have said, their role is for the moment insignificant and Neo-Classicism has so far showed itself mainly in non-domestic architecture, this most recent excursion could have been anticipated. So we shall now return to the early 1880s and follow the thread of the development of the modern English house from that time onwards.

Popular motifs in architecture

In the small and medium-sized houses which he built in large numbers throughout his career in addition to the larger buildings that we have already discussed, Norman Shaw retained the motifs of the old, indigenous domestic architecture. The Hallams, a fine house in Surrey, built in 1896, shows how fresh his approach in this respect remained to the end of his days. Plain brick walls, pantiled roof, tile-hung gables, chimney-stacks that rise at the side of the house, white-painted woodwork surrounding windows and doors and, above all, the extraordinarily attractive motifs of the windows that he took from early domestic architecture – such was the repertoire he used to obtain his effects for this type of house.

It was, perhaps, in his ideas about windows that he influenced his period most powerfully. The window in northern architecture is, of course, fundamentally different from its counterpart in Italy. Italian art uses windows as mere holes in the wall to be distributed regularly over the façades. The hole-like quality of the window was further emphasised by cornices that cast shadows and, for the sake of symmetry, holes were also placed at points where they were not needed. How different was northern architecture! By grouping windows together, by relating the window closely to the requirements of the room it was intended to light, it made it the most eloquent vehicle of expression, made it proclaim the character of the house. From the beginning Norman Shaw had been the first to recognise this great truth once more. He was responsible for making the English type of deep bay window with glazing all round, the continuous rows of little windows uninterrupted by mullions, and indeed, groups of windows of all sorts thoroughly at home in England again. He rediscovered these gems of northern popular art and offered them to the contemporary world. Windows are always the main feature of the house and often the only one.

The small house. Bedford Park

There had been until now, i.e. for the twenty years during which Philip Webb, Eden Nesfield and Norman Shaw had begun to extend their interest in its direction and to bring new ideas to bear upon it, little real progress in the small house; or at least it had not yet become popular in its new form. It was still the exception and not the rule. Furthermore it was reputed to be expensive and those who wished to build cheaply from either choice or necessity, felt obliged to stick to the old pattern. The credit for having intervened to ease the situation and for having made the new type of small house completely at home in England must again go to Norman Shaw. His means to this end was the garden suburb of Bedford Park on the outskirts of London. In the mid-1870s Jonathan Carr, an enterprising man with an understanding of art, had bought the land west of London and immediately behind the suburb of Hammersmith on which an old country-mansion named Bedford House had stood; this land was now ripe for development and Carr wished to put up houses for the lower middle classes.* He consulted Norman Shaw, who eagerly set about developing a series of types of small house which were to meet all the demands of comfort, convenience and even artistic design and still be cheap enough to compete with the normal run of speculative buildings. The success of the experiment exceeded all expectations. The ground was parcelled out in such a way as to preserve as many as possible of the fine old trees and there was no reluctance to leave old trees standing at the roadside or to carry the pavement round them. Streets were pleasantly winding and care was taken to see that the houses faced in the best possible direction – south-east to south – and every house had its smaller or not so small garden shaped as agreeably as possible. Most of the houses were detached, a few were semi-detached and there were also a few terraced houses, for the planners were aware that where extreme cheapness was required, this could only be achieved with terraced housing. A carefully calculated variety – which yet managed to avoid the trivial and the picturesque, into which such attempts may easily degenerate – ensured that even the terraced houses made a pleasant impression. And this they most certainly did. Apart

*Carr (1845–1915) was a cloth merchant who bought 24 acres of land in Turnham Green, Chiswick, including three Georgian villas built by the Bedford Brothers. His first architect was E. W. Godwin whose designs date from 1875. Shaw's appointment as Estate Architect to Bedford Park began in 1877. [DS]

even from its cheapness, the estate was a complete revelation to the contemporary world. These streets with their cheerful little houses nestling amid the greenery seemed to bespeak quiet comfort and a refreshing *joie-de-vivre*. Such a thing had never been dreamt of before, but least of all was it expected in a new quarter of a city built for the lower middle-classes. But naturally the novelty of the venture could not fail to provoke scorn in many forms, for this is always the means of escape for the majority in the face of the unfamiliar in art. The estate became linked in the public mind with the aesthetic movement that was flourishing at the time and became a favourite butt of witticisms in the variety theatre and in comedy, just as – or perhaps even more so than – fun is poked today in certain circles at the new artistic movement on the continent. The similarity between the movement of that time in England and the present one that started twenty years later on the continent is in every sense most striking. The master's experiment in building an estate of smallish houses on artistic principles could not fail to be an immediate success. Bedford Park became the refuge of the aesthetes. They found what they wanted there and were happy. It was not long before the estate became a meeting-place not only for painters, writers and actors but also for art-loving lay people who shared their aims. Soon Bedford Park actually became a sight which no American passing through London could miss seeing. And, considering the circumstances of that time, one has to admit that

it richly deserved such attention. There was at the time virtually no development that could compare in artistic charm with Bedford Park, least of all had the small house found anything like so satisfactory an artistic and economic solution as here. And herein lies the immense importance of Bedford Park in the history of the English house. It signifies neither more nor less than the starting-point of the smaller modern house, which immediately spread from there over the whole country.

The Bedford Park houses

Looking more closely at Bedford Park – which even now is a sight worth seeing – one hardly realises that there are only nine different types of house. They are so successfully mixed that one does not notice the repetitions but has the impression of an inexhaustible variety. Most of the types were designed by Norman Shaw, a few by E. W. Godwin.* It is worth reproducing the plans of a few of the houses (Figs. 38–43). The most striking point about them is their great saving of space, which does not, however, detract from their convenience and comfort. The rooms are all of medium size, the largest measuring 4.5 to 5.5 m.; the rooms – the houses are all two storeyed with attic rooms – measure 3 m. in height on the ground-floor, 2.75 m. on the first floor and 2.5 m. clear in the attic. But as a general principle the kitchen is on the ground floor. The houses have no basements apart from a small, low-ceilinged excavated area for storing coal and wine. At ground-floor level and at first-floor level when they are not tile-hung, the outside walls measure $1\frac{1}{2}$ bricks (35.5 cm.) in thickness and where they are so hung one brick in thickness. A house of this type may be rented for 1000–2000 M.† As is the custom in England, the houses are on leasehold land and can therefore be bought for a very moderate price (10,000–16,000 M),‡ plus a fairly low annual ground-rent for the land. There are a shop, a church, an inn, a club-house and various schools, including a school of art, on the estate. In addition to the small houses, several of the inhabitants have built themselves larger ones, but these have been kept in character with the others. The estate originally comprised some five hundred houses built between 1877 and 1881; new, mostly bad speculative, buildings have recently sprung up round the original nucleus.

*Further types were added by later architects after this book was written. [DS]
†Approx. £50 and £100 at the time; £1 was worth about 20 Marks in 1906 [DS]
‡Approx. £500 and £800 at the time. [DS]

37–43 Garden suburb, Bedford Park, nr London. By R. Norman Shaw, *c*.1880. Houses.
Plans of a semi-detached house. Plans of a detached house

1 Scullery
2 Kitchen
3 Dining-room
4 Hall
5 Drawing-room
6 Vestibule
7 Bedroom

1 Coal
2 Cleaning-room
3 Meat-larder
4 Kitchen
5 Drawing-room
6 Dining-room
7 Scullery
8 Library
9 Bedroom

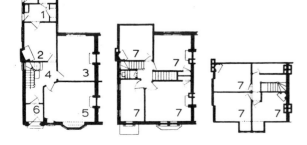

44 Houses in Bedford Park

45 Houses in Bedford Park

The importance of Bedford Park

The pointers given by Norman Shaw at Bedford Park were of the utmost importance. It may indeed be that these small houses, on which he himself spent little time and which were in a way extra to his main work, represent one of the most fruitful ideas that he threw out to his contemporaries. The problem facing house-building in the world of today is that of the middle-class house. This class gained an undreamt-of importance during the nineteenth century and economically speaking is now at the top of the social order. It is clamouring loudly for its art. Compared with this more momentous question of our time it matters little whether a dozen or two more or less large country-mansions or princely palaces – which in earlier centuries accounted for almost the whole picture of house-building – are built. The important thing is to find a satisfactory solution to the problem of the small house – and this is just what Norman Shaw did for the first time for England at Bedford Park.

Thus this great architect touched every nerve of his age with beneficent hand; he moulded every aspect of art that came his way; he found an architecture for his age, developed it and brought it to maturity; indeed, he may even have moved too fast and – in his last sternly classicising works – almost carried things to excess.

John Douglas

Although in effect Norman Shaw considerably dwarfed his contemporaries, he was not an isolated figure. There were a number of skilled and extremely efficient fellow-architects, who shared his aims. One thinks first of John Douglas in Chester. Born in 1829, he was two years older than Shaw. His houses gave the newer parts of Chester its character and he also built many large country-mansions and smaller houses round the outskirts of the city and up and down the country. Like the triple constellation Webb-Nesfield-Shaw he closely followed the traditional native style, remaining constant to it throughout his life. Born and resident in Chester, the home of true half-timbering, he devoted himself most lovingly to the re-introduction of the style, mastered it down to the last detail and produced buildings of great charm. Yet he also handled brick and stone with great skill. His buildings always reflect consummate mastery of form and are yet simple enough in feeling and natural-looking fitness for purpose to stand comparison with the old houses. His most charming creations include a whole series of small buildings (lodges, farm-buildings (Fig. 46), workmen's houses, schools, etc.) in the vicinity of Eaton Hall, the Duke of Westminster's seat in Cheshire, where their fresh and natural character shows them up to great advantage against Alfred Waterhouse's main house. These

46 Cheese-dairy on the estate of the Duke of Westminster, nr Chester. By John Douglas

48 Flete Lodge, Holbeton, Devon. By John D. Sedding, 1887

buildings amply repay an outing from Chester. The best-known of Douglas's larger houses are Barrow Court, near Chester, and Abbeystead, Lord Sefton's country-seat near Lancaster (Fig. 47).

John D. Sedding

John D. Sedding (1837–91) was in fact one of the Gothicist church architects and only occasionally turned to house building. But the houses that he did build are as brilliant as his churches. It would be hard to imagine a more delightful house than the little Flete Lodge of 1887 at Holbeton (Fig. 48), which, despite a lingering Gothic feeling in its forms, is yet entirely modern in spirit. His most important work in the field of domestic architecture was the alteration of Netley, a Gothic mansion near Southampton, the exterior and interior of which are illustrated in Figs. 49–51.

Ernest George

Ernest George (b. 1839) was by far the most important of the generation of domestic architects slightly junior to Norman Shaw who followed in his footsteps more or less in the direction mapped out by him and his fellows. George worked in the same good idiom of plain brickwork and homely interiors, yet he occupies a special place among English architects. From early youth onwards he accompanied his father on his travels in Europe, where, then as now, he enjoyed sketching in the cities of the continent. He likes to come over every year for a sketching tour in some region where there are picturesque towns or villages. He has published the fruits of these travels in several portfolios of etchings ('on the Moselle', 'on the Loire', 'of Belgium', 'of Venice') which have enjoyed great popularity. The influence of these trips is also reflected in his buildings, especially in the best-known among them, the rows of houses in Collingham Gardens (Fig. 52), Harrington Gardens and Sloane Square in London.[7] In his no less numerous country-houses he

[7] All these houses have been published in my *Die englische Baukunst der Gegenwart*.

49 Netley, Hampshire. Gothic house altered by John D. Sedding, *c.*1889

33

adhered more or less closely to the English tradition, but in these town houses we find a number of foreign influences, especially Dutch and German, such as are found nowhere else in England. The gabled houses of Holland, in particular, made a great impression on George. But he transformed these impressions most successfully, never copying slavishly what he had seen, and the residential quarters that he built are among the finest examples of domestic architecture to be seen in London. These houses are admirably fresh in design, versatile in conception and sure in detail. Compared with the strict practicality and the often almost puritanical plainness to which one is accustomed in other English buildings, the dominant mood of these houses is almost romantic, fantastic. This is George's characteristic quality. It occurs in nearly all his buildings, in the many charming workmen's houses that he built on the estates of the great landowners (Fig. 53), in his country-houses large and small and in his town houses. Though the motifs of earlier architecture with all their variety of forms are no longer entirely appropriate to the culture of today and their many-sided qualities seem merely sentimental to us, they suit George admirably. He enjoys using old towers and outbuildings, outside staircases and broad

50, 51   Netley. Drawing-room and hall

52   Town house, 17 Collingham Gardens, London. By E. George and Peto, 1887

53 Workmen's houses, Leigh, Kent. By E. George and Peto, *c*.1885

54 Clencot, Gloucestershire. By E. George and Peto, *c*.1885

55 Below: Clencot. Hall
56 Right: The architect's house, Totteridge, nr London. By T. E. Collcutt, 1898. Plan

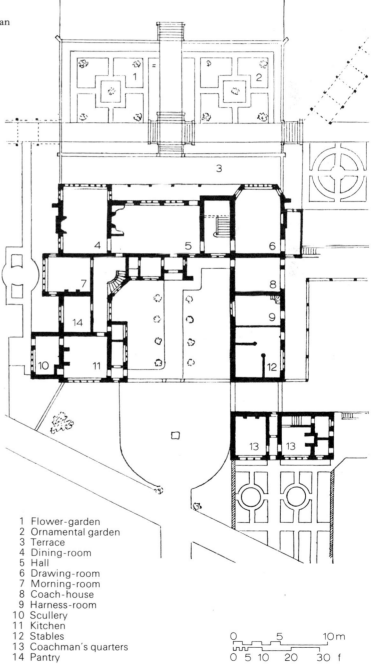

57 View of T. E. Collcutt's house at Totteridge

1 Flower-garden
2 Ornamental garden
3 Terrace
4 Dining-room
5 Hall
6 Drawing-room
7 Morning-room
8 Coach-house
9 Harness-room
10 Scullery
11 Kitchen
12 Stables
13 Coachman's quarters
14 Pantry

58 House at Fifield, Oxfordshire. By T. E. Collcutt, 1894 (after a drawing by the architect)

gateways, elaborately worked, unconcealed roof-timbers and profusely ornamented overmantels. He never misses an opportunity in large country-mansions of reviving the medieval hall in all its spaciousness, including the dais and the minstrels' gallery.

This means, of course, that he has done little to further the development of modern ideas. Such was probably not his intention. He took all the richness of accumulated experience from the large English mansion and used it skilfully to build new houses which he intended should equal the old in comfort and romantic character. He lacked Norman Shaw's flair for the new and unusual. Nevertheless his plans are among the best achievements of contemporary architecture. They have a consistent clarity and simplicity which is pleasing. As regards style, George adhered to Elizabethan forms, never forsaking them for Palladianism. In this respect too he is a northern Romantic who has never been tempted by Italian brilliance and rhythm.

During a career that has been full and marked by great personal industry Ernest George has built a whole series of great English country-mansions. The most important are Studleigh Court and Rousdon in Devonshire, Motcombe in Dorsetshire, which we shall discuss in detail later in the book, Clencot (Figs. 54, 55), Batsford and Edgeworth Manor in Gloucestershire, Monk Fryston in Yorkshire, Poles and North Mymms in Hertfordshire, Buchan Hill in Sussex, Dunley Hill in Surrey and Shiplake Court in Oxfordshire.

T. E. Collcutt

The houses of T. E. Collcutt (b. 1840) are distinguished for the energetic yet pleasing design which is so refreshing in his other buildings. Collcutt's means of expression, like George's, are Elizabethan in form, but he is more personal in his use of these forms which he displays in sharply outlined, fairly modern-looking buildings. However, by far the greater part of his work and importance has been in the sphere of public buildings rather than of dwelling-houses. The most charming of the latter must surely be his own house at Totteridge, near London (Figs. 56, 57), the plan of which is also distinguished for its unusual articulation and spatial arrangement. The character of the main living-room in the house is modelled on the hall and forms the central point of the building, which lies in a horseshoe shape round an entrance court. The main rooms on the garden front look on to a formal flower-garden, beyond which stretch broad, green lawns. A little house for a coachman stands guard at the front of the house. Viewed from the road the whole complex has a picturesque, intimate appearance (Fig. 57). The proportions of the house at Fifield in Oxfordshire (Fig. 58) are more modest, as befits a rubble-walled building, and the broad, flat areas of roof form an unusually pleasing group.

B. The development of the modern English house under the younger architects

Earlier position of architecture in relation to arts and crafts

An important phase of English domestic architecture ends with the architects we have been discussing. We have already stressed the fact that Morris's Arts and Crafts movement and the movement in architecture had in fact nothing to do with one another. Sedding was the only architect of those of the older generation whom we have discussed who actually came into contact with the Arts and Crafts; Philip Webb, who is anyway and in all respects exceptional as an architect, was the only one who was fully involved in both movements. Nesfield, Norman Shaw and George, in short the typical architects of the period from 1860 onwards, remained entirely ignorant of Morris and the Arts and Crafts movement. It is true that they persuaded the clients for whom they built houses to allow Morris to do the furnishings, from which it appears that they regarded Morris's work as the best of its kind. But the important point is that they took little or no part in the actual appointing of the house, especially as regards the movable objects such as furniture, materials and carpets. They believed that once the house was built their work was done. Thus the actual Arts and Crafts movement proceeded in parallel with architecture but had no contact with it. The new Arts and Crafts had sprung from painting: Rossetti's school was its foster-mother; its first disciples were painters, its adherents aesthetes in general, not architects. Architects were above such matters, they regarded handicrafts as beneath them.

Not that architects of an earlier generation had not been willing to take up the cause of handicrafts. The Gothicists with the brilliant Pugin at their head had bent all their energies towards their reorganisation. But they had been concerned only with a medieval vocabulary of forms and today we can safely admit that they were unsuccessful to the extent that they were set on a superficial imitation of styles. Sedding was the first to recognise the full implications of this. He regarded stylistic considerations as of secondary importance and just as in his architectonic creations all historical forms – which he used entirely as he pleased – were equally acceptable to him, so in handicrafts he admitted every form of expression. But one thing he did above all else: he zealously returned to nature for inspiration. Like Pugin, Sedding was centrally involved with handiwork, he was its enthusiastic friend and powerful supporter. But as he was almost exclusively employed in building churches, his very progressive efforts on behalf of handicrafts had little influence on the house. Nevertheless he forms the first bridge between the architects' camp and that of handicraft proper. In so far as handicraft relates to the furnishing of the house, it was virtually bound to develop into the requisite new form by following Morris's lead; and, as we have already stressed, the development took place within a small group which gradually grew into the Art Workers' Guild, the members of which organised the Arts and Crafts Exhibitions from 1888 onwards.*

New approach to the artistic movement

The younger generation of architects adopted a fundamentally different approach to the Arts and Crafts movement from that of their elders. The movement was already in existence and was,

*The Art Workers' Guild was formed in 1884 with Walter Crane as its first President. He was also President of the Arts and Crafts Exhibition Society (founded in 1888) from 1888–1890. [DS]

indeed, an essential item on the agenda of problems of the day. They grew into it and it was inevitable that they should be, if not entirely absorbed, at least powerfully stimulated by it. So the best elements of this younger generation now became active followers of the Arts and Crafts movement. Indeed, they felt more or less in agreement with it and the great majority of those who shared this feeling were architects involved in building churches and houses; and among the domestic architects in particular nearly all were pupils of Norman Shaw. New aims now arose; by and large they were the ones proclaimed so vehemently and at every opportunity by Ruskin and Morris, which concerned the qualities of material and labour. The idea began to take root that the value of a piece lay mainly in its execution, which must be technically correct and appropriate to the material and workmanship. All the prerequisities for every man-made object should lie in its material, purpose and construction, its form should be consequent upon these prerequisities and not upon an independent preconceived idea. But above all, workmanship should be as sound as possible; this became the indispensable condition and it was here that the influence of Morris was so important. These were the principles of Ruskin's theories, which have since become so familiar and at the heart of which one can see the awakening of a northern, Germanic view of art contrasting with the Italian, classical view. Only one aspect was ignored in the formulation of these principles; this was the purely sentimental qualities, such as mood, poetry, rhythm, symbolism and fantasy, that underlie all human creativity. But it did not matter that the tangible requirements were so heavily weighted at the expense of the sentimental ones, since these make themselves felt anyway. The movement that returned so wholeheartedly to ideals of pure craftsmanship may be described as a kind of materialism; a similar movement sometimes occurs in painting after periods of lofty idealism during which reality may easily have been lost to sight, in order to re-establish contact with basic principles.

First consequence of the movement. Purist aims of architecture

The first consequences of this movement to architecture were not an immediate readiness on the part of architects to take over the whole interior furnishing of the house, but primarily a strong purist development in architecture itself. Architects now aimed at a maximum of formal reticence and the strictest simplicity. In fact, they returned to the bare brick walls of the terraces in Gower Street, London, which had been built some hundred years previously on land leased from the Dukes of Bedford and Portland and which, in their total lack of anything resembling art or architecture, were the ultimate in artistic restraint. In reality certain merits, if not beauties, were beginning to be recognised in such buildings. And it was believed that by adding a very small amount of atmosphere, the architecture of the modern house could be shaped out of their spirit. These trends are quite strongly expressed in the better examples of the domestic architecture of the past ten to fifteen years, as can be seen from a glance at the illustrations from here onwards. These houses do not on the whole appeal to the continental eye. They appear sombre, hard, secretive, inartistic and indeed almost repellant. Dark masses of brick rise from the ground without any form of articulation. There are no mouldings to enliven the undecorated surfaces, the walls continue upwards as parapets beyond the point where the roof begins and are cut off square at the top, ending in straight-edged gables on the narrow sides. Great rectangular chimney-stacks tower in isolation into the sky. Only the framework round the windows, painted white in contrast to the dark mass, lightens the impression somewhat. But even here

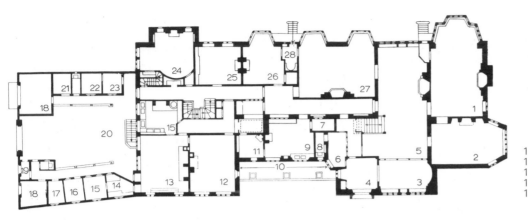

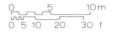

1 Drawing-room	15 Scullery
2 Library	16 Meat-larder
3 Front hall	17 Washing-place
4 Vestibule	18 Coal
5 Hall	19 Refuse
6 Cloak-room	20 Kitchen-court
7 Silver	21 Wood
8 WC	22 Cleaning-room
9 Butler	23 Lamps
10 Single-storey projection	24 School-room
11 Bedroom	25 Steward
12 Servants' hall	26 Man of the house's room
13 Kitchen	27 Dining-room
14 Pantry	28 Entrance from garden

59–62 Avon Tyrell, nr Salisbury, Hampshire. By W. R. Lethaby, for Lord Manners. Plan of ground floor. View from south-west. View from the forecourt. Garden front

there is no effect of variety or chiaroscuro, they lie flush with the wall surface. There is something austere, gloomy, almost joyless about the whole thing. Yet there is also something unusually powerful and confident about it. Reserved, tough and embattled, these houses stand in the foggy English air, the dark colossi march proudly beneath the eternally overcast sky as the lowering clouds race past. What would be the good of the smiling, sunny architecture conceived beneath Italian skies here? Despite many borrowings from abroad, English architecture has frequently returned to this heavy sombre, unadorned style. There can be no doubt that it embodies a national instinct. This may perhaps also be why after years of acquaintanceship with England and its art, this particular type of architecture should seem so uncommonly appealing. Philip Webb was the first to reintroduce it in modern times and the growing respect in which the master has been held by younger architects in recent years is the best proof that the seed he sowed has taken root. Norman Shaw, who handled the whole range of architectural expression with brilliance, not to say with virtuosity, used it in his best period. And of the generation that is now at the helm it is primarily his pupils who still use it. It is remarkable that none of them followed the master in his final swing towards Neo-Classicism but all adhered to the ideals of his best period: the struggle for simplicity, freedom from decoration, grandeur of conception.

W. R. Lethaby

Of Norman Shaw's pupils, William Richmond Lethaby undoubtedly deserves first mention.* He has remained little known because of his great dislike of publicity, a characteristic which he shares with other members of the Arts and Crafts movement. But those who know his houses must immediately recognise that he is one of the architects who today uphold and continue the best traditions of English house-building. He brings a delicate, distinctive atmosphere to the sombre grandeur of the English house. Modern in the best sense in thought and sensibility and certainly hostile to any hint of romanticism, he cannot help imbuing his buildings with an exalted aesthetic and spiritualised atmosphere which immediately charms the spectator. The number of his houses is not large but all appear to be masterpieces. His aims are perhaps embodied in their purest

*William *Richard* Lethaby (1857–1931) and not as Muthesius has it 'Richmond'. Lethaby still remains little known as an architect. As Mumford pointed out in his introduction to the Oxford republication (1957) of Lethaby's *Form and Civilization* his 'great importance in the history of British architecture derived . . . from the fact that he carried the Arts and Crafts doctrine beyond the stage of pious medievalism and blind mechanophobia'. [DS]

63 Avon Tyrell. Drawing-room

64 Avon Tyrell. Hall

form in the country seat Avon Tyrell built for Lord Manners and fully illustrated here (Figs. 59–64). Though the entrance front appears earnest and stern, the garden front with its terraces and three white bay windows projecting from the dark brickwork is lively and inviting. Lethaby's sole aim for the interior has been restfulness and comfort; the only decoration is the real hand-worked stucco on walls and ceilings; apart from the carpets there is no colour, walls and ceilings are plain white. Lethaby likes to construct his fire-places of plain, flat marble slabs and attaches the highest importance to the choice of finely marked stone. Forms throughout are most restrained and all his designs are strictly practical in character.

Much more powerfully, perhaps, than in architecture, Lethaby influenced his period in the sphere of artistic handicrafts, for he was the director of the Central School of Arts and Crafts in London, which had been founded in 1896 and where he was the first to stand for the aspirations of the workshop, both in principle and in all their implications. Nowadays all the schools of arts and crafts in England follow Lethaby's extremely worth-while example.

Ernest Newton

Another of Norman Shaw's pupils who achieved considerable prominence, Ernest Newton,* shared Lethaby's aims, though he was less closely involved in Arts and Crafts. He is one of the busiest architects in England and therefore represents the good principles of current thinking about the house in perhaps its most accessible form. Like Lethaby, he designs in broad, plain masses and, as with Lethaby, one is surprised to find in him the most sensitive understanding of the effect of material and workman-like treatment. This is why it is difficult to tell from photographs what his houses are like and it is a surprise to see them in reality. Our interest is immediately engaged by the masterly way in which the qualities of the material are handled and shown to advantage, the excellent work in every material, the subtle juxtaposing of colour in the different materials. Although

*Ernest Newton (1856–1922) [DS]

they are far removed from any elegance, they reflect a high level of refinement. The question as to what gives these men their extraordinary sureness in these matters is easily answered: they have devoted painstaking and assiduous study to the old techniques of their country. They have made great efforts and have succeeded in recovering the accumulated traditions which had been preserved by the old guilds, each in its own technique, and which had been lost for a time when the guilds were dissolved. They sought out, applied once more and developed further all the old techniques, such as decorative lead-work (in which the decorative motifs are partly coloured), the old style of brick-laying, stone-carving, plastering, the metal-working techniques, etc. The operation entailed a vast amount of painstaking work, which has demanded much personal sacrifice from individuals. There is at the moment a strong feeling among English architects for detail of this kind and it is probably true to say that the secrets of the old guild tradition have been studied and adapted to modern use more widely in England than in any other country. Apart from their unadorned naturalness of interpretation, it is this that makes modern English buildings so impressive. Recently, especially, Newton has moved steadily closer to the entirely undecorated, broad style with strong emphasis on the effects of material and natural colouring; in his earlier buildings he was still somewhat fantastic and romantic. The most important of his recent larger houses are Bullers Wood in Chislehurst and Red Court near Haslemere. His other houses may be numbered in hundreds and are scattered all over England. Of the two illustrated here, Steephill on the island of Jersey (Figs. 65–68) is unusual in being rather southern in character, as befits its geographical position. One can tell from looking at the house that it occupies a sunnier site than England, also it has verandas and balconies and a generally cheerful appearance. Red Court, near Haslemere (Figs. 69, 70), is entirely different. It illustrates Newton's plain, broad, austere manner and in its general appearance is an ideal example of what is called in England today a good house. The ground-plan is arranged simply round a northern service yard in such a way that all the living-rooms face the sun, the layout of the front court and surrounding gardens is strictly geometrical, as is commonly the case in England today.

65 Steephill, Jersey, Channel Islands. By Ernest Newton. Front view

1 WC
2 Washing-place
3 Hall
4 Study
5 Drawing-room
6 Library
7 Dining-room

8/9 Butler's rooms
10 Servants' hall
11 Kitchen
12 Scullery
13 Meat-larder
14 Cleaning-room

66 Steephill. Plan of ground floor

67 Steephill. Another view

68 Steephill. Library

Other pupils of Norman Shaw

These are the most prominent of Norman Shaw's pupils but there are a number of others of high standing among present-day domestic architects. The most important are: E. J. May, G. C. Horsley (Figs. 71, 72), Edward S. Prior and Mervyn Macartney. They all follow more or less closely in the steps of Norman Shaw in his best period, which can be summed up as an individual use of native forms. Admittedly the emphasis in the master's work was on the individual use, whereas in that of the pupils it is rather on the native forms. When all is said and done the master stands unrivalled among his pupils, none of whom can touch him for brilliance. They are perhaps a little too much obsessed by notions about material and craftsmanship or perhaps the Arts and Crafts movement has had too restrictive an influence on them. This is always a danger with realistic movements in art. Artists cannot concentrate all their attention on matters of pure craftsmanship and at the same time allow the imagination free play to create noble works of art. Indeed, S. H. Barnsley, an able pupil of Norman Shaw, has gone so far as to practice joinery with his own hands; he finds craftsmanship entirely satisfying and takes pleasure in making kitchen or farmhouse furniture of a primitive kind which he sends in to the Arts and Crafts Exhibitions. Yet it must be said that this practical movement which began in England as the product of the union between architecture and handicraft has done a great deal of good, especially in house-building, where one readily sacrifices great flights of the imagination; it has also had an extremely beneficial influence in the direction of honesty, sterling quality and especially in the education of public taste towards simplicity and unpretentiousness, and so towards a measure of improvement of taste in general. If taste for the vernacular has become somewhat excessive in England today, this is altogether preferable to the stage of parvenu taste that is still so cosily entrenched in Germany.

69   Red Court, nr Haslemere, Surrey. By Ernest Newton

70   Red Court. Plan of ground floor

1 Conservatory
2 Billiard-room
3 Washing-place
4 Service area
5 Workshop
6 Scullery
7 Coal
8 Servants
9 Kitchen
10 Meat-larder
11 Pantry
12 Dining-room
13 Hall
14 Porch
15 Drawing-room
16 Study
17 Forecourt

Second consequence of the connection with Arts and Crafts: new vocabulary of forms

Another consequence of the close contact between architecture and artistic handicrafts in England was the tendency that grew up among several architects to abandon historical forms in architecture and to work in so-called new forms. Norman Shaw's pupils are all entirely at one with him in not wishing to develop new forms. They are quite content with historical forms, indeed they restrict themselves to native English forms, even to the extent of following the local traditions of the areas in which they build. Thus this second group of architects forms a striking contrast to them. It has adopted much the same attitude to historical forms as the new movement on the continent, which began by throwing tradition to the winds. It must be said at once that this group of domestic architects is small in England. Not counting the Scottish architects, most of them fairly young, whom we shall discuss later, they number barely half-a-dozen in London. Like Shaw's pupils they belong to the Art Workers' Guild, forming the other half of that group, and from their midst sprang the new vocabulary of forms that so greatly astonished the continent during the first half of the 1890s. Incidentally, in the course of time the work of the other party had moved spontaneously towards characteristic forms of its own, only that these were now sought for their own sake, came indeed to be considered indispensable.

If one examines this new vocabulary of forms in detail it becomes apparent that from the purely formal point of view its constituents are extremely simple. The author of a humorous article in *The Artist* reduced them to three forms: a rectangular vertical tapering towards the top, a very elongated simple cyma moulding and a motif of a little tree. All today's competitions can be won with these three elements, says the writer, and this whole new art can be mastered in five minutes. There is a grain of truth in his sarcasm. In particular it is a good description of the primitivism which the new English artistic community embraces so ardently. But the point on which it is silent is that the new element that speaks to us out of these creations does not lie so much in mere form. It is rather a question of new ideas about the surface, the relationship between decorated and undecorated areas, and colour. To make as much of external forms as is often done is to misunderstand the situation because it means judging by purely external, superficial standards.

New understanding of the house and its contents as a single entity

Thus it is new ideas, rather than new forms, which make the work of this group so interesting and give it a civilising significance; it is also due to it that the whole continent has been so powerfully influenced by England. This group cherished the same ideals of craftsmanship as the group of Norman Shaw's pupils, with whom its members were on friendly terms in the Arts and Crafts movement. But with the moderns more than with the Norman Shaw school there was from the first a feeling that the house and its whole contents should be regarded as a unity. This heightened sense of responsibility was the real innovation that they brought with them. The work of Voysey in particular among the members of the London movement was extremely influential; although within a fairly narrow framework, he was the first to achieve a complete synthesis between the work that had been the province of William Morris and that which had belonged hitherto to architects. He not only built houses but also designed furniture, carpets, wallpapers and appliances. This then, this very synthesis of the house and its contents, was the second step in the development of the English house. The same designer is now responsible for both.

C. Harrison Townsend

If he had had more opportunities to build houses C. Harrison Townsend would have had to be regarded as the most important member of this group of architects and discussed first.* Most of his work, however, has been concerned with public building. In this field he is undoubtedly the architect who has achieved the finest results in the endeavour to find a characteristic style based on a personal vocabulary of forms. Cliff Towers in Devonshire, which has unfortunately not yet advanced beyond the planning stage, is the most interesting of his dwelling-houses; he has used more conventional forms for his house Dickhurst in Surrey. Townsend has also designed wallpapers, furniture, etc.

C. F. A. Voysey

By far the most active and best-known architect of this group is, however, C. F. A. Voysey. He has devoted all his energies to

*See Alastair Service's article on C. H. Townsend (1851–1928) in *Edwardian Architecture and its Origins*, London: Architectural Press, 1975, for the whole range of this architect's output. Townsend, as Service points out, worked with Nesfield and was an active member of the Art Workers' Guild. [DS]

71 Balcombe Place, Sussex. By G. C. Horsley. Hall

72 Balcombe Place. Music room

house-building and his fecundity in this field is comparable with that of Ernest Newton. He tends to specialise in small houses, though he has also built larger ones. In both interiors and exteriors he strives for a personal style that shall differ from the styles of the past. His means of expression are of the simplest so that there is always an air of primitivism about his houses. This lends them their charm, for deliberate originality in architecture can lead those who are less than brilliant into absurdities. Yet Voysey's total abandonment of historical tradition does rob his houses too of that firmly established conviction that we admire so much in the houses of the Norman Shaw group. Voysey almost invariably uses rough plaster on his walls and English slate for his roofs. He often places broad, tapering buttresses at the corners, his roofs project a long way beyond the walls and usually rest on slender wrought-iron brackets. His fenestration consists of strips of small, narrow windows, the frames of which are painted green or white. Chimney-stacks are white and slightly tapering. The proportions of the houses are decidedly long and low, this being the architect's main aim in planning the masses. The cottage is his ideal, even when he is building houses of a size and luxuriousness more appropriate to a palace than to a cottage.

His characteristic manner. Simplicity. Low ceilings

Voysey's ground-plans are always as compact as he can make them while still providing in a masterly way for a maximum of comfort. Since of all the English architects he is the one most interested in economy, he prefers his plan to be rectangular, especially in small houses. At the same time this always gives the exteriors of his houses a pleasing simplicity. Inside he saves as much space as possible in passages and less important areas, but he never skimps the main rooms unnecessarily. His real hobbyhorse is the low ceiling, as low as he can make it. He regards a height of 2.75 m. (9 ft.) as the maximum for the main rooms and 2.44 m. (8 ft.) or even 2.36 m. (7 ft. 9 ins.) as still entirely admissible, even desirable. He is opposed to tall rooms in general and refuses to work for clients who will not agree to low rooms. In laying so much stress on low rooms, Voysey is, however, only voicing an opinion that is general in England today, if not always expressed so bluntly. Norman Shaw had

already built rooms as low as 3.05 m. (10 ft.) in his simpler houses. A taste for far lower ceilings has developed since. Leading architects of today regard 2.45 m. clear as the proper height for ordinary living-rooms. And here they are thinking less of economy than of aesthetic effect: low rooms always look comfortable and give the room a compact, unified appearance; they make them look large at floor-level and in general they halve the work of furnishing, especially the treatment of walls and ceiling. From the point of view of economics this is one reason why the English house is cheap. And they are therefore a welcome aid to Voysey in his efforts to build as economically as possible. His extreme simplicity is another means to this end. He is quite willing to renounce all forms of ornament and achieves his effects by means of proportions and the simplest of colours. In his interiors even the strips of small windows contribute to an artistic effect which cannot be achieved by other means. He also takes special care over fire-places. Where means are available he likes to panel the walls, preferably with oak, which he leaves untreated. His furniture is also of unpolished oak, yet in form it has a certain gracefulness of line. He is able to call on the very best resources for wall-coverings, carpets and materials, since these are made to his design: English industry has benefited largely from Voysey in this field, in which he has almost become Morris's successor. But he uses pattern in his interiors less than the delight in ornament reflected in his materials and carpets might lead one to expect and his rooms have an air of pleasant restfulness in form and colour. Their underlying atmosphere is one of delicate, almost timid, modesty that recoils in horror from sudden flights of fancy. Voysey has built a very great number of larger, and especially of smaller, houses. Broadleys on Lake Windermere is an example of a medium- to small-sized house and will be discussed in greater detail (Figs. 73–80). It is a house to be lived in during the summer and its terraces command a magnificent view of nearby Lake Windermere. Voysey has made the hall the main living-room and has therefore given it a large bay window and a spacious fire-place; a billiard-table stands in the middle of the room. The other rooms are of moderate size. The appointments and furnishings of the interior demonstrate Voysey's extremely simple but intimate and tasteful handling of such matters at its best.

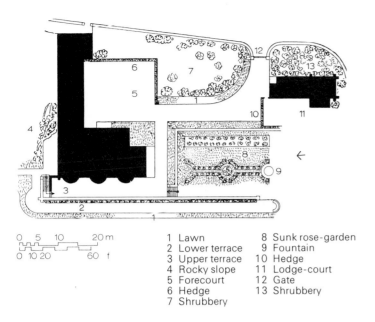

1 Lawn	8 Sunk rose-garden
2 Lower terrace	9 Fountain
3 Upper terrace	10 Hedge
4 Rocky slope	11 Lodge-court
5 Forecourt	12 Gate
6 Hedge	13 Shrubbery
7 Shrubbery	

73 Broadleys on Lake Windermere, Westmorland. Built and designed throughout by C. F. A. Voysey. Site plan

1	Dining-room
2	Pantry
3	Larder
4	Kitchen
5	Servants
6	Meat-larder
7	Cleaning-room
8	Coal
9	Veranda
10	Drawing-room
11	Hall
12	Billiard-table
13	Washing-place
14	Terrace
15	Sun-dial
16	Seat
17	Courtyard

74 Broadleys

75 Broadleys. Plan of ground floor

76 Broadleys. Terrace

Voysey has been a considerable influence on the younger generation. It may be due to him that rough plaster has become the fashionable finish for exterior walls, perhaps too it was his influence that has produced so many advocates of the low ceiling, of which he was so fond. Some of Voysey's external features, such as corner buttresses, have also been imitated. At all events Voysey is the most individualistic of the busy domestic architects in London today, and his courage in seeking new ways and displaying his own personal art to good advantage is as rare as it is refreshing in the prevailing conservatism of the London movement.

Walter Cave

Walter Cave, another member of the inner circle of the Art Workers' Guild, uses forms of expression that are close to those of Voysey. Like Voysey, he favours certain characteristics of the 'new art', such as tapering uprights and elongated mouldings, closely-set supports for banisters, rough plaster and slate roofs for exteriors. The external appearance of his houses (Figs. 81, 83) is almost more successful than Voysey's, his surfaces have a

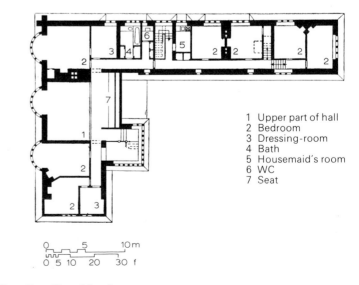

1	Upper part of hall
2	Bedroom
3	Dressing-room
4	Bath
5	Housemaid's room
6	WC
7	Seat

77 Broadleys. Plan of first floor

78 Broadleys. Dining-room

79 Broadleys. Another view of dining-room

80 Broadleys. Drawing-room

81 Belgaum, Woking, Surrey. By Walter Cave. View from the north

broader sweep and the whole is more expressive. Cave has also had great success with his designs for furniture and the delicacy and grace of his pieces within their somewhat primitive forms have earned him unqualified praise. He has built a number of extremely pleasant houses in the Surrey countryside and other parts of England.

W. A. S. Benson

Another architect who must be mentioned in this group is W. A. S. Benson. He has, of course, worked only intermittently as a domestic architect but has become well-known for his tasteful lamps and metalware, for which he uses plain metal surfaces to great effect. For twenty years now he has been using entirely new forms thanks to which his fertilising influence has spread widely. His architecture, and especially his interior decoration, is equally down-to-earth, though his work is sometimes still strongly tinged with the Morrisian love of pattern. Again, some of his interiors, such as the hall in a smallish country-house (Fig. 86), are extremely plain but nonetheless pleasing.

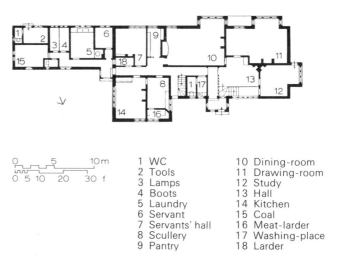

1 WC	10 Dining-room
2 Tools	11 Drawing-room
3 Lamps	12 Study
4 Boots	13 Hall
5 Laundry	14 Kitchen
6 Servant	15 Coal
7 Servants' hall	16 Meat-larder
8 Scullery	17 Washing-place
9 Pantry	18 Larder

82 Belgaum. Plan of ground floor

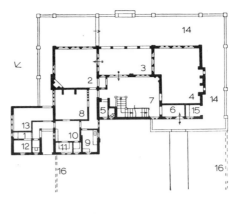

1 Knives
2 Dining-room
3 Loggia
4 Drawing-room
5 Washing-place and WC
6 Porch
7 Hall
8 Kitchen
9 Pantry
10 Scullery
11 Meat-larder
12 Coals
13 Bicycles etc.
14 Terrace
15 Sitting-out area
16 Hedge

83, 84 Warren Mount, Oxshott, Surrey. By Walter Cave. View and plan of ground floor

85 Warren Mount. Hall

86 Maltman's Green, Gerrard's Cross, nr London. By W. A. S. Benson. Hall

Henry Wilson. C. A. Nicholson

Henry Wilson, the well-known and brilliant architect, has built few houses. However, what one can see of his work at Welbeck Abbey, the Duke of Portland's great country-seat, is on a level with his usual high-flying, intensely personal art. His splendid design for the library (Fig. 87) was unfortunately not carried out according to the original project, so we can only admire it in the drawing exhibited at the Royal Academy in 1893. It is a matter of profound regret for English art that an artist of Wilson's brilliance has not found greater opportunity to exercise his splendid artistic powers. C. A. Nicholson's work is equally fine, but, like Wilson, he has little to do with house-building; his province is church architecture.

Leonard Stokes

Although not a member of the Arts and Crafts group, Leonard Stokes must be mentioned in this context, despite the fact he has recently developed a liking for eighteenth-century English forms – which he handles with his own peculiar breadth of vision and scintillating power. Leonard Stokes is certainly one of the most

interesting and talented architects in England today. His buildings are always arresting because of the reposefulness of their broad surfaces and the spacious, robust placing of the masses. This is well illustrated in his own house at Woldingham, Surrey (Figs. 88, 89). In his non-classicising houses at least, he also treats the few details entirely as he pleases, in a free and witty manner that is attractive in its mixture of forcefulness and charm. His ground-plans are no less lucid and definite than his architecture: the same bold, steely thread runs through them, as the plan of Cold Ash, near Newbury, so beautifully shows (Fig. 90). The large house at Streatham Park, near London (Figs. 91, 92), is built on a rectangular plan (the central area has top light) and shows how he uses the compact Palladian form and is even unafraid of making small sacrifices in the layout.*

Other architects with similar ideas

Architects such as A. Dunbar Smith and Cecil Brewer – best known for their charming design for the Passmore Edwards

*Illustrated in *Academy Architecture*, London, 1893, edited by Alexander Koch, p. 41 (ill. 1623). [DS]

45

87 Design for a library at Welbeck Abbey, Derbyshire, seat of the Duke of Portland. By Henry Wilson (drawing by the architect)

88, 89 The architect's house, Littleshaw, Woldingham, Surrey. By Leonard Stokes. View and plan of ground floor

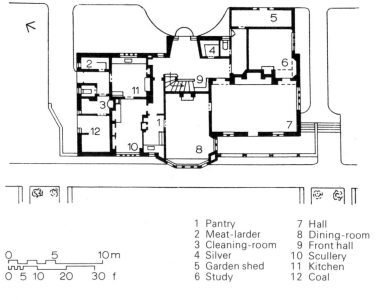

1	Pantry	7	Hall
2	Meat-larder	8	Dining-room
3	Cleaning-room	9	Front hall
4	Silver	10	Scullery
5	Garden shed	11	Kitchen
6	Study	12	Coal

1	Veranda	10	Scullery
2	Man of the house's room	11	Larder
3	Drawing-room	12	Store-room
4	Hall	13	Servants' hall
5	Dining-room	14	Coal
6	Washing-place and WC	15	Side entrance
7	Entrance	16	Milk-larder
8	Pantry	17	Knives
9	Kitchen	18	Forecourt

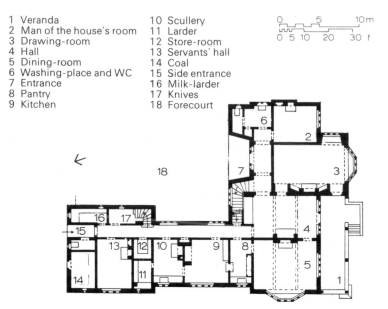

90 Cold Ash, nr Newbury, Berkshire. By Leonard Stokes. Plan of ground floor

Settlement, a home for crippled children in London – used a lighter, more pleasing form than those we have just mentioned. Their works show extreme tastefulness together with a primitive simplicity that borders on the vernacular. A house named Fives Court in Pinner, near London (Figs. 93, 94) illustrates Cecil Brewer's distinctive style. C. J. Harold Cooper depends more on historical forms, but the general impression of his work is modern. The following subscribe to entirely independent forms and are for the most part concerned with interior decoration and furniture design: W. J. Neatby, Charles Spooner, Ambrose Heal junior and that master of the pen-and-ink drawing C. H. B. Quennell. C. R. Ashbee, universally celebrated as an artist in metal, has built a number of houses in Chelsea, London, that have a certain distinctive quality though they are not always free of affectation. Ashbee is mainly occupied in directing his well-known Guild and School of Handicraft, with which he has now moved from London to the country. The pieces he makes there include domestic appointments such as furniture. His real strength, however, lies in the realm of metal utensils, for which he is justly celebrated.

Edgar Wood

It is pleasant to be able to end the list of this largely London-based group of architects with a representative of a similar movement in Manchester, Edgar Wood. Wood is one of the best representatives of those who go their own way and refuse to reproduce earlier styles.[*] He has tried to express his position clearly in a few churches, schools and public buildings. They are exceptionally interesting for their individual spirit and characteristic manner of interpretation and decoration. His individuality is even more clearly apparent in his many dwelling-houses. The best example, perhaps, is a rather large house at Edgerton, near Huddersfield (Figs. 95–102). Its exterior of rough-hewn stone exactly matches the character of the ordinary houses of this hilly area. Inside, however, it reveals in both the arrangement of the rooms – all of which are extremely comfortable and attractive in shape – and in their colour-schemes and decoration, a great creative power in which a certain

[*] Edgar Wood (1860–1935) has been studied in depth by John Archer of Manchester University, whose book on the architect is due for publication shortly. See: Section in *Edwardian Architecture and its Origins*, London, 1975, edited by Service, A., pp. 372–385. [DS]

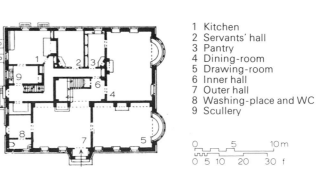

1 Kitchen
2 Servants' hall
3 Pantry
4 Dining-room
5 Drawing-room
6 Inner hall
7 Outer hall
8 Washing-place and WC
9 Scullery

91, 92 West Drive, Streatham Park, nr London. By Leonard Stokes. View and plan of ground floor

93 Fives Court, Pinner, nr London. By Cecil Brewer

94 Fives Court

poetic gift is dominant and actually lends the rooms their essential quality. Edgar Wood's rooms do not merely interest or stimulate, they transport one into an agreeable, warm atmosphere, to which one is glad to submit. Every room has its extremely attractive fire-place in the form of an ingle-nook, in which a sculptured overmantel is the *pièce de résistance* and central point of the decoration. One of Wood's favourite notions is the painted figural frieze. Elsewhere his ornament consists of freely treated plant compositions; but he always follows the basic rule of sharply concentrating the decoration at vantage-points so that it contrasts with undecorated areas. He follows his own bent in design just as he does in architecture. In the field of design he favours a broad, generous treatment, often with inlaid work, especially checker-board edgings and bands (he may be the originator of the present fashion for such things). His steel or bronze fittings also display broad metallic surfaces. He follows his guiding ideas of broad surfaces throughout, but avoids the hard, cold appearance that could easily result from an exaggerated use of this method by using engaging little devices to break up the surface. This attractive quality combined with a pervasive poetical overtone in his designs sets him apart from the great majority of the London Arts and Crafts people, the dominant note of whose work is plainness.

The poets among the domestic architects. M. H. Baillie Scott

Edgar Wood forms the bridge to the poetical and imaginative north of the British Isles, to Scotland, where the Gaelic vernacular element predominates. On the way thither we encounter an architect who plays a very large part in house-building in England today. He is M. H. Baillie Scott,* who lived until recently on the Isle of Man and now resides in Bedford, not far from London. All the coolness and naked rationality which distinguishes the Anglo-Saxon south seems already to have vanished. We seem already to have stepped into the world of fantasy and romance of the ancient bardic poetry that was once supposed to have been the legacy of the misty figure of Ossian and gave the world a new thrill of emotion from the heart of Scotland. With Baillie Scott we are among the purely northern poets among British architects.

Baillie Scott is one of those architects who have discovered entirely personal forms of expression. Externally, however, his

*For the most recent and extensive study of Baillie Scott's work see: Kornholf, J. D. *M. H. Baillie Scott and the Arts and Crafts Movement*, Baltimore and London, 1972. [DS]

47

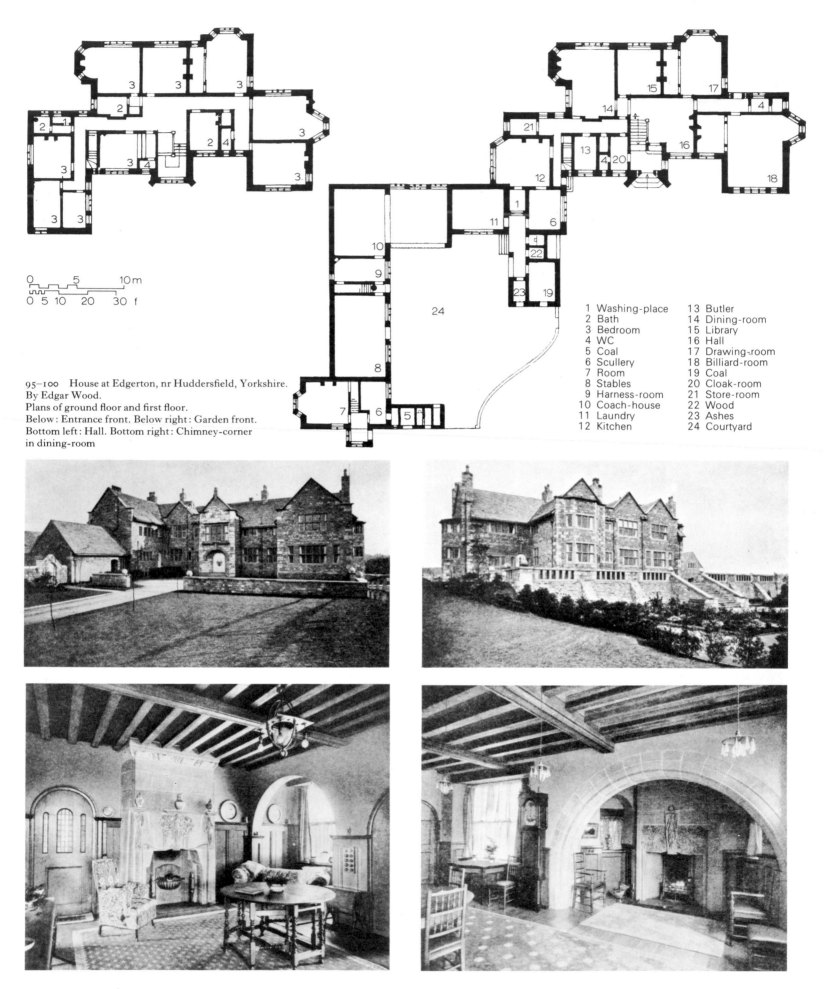

95–100 House at Edgerton, nr Huddersfield, Yorkshire.
By Edgar Wood.
Plans of ground floor and first floor.
Below: Entrance front. Below right: Garden front.
Bottom left: Hall. Bottom right: Chimney-corner
in dining-room

1	Washing-place	13 Butler
2	Bath	14 Dining-room
3	Bedroom	15 Library
4	WC	16 Hall
5	Coal	17 Drawing-room
6	Scullery	18 Billiard-room
7	Room	19 Coal
8	Stables	20 Cloak-room
9	Harness-room	21 Store-room
10	Coach-house	22 Wood
11	Laundry	23 Ashes
12	Kitchen	24 Courtyard

101, 102　House at Edgerton. Billiard-room and staircase

[8] A good idea of Baillie Scott's furniture may be gained from the catalogue of the furniture-maker John White of furniture made to the artist's designs. The catalogue is for sale.

earliest houses on the Isle of Man are still based on historical forms. Yet one of his characteristics had already emerged; this was his strong tendency to design unusual ground-plans. It cannot be denied that the interior planning of the average house is to some extent conventional, not to say schematic. Though this may suit the average man, one certainly cannot blame those who like to control their own lives for making a break. But it is occasionally desirable to make changes even to the schematic arrangement of the average ground-plan; for, as we shall see, the small English house suffers from the disadvantage of being a modification of the large house, whereas it ought to embody the true life-style of the middle-classes. Baillie Scott has given the scheme a jolt and continues to do so with each fresh commission. Instead of the usual humdrum box-like division of the rooms, he sometimes throws several rooms into one, making one large room within the framework of the small house; sometimes he makes one room do duty for two by means of a low, projecting bay; elsewhere he concentrates the life of the house into a large central hall, off which all the other rooms open, as the rooms in a Roman villa opened off the atrium. At the same time he invests all his rooms with the most intimate, poetical and concentrated feeling that they are for living in. He never thinks in terms of rooms without furniture, but in planning always imagines the room as it will be when it is fully furnished and occupied. Thus every square foot of space is considered in the light of its suitability for living in: no door is positioned arbitrarily, no window is in anything but the correct relationship to the room it has to light. For his exteriors Baillie Scott has slowly but surely abandoned historical motifs, he omits details and builds as simply as possible. The walls of his houses are entirely unarticulated areas of rough plaster, the roofs are absolutely plain in shape and are enlivened only by the tall white chimney-stacks that straddle them. A note of cheerful colour is struck inside, but again forms are kept to a minimum. Wooden panelling stained green in the hall and dining-room, white background colour in the drawing-room and bedrooms form the basis of the colour-scheme. Colour means everything to him, he thinks in colour from the beginning. In his simpler pieces of furniture the shade of the untreated oak is allowed to stand, others are stained more colourfully (green, red or blue) and are decorated with simple painted ornament. Yet more luxurious pieces have polychrome ornament inlaid in finely coloured woods. He likes to paint the insides of his pieces in bright colours, even – or rather, especially – when the exteriors are left plain. Baillie Scott derives his decorative motifs from plants, except when he uses a geometrical pattern for edges, etc. His furniture is always primitive or rustic in form. Yet he manages to give it a feeling of quite sophisticated intellectual culture.[8] His pieces breathe a poetry and intimacy that is not dissimilar from the songs of Robert Burns, the peasant-poet who sang in the country that faces the island of Baillie Scott's birth on the mainland of Great Britain. The general tone of Baillie Scott's work is a tender and intimate but refreshingly healthy pastoral poetry. One senses the earthy smell of ploughed fields but it is mingled with a soft scent of meadow flowers in bloom.

We can gain an idea of the artist's manner from Blackwell (Figs. 103–108), a handsome house in beautiful surroundings on Lake Windermere. The house combines dignity with great comfort and a poetical atmosphere within. Since it is largely intended as a summer residence, the main emphasis is on the hall as the principal room for sitting in. Dark woodwork (the wall panelling came from an old church) gives it a rare feeling of well-being and its custom-made ground-plan provides delightful areas for rest, conversation and games. Halfway up the stairs is a landing with a view on to the hall, which also serves as a small smoking-room.

103–106 Blackwell on Lake Windermere, Westmorland. By M. H. Baillie Scott. Top left: Garden front. Top right: View from forecourt. Above: Hall. Above right: Fire-place in drawing-room

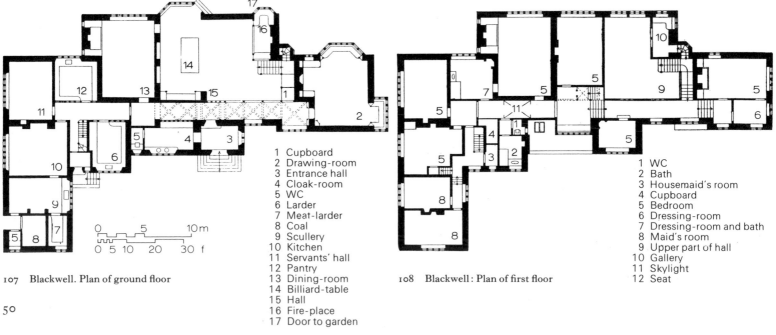

107 Blackwell. Plan of ground floor

1 Cupboard
2 Drawing-room
3 Entrance hall
4 Cloak-room
5 WC
6 Larder
7 Meat-larder
8 Coal
9 Scullery
10 Kitchen
11 Servants' hall
12 Pantry
13 Dining-room
14 Billiard-table
15 Hall
16 Fire-place
17 Door to garden

108 Blackwell: Plan of first floor

1 WC
2 Bath
3 Housemaid's room
4 Cupboard
5 Bedroom
6 Dressing-room
7 Dressing-room and bath
8 Maid's room
9 Upper part of hall
10 Gallery
11 Skylight
12 Seat

The drawing-room is white throughout, with delicate relief decoration on the frieze and ceiling. The other rooms are all designed down to the last detail in the same careful manner, so that the house may be regarded as one of the most attractive creations that the new movement in house-building has produced.

The new concept of the room

Baillie Scott's concept of the house is already that of an organic whole to be designed consistently inside and out. Architect and interior designer merge, so that one is unthinkable without the other. This is an advance on the London movement. It is true that Voysey works to a similar pattern. But as the emotional overtones are less emphatic in his work, his rooms, even those he has furnished himself, are not so very different from the old idea of assembling good interiors from whatever scattered material happens to be available. Morris too worked more or less in this way, though he naturally used only articles such as carpets, materials and furniture that he had made himself. But in Baillie Scott's work each room is an individual creation, the elements of which do not just happen to be available but spring from the over-all idea. Baillie Scott is the first to have realised the new idea of the interior as an autonomous work of art. From now on it springs suddenly to life in several places at once – in particular it emerged soon after this on the continent where the movement virtually began with this idea. London, and in fact England as a whole, remained stationary at the point to which Morris had taken it. Scotland, however, started out in the new direction at the same time as the continent, though with the poetical and mystical local colouring that, as we have seen, always marks Scottish work.

The Glasgow movement

The new ideas were given shape in Scotland by a small circle of quite young people around the mid-1890s, that remarkable period during which so much that was new was seething and rumbling unseen as it struggled for expression. The public at large gained their first sight of them at the Arts and Crafts Exhibition of 1896, where they suffered the ridicule that is always levelled at important artistic achievements. Few could make sense of the dream-like designs of the beaten copper panels, the strange tangle of lines in the figural compositions, the stark forms of the furniture. Indeed, the London camp raised open objection that reached such a pitch that at the next exhibition in 1899 under the presidency of Walter Crane their pieces were refused. Thus the London movement made its position clear: it would in future take no part in furthering the new ideas, a stance it has steadfastly maintained since the death of William Morris in 1896 until the present day. Not only, however, did the Scots receive the liveliest recognition on the continent from the moment they appeared there, but they had a seminal influence on the emerging new vocabulary of forms, especially and most continuously in Vienna, where an unbreakable bond was forged between them and the leaders of the Vienna movement over England's head. Just as fifteen years earlier England had failed to understand the new movement in Scottish painting and had allowed it to pass unrecognised, so now it adopted a negative attitude to the new Scottish movement in the tectonic and decorative arts. So it has remained until this day. Here, as so often, England has played the strange part of developing new ideas up to a certain primitive form but then being unable to carry them to completion. Our very recent movement builds on the experiences that evolved in complete silence in England during the period from 1860 to the mid-1890s. England has forborne to draw the ultimate conclusion that must consist in regarding the interior with all its contents as an autonomous work of art. A complete room has never yet been exhibited at an Arts and Crafts movement exhibition in London. The movement is still content to trot out little boxes, embroidery, designs for wallpapers and materials, metalwork and furniture as before.

Charles R. Mackintosh and his circle

The real driving force of the Scottish movement is Charles Rennie Mackintosh. The other members of the small original circle, Herbert McNair and the former Misses Margaret and Frances Macdonald, now Mrs Mackintosh and Mrs McNair, form a group around him. They all speak the same artistic language with great conviction, so that, although on closer inspection they differ from one another, they could work together on the same project without in any way destroying its unity. Mackintosh is an architect to his fingertips; his numerous architectural creations, both as a member of the firm of Honeyman, Keppie and Mackintosh and under his own name, including business premises, churches, schools, etc. and, most particularly, his many competition designs, mark him as one of Britain's, if not one of *the*, most outstanding younger architects of the day. Mackintosh's architectonic sensibility brings to the group's creations those strict tectonic foundations that are apparent despite all their imaginative qualities. Herbert McNair, now professor in the Department of Art at Liverpool University,[*] is a figural draughtsman but has worked as a furniture designer and in all kinds of small works of art. The two lady members are responsible for ornament proper, such as embossed panels, embroidery, wall paintings and appliqué work. Their principle is not simply to produce the design but to execute everything themselves, thus giving their efforts the only valid hallmark of the genuine work of art. The central aim of these members is the room as work of art, as a unified organic whole embracing colour, form and atmosphere. Starting from this notion they develop not only the room but the whole house, the sole purpose of the exterior of which is to enclose the rooms, their central concern, without laying any particular claim to an artistic appearance itself. Nevertheless Mackintosh with his strong architectonic sense sees to it that proper architectonic values are maintained here too; and his ground-plans are models of practicality and comfortable, convenient planning (Figs. 110, 113, 114).

Essence of the art of the Glasgow group

Yet the essence of the art of the Glasgow group in fact rests in an underlying emotional and poetical quality. It seeks a highly charged artistic atmosphere or more specifically an atmosphere of a mystical, symbolic kind. One cannot imagine a greater contrast in this respect than that between the London architects working in the new forms, the most sedulous of whom is Voysey, and the Scottish architects round Mackintosh. The former seek extreme plainness in which imagination is suppressed, the latter are virtually governed and led by imagination. Common to both, however, is a strictly tectonic underlying factor that holds qualities of material and construction sacred and in this respect never descends to the unnatural and artificial. Sound workman-like construction and design within the natural limits of the material (so that wood, for example, is not treated like rubber or cast iron) are the basic stipulations of both groups – in which both contrast with certain sections of the continental movement, in particular that which originated in Belgium. The special character of the Mackintosh group rests as much in form, especially in their ideas about the relationship between surface

---

* Herbert McNair was not in Liverpool University. [DS]

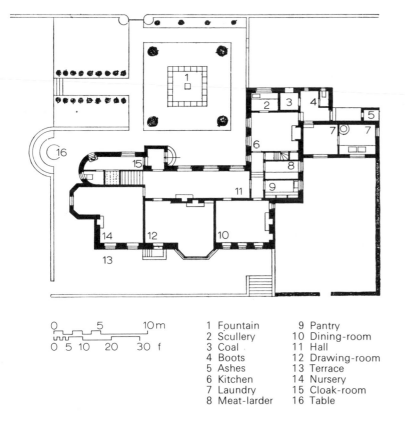

109, 110 Windyhill, Kilmacolm, nr Glasgow. By C. R. Mackintosh. View from courtyard and plan of ground floor

0 5 10m	1	Fountain	9 Pantry
0 5 10 20 30 f	2	Scullery	10 Dining-room
	3	Coal	11 Hall
	4	Boots	12 Drawing-room
	5	Ashes	13 Terrace
	6	Kitchen	14 Nursery
	7	Laundry	15 Cloak-room
	8	Meat-larder	16 Table

and decoration, as in colour. In both connections the keynote is a spacious, grandiose, almost mystical repose, broken only here and there by the application of a small decorative area, which has the effect of a precious stone. Repose is achieved by the use of broad, unarticulated forms and a neutral background colour, such as grey, white or a dark brownish-grey. The strictly architectonic character stems from strongly emphasised rhythmic sequences, such as vertical elements or series of any similar elements (e.g. box-like lampshades). Patterned materials are taboo, as is all mechanically produced ornament. The few decorative devices appear in the form of hand-made panels, appliquéed work, inlays, stencilled patterns, but they are always used sparingly and at isolated points. They are never more than mildly unexpected within the great, restful whole. The

decorated areas are vividly coloured in bright green, dark pink or purple. This colour-scheme reminds one of the grey paintings of Velasquez, in which touches of colour stand out as effectively as here. Alternatively one may say that the Glaswegians have borrowed the idea that Whistler introduced into painting for the decoration of their rooms. At all events the refinement that is achieved is convincing and by comparison the earlier habit of juxtaposing dark rich colours to form the basic colour-scheme immediately seems awkward and ill-conceived. In a way, colour is now raised to a higher level since it is used more sparingly. It is looked upon like festive occasions in life: the rarer they are the more we enjoy and desire them. One has to see these rooms, for example Mackintosh's drawing-rooms in Glasgow (Figs. 111, 112), to appreciate the tremendous effects that can be achieved by such means.

There are still many misguided opinions of the Mackintosh group. Their work is known either from journals, which always give a distorted picture, or from the tedious exhibitions which tempt even the best to overstep the limits of good sense, of what can be tolerated in life. One must see Mackintosh's real rooms, those intended to be lived in, such as those drawing-rooms in his house in Glasgow, and one's opinion will change. At all events, Mackintosh has enormously enriched the repertoire of ideas affecting interior decoration. Not only has he introduced new means but he has raised the level of its whole interpretation. Once the interior attains the status of a work of art, that is, when it is intended to embody aesthetic values, the artistic effect must obviously be heightened to the utmost. The Mackintosh group does this and no one will reproach them on this particular point. Whether such enhancement is appropriate to our everyday rooms is another question. Mackintosh's rooms are refined to a degree which the lives of even the artistically educated are still a long way from matching. The delicacy and austerity of their artistic atmosphere would tolerate no admixture of the ordinariness which fills our lives. Even a book in an unsuitable binding would disturb the atmosphere simply by lying on the table, indeed even the man or woman of today – especially the man in his unadorned working attire – treads like a stranger in this fairy-tale world. There is for the time being no possibility of our aesthetic cultivation playing so large a part in our lives that rooms like this could become general. But they are milestones placed by a genius far ahead of us to mark the way to excellence for mankind in the future.

The influence of the Mackintosh group is far-reaching. Its influence in its native city is already so generally obvious that Mackintosh's repertoire of forms may almost be said to have created a local style.

George Walton

George Walton is another Glasgwegian, now resident in London, who must be considered the second member of the Scottish movement, for although he is probably fairly independent of the Mackintosh circle, his work has something in common with theirs. He had been a bank official until his middle years when for the first time he was able to realise his wish to devote himself to interior decorating. Almost from the beginning his work had a delicate, mature, solid and pleasing quality. He is more down-to-earth, that is, the demands of pure utility are more to the fore in his work than in that of the Mackintosh group, but he is nonetheless a poet from whose creations a subtle spiritual atmosphere always radiates. His vocabulary of forms is always independent, but he is not afraid of historical echoes and does not ignore the results of historical development. His colour

111, 112 The architects' flat, Glasgow. By C. R. Mackintosh and Margaret
Macdonald-Mackintosh. Two views of the drawing-room
113, 114 Blackhill, Helensburgh, nr Glasgow. By C. R. Mackintosh. Plans of
ground floor, first floor and part of attic floor

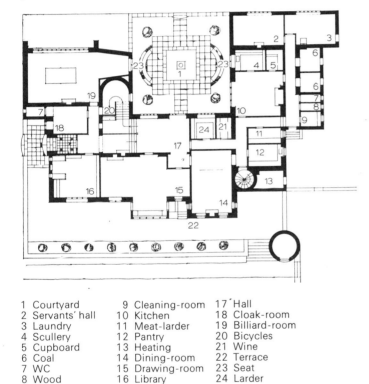
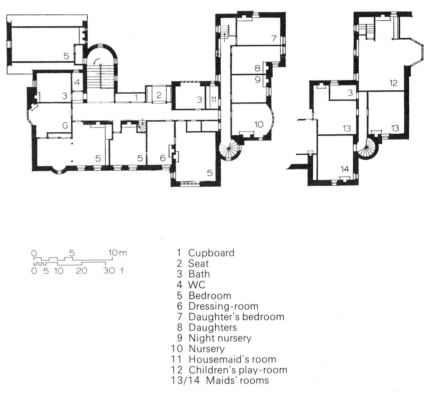

1 Courtyard	9 Cleaning-room	17 Hall
2 Servants' hall	10 Kitchen	18 Cloak-room
3 Laundry	11 Meat-larder	19 Billiard-room
4 Scullery	12 Pantry	20 Bicycles
5 Cupboard	13 Heating	21 Wine
6 Coal	14 Dining-room	22 Terrace
7 WC	15 Drawing-room	23 Seat
8 Wood	16 Library	24 Larder

1 Cupboard
2 Seat
3 Bath
4 WC
5 Bedroom
6 Dressing-room
7 Daughter's bedroom
8 Daughters
9 Night nursery
10 Nursery
11 Housemaid's room
12 Children's play-room
13/14 Maids' rooms

is neutral like that of the Mackintosh group. But he likes broad
patterned surfaces and does not spurn mechanically produced
patterns for this purpose in carpets, wall friezes and furnishing
materials. The workmanship of his furniture and all his other
pieces is meticulous down to the last detail; for furniture he likes
the colour of the natural wood, for metalwork an absolutely flat
matt surface. The colours of his rooms are stronger and the
furniture is quite differently shaped from that of Mackintosh.
Yet there is a certain similarity between the two; the fact that
they both grew up in Glasgow is reflected in the work of both.
Next to the Mackintosh circle, Walton is the artist who has
understood the idea of the interior as work of art best and he has
pursued it most consistently of any artist in Great Britain. The
house known as The Leys at Elstree near London (Figs.

115–119), which he built and furnished, is an example of his
work. The hall does double duty as a billiard-room. The
splendid architectonic effect of the long dining-room is
particularly successful.

Other Glasgow artists

The Mackintosh group and Walton are the leaders and founders
of the Glasgow movement. They have been followed by a whole
host of other artists, mostly younger men, who have recognised
the high ideals in the work of their masters, to whom they were
devoted body and soul but whom they have so far been unable to
equal. Ernest A. Taylor is probably the most talented interior
decorator among this following; he creates rooms of great
refinement and charm but lacks the virile power of the

115–117 The Leys, Elstree, nr London. By George Walton. Rear view and plans of ground floor and first floor

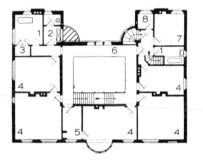

1 Bath
2 Washing-place
3 Cupboard
4 Bedroom
5 Dressing-room
6 Gallery
7 Maid's room
8 Housemaid's room
9 Meat-larder
10 Scullery
11 Kitchen
12 Serving-room
13 Dining-room
14 Vestibule
15 Drawing-room
16 Morning-room
17 Library
18 Washing-place and WC
19 Hall
20 Terrace
21 Porch

Mackintosh group (Fig. 120). He is more colourful than Mackintosh and does not exercise his wise self-restraint in the matter of vivid hues. Other members of this group who are searching for original design are the architects James Salmon & Son, especially James Salmon the younger and the architect J. Gaff Gillespie who have joined the new movement. Their aspirations as regards interiors are much the same as those of the Mackintosh group: broad surfaces, strong rhythm, neutral colour, spare concentrated ornament, a mystical air. As to their exteriors they are often merely on the look-out for originality, which must damage any favourable judgment of them.

The nature of the Glasgow movement

The influence of the Mackintosh circle is also apparent in Glasgow in several quite outstanding practitioners of minor arts of various kinds; they include especially J. R. Newbery, the excellent embroidress, her pupil Ann Macbeth and Jessie King, the book illustrator. All aspire to the same romantic, poetical goals and exercise the same subtle mixture of stringent reticence and far-ranging imaginativeness. The Scottish movement is a reaction against the insistent utilitarian and rational principles of the Arts and Crafts camp in London. They preached death to romanticism and were thinking mainly of the stylistic chaos, the meaningless ornament and the forgotten considerations of material and craftsmanship that marked the art of the nineteenth century. The Scots replied that without imagination there is no art. Here again are the two poles of realism and idealism between which a developing art vacillates so freely. Realism is the refreshing dip which is salutory from time to time if art is to remain in touch with the world, to keep its feet on the ground. But the ultimate goal of art can never be other than idealistic.

The outstanding features that we have described would suffice to give a general picture of the aims and development of the English house in modern times. But it includes only the work of those men who pointed the way for this development and we have still to mention several other architects who have contributed able, even excellent, work. Some of them are content to draw upon the experience of the past and are satisfied with well-built houses; some others are only just beginning their careers, they may become influential in the future but for the present this must be a matter of surmise.

118 The Leys. Dining-room

119 The Leys. Hall

E. L. Lutyens

First among these must be E. L. Lutyens in London. He is a young man who of recent years has come increasingly to the forefront of domestic architects and who may soon become the accepted leader among English builders of houses, like Norman Shaw in the past. Lutyens is one of those architects who would refuse to have anything whatever to do with any new movement. His buildings reflect his attachment to the styles of the past, the charms of which he finds inexhaustible. Anyone who visited the last Paris world exhibition will recall from the example of an English house which Lutyens built on the Quai d'Orsay the lengths to which he will go. The house was so archaic in appearance that it gave an entirely false impression of the situation in England; indeed, the whole exterior and most of the interior were directly copied from an old house. In this way he propagated the view that is so widespread in England that this old art cannot be bettered. But just as a really important artist cannot ignore the demands of his time, so Lutyens's new buildings do not really look ancient at all. On the contrary, they have a character that, if not modern, is entirely personal and extremely interesting. As regards the ground-plan, he seeks unusual solutions by introducing, or rather re-introducing, the idea of the enclosed courtyard; in siting a house he seeks to relate it as closely as possible to the surrounding terrain by developing the architectonic idea in the form of terraces, flower-beds, pools, box hedges and pergolas. In this connection he is the most zealous champion of the new movement in gardening, to which we shall return. The surprising thing about his exteriors is their unusually simple and spacious style and his excellent treatment of the material, in which he is the undisputed master. He manages to give an unexpected charm to a simple stone wall, a brick or a half-timbered wall. He prefers stone but can also use rough plaster to the same good effect. Small strips of windows are a favourite device and he likes to place his chimneys obliquely to the façade (so that they are turned through an angle of 45°), and, especially in courtyards, he favours loggias with broad spreading semi-circular arches. His houses are as convincing in their workmanlike efficiency as in their intimate, pleasing appearance and are undoubtedly among the best being built in England today. He is less interested in making the interior a work of art. He is content with the extreme simplicity of the country cottage, or where luxury is called for, imitation of an earlier style. His furniture too is anything but modern; he loves the lathe-turned forms of the period of James I and uses the furniture of that time. But these borrowings always reflect the characteristics that distinguish all he does: a forceful efficiency and a reassuring willingness to get to the heart of the problem facing him.

Despite Lutyens's youth, he has already built a considerable number of houses and for most of them he has had the good fortune to find artistic clients who have given him much assistance, so that his houses have almost become models of their kind. There is a whole series of such houses in Surrey alone, each one of which is worth the effort of a day's excursion. The Orchards, near Godalming, one of the most attractive, is illustrated in detail (Figs. 121–125).

W. H. Bidlake

Although W. H. Bidlake is considerably older than Lutyens, his work shows a certain similarity to Lutyens's. He is not so exclusively committed to house-building as Lutyens, nor does he depend as closely on earlier styles as he. Indeed, in his more recent houses, especially in their interiors, he has found a very independent, novel interpretation. But he has the same naturalness and breadth of interpretation as Lutyens. The new estate of Four Oaks, near Birmingham, is well worth seeing and some of the best villas there were built by Bidlake. They are immediately recognisable from their very simple style and the great honesty that they express. Their characteristic features are: the plainest of brick walls, broad sweeping masses for the roofs, small white-painted windows separated by stone mullions and nearly always in strips, pleasant groupings, the larger ones centred on a courtyard. Bidlake detests eye-catching devices of any kind, such as exaggerated forms of bay window, etc. and inside as well as outside everything is extremely natural. Yet though his means are of the simplest, he manages to create interiors of great intimacy, as is most clearly demonstrated in his larger houses, Garth House at Edgbaston and Yates House at Four Oaks near Birmingham, the latter of which we illustrate (Figs. 127–131).

Bateman & Bateman. Arnold Mitchell

Another firm in Birmingham is much involved in house-building. The architects Bateman & Bateman build larger and, most particularly, a great many smaller houses, indeed they specialise in the smaller house. Economic factors which always play such an important part in the smaller house are a major consideration here, though they have not been allowed to impair the artistic effect. Arnold Mitchell in London works on similar lines, laying great stress on the economic aspect. His ground-plans are always practical and interesting, especially in their skilful arrangement and balanced proportions. His vocabulary of forms is less personal and usually tends towards Neo-Classicism.

A. N. Prentice

An artist who has moved steadily closer to this latest classicising trend is A. N. Prentice, who first made his name with his fine drawings of Spain. One must regret this change of heart all the more since in his first projects Prentice raised great hopes of a more independent attitude and at the beginning was in every way one of the most promising talents. His taut, forceful style of drawing, of which he is an undisputed master, has had a great influence on the youngest generation. His ground-plans are always extremely lucid and precise.

120   House in Leeds. Drawing-room designed by Ernest A. Taylor

121–125 The Orchards, nr Godalming, Surrey. By E. L. Lutyens.
Top left: View of entrance. Top right: View from garden (south-east).
Above: Loggia. Above right: Dining-room. Right: Plan of ground floor

1 WC	15 Gateway
2 Coal	16 Servants' hall
3 Larder	17 Pantry
4 Meat-larder	18 Veranda
5 Scullery	19 Dining-room
6 Kitchen	20 Hall
7 Kitchen-court	21 Porch
8 Coal	22 Courtyard
9 Wood	23 Man of the house's room
10 Boots	24 Washing-place
11 Harness-room	25 Loggia
12 Living-room	26 Studio
13 Stables	27 Carriage-entrance
14 Coach-house	28 Lodgekeeper's quarters

126 Home for sailors, nr Greenock, nr Glasgow. By E. L. Lutyens

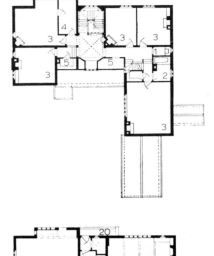

1 WC
2 Bath
3 Bedroom
4 Dressing-room
5 Cupboard
6 Yard
7 Coal
8 Boots
9 Kitchen
10 Scullery
11 Meat-larder
12 Coach-house
13 Stables
14 Serving-room
15 Dining-room
16 Hall
17 Study
18 Drawing-room
19 Inner hall
20 Terrace

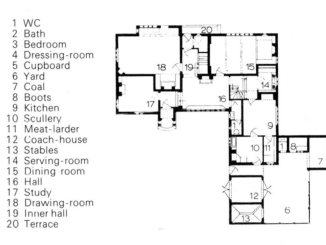

127–131 Yates House, Four Oaks, nr Birmingham. By W. H. Bidlake.
Left: View. Above right: Plans of ground floor and first floor. Below left: Hall.
Below: Dining-room

132 Brockhampton Park, Gloucestershire. By Atkinson. Hall

Other London architects

Finally, mention must be made of certain other outstanding domestic architects working in London: Niven and Wigglesworth work within the old vernacular tradition; Basil Champneys belonged originally to the Gothic camp, but all his houses are simple brick buildings; T. W. Cutler[9] and R. A. Briggs[10] are best known for their published projects for simple country-houses. There are also E. Goldie, Frank Baggallay and W. Flockhart, all of whom represent the good, new type of house and have done much interesting work; and John Belcher and Reginald Blomfield, who are entirely on the side of classicising historicism. Young talents who promise well include E. Guy Dawber, and L. B. Griggs and W. Curtis Green, both of whom are fine draughtsmen.

Other architects outside London

There are many fine talents in the provincial cities of England. We have already mentioned the Birmingham architects Bidlake and Bateman & Bateman, to whom we should add Crough & Butler. Edward Burgess (not to be confused with W. Burges the well-known Goth who died in 1881) in Leicester has for many years been producing distinguished work similar in conception to that of Norman Shaw and Douglas; also in Leicester is James Tait, who uses very independent and powerful forms. Altogether Leicester can boast much good villa architecture. Arthur Marshall and Brewill & Baily produce good work in Nottingham; Grayson and Ould are in Liverpool, William & Segar Owen in Warrington; in Chester, besides Douglas & Minshull, there are the architects Lookwood & Sons; and in York Penty & Penty and W. H. Brierley. Besides Atkinson, one of whose interiors we illustrate (Fig. 132), Leeds has Bedford & Kitson, a firm of very promising young architects who have already built a number of country-houses which are among the best works of recent years. Their exteriors are more or less traditional in design, but inside they experiment in more independent ways, though without becoming fantastic, and create rooms which are striking for their comfort and their pleasant appointments and furniture and give an impression of quiet refinement. To judge from their work to date we can expect much of them.

The workmen's villages of Port Sunlight and Bournville

There is no better way for those who wish to take a quick and pertinent look at the achievements of the English architects of today than to visit the workmen's village of Port Sunlight,[11] near Liverpool. Certainly these are only factory workers' houses. But they contain the whole repertoire of contemporary means of expression in such accomplished form that the estate may be considered the flower of the small modern house in a small space. The existence of the estate is due to the enthusiasm of W. H. Lever, owner of the Sunlight factory.* Lever, a great lover of architecture, allocated a certain proportion of the profit of his fast-growing business to the erection of fine workers' houses. With this intention he approached the best architects in the country, who all contributed to the creation of a model estate (Figs. 133–135). It was easier for him than it usually is to think of such a thing since he did not have to worry as much about profitability as is normally necessary with workers' dwellings; Lever built the houses and calculated the rent simply on the cost of maintenance.

In one sense Port Sunlight may be regarded as the present-day outcome of Norman Shaw's pioneering work at Bedford Park thirty years ago for it is a solution of the problem of the small house and a grouping together of houses to form a residential area in a way that is modern and satisfies all practical and artistic requirements. In both places the architects drew upon early vernacular architecture, the motifs of which offered the best source for the design of the houses and the layout of the streets. In both instances the layout of the streets was not merely planned on the drawing-board but was closely harmonised with the terrain, which included siting the houses in the sunniest positions; in both places the result was surprisingly good. However, the exteriors at Port Sunlight differ radically from these at Bedford Park in that there are many more different motifs. One can see how much work has been done during the past thirty years in enlisting all the usable ideas from earlier art. It was in the ground-plan, at Port Sunlight as at Bedford Park, that the real innovation lay, because it was here that the economic conditions of the time set the guide-lines. In this respect the houses at Port Sunlight did for the workman's house what those at Bedford Park had done for the lower middle-class home; they provided an ideal combination of comfort, ease and artistic quality with the economic possibilities appropriate to their status. The smallest of the workmen's houses contain only a living-room and a few bedrooms, but the layout of these rooms could scarcely be more convenient. As regards hygiene, we should add that every house, down to the smallest, has a bath. There is the economic drawback at Port Sunlight that, as we have said, the rent of the houses does not cover the cost of construction.

[9] T. W. Cutler: *Cottages and country buildings.*
[10] R. A. Briggs: *Bungalows and country residences.**

*Cutler's book was published in London in 1896. Briggs' book in London in 1891. (The fifth edition of this popular book appeared in 1901.) [DS]

[11] Described at length in my *Die englische Baukunst der Gegenwart* and the *Centralblatt der Bauverwaltung*, Vol. for 1899, p. 133. A monograph containing plans and illustrations by W. H. Lever (*Cottages and other buildings erected at Port Sunlight and Thornton Hough*) has appeared recently.

*The book by W. H. Lever (the Lord Leverhulme) was published under the title *Buildings erected at Port Sunlight and Thornton Hough*, London 1902. [DS]

136–138   Workmen's village, Bournville, nr Birmingham. By Ralph Heaton. Small houses and street view

133–135   Workmen's village, Port Sunlight, nr Liverpool. By various architects. View of smaller houses

This important problem has been solved, however, in another similar estate which has recently been built at Bournville, not far from Birmingham, in association with G. Cadbury's cocoa and chocolate factory. This estate has been set up on an absolutely sound economic and commercial basis: in cases where the occupants are only lease-holders, the rent exactly covers the cost of construction; in cases where they become owners the purchase-price equals the value. The drawbacks of the English system of ground-rent – to which we shall return – are also avoided, because the lease runs for 999 years, which means that the house-owners as good as own their land themselves. In either case, however, the company that heads the Cadbury enterprise does not seek profit, it merely expects interest at the lowest prevailing rate. Furthermore, its statutes lay down that any surplus that may accrue is to be used to develop the enterprise and is not to be withdrawn as profit. All the houses at Bournville (Figs. 136–138) are by the same architect, Ralph Heaton, but have been built on the same principle as Port Sunlight. The appearance of the estate is therefore not quite as varied as Port Sunlight; nevertheless it is another extremely attractive creation and again one that more than satisfies every artistic demand. These two are at present the only estates of their kind in England, in both social and artistic respects; their special achievement is to have satisfied in an almost ideal fashion a demand that is often heard today: that of bringing art to the life of the working-classes.

The 'garden-city movement'

Indeed, both experiments were so successful that they encouraged further advances. In his book of 1898[12] Ebenezer Howard analysed the conditions under which the misery of the cities, especially as it affected the urban working-classes, could be alleviated. He concluded that it could be done by moving industry into the country and building new cities with healthy detached houses on an open system. So successful was the book that a society was soon formed, first to give wider circulation to the author's ideas and then to progress to the founding of a new town or 'garden city' in a suitable locality. Lever and Cadbury, the founders of Port Sunlight and Bournville, have taken up the movement and have held meetings on their estates. It is now growing fast and the first attempt at establishing a new town has been made at Letchworth Garden City in delightful country to the north of London, where it is developing apace.

Working-class houses in London

Thus in the sphere of the small house in England social questions have been firmly linked to questions of art and it must be said that this has been greatly to their advantage. If the ideals that are in the air can be successfully realised, art will gain as much as the social movement has done. Naturally there is as yet no chance whatever of suddenly siphoning the lower classes of the population out of the cities. And a solution of the problem of working-class dwellings, which has been a burning issue in England for decades, cannot be expected immediately on the basis of the Garden City Society. Conditions are becoming steadily more urgent in the cities, particularly in London, and the authorities are faced with the enormous task of finding new and healthier dwellings for thousands of people every year. Since the present London County Council has made itself responsible for the matter it is going forward in an economically successful and artistically very satisfactory manner. The most recent quarters in Bethnal Green (Boundary Estate) and Pimlico

139   County Council Houses, Boundary Estate, London. By LCC architect T. Blashill

(Millbank Estate) especially are almost model developments as regards the artistic interpretation of these important problems. Obviously in this case the artistic answer cannot consist in a display of forms. Architects have searched and have happily found it (Fig. 139) in an extremely simple distribution of masses, excellently balanced proportions, pleasing grouping of buildings, combined with colour in the shape of rich red brick walls and roofs, against which the window-frames stand out vividly. Considering the good results that London has now achieved in this field, one has great hopes that the plan to build a whole district of ninety-one hectares with houses for workers at Tottenham, a two-hour journey north of London, will be realised. This enterprise is entirely in keeping with the aims of the Garden City Society, for there is a growing realisation that the erection of large workers' barracks in the centres of towns leaves the root of the question of the wretched housing of the lower classes untouched. A real remedy can only come through depopulating the large cities, through the removal of the urban population to the open country. England may be the first to solve the problem because the English of all classes have retained their natural love of country life to a greater extent than any other people.

New move to the country

This love has always existed in England but perhaps never as strongly as now. For the past ten years there has been a very active movement towards a closer contact with nature. A number of excellent journals (e.g. *Country Life*, begun 1897) dealing in detail with everything connected with life in the country have begun publication. There has been a great increase recently in trips into the country, especially those that last from Saturday to Monday, summer holidays in the country and removals to the country in general, often to parts remote from the cities. Another significant sign of the movement is the preference for types of sport (e.g. golf) that necessitate a stay in the open country; and finally a great love of gardens, of growing plants and flowers and all that this entails has developed and is perhaps the most significant of all these signs. The English have always been great garden-lovers, yet the past thirty years have seen a complete

[12] *Tomorrow: a peaceful path to real reform*; a second edition appeared in London in 1902 under the title *Garden cities of to-morrow*.

revolution in this field. This point, which is so intimately connected with the house, will be discussed later.

Recent house-building in Scotland

We must first take another look at Scotland, for so far we have discussed only a small section, the Glasgow group of poets of the modern interior. Anyone who has had anything to do with the circumstances of British art will know that developments in Scotland have always differed radically from those in England. The two countries are separated by differences of thought and feeling that neither a common language nor unification into a single kingdom can eradicate. Moreover, Scotland's influences on England have been more numerous than vice versa (e.g. poetry and painting). On the whole, however, developments have gone ahead independently. Again, some degree of influence has always been transmitted from France to Scotland without affecting England, perhaps as a result of ancient sympathies that have existed between the two countries, as historical events have clearly shown.

Buildings in Edinburgh were in the classical mode, those in outlying areas were romantic in the old, still strongly fortress-like character of the country. The outer dress of these buildings is still strongly reminiscent of the superficiality of the stylistic historicism that affected our whole culture in the nineteenth century. Men saw the 'picturesque' but did not grasp the meaning of the features which they felt to be picturesque. They mistook them for objective reality and the result was the characteristic quality of all stylistic imitation: meaninglessness, superfluity and falsity. Scottish architecture around the middle of the last century vacillated between the two extremes of classical and romantic. We have already remarked, however, that at about this time Scottish architects, with what might be called their scientific development of the ground-plan, had very largely assumed the upper hand in Britain. And this was certainly an important cultural achievement.

One effect of the prominent position occupied by France in the more recent development of architecture was that from this time onwards many young architects went to study at the school of the Académie des beaux-arts. They returned to Scotland without having acquired anything worth mentioning in return for the native architecture that they had given up. To have studied in Paris is almost the badge of the 'leading' Scottish architects of today. Just as Americans go to France to finish their education, so in Scotland it is a mark of *bon ton*, and it is certainly a powerful recommendation for a young architect to have been at the Ecole des beaux-arts.

The following are regarded as the leading architects in Scotland today: Dr Rowand Anderson (the Nestor of Scottish architects), Hippolyte J. Blank, Washington Brown, W. Leiper, John Burnet, Son & Campbell, Honeyman & Keppie (this firm has recently taken C. R. Mackintosh into partnership, since when their work has become very uneven). Many of these men have studied in Paris. The result is that their exteriors are a mixture of Ecole des beaux-arts art with Scottish overtones, while their interiors are either decorated entirely in the French manner or, more usually, they are compromises. The fact that their handling of forms often reflects good schooling does not compensate for their lack of national character. There is some very good work in business premises, public buildings and particularly in churches of much the same kind as we find in continental cities. Indeed, in general the circumstances of building in Scotland have much in common with those of the continent, especially inasmuch as most of the residential accommodation is rented and is in multi-storeyed buildings. In the present context, therefore, they would still be less influential than the English, even if the group of leading architects whom we have named had had been less academic and eclectic, had been less fond of imitating early styles than they are. As regards ground-plan and layout, however, their houses are of the highest order.

The great movement that began in England in the 1860s and drew with such good results on earlier vernacular styles of building found no response in Scotland. And it is interesting to note that Norman Shaw, the leading spirit of the movement in London, is himself a Scot who has settled in England. While Morris's work remained unknown in Scotland, his influence, as reflected in the present-day Arts and Crafts movement, did become accepted there, though not much before its first awakening of new ideas on the continent. It is most important to note, however, that the English movement spread only to a very limited extent; indeed, R. S. Lorimer is its only true representative. A few other architects, such as Sidney Mitchell & Wilson, do from time to time build country-houses in the current English forms. One such is Mitchell's own house at Gullane (Fig. 140), which is one of the good examples of British houses.

140   The architect's house, Gullane, nr Edinburgh. By Sidney Mitchell. Hall

141   Duntreath, nr Glasgow. By Sidney Mitchell & Wilson, Edinburgh. Hall

In other houses, such as the mansion of Duntreath, near Glasgow (Fig. 141), they work in Scottish baronial or other historical styles. A few younger architects, such as L. Rome Guthrie, H. E. Clifford and Alexander N. Paterson are closer to the London movement. James A. Morris is a good architect who works in simple, modern-looking forms while yet maintaining his own personal style (Fig. 142). And James Miller, who made his name mainly with his exhibition buildings at the Glasgow Exhibition of 1901, has also had successes with houses. These names, together with those of the Mackintosh group, largely complete the list of architects who have been stirred by the wind of modernity. Most of them are young, or very young.

Dependence on vernacular building styles. R. S. Lorimer

Scotland might have been expected to follow the English example and to imitate the old vernacular styles of building as was done in the south, for the successes there must have been obvious to everyone. But in fact imitations of this sort, in which the architect has penetrated to the root of the problem, have all been very recent and are due to the work of a single architect, R. S. Lorimer. He was the first to recognise the charm of unpretentious old Scottish buildings, with their honest plainness and simple, almost rugged massiveness. He saw no necessity for imitations of early Scottish styles, with pinnacles and towers and projecting bartizans; he had steeped himself in early art sufficiently to recognise and re-assess its more intimate charms. In short, Lorimer has begun to do in Scotland what Norman Shaw's group did in London thirty-five years ago. Lorimer's achievements in house-building in Scotland today are by far the most interesting of any that can bear comparison with the Mackintosh group. He has built a whole series of smaller houses in the charming, unpretentious forms of old Scottish vernacular building in the Edinburgh suburb of Colinton. Fig. 143 gives a good idea of his style. He has enlarged a few old manor-houses, such, for example, as Earlshall Castle in Fife where he seems to have had ample means at his disposal to carry out his outstandingly tasteful work in the style of the original; on this occasion he was also responsible for the interior, including the furniture, and he gave of his best. He also redesigned the garden in the old Scottish geometrical style and has in general devoted the closest attention to the old Scottish art of the garden.

Scotland will not achieve what England has already achieved – a completely national style of house-building based on the old vernacular architecture – until it follows the lead given by Lorimer.

142   Hinton House, Ayr, Scotland. By James A. Morris. Entrance hall

143   Brigland, Kinrosshire, Scotland. By R. S. Lorimer

Conclusion

Current ideas about the English house

Present-day English architecture has grown out of the revival of the traditions of early vernacular building and the modern Arts and Crafts movement. But, be it repeated yet again, the modern movement in England has none of the fantastic, superfluous and, often, affected quality which still characterises some of the products of the continental movement. Far from it, it rather clings to the primitive and the vernacular and in this it closely follows the type of the traditional country-house. Furthermore the result genuinely suits English taste, which values unadorned simplicity above all else, finds poetry in the primitive because it gratifies its yearning for the country and detests flights of fancy most bitterly when it is expected to live in their midst day after day. When an Englishman lives in a house he expects to find peace there. He looks for neatness, homeliness and all comforts. He seeks a minimum of 'forms' with a maximum of restful, relaxed yet fresh atmosphere. His ineradicable preference is for the rural and the unsophisticated. He regards every reminiscence of these qualities as a bond with his beloved mother Nature, to whom, for all their advanced culture, the English people have remained truer than any other race. The house of today is a witness to the fact. The English house lies in the midst of flower-gardens, facing far away from the street, looking on to broad green lawns which radiate the energy and peace of nature; the house lies long and low, a shelter and a refuge rather than an essay in pomp and architectonic virtuosity; it lies hidden somewhere in the green countryside remote from any centre of culture and demanding of its occupants the daily sacrifice of long journeys, a sacrifice they make willingly for love of the house; and the house itself, with its cheerful colours and solid forms, fitting so admirably into the surrounding country stands as a witness to the sound instincts of a people, which, for all its wealth and advanced civilisation, has retained a remarkably strong feeling for nature. Urban culture with its distorting influences, its senseless speed and pressure, its hot-house forcing of the emptiness that is latent in human nature, its excitements raised to the point of unnatural sophistication, neurosis and morbidity – all this has scarcely touched the English people. The intellectual leaders of the people are the very ones who choose to live in the country, the same people who in Germany are most liable to succumb to city-life.

There is an expansive, easy-going quality about the English way of life. The Englishman's existence is far more old-fashioned than modern; in all its facets it bears the marks of a peaceful, traditional culture grounded in an old-established prosperity. This prosperity has long since outgrown the parvenu stage through which all affluence passes and through which some of the German rich seem to be passing now. This stage may have been reached in England at the time of the Palladian ideal of the house with its passion for external display.

There is no trace of this in the house of today. In every aspect it proclaims an unostentatious, indeed a modest, outlook, the outlook of a mature man whom life has taught that the contentment he craves is to be found in himself alone and not in the ways of the world. He must concern himself with these at his work; peace and contentment he seeks in his house, which is both the stronghold of his family-life and his link with nature. He draws love and happiness from the heart of his family, but from unspoilt nature he derives that strength that constantly renews itself, for which nature is itself the best symbol. Love and strength are the things in life that awaken us to action and are essential to spiritual and physical wellbeing. It follows that domestic life at its best is the source of the most consummate health.

Part II: Layout and construction

Some of the local determinants of the English house

A. Geographical determinants

The English house in its present form cannot be explained simply in terms of its historical development, in which fluctuations of sensibility and fashion in art from generation to generation have provided the *leitmotiv*. There have always been other forces at work moulding it, forces deep within these trends but more stable and more easily measured. They are the local determinants of the English house.

We have already suggested (p. 8) that they have been generally responsible for the custom of living in houses in England and it now remains to indicate the extent to which they contributed to the development of their characteristics. We shall now, therefore, briefly set out the relevant facts, which will be discussed in greater detail in the course of the following chapters.

Geographical influences. 1. The mild climate

The strongest of these influences always lie in a country's climatic and geographical conditions. The English climate is fundamentally different from that of the continent; in particular, it is milder, the air is extremely damp and it is generally inhospitable – all basic characteristics of the maritime climate of the country. It is extremely rare for snow and ice to persist in England, and the day-time temperature in winter seldom falls below freezing-point. There are short spells of great heat during the summer, but in general summers are rather cool, so that in both seasons the temperature remains much closer to the annual average (12° in the south, 7.4° in the north) than it does on the continent. The mildness and evenness of the climate account for the insubstantial structure of the English house, especially the meagre thickness of the walls, the absence of cellars, of double-glazed windows, the negligible care bestowed on ensuring that windows and doors fit snugly, the frequent absence of an entrance porch, the universal habit of using the whole attic floor for living accommodation and the heedless exposure of supply pipes and drain-pipes, for the building regulations prescribe that the latter must be on the exterior of the house. As regards the design of the exterior, there is no need to consider the possibility of snow piling up, therefore all forms of roof are permissible, e.g. parallel roofs that meet in a dip which are inadmissible with us since they allow a pocket of snow to form.

2. Damp. More ventilation required

Open fires are the only means of heating the house. The many advantages the fire-place is deemed to possess (not least its aesthetic advantages, some of which, it must be admitted, exist only in the imagination) so completely convince the Englishman of its superiority to all other forms of heating that he never even remotely considers replacing it with the more efficient and more economical stove. One presumes that the mild climate is also responsible for the fact that the English have made scarcely any use at all of central heating. And even when it is installed it never replaces the open fire, for to the English a room without a fire is like a body without a soul.

However, the fire-place in England serves another, extremely important, purpose. I refer to ventilation. Much ventilation is needed, largely because of the high humidity of the atmosphere. Humidity is the most marked of all England's climatic features: it accounts for the frequent fogs, for the distances in which all is veiled in a light mist, for the luxuriant green of the plant-life, which lasts the whole year round. As regards its effect on people, it is responsible for that permanently chilly feeling that so often causes visitors to catch cold. In enclosed spaces it induces the fusty, musty smell that affects any room that is not thoroughly aired every day. It necessitates extremely powerful ventilation, which, indeed, the fire-place admirably provides. At all events, its justification in England lies in its capacity to ventilate far more than to heat, as is demonstrated by the English belief that every bedroom must have its fire-place, even if the fire is rarely lit. The large diameter of the flues gives some idea of the great volume of air that the fire-place when hot continuously extracts from the room; the old diameter was 23–35.5 cm. (1–1½ bricks); nowadays, however, they are often as small as 23 cm. Every fire-place has a flue of its own, which accounts for the immense chimney-stacks on English houses.

The need for adequate ventilation also influences the construction of the house in many other ways. It accounts, for example, for the Englishman's fondness for sash-windows, for there is no window that can regulate the ventilation as minutely as the English sash-window. Both halves can be pushed up and down to let air in at the top or bottom; thanks to a counter-weight in the suspension the light sticks at any position to which it is pushed. Again, the possibility of creating a draught through the whole house is often considered at the planning stage; in the case of blocks of workmen's flats this idea becomes one of the most important points to be considered. The large amount of ventilation is the cause of the famous draughtiness of the English houses, which has already provoked many a harsh word from foreigners. But the blazing fire in the grate is solely responsible for continuously sucking a powerful current of air through cracks in doors and windows, towards the fire-place. The English are more or less impervious to the draught, partly because they are used to it, partly because they take the precaution of wearing warm underclothing. They have a highly-developed need of fresh air. They usually sleep with the window open, open the windows in unheated railway compartments in winter and, in general, have nowhere near the same need of warmth as we on the continent with our over-heated railways carriages and the tropical temperatures in our rooms.

Questions concerning the subsoil

The battle against damp is expressed in other ways, most importantly in the choice of building sites. The first and most important point to be considered when assessing a site is whether the subsoil is clay or sand. Sandy soil is considered by far the better and the more worth looking for of the two.

Sandy soil allows rain-water to filter through immediately to a lower, impermeable stratum, whence it finds its way naturally to the water-courses and basins. This is why sandy paths dry quickly after rain. Clay, however, retains water on the surface, where it must evaporate. In this way it increases the humidity of the atmosphere even more by absorbing latent heat when the temperature of the air falls significantly, so that clay building land is always colder than sandy ground. Chalky soils are usually porous and behave in the same way as sand. In England recently so much attention has been paid to questions of the subsoil that it is now almost the first consideration for anyone choosing land for a house or buying a house, with the result that round London houses and rented property on sandy soil cost twice as much as those on clay. These popular assumptions are, of course, only partly true. Thus, for example, sandy soils are only dry when the impermeable lower stratum really does allow the water to drain away. There is little advantage if it holds the water, as it may do in a basin with a closer-grained subsoil. And again, in certain circumstances, for example when it slopes in the direction of a run-off, there is no danger in a clay subsoil. The English authorities have recently found it expedient to publish their views on the question of subsoils in building land and, in so far as London and its environs are concerned, to explain the situation in detail and in popular form, an enterprise which, in view of the traditional passivity of the English authorities, must be doubly commended.[13]

3. Inclemency of the weather

The perpetually damp atmosphere must also be at the root of the Englishman's unwillingness to live by a river or lake. He much prefers to live on a hill. Water is not the attraction in England that it is in dry countries and it is significant in this connection that fountains and ornamental pools play a minor part in English gardens, just as swimming has little place in the immense variety of English sporting life.

Like the humid atmosphere, with which it is to some extent linked, the inclement weather affects the layout of the English house. There is little sunshine, hence no real need for shady places, such as covered areas for sitting out, loggias, open halls, etc.; and the impossibility of remaining outside eliminates balconies, verandas and the facilities for relaxing in the open and enjoying the fresh air without leaving the house, which delight continentals in the warm season. As one might expect, all these things were introduced into England in plenty during the period of the domination of the Italian house-plan. But they never became anything more than lifeless appendages and they disappeared automatically when England returned to its native style of house. The balconies that were attached to London houses during the Neo-Classical period were so far from being intended for use that they often collapsed under the weight of any more than a handful of people, so the authorities always insisted on their being supported by wooden sub-structures when street processions and the like were due to take place.

Bay windows are the substitutes for seating in the open air in the true English house and for centuries English architects have shown a special fondness for them. The English bay, which is deeply bowed, is very different from the continental form. The English wanted all the advantages of the uninterrupted view that open-air balconies and the like provide while remaining in the shelter of the room.

Situation of the house in relation to the sun

The sun's rays but rarely penetrate the cloud-cover that hangs in English skies and the most far-reaching reflection of this in the English house is the extreme care that is lavished on the choice of site, a matter which we shall consider later. The ideal would be, of course, for all the rooms to face the sun, but this is seldom possible. It must therefore be a question of calculating exactly how much sunshine to give each room according to its purpose, from which a whole science of correct layout has evolved. On the continent too, of course, architects consider the houses' orientation in relation to the sun. But it is not half as important to us as it is to the English. Usually also, we are bound by the belief that the principal rooms must look on to the street, no matter in which direction it lies. In England, however, the first consideration when building a house is always that it should be in a sunny position; and the merits of a house are judged very largely by the extent to which it meets this requirement.

Building materials. Local usage

The materials afforded by the country itself must, of course, be an important element in any consideration of the geographical determinants of the house. In the past, when means of transport were rudimentary, each district was restricted to the materials that occurred there naturally, with the result that architecture always had a pronounced local character. Thus in the north of England buildings were traditionally of stone, in the midlands and part of the south they were made of wood, while those round London were of brick, and these characteristics were quite strictly localised. In the course of development these local differences diminished in proportion as transport became less difficult. But in fact the present-day school of architects is seriously trying to reintroduce local materials. The purpose of the attempt is first and foremost the aesthetic one of ensuring that a house is visually in keeping with the ground on which it stands. But the selection of materials afforded by the land does not contribute to this effect solely because they can be seen to have been used in the place where they occur naturally but also because the new buildings harmonise so well with the old.

Natural and artificial stones

Of native stone, granite is obtainable in quite large quantities in the south-west and in Scotland. Bath and Portland produce large amounts of limestone. Portland stone weathers extremely well and is double the price of Bath stone, which is of poor quality in its natural state and can only be used when it has been impregnated with silicates. Most of London's monumental buildings are of Portland stone, one of the qualities of which is that it takes on a pleasing silver-grey colour amid the black smoke of London. There is no sandstone in England, but much, of good quality, in Scotland. It is rarely seen in England itself. On the whole, England is poorly endowed with stone for building, but there are rich and easily accessible deposits of clay, so that by nature England is a brick-using rather than a stone-using country. Brick is the favourite material for building nowadays and will be discussed in greater detail later.

Some forty years ago an unusual terracotta technique was evolved; terracotta blocks as large as moderately sized dressed stone blocks are placed in position after the blocks, which are hollow, have been filled with concrete. This method is used primarily for urban buildings and is justified by the fact that smoke from coal, which is very thick in English cities because of all the open fires and the many industrial plants, cannot settle on the smooth surface of the terracotta, whereas it rapidly blackens dressed stone and brick.[14] Terracotta is used rarely or not at all

---

[13] H. B. Woodward: *Soils and subsoils from a sanitary point of view, with especial reference to London and its neighbourhood*, 1897. (Official publication.)

[14] I have described the English methods of building in brick and terracotta at length in the *Zentralblatt der Bauverwaltung*, vol. for 1898.*

*In ZB XVIII, 1898, p. 265ff., 277ff., and ZB XVIII, 1898, p. 581ff., 593ff., 605ff., 622f. [DS]

for building houses in country districts and there has been a considerable cooling of the extravagant enthusiasm that it has enjoyed during the past decades.

Wood for building. Half-timbering

England is very poor in timber for building and has to rely almost entirely on imports from Russia, Finland, Sweden and north-east Germany. The high price of timber probably accounts for the flimsy construction of the roofs. A large selection of woods for interiors comes from America and the colonies. One notices that furniture is almost exclusively made of mahogany, which is about the same price as oak, only the so-called Spanish mahogany being more expensive than oak. Oak is the only wood that is still felled in England. In the Middle Ages, however, large areas of England were covered by forest, which explains the English fondness for half-timbering. Indeed, half-timbering was revived not long ago, but there is growing opposition to it based on the undeniable fact that present-day circumstances no longer favour it.

B. Determining factors in social life

Immutable patterns of life

The most striking characteristic that the foreigner notices about the English is that their patterns of life are immutable and fixed for all time. They are the outcome of an ancient culture that can look back over a lengthy evolution, combined with a long inheritance of prosperity; in short, a natural product of English history. The immutable patterns which enable the English in all situations to do the right thing – right because everybody does the same – doubtless have their uses. For they give the individual immense self-assurance (even Goethe was struck by the young Englishmen, whose 'bearing and behaviour is so confident and easy-going that one would think that they were lords of all they surveyed') and ease him over many little contrarieties that arise out of the differences of custom that prevail with us. An Englishman is never in doubt about what clothes he should wear or how he should behave in any given circumstance. Indeed, the rules have assumed so much of the force of law that foreigners often find them tyrannical. This opinion is not shared in England. It is probably truer to say that these immutable patterns are in general a dispensation that obviates the necessity of thinking about formalities, since these have been fixed once and for all by mutual agreement.

Like the customs of everyday life in England, those that govern the household are fixed and unshakeable. Not only is the domestic routine in the individual house unvarying and as punctual as clockwork throughout the year but all households of similar economic standing are as like one another as peas in a pod. So one can classify the households of England according to income and know at once precisely how things will be done in a household of a given class. They have the same number of servants and the work is apportioned in exactly the same way, they have the same rooms, the same meals, the same daily routine for the inmates. This has advantages; for example, new servants entering a household know in advance exactly what their work will entail and follow it with unquestioning precision. But woe to the lady of the house who seeks to change things by one iota (only foreigners attempt this). No servant would tolerate it but would leave immediately.

Although these rigid patterns have undoubted advantages, there can be no denying the fact that the obstinacy with which the English observe the minutest conventions often tends to be exaggerated. It is part of a tendency towards the mechanical, which is deeply rooted in every English head and which is more apparent than ever today. This tendency runs through the whole of English culture; we find it in trade, in industry, in school-life, in government institutions, and the observer is left with the impression that England is beginning to suffer from a certain hardening of the arteries. She resembles an old man, who, though still sprightly, prefers to take things quietly, wants no more changes and would leave things as they are, because he fears that any deviation from habit would upset him.

Wealth and housing standards

The country's proverbial wealth must naturally find expression in the style in which its people live. Yet it must be stressed that there is nothing ostentatious about this, they display the very opposite of a desire for extravagance and ceremony. Compared with continental, especially German, standards, the English standard of housing is decidedly simple and modest. This can be seen at once from the fact that the proportion of expenditure on housing to total expenditure is not nearly as high as it is in Germany. In England they reckon that rent accounts for no more than one-tenth of annual outgoings. Add to this the rates and taxes on the house (they are high, amounting to between a quarter and one-third of the rent) and outgoings on the house, according to present opinion in England, come to no less than one-tenth and no more than one-sixth of income, which would mean for the rent itself only between one-thirteenth and one-eighth of income. From this it follows that the outgoings of an English household are distributed quite differently from those of a German household. Proportionately less is paid for the house but more for certain amenities of life, such as service, travelling, books and periodicals, hobbies etc. It will be instructive to look at a schedule of expenditure for an English household, for example for a family spending 20,000 M a year. The items are as follows:

Rent	2000 M
Rates and taxes	660
Repairs, etc.	1000
3 servants	3000
Maintenance for husband and wife	2000
Drink	250
Clothes and personal expenses for wife	1500
Clothes and personal expenses for husband	2000
Coal	500
Life and other insurances	1000
Fares	600
Laundry	720
Unforeseen	4770
Total	20,000*

The margin of 4770 for unforeseen expenses is large. But it should be remembered that it covers entertaining and hospitality, amusements (such as visits to the theatre and concerts), charity (this form of expenditure in England, where many public institutions, such as hospitals, etc., are supported entirely by voluntary contributions, is always very high), doctor's bills etc. The fact that only three servants are kept, which is unusual for a house costing 20,000 M to run, shows how small this particular house is. There are, of course, no children. A further 1000 M is reckoned for each young child.

*English value at the time £1000. [DS]

The English household proves the rule that expenditure on essential needs diminishes with increasing prosperity, while expenditure on comforts and luxuries increases. Expenditure on luxuries, not on necessities, indicates the value of money. In England at present this is about half as high as in Germany, which means that one thinks as little of giving two shillings there as we do of giving one mark. This is a fairly accurate reflection of the country's prosperity, which is at the moment about double that of Germany.

Hospitality

Standards of home-life in England are as simple as standards of housing and the naturalness of the English style of hospitality in particular comes as a pleasure. The habit of entertaining large numbers to great feasts which is so common in Germany and which is often so inexplicable and difficult to justify in terms of the host's expenditure on other things, is virtually unknown in England. From time to time, of course, a few friends are invited to a meal, but they are kept to a minimum so that they shall not greatly outnumber the members of the family. These occasions are simple, especially as regards the drinks that are served. The desire to impress his guests with special kinds of food and drink or to outdo, or even to try to rival, others is entirely alien to the Englishman and would be regarded as a mark of bad taste. Yet, as we shall show, considerations of hospitality play a by no means unimportant part in the layout of the English house. Unlike his colleague in Berlin, the English architect has no need to ask his client how many people he wishes to seat but can content himself with ascertaining the style in which he proposes to live. Sociability is a rather different thing in England from what it is in Germany. The English are certainly less sociable by nature than the Germans. Yet the scope of social life is wide and everyone can have as much of it as he wishes.

The commonest form of entertaining among the middle-classes is the 'At Home', which takes place either at nine in the evening or in the afternoon (when it is attended mainly by women). Refreshments are of the simplest, even the most primitive, kind, indeed, a German would pronounce them positively inadequate : they consist of coffee, tea, fruit-cup, cakes and sandwiches. But one has the feeling that no one would come on account of the food or attach any importance to it. Sometimes a few friends, as many as can be seated without difficulty, are invited to dinner, while a larger number arrive later for an evening reception. Besides 'At Homes', women entertain among themselves by visiting one another on their respective reception days. Visiting takes place in England only between three and six o'clock in the afternoon. Visits are not paid, nor, as a rule, received, outside these hours. Married men do not visit at all: it is assumed that they are too busy, but when a wife visits, she always leaves her husband's card as well. It is understood in the English house that social life is the wife's province, over which she has sole sway, thereby freeing the husband, who is fully occupied by his work and need only accompany her. The husband more often sees business friends or those with whom he shares some specific interest, in his club, a kind of male *pied à terre* in town. Short discussions often take place over lunch at the club, after which the men exchange many entirely non-commital and informal invitations.

Staying with friends

If entertaining in the English house is rather meagre, another form of hospitality is far more highly evolved: I refer to invitations to stay. Every house is equipped to accommodate one or more house-guests and it is amiably taken for granted that no special arrangements will be made for the visitor. He is one of the family and can do or not do as he wishes, like any of the others. His host does not feel obliged to drag him round the sights of the neighbourhood, nor his hostess to put special delicacies before him. Everything goes on as usual and the visitor is spared the embarrassing feeling – that ultimately obliges him to leave – that he is upsetting the routine of the house. And, as is so often the way, true courtesy lies in the very absence of conspicuous marks of it. The Englishman's highly developed sense of hospitality has evolved through living in the country and still to this day it appears in its most striking form in country surroundings. Country-houses are essentially planned with visitors in mind and are equipped for entertaining them, not only in the provision of spare rooms, but also in domestic offices and outbuildings designed to cater for temporary large increases in numbers.

Size of the domestic offices

In fact the English country-house is a world in miniature. The old patriarchal conditions of the isolated farmhouse still prevail. Considerable stores against all eventualities, horses and carriages and adequate staff are essential even for small houses in the country. The house should preferably have its own small farm to provide the most important raw materials for food. These circumstances also account for the large area occupied by the domestic offices, a peculiarity that has spread from the country-house to the house in general. In town houses, which in England are never regarded as fully evolved entities but merely as temporary expedients, all the domestic offices are in the basement. The basement, however, extends underground to the front of the house and behind it, forming cellars under the pavement and increasing the space to the front, while at the back it provides room for domestic purposes under all the courtyards. By this means extra space, which at least comes somewhere near conditions as they are in the country, is gained.

Numerous servants

The large numbers of servants in the English house are also largely accounted for by the conditions of household management that have developed in the country. It may be assumed that in the smaller English house at least one more, and in larger houses, several more, servants are kept than in corresponding German houses. The reason lies partly in the Englishman's higher standards of physical comfort, partly in the fact that English service is more specialised, which makes it impossible for one servant to do anything except the particular work for which he was engaged, even if there is little for him to do in his own department. There is also the fact that the lady of the house merely presides over the household without taking any active part in it. The lady of an English house never sets foot in the kitchen and the cook would not want her to do so. She sends for the servants when she is ready to give her orders. In the English view, a household designed to cost between three and four thousand marks a year requires one servant, one costing 6000 M two servants, one costing 10,000 three (a cook, a housemaid and a boy, perhaps), one costing 15,000 also three, at a pinch (cook, housemaid and under-housemaid), one costing 20,000 four (cook, housemaid, under-housemaid, man-servant). In regard to these figures, it must be remembered that corresponding households in Germany would be those only that cost about half. In all these cases it is assumed that there are no children, if there are children there will be one or more nannies as well.

Duties of the individual servants

In a very large English household, such as the country-seat of a nobleman, there are, of course, more servants, both male and female. As has been said, the duties of each individual servant are specialised down to the last detail and each one is regarded as a matter of course. Both male and female servants have a head, the butler being the head man-servant, the housekeeper in charge of the women. Both occupy positions of responsibility and trust and are paid accordingly (the butler receives about 1200–2000 M, the housekeeper about 800–1600 M). The butler is in charge of the silver and the wine, serves at table with a footman and is responsible for seeing that all the men-servants fulfill their duties punctiliously. The housekeeper is the representative of the lady of the house; she keeps an exact account of all expenses, superintends the household washing and engages, supervises and, if necessary, dismisses the maid-servants. Next in the hierarchy are the husband's valet and the wife's personal maid. These four senior servants eat separately from the others in the housekeeper's room, which must always, therefore, be of a suitable size. One of the junior kitchen maids waits on them. All the other servants eat together in the servants' hall. Their table, like that of the four others, always has a clean cloth and is fully laid, a praiseworthy custom which is observed even in the smallest English households where only one servant is kept. The servants eat at entirely different times from the gentry. English meals, which are exactly the same throughout the country, are, as is well known, a hot breakfast with meat dishes at nine o'clock, a simple hot lunch at one o'clock, tea with bread and butter at four o'clock and a generous main meal (dinner) at seven o'clock. The servants, however, have breakfast at eight, lunch at twelve, a generous meal with tea at five and cold supper at nine o'clock.

The duties of the servants from the cook and the first footman downwards follow naturally. The cook has one or two kitchen-maids to help her (the second, when present, is called a scullery-maid). The house, that is, mainly, the cleaning, is the province of the head housemaid and one or more under-housemaids. Of the ordinary men-servants, the first footman remains in the hall to open the door to visitors (except during the gentry's mealtimes), the second sees to the rooms, while the third does the rougher housework, such as cleaning the knives, boots, windows, etc. When there is only one man-servant he has to do all these jobs alone; but in many households another maid is kept, a so-called parlourmaid, instead of the solitary man-servant; she takes over at least the less heavy jobs that otherwise fall to the man and special help is brought in to do the cleaning.

Separate service in the nursery

The nursery in the English house is always run and served quite separately. Except when they are driven out or taken for a walk, the children spend the whole time in the nursery under the supervision of women engaged for the purpose and contact with their parents is far less frequent than in continental households. The only connection between the nursery and the rest of the household is that the cook prepares the meals for the inmates of the nursery. Otherwise everything, including meals, is separate. In large households there is a nursery governess for the very small children: she may be regarded as the mother's help. Her presence does not render the real head of the nursery redundant. The real head is the nurse, who looks after every aspect of the children's personal well-being. In addition there are one or more nursery-maids to do the heavy work. In smaller households either the nurse does everything herself or a housemaid helps her to fetch and carry. The nursery staff take their meals together in the nursery, after the children have had theirs. The nurse herself occasionally takes a meal at the housekeeper's table by way of a rest, but she is in duty bound not to leave the children for an instant by day or night, which means that hers is the most arduous job in the whole household, as, of course, by the nature of things, her position is the most responsible.

Children are extremely well looked after in England. This has to be admitted even though one knows that it makes relatively few demands on the parents, who delegate it to employees. But extreme punctiliousness and order and close and constant supervision and guidance ensure that a generation will rise that will be sound in body and mind and whose strength will lie in stability, toughness and steadfastness of character. The ways of the English nursery make an appropriate start to the development of these qualities.

C. Laws of land-tenure

Origin of tied land

If anything will bring home to the English every hour of every day the fact that their history has continued without a break for close on a thousand years, it must be the present conditions of land-tenure. In all essentials they possess today the character given them by William the Conqueror when he seized England. Everyone knows how he confiscated land and gave it to his barons in fief. Under the Saxons most of the country had been folkland but when William transformed it into king's land it ceased to be common property and became the property of the crown. Since then the notion has persisted that in the last analysis all land belongs to the crown and the owner for the time being is only the tenant. Even today, when no heir to a piece of land can be found, it reverts to the crown. Even the owner (in our sense) of the land only holds it in freehold, which means that he enjoys it literally freely, i.e. unconditionally.

William's barons were granted land in return for military service, thus every feudal lord originally only held his fief for life. But it soon became hereditary and in particular, from the beginning, the feudal lords strove to make it not only hereditary but inalienable from their descendants, thus securing the prestige of their families by preserving its real bases. This gave rise to settlements similar to the German fidei-commissions, by which nearly all landed property in England became inalienable. When the process of industrialisation began in England this was found to be an obstacle and a restriction and there was an attempt to make it impossible for families to possess land in perpetuity. Thenceforth ownership of land was restricted by the judiciary to living persons and, after their day, for a further twenty-one years (which meant to a future generation, as yet unborn). This unwritten law was confirmed by legislation but evasion was so simple and widespread that nothing was gained by its introduction. The next heir would dissolve the family settlement (which he can do legally with the assent of an heir who has reached his majority) and entail the estate afresh. This usually takes place in the presence and under the direction of the first owner in his lifetime and is repeated in each generation, that is, on average, every thirty years.

Present position

By and large, therefore, land is still as inalienable as it ever was. A good two-thirds of the land in the United Kingdom is still entailed. This means that half of England is owned by 150 landlords, half of Scotland by seventy-five and half of Ireland by thirty-five. When one speaks of estate in England one therefore always distinguishes between freehold and leasehold or, as we understand it, between ownership and tenancy. In the great majority of cases the owner for the time being or the user merely has a lease on the land, with the result that freehold property is valued very much more highly. As we have said, freehold ownership is mostly only found in entire areas of some size. Freehold may either be absolute (when the estate is held in fee simple) or part of a family settlement (when the estate is said to be entailed), or there may merely be a life interest in an estate. In addition to these main types of land-ownership, there are several sub-groups. The matter is extremely complicated and the continental finds himself confronted by a system that is difficult to grasp, has become highly involved and is bedevilled by its own most archaic technical jargon. But in England it is universally understood, for it affects every individual's closest interests daily. The person who most strikingly and obviously comes up against this colossus of legal involvement and hair-splitting is the house-owner whose house stands on leasehold land.

Leasehold land

The practice of building on leasehold land is very general in England and is the rule in London. Most of the land in London belongs to a few owners of large estates, the most important of whom are the Dukes of Westminster and Bedford and Viscount Portman. All three families are of comparatively recent creation, but because the houses of the great city have washed over their lands like ocean rollers they have become the richest families in the world and still put the American millionaires into the shade. Like that in other parts of England, the leasehold land of London came into existence simply because the owners of land that had become ripe for development were, like all the owners of great estates in England, unwilling to sell in any circumstances. So the only path open to those who were eager to build was to lease their land. The land was therefore divided into small blocks and leased for building; leases were long and were granted on condition that at termination both land and buildings were to revert to the landlord. The large estates in London belonging to the three families we have named were developed in this way about one hundred years ago. For the past twenty years they have been gradually reverting to the families, bringing in undreamt-of riches. Ninety-nine-year leases were granted when these districts were developed. This period was fixed to conform to an existing law governing church land, by which it could not be sold but could be leased for a period not exceeding ninety-nine years. The ninety-nine-year lease which then became customary has diminished steadily in recent years as land has been developed in and around London and leases with similar conditions have been granted for eighty, sixty and even forty years. The term of ninety-nine years has been reduced less generally outside London than in the capital; indeed, in many places there has been vigorous opposition even to this term and landowners have frequently been persuaded to grant leases of 999 years. The effect of so long a lease is exactly that of ownership. In Scotland the long lease (known as feu), similar to ownership, is the rule, so that the Scottish house-owner suffers from none of the disadvantages associated with short leases.

Operation of the lease

Landowners in England lease building-land in return for an annual rent which is very variable but is in general never less than five per cent of the selling value. They impose certain conditions on the leaseholders regarding the buildings to be erected. They stipulate, for example, that houses must be of a certain size, that only good materials must be used and that they must be well built; they exercise not only legal supervision of the new buildings but also a kind of continuous control over all the building operations on their land. Larger landowners always retain an architect who devotes all his time to these matters. Thus in certain areas south of the South Kensington Museum (Collingham Gardens (cf. p. 33) and Cadogan Square) residential districts of great architectonic importance have been developed in the past fifteen years because the owner of the land made it a condition that the houses must be built by certain good architects.

Condition regarding reversion

In other cases, however, no burdensome conditions of any kind are imposed; in particular this is so, when, as usually happens, a speculator develops a whole area as an investment. In this case the owner plays on the very mildness of his conditions to extort a higher rent from the speculator. The speculator runs his houses up hurriedly and sells them as quickly as he can (together with the condition relating to ground-rent). In such cases, which are common, there is no good influence on the style of building exercised by the terms under which the houses are built and the situation is the same as in the case of the large tenement blocks that go up in continental cities. They are jerry-built, to as low a standard as will pass muster. But for the house-owner who later buys such a house it is almost tantamount to calling down a curse on his head. For in English usage a house that stands on rented land is always encumbered by the condition that at the termination of the lease it must be returned to the owner of the land in good habitable order.

It is in fact this condition that makes the leasehold situation in England oppressive, indeed almost a national disaster. Even if the date of surrender is long after the death of the owner for the time being, the condition is quite palpably reflected in the premature depreciation in the value of the house, especially when a change of ownership is involved. It is possible that a very badly built house may not survive the eighty or sixty years that the lease has to run. Nevertheless, the last occupant still has to return it in good habitable order. Thus, if he is thinking of selling, each intermediate owner must see that he hands on a good house, because the last owner has to deliver up such a house. For the unfortunate final owner, this surrender is often like a Last Judgment. Dilapidations are fixed by assessors appointed for the purpose and in perfectly normal conditions they always amount to many thousands of pounds. There is a whole literature on the important question of dilapidations and innumerable court cases have arisen out of it. But, whatever the cost, the Englishman would ten times rather pay it than be taken to court, since legal costs are always enormous. Anyone who lets himself in for a law-suit in England risks a fortune.

Thus, even when they are well built and in good condition, the value of houses on leasehold land diminishes as the date of reversion draws nearer, until finally their selling value is nil. There are special tables that show the value of a house in each year of the lease. In the case of houses in rapidly developing urban areas, areas that may be becoming fashionable, increasing market values naturally counteract the falling value of the house. In such cases the true selling value is the product of the two forces.

New agreements after termination

Once the lease has terminated, the relationship of the ground landlord to the house changes completely: he ceases to be merely the owner of the land and henceforth owns the house as well. Most former occupants will wish to continue to live in their house. So the landlord enters into an agreement which enables them to go on living there. The conditions under which this can be done are hard. An actual example will explain the procedure. In the case of a house attracting a rent of 4000 M, the landlord lets it to the man who has been living in it for a further forty years on payment of a premium of 28,000 M, an annual indemnification for loss of rent of 1600 M and makes him liable for adding an extra storey and 'modernising' the house throughout. More specifically, modernisation entails laying entirely new supply and drainage pipes, putting in new windows and redecorating throughout. This involves an expenditure that cannot amount in London to much below 30,000–35,000 M, let us say a round 32,000 M. Thus he has to lay out 60,000 M down, which at four per cent interest makes 2400 M annual interest. Added to the annual rent of 1600 M, this comes exactly to the 4000 M rent which the house is worth. At first sight this does not look too unfavourable a deal for the house-owner. However, he has spent this whole sum on a house which does not belong to him and which he has again to turn over to the landlord in good habitable order at the end of forty years. The value of the new work again decreases hourly, but does so more quickly this time because the lease is only of forty years' duration and if the owner moves house within this period he probably makes a considerable loss. Thus the advantage of the agreement has all been on the side of the landlord. Moreover, the contracts which the landlord makes with his individual tenants differ widely. If a tenant is particularly anxious to remain in his house, perhaps because he conducts a business that depends on local custom, conditions are made harder for him. One hears stories of extremely harsh practice on the part of landlords in this connection. But from the purely commercial point of view it is only natural that both parties to the deal should try to get as many advantages for themselves as they can.

Influence of leasehold

Nor must it be forgotten that over a long period the landlord has been receiving rent fixed ninety-nine years previously and that, if the district has improved meanwhile, his income must have been too low for decades. He is therefore justified in indemnifying himself when the lease falls in. One of the main results of this state of affairs has been that leases have recently been shortened in order to enable landlords to take more advantage of increases in market values. But in no sense does this mean that artificial restraint of increasing land values is to the advantage of the population. Valuable leasehold sites in city centres are as much involved in the increase in market values as if they were freehold plots. A house-owner can sell his house, with its liabilities, any day and obtain the market price for it. The price will, however, always be influenced by the peculiar leasehold situation in so far as it is only the unlapsed part of the lease that can be sold. But this makes little difference in highly developed urban areas, especially in shopping streets, since a shop that flourishes because it is in the right position can quickly recoup a heavy outlay by correspondingly high earnings. This is why purchasers risk heavy outlays despite the fact that their ownership of the premises is only temporary. The two conflicting forces that go to fix prices – the steady depreciation of the house as the date of termination of the lease approaches and the steady increase in the value of land as a result of the development of the urban area – are expressed in this instance by the former dwindling to almost nothing by comparison with the latter, with the result that in shopping streets in the inner city, for example, it is entirely disregarded. And so the only effect of the leasehold system is that the leaseholder is not free to dispose of the property, which means that no house-owner will undertake any large constructional project because it is not worth putting up a permanent building for a limited period. As regards residential districts, the development of the neighbourhood does not counterbalance the depreciation of the house, or at least not to nearly the same extent as in commercial districts. Yet even here, particularly in the case of a district that is becoming fashionable, it gives a house a market value that is strongly influenced by the trends of the day. It is in the nature of things that in both cases the speculator comes between the house-owner and the intending purchaser, though without affecting the landlord, and exploits the fluctuations of the market, drives up the price and so on. Those who are familiar with the situation say that there is no possibility that the existence of tied, leasehold land in improving urban districts will put an end to speculation. Speculation enters in here just as if leasehold did not exist, though conditions are less clear and, especially as the lease nears its end, become extremely involved.

Advantages of the English leasehold system

Although these circumstances show that the leasehold system, as it has developed in England, is by no means an ideal arrangement, we must not fail to recognise that in many respects it has great advantages. Chief of these is that it enables many people to possess a house, who, if they also had to purchase an expensive building plot, would have no house to call their own. This advantage is very obvious and quite beyond doubt in England. Economically speaking, it is a simple matter to build a house since the house-owner is entirely relieved of the building costs and his only connection with the land is expressed in the form of a moderate ground-rent. Thus the future house-owner takes upon himself only half the worries. In fact this relief explains why thousands upon thousands of people in England build their own houses who could not dream of doing so in Germany.

Now it could be objected that this relief exists in the imagination only since the ground-rent comes to the same as the interest on a mortgage on land. This would be true if the English owner of land rated his land as highly as we do in our real estate market. But this he cannot do because, as a result of the inalienability of land in England, there are no market increases and forcing up of prices. The situation is much more stable, more permanent, more exclusive and land remains outside the activity of the market and the speculators. There are no property dealers who grow rich on land on which humanity needs to live. Although in developed parts of the city the influence of increasing commerce and other economic increases cannot be averted and speculation itself cannot be stopped, there is no sign at all in suburban areas of land values being driven up in the way that they are in Germany, and even less in the remoter environs of the city and in the country. Whereas half or more of the sum laid out on his house by the German who lives in a suburb goes on the plot, the fraction in England in equivalent circumstances amounts to perhaps only a tenth. Thus, although in other respects the cost of living is higher in England than it is in Germany, housing is much cheaper, only two-thirds or even half the price in the suburbs. The consequences are obvious. They are clearly expressed in the ubiquity of the private house, in the superior style of the accommodation in general and in the beneficial influence of all this on family life, on health and manners, on the whole culture of the population.

It is also true that an unselfish and high-minded landlord who builds decent, solid houses can do a great deal of good.

Disadvantages

But these advantages in England are purchased at the cost of sacrifices on the part of the house-building public and there are many intractable circumstances – indeed, the leasehold system as a whole can hardly be said to be distinguished by overmuch rationality. The most serious aspect of the situation is that the house-owner can never enjoy complete control of his house, for he depends on the landlord's assent if he wishes to rebuild, change use or the like; and there is also the fact that, as we have seen, he must hand over the house in good, habitable order on termination of his lease. Thus although the house is his, the house-owner can never feel that he is in the true sense master of a house, for he is in effect using his money on behalf of someone else, by whose permission he lives there. The consequence is that when he builds himself, he too will build more flimsily, less well, in short, with less interest, than if he were building on his own land. Moreover, in a developing city like London, the leasehold system is most palpably inhibiting the evolution of the city. The old-fashioned, confused appearance of London is probably closely connected with the prevailing system of leasehold. Nor can there be any advantage in the fact that, as in the case of the ninety-nine-year leases in London, the true value of the land lies hidden for decades because of an ancient agreement and then suddenly rises to unheard-of heights as soon as the lease falls in. This is often disastrous in the way that it tests the economic situation of the occupants. In the final analysis, it must be regarded as a doubtful gain that not only the fate of the urban scene in a whole district but also that of a whole section of the population becomes dependent on the will of an individual. The free development of a city, even accepting that there will be property speculation, is surely preferable to that.

The main point to remember when considering the situation is that the English leasehold system was not invented to serve the interest of the house-building public, but that of the large landowners. In plain terms, they have a monopoly of the land. But a monopoly always means crushing free development. In a city like London it cannot be considered anything but a most serious drawback.

Thus there has been much talk during the past decades of some kind of legal annullment of land rights in developed areas; indeed, as time has passed, this has become one of the most burning questions in an England in need of many reforms. But with the preponderance of plutocratic elements in Parliament, no change can be expected for the time being. The present state of affairs is the result of two specifically English national characteristics: the tendency to cling to tradition and the disinclination of the public at large to think of the long term or even to protect their interests.

Conclusion

So if the traditional English handling of the system of leasehold has its darker, as well as its lighter, sides, it cannot in any sense be maintained that the present shortcomings have cast doubt on the question of leasehold as such. The only shortcomings are that contracts between landlord and tenant lay too much emphasis on the rights of the one to the detriment of the other. The ominous aspect of these contracts stems, perhaps, from the fact that they remain in force beyond the span of a human life. Family tradition enables the landlord to give prudent thought to the future, whereas the tenant, belonging as he does to a poorer class of the population, enters lightly into his obligations, both present and in the distant future. He is, moreover, entirely dependent on the landlord who has the monopoly on the land in question.

If it were possible to divide the obligations fairly between both sides, the system of leasehold would be well worth imitating. New legislation could perhaps ensure that contracts must only contain fair conditions that take account of the interests of both parties. An even better system has already been adopted here and there on the continent whereby the local authority and the state act as landlords and lease building land so that everyone benefits. The conditions can then accommodate the tenant in a way that cannot be expected of an individual landlord. If local authorities and large groups would develop a consistent policy along these lines, they would do an immense amount of good. They would also help to solve the steadily deteriorating housing problem in a way that could be of fundamental importance for both the healthy development of the cities and the rehabilitation of our living conditions; in particular they might extend the practice of living in private houses.

D. Legal determinants

Law of 1894

The first legal determinants that we must mention are the London building acts[15] relating to dwelling-houses, for not only do the London acts affect a large proportion of the population of England (over six million) but they also form guidelines for all the other building acts in the country.

Absence of regulations governing construction

The current Building Act was drafted in 1894 (a few additional clauses were added in 1898) and has been in force since 1 January 1895. But it leaves many clauses in other local laws unaltered and, as regards health in particular, is extensively supplemented by the well-known Public Health Act of 1875 that legislated for England apart from London and was amended in 1891, when the conditions of the capital were taken into consideration. The most striking difference between the English and German building laws is that the English legislate basically on points of health and fire hazards and virtually ignore construction. They do, of course, stipulate minimum thicknesses for walls, together with a few constructional measurements, such as those for the bearing surfaces of joists, but from the point of view of fire precautions, not of statics. In England no statical information is required in applications for permission to build (nor would the ordinary English technician be likely to be capable of giving it). This is an instance of the English contention that each individual must bear responsibility for the consequences in case of careless practice. The only jurisdiction the authorities have over constructional matters is in the clause dealing with so-called 'dangerous structures'. If notified of the existence of a dangerous structure, the district surveyor is bound to examine it and if he finds the allegation to be correct, he can order the owner to remove it. The so-called model by-laws issued by the Local Government Board as a result of the health laws, which have been adopted by many cities, and the relevant local regulations for London of 1891, do indeed give guidance about the quality of the materials to be used, yet here again considerations of health have obviously been the ruling ones. It is so diametrically opposed to popular English

[15] Two excellent commentaries on these acts may be recommended: *The London Building Acts 1894 and 1898, a text book for the use of architects*, 23 plates 3rd edition, 1901, by Banister Fletcher and *The London Building Act 1894, with introduction, notes, etc.*, London 1894, by W. T. Craies. The first illustrates and examines the subject in detail, rather from the technical angle, the second more from the legal point of view. The study of these regulations is no easy matter. It would probably be altogether impossible for the foreigner were it not for Banister Fletcher's book, in which all the basic regulations are explained by drawings. For, like most English laws, these are expressed in innumerable clauses of official jargon of the most mystifying kind that seems like something out of the Middle Ages in the midst of the otherwise refreshingly lucid English prose style.

belief that there should be official supervision of these details of building procedure that it would be a rare official who would dare to intervene in such matters, even if he possessed express powers to do so.

The planning of streets

Another peculiarity of the English regulations is that they all begin with the planning of the streets. This arises from the practice of leaving the planning of the areas to be developed entirely to the ground-landlord or the developer. The local authority only reserves the right to approve the resulting new streets, for which purpose plans must be submitted. But here again its hands are tied to a considerable extent. The authority can only refuse permission if carriage-ways are less than 40 ft. (12.20 m.) and pedestrian walks less than 20 ft. (6.10 m.) wide, if culs-de-sac are longer than 60 ft. (18.3 m.) and carriage-ways steeper than 1:20. In certain cases the authority can also require pedestrian walks to be converted into carriage-ways and main streets to be widened to 60 ft. (18.3 m.). It needs little explanation to see what an obstacle to the general development of cities and towns these regulations must represent. The continental procedure, whereby the municipality plans in advance the areas to be developed, certainly has its darker aspects in the way in which it usually works, but the English procedure of caring not at all about these important matters is clearly an immense defect and an incomprehensible sign of backwardness. The result is the English cities with their inextricable confusion of lanes and alleys, those suburbs in which one inevitably gets lost unless one keeps strictly to the single main streets, those pointless meanderings known as crescents (not until the law of 1894 was it decided to prohibit roads in London that lead back into the same thoroughfare without opening into other streets) and many other arrangements established without the slightest forethought. If the street systems were laid out by men who knew what they were about, such as the few isolated instances in which this has been done by architects (e.g. in Bedford Park by Norman Shaw, see p. 30) this freedom would be an advantage. Regrettably, however, the basic planning of most areas for development is entrusted to the intelligence of ordinary developers and in nine cases out of ten the result is bound to be unfortunate.

Light and air, height of street front

The most important section of any building act, the clauses concerning the access of light and air to the building, is formulated very strangely. The height of the building is influenced only by the width of the street and also by the size of the empty space behind the building. To take the influence of the width of the street first: the London regulations specify that in new streets the houses shall not be taller than the street is wide. But this restriction applies only to streets under 50 ft. (15.25 m.) wide. As soon as a street measures 50 ft. or more houses may be built to a maximum of 80 ft. (24.40 m.). Thus the moment the width of the street extends from 49 ft. to 50 ft., the height leaps up by 30 ft. (9.15 m.). However, if an existing building is higher than this and is replaced by a new one, the new house may be built to the height of the old one, however narrow the street. The height is always reckoned from the pavement to the upper edge of the roof parapet or cornice and it is always possible to accommodate two more habitable floors in the roof that rises from this point.

Height of the rear parts of the house. Courtyard space

The fact that the height has been made to depend on the empty space at the back shows clearly how the English situation differs from that of the continent, where the usual large block surrounded by buildings on all sides has prompted entirely different ideas. The regulations in England are derived from the case of a house that is not built round a courtyard, which we shall here assume to be the norm. The rule is that the space remaining behind the house shall never be less than 10 ft. wide (3.05 m.), that it shall extend along the full width of the back of the building and shall not be smaller over all than 150 sq.ft. (13.94 sq.m.). Only dust-bins and lavatories may be built in this empty space and these may not exceed 9 ft. (2.75 m.) in height. If there is a habitable basement, it must have at the back, besides the light of the area at the front – to be discussed later – enough light and air from a yard lying at the level of the basement floor and measuring at least 100 sq.ft. (9.29 sq.m.), the shortest side of which must not measure less than 10 ft. (3.05 m.). The stipulated height of the building depends on the empty space at the back and is calculated by drawing an imaginary straight line from the rear boundary of the site sloping towards the house, no part of the building to project beyond this line. The legally prescribed angle of inclination is $63\frac{1}{2}°$ (the draft bill suggested $45°$, but the large landowners who sit in Parliament forced through this radical amendment that nullifies the whole intent of the law). The angle of $63\frac{1}{2}°$ is that of an upright right-angled triangle, one of the sides of which is double the length of the other two. The angle springs from the point at which a horizontal line drawn through the centre of the building at right-angles to the front and running through the upper edge of the pavement meets the rear boundary of the site. If the site slopes towards the street, the horizontal runs from the higher level at the back. Fig. 144 illustrates an instance of this, and also shows how the back of such a house is constructed to make the most of the permitted development of the site. If there is no yard behind the building but another street or an empty space, the angle springs from the centre of the street or the outer boundary of the empty space. But certain exceptions to the rule are permitted in individual cases. If the ground-floor is not used for residential purposes (if it is a shop, for example), buildings may be put up in the yard to an extra height of 16 ft. (4.88 m.), i.e. the empty space does not begin below the level of 16 ft. (though the angle still springs from below at the point previously fixed). In such a case even an inhabited basement is permitted, provided only that this has the yard measuring 100 sq.ft. For houses built in old streets, the whole springing-point of the angle is moved up 16 ft., so that the terracing of the backs of such houses begins higher than is the case with houses in new streets. Only in the cases of 'workmen's houses' this exception is not permitted. The definition of a workman's house in the special regulations applicable to the building of such houses is a house that either as a whole or in part brings in a low rent of a fixed maximum (400 M in London and 260 M in Liverpool).

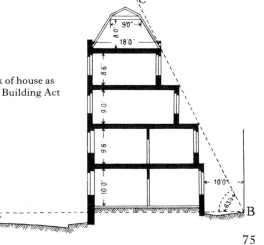

144 Open space at back of house as required by the London Building Act of 1894

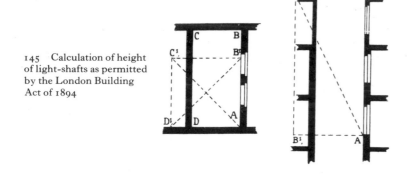

145 Calculation of height of light-shafts as permitted by the London Building Act of 1894

Light-wells

As we have said, an inner courtyard is an exception in the English house. At best it takes the form of a small light-well. A regulation governing this type of structure is well worth imitating: the lower part that serves as an air vent must have effective access to the outer air if the height of the light-well, measured from the ceiling of the ground floor, is greater than its length or breadth. There are no minimum measurements for this type of light-well. But it is stipulated that when windows of habitable rooms (see below) are to open on to a light-shaft that is enclosed on all sides, the distance between the opposite wall and the window must be at least half the height of the light-shaft measured upwards from the sill of the window in question. But the law is relaxed in the case of light-wells in which one side of the base does not exceed twice the length of the others; reckoning the height instead of the actual distance, as mentioned above, the length of the side of a rectangle of the same area as the base of the light-shaft may be assumed (Fig. 145). In light-wells with bases in which the length is more than double the breadth but which are enclosed on three sides only, the height measured from the window-sill of the first floor (not of the ground floor) may be at most double the distance of the window from the opposite wall. Obviously only moderate lighting was considered when these regulations were drafted: light-wells of this kind were not very common in private houses of the old sort. But they occur frequently in the multi-storeyed houses that are going up nowadays.

Wall thicknesses, fire-resisting walls, cornices, parapet walls, bay windows

The thickness of a well must depend on its length and height. It is a striking fact that with external walls of up to 50 ft. (15.25 m.) in height and up to 30 ft. (9.15 m.) in length, the upper floor need be only one brick (i.e. $21\frac{1}{2}$ cm.) thick. Party walls (fire-resisting walls) between two houses (the legal aspects are controlled in detail) are permitted in all cases and must be as thick as the external walls. The fire-resisting walls must exceed the height of the roof by 38 cm. Wooden cornices and barge-boards are permitted. But in no circumstances may a cornice project beyond 76 cm.; so a designer who cannot fit his design into this limit must move back behind the building line for the sake of his cornice. Where gutters are not solidly constructed, the front wall must pass up above the eaves gutter; it must be one brick thick and must rise to at least 30 cm. above the highest point of the gutter. This front wall that passes up beyond the eaves gutter is the real old traditional – one may almost say the national – English style of building. The parapet wall is almost ubiquitous in London.

Balconies may not project more than 75 cm. towards the street. In streets over 40 ft. (12.20 m.) wide, bay windows standing on land belonging to the owner of the house may extend to a total width of three-fifths of the width of the front of the house; they may not project more than 3 ft. (92 cm.) and may not extend upwards above three storeys; nor must they be closer to the neighbouring boundary than a distance equal to the distance they project. Oriels or towers projecting from upper floors must not jut out more than 92 cm. over the householder's own land or 30 cm. over the street; the projection must begin at least 10 ft. (3.05 m.) above the pavement; it must not extend beyond three-fifths of the width of the front.

External waste-pipes

The regulation which says that all waste-pipes must be on the outside of the house, which was introduced in London in 1891 and adopted by other cities, has had a powerful influence on the exteriors of houses. For purposes of ventilation they must also extend above the roof at full diameter. Ever since this regulation came into existence one has seen a strange assemblage of waste-pipes on the faces of houses in general and especially those of the barrack-like tenement-houses that contain many small dwellings. These pipes are now universally attached to external walls, even those of houses that do not come under the jurisdiction of municipal building acts. This measure would obviously be unthinkable in any climate but the mild English one. In continuous hard frosts the pipes would simply freeze.

Room heights. Window measurements

There are detailed health regulations governing the interior arrangements of the house. The most important are those that apply to the height of rooms. Until 1894 the minimum height was 7 ft. clear (2.14 m.), but the new legislation has raised this to $8\frac{1}{2}$ ft. (2.59 m.). Further, every habitable room must have a window opening on to fresh air (or on to a conservatory); and this window, clear of the wooden frame, must measure the equivalent of at least one-tenth of the floor area of the room; it must be possible to open at least one-twentieth of the area of the window. A habitable room means one which someone 'inhabits' during the day or in which someone spends the night. If the authorities suspect that a room meets one of these conditions they can classify it as habitable until the owner proves the contrary.

Habitable rooms in attics

There are special relaxations for habitable rooms in attics. As we have said, it is one of the peculiarities of the English house that the attics are always converted into habitable rooms. The Building Act favours this custom by permitting attic rooms to be slightly lower, i.e. 8 ft. (2.44 m.) instead of $8\frac{1}{2}$ ft., and the window area to be one-twelfth instead of one-tenth of the floor-area of the room. Whereas in other rooms the openable parts of windows must extend to at least 7 ft. (2.13 m.) above floor-level, this may be reduced in attics to 5 ft. (1.55 m.). Furthermore, a horizontal ceiling need cover only half the area of the floor, which means that it may slope for the other half. Under the present law there may not be more than two floors in the roof.

Rooms below ground

It was not until the passing of the Public Health Act that stringent regulations governing habitable rooms in a basement which is partly below ground first came into force in England. The Act of 1891 for London provides that there shall be a light-shaft or area at least 4 ft. (1.22 m.) wide in front of every such room, that its base must lie at least 15 cm. below the level of the floor of the room and that it must be properly drained. The room must be at least 7 ft. high (this figure has been increased for London by that city's Building Act and raised to the minimum for habitable rooms in general, i.e. $8\frac{1}{2}$ ft. (2.59 m.); and they must rise to 3 ft. (92 cm.) above the pavement if the area is not at least as wide as the part of the space below the upper surface of the pavement is high. But if this is the case, it need be only 1 ft. above the pavement. The external walls of the room must be insulated from the ground. The floor must be hollow-laid and the space beneath it must be ventilated. But the London Act also permits the laying of wooden floors in cement, a method of construction that is in fact in general use in England for floors of this kind. Each room must have a fire-place and proper ventilation must be allowed for. In addition to these requirements – which, however, do not apply in the Public Health Act of 1891 to new buildings only but must also be met by all existing basement rooms – the London Building Act of 1894 stipulates, as we have seen, that there must be a yard measuring 100 sq.ft. outside the back basement rooms.

Levelling of the floors. Insulating courses. Precautions against damp

To exclude rising damp the whole area of ground below the building must be levelled off with a layer of good concrete carefully rammed down and not less than 6 ins. (15 cm.) thick. This regulation is extremely important for England because, as we have seen, houses other than those in the centres of cities do not as a rule have cellars. The space between the layer of concrete and the lowest floor must be ventilated. Insulating courses are naturally required. But vertical air ducts are not encouraged, because the regulation says that such may only be laid horizontally in the wall, the minimum thickness of which must not otherwise be touched. The reason for this lies presumably in the steadily growing belief that ventilation of this kind harbours vermin and must be opposed. The last six courses of the upper edges of free-standing walls, such as parapet walls, chimney shafts, etc. must be built up and thickly coated with cement to prevent damp seeping in. These are the most important of the regulations governing housing in the London Building Act.

Regulations governing drainage

The last chapter of this volume will be devoted to the fairly detailed regulations relating to drainage systems in houses.*

Regulations for rural areas

As we have said, the London regulations were often used as models for other cities, although there was, of course, nothing to prevent their introducing changes. Indeed, the influence of the London Act reaches right out into the country. The first Public Health Act of 1875 permitted rural districts to introduce building regulations for which the Local Government Board had drawn up 'model by-laws', the final form of which was subject to its assent. These model by-laws and the local regulations based on them have since proved a source of widespread dissatisfaction in England. For they entailed applying measures appropriate to an over-populated, densely built-up city to smaller towns and, indeed, to isolated houses, and if Goethe's words 'reason turns to madness, good deeds to torment' apply anywhere they apply here. Many local authorities therefore preferred not to use the powers given them in the Public Health Act and to dispense with building regulations altogether.

Vigorous agitation against the model by-laws continued for a number of years. Architectural associations passed resolutions against them and the press took the matter up with fervour. In the end, in 1901, the Local Government Board felt obliged to supplement their existing regulations with others specifically designed for country districts.[16] These were only intended as guide-lines to the most important requirements in matters of health; points relating to construction and fire precautions and recommendations regarding the planning of streets are omitted. The earlier model by-laws for cities exist for those municipal bodies that wish to pass wider-reaching regulations in these fields. The new regulations relate to dwelling-houses only. They prescribe such measures as covering the ground with a layer of concrete (but only in cases in which damp is suspected), provision of insulating courses to guard against damp, etc., but otherwise they give complete freedom in matters of the thickness of walls, quality of materials, size, and even height, of rooms. The regulations relating to the provision of light and air are also very mild. They stipulate a minimum width for streets of a mere 24 ft. (7.32 m.) and say simply that if narrow streets are already in existence, new buildings must lie 12 ft. back from the middle of the road. As regards yards, each house must have a yard of at least 150 sq.ft. (13.94 sq.m.) in area, and the house must lie at least 15 ft. (4.58 m.) from the adjoining boundary at the rear; but if the house is 25 ft. (7.63 m.) in height, this distance is to be increased to 20 ft. (6.10 m.) and if it reaches 35 ft. (10.68 m.) and above, it must be increased to 25 ft. (7.23 m.) (the height is to be measured to either half-way up the roof or to the parapet, whichever is the greater). Regulations regarding window areas are the same as in London. It is also laid down that the space between the ground floor and the ground must be ventilated and, furthermore, if the ground is not covered so as to exclude damp, the space must measure 9 ins. (23 cm.) in depth. Habitable rooms without fire-places must have a ventilating shaft of at least 18 cm square.

The remaining model by-laws deal with the installation of lavatories, rubbish-bins and the drainage of houses.

Conclusion

The most antiquated of the London regulations are those that deal with the planning of streets. Their inadequacy is recognised by discerning professionals and there is a movement to work towards introducing the continental practice. Although present regulations governing the lighting and ventilating of buildings represent an advance on the earlier ones, provisions are less adequate than continental opinion requires. The angle of $63\frac{1}{2}°$ for light at the backs of houses is as insufficient as light from a street 50 ft. wide lined with houses 80 ft. high. Dark passages are much more common in English town houses than they are in the new districts in continental cities.

But one may single out as worthy of imitation the freedoms permitted in construction and the mild regulations governing heights of rooms and the facilities in the layout of attics are worthy of our attention. One is also agreeably impressed to find none of those unreasonable requirements that appear in German regulations governing country-houses in areas where detached houses are built, regulations which one can only regard as deterrents to the building of private houses. Nowhere is it forbidden to erect connected groups of houses, nor do we find that strange rule whereby front gardens must be left in full view that obliges every house-owner to maintain part of his land – which he has often acquired at considerable expense – as a show-piece for the benefit of passers-by in the streets, thus dismembering his property and surrendering it to the public. Such measures would be impossible in a country in which the private house is something other and more important than a rich man's luxury obstructed by officialdom.

* This section has been omitted. [DS]

[16] Local Government Board. *Model by-laws. IV. Rural districts. New Buildings and certain matters connected with buildings*, 1901.

The regulations governing drainage and other sanitary installations are also thoroughly admirable. Viewed as a whole, the difference between the English and the German regulations may be said to lie in the fact that the German regulations, with anxious protectiveness, concern themselves with every conceivable matter except sanitary arrangements, while the English permit the greatest freedom over points of construction but are extremely stringent in requiring care in the installation of sanitary equipment.

The new model by-laws issued by the Local Government Board for rural districts deserve praise for their great mildness and the freedom allowed the individual to design his house in a sphere in which there is no need to consider the evil consequences of overcrowding. For this reason they were also given a ready welcome everywhere in England. Architects too have most gratefully acknowledged the absence of all restrictive measures in the fields of construction and materials; they are even permitted to use thatched roofs again. It would surely be hard to surpass these regulations in leniency and broad-mindedness.

The English building laws possess the distinctive feature shared by many other public activities in England: they confine themselves to essentials. They do not pretend to anticipate, they merely follow what has convincingly proved itself to be needful. This leaves the way open to much misunderstanding, but also avoids the artificiality and severity inherent in many of our German building laws with their experiments, at once tentative and dogmatic, and their studied intentions that do not always succeed in their aims.

The layout of the English house

So numerous are the forms of the English house that as soon as one begins to consider its plan in greater detail it becomes necessary to sub-divide the material. For the conditions underlying the country-house obviously differ from those of the town house, the rich man's mansion from those of the workman's cottage; and these conditions must create different basic forms of house. Before we describe these it would seem practical to mention a few of the characteristics of the ultimate unit that is common to all, the English room.

The English room. Its seclusion

All sorts of influences, some of which we have already mentioned, combine to make the English room essentially different from the continental. Perhaps the most striking difference is the lack in England of communicating doors between the rooms, which means that the only access to a room is from a passage or hall. Thus the English room is a sort of cage, in which the inmate is entirely cut off from the next room. Englishmen usually shake their heads at the sight of a continental ground-plan with its ubiquitous communicating doors and in a continental house they might feel as though they were perpetually sitting out in the street. They would see this as an interference with one of their most conspicuous needs, their desire for privacy, for seclusion. Though we are so different, though we like to have access to the adjoining rooms, like continuous suites of rooms with their long vistas, we should not overlook the fact that this desire for privacy is only the final outcome of the feeling that has driven the English as a people instinctively towards living in their own houses: the sense of being their own masters. It must also be the final outcome of the process of division and separation that we have found in the development of the plan of the English house. A hundred years ago the rooms in the English house intercommunicated to the same extent as ours on the continent today. One of the factors that contributed to the gradual shutting-off of separate rooms was the diminishing desire for sociability. As time went on, it was replaced to an ever greater extent by the desire to live quietly, in self-sufficiency, secluded from the hubbub of the city. Just as the Englishman plans the layout of his house without giving a thought to banquets and celebrations, but rather to fulfil all his residential needs as intimately as possible, so he wishes his room to be designed less for the general coming and going of the house than for the special use for which it is intended. Communicating doors obviously rob the room of part of its specific character. Communicating doors make a living-room not so much a living-room as a reception-room.

There is, moreover, one undoubted advantage in the separate room: it leaves very good wall spaces. In the English room there are almost always two entire walls without openings, whereas we in Germany are only too fond of sacrificing wall-surfaces to communicating doors, which is a grave disadvantage when it comes to furnishing and giving the room a homely atmosphere. For openings in the walls are not in the least desirable and can only be considered necessary evils. Windows and doors are sources of draughts, doors let in noise from adjoining rooms and restrict the space available for wall-furniture. Artistically too they destroy the unified effect of the room, so that it looks dilapidated and full of holes. So we should support any attempt to limit those necessary evils (both in number and in size); but this does not mean that we need go as far as they do in England. Fortunately, however, at least the two-winged door, that most obtrusive witness of an empty love of grandeur that lacks all homeliness, is steadily disappearing. It is quite unknown to the Englishman in his present-day home; he insists on having as few openings in his walls as possible. There are only a handful of cases in which exceptions are made to the rule, as, for example, in rooms that by their nature belong together, like bedrooms and dressing-rooms, kitchens and sculleries, etc. Sometimes also a client will decide that he wants the two main rooms of the house such as the dining-room and drawing-room or the hall and drawing-room, to communicate by means of folding doors (sliding doors are seldom seen). But this reflects a particular liking and in no way alters the proposition that the English room is a secluded one.

Position and opening of the door

Not only are openings in walls made as sparingly as possible but the greatest care is exercised in choosing a position for the door. In the ordinary German house walls are often pierced here and there, entirely arbitrarily; and communicating doors are usually situated in the centre of the wall, generally the worst possible position. It is otherwise in England: both matters are considered with the greatest care since they are of paramount importance to the comfort of the room. For one thing, the draughtiness of the English house ensures that care will be taken to site the door so that parts of the room can be reserved for people to sit where the draught cannot reach them, an important point here being that the sitting area must be some way away from the source of the draught. The greatest care is also taken to see that those seated in the room are disturbed as little as possible by the opening of the door. The most important point is that people should not be disturbed and this is reflected mainly in the direction in which the door opens. The rule known to every Englishman says that the door must open towards the main sitting area in the room, which usually means towards the fire-place; in a study it opens towards the desk, in a bedroom towards the bed. The idea behind this is that the person entering shall not be able to take in the whole room at a glance as he opens the first crack of the door but must walk round it to enter the room, by which time the person seated in the room will have been able to prepare himself suitably for his entry. The ground-plans of the country-house Cavenham Hall (Figs. 146, 147), in which the openings of the doors are marked, should help to clarify these remarks. The striking feature about the opening of the doors as it appears there is that the person entering seems at first to be walking into a wall and sees nothing inside the room until he opens the door wide. In fact it is not at all unpleasant to enter a room in this way. It is only like passing through a kind of porch or small vestibule.

Position of the fire-place

By far the most important feature in the English room is the fire-place. We have already mentioned the justification for its existence in the English climate. We shall discuss the way in which it determines the whole arrangement of the room at a later stage. But even in the general plan of the room it is the most

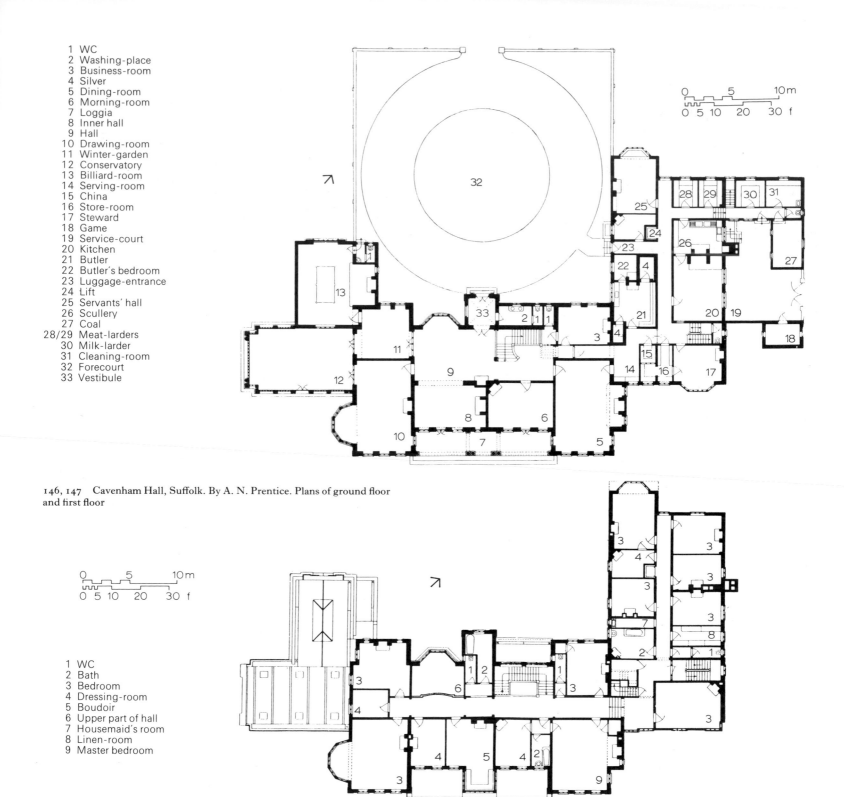

1 WC
2 Washing-place
3 Business-room
4 Silver
5 Dining-room
6 Morning-room
7 Loggia
8 Inner hall
9 Hall
10 Drawing-room
11 Winter-garden
12 Conservatory
13 Billiard-room
14 Serving-room
15 China
16 Store-room
17 Steward
18 Game
19 Service-court
20 Kitchen
21 Butler
22 Butler's bedroom
23 Luggage-entrance
24 Lift
25 Servants' hall
26 Scullery
27 Coal
28/29 Meat-larders
30 Milk-larder
31 Cleaning-room
32 Forecourt
33 Vestibule

146, 147 Cavenham Hall, Suffolk. By A. N. Prentice. Plans of ground floor and first floor

1 WC
2 Bath
3 Bedroom
4 Dressing-room
5 Boudoir
6 Upper part of hall
7 Housemaid's room
8 Linen-room
9 Master bedroom

important element, and as the architect develops each individual room in his plan, deliberations over the best position for the fire-place, and in particular over its relationship to the wall-space and to the doors and windows, are the most important of all. The fire-place is the focal point of the room. People naturally like to sit close to it to enjoy its warmth. But it also has the disadvantage that it continually sucks vast volumes of air out of the room through its broad flue; this must be replaced by fresh air entering through cracks in windows and especially in doors, so creating a draught. The path of the draught can be accurately plotted by drawing straight lines from door and windows to the fire-place. What must now be done is to reduce the draughtiness of the fire-place as far as possible by positioning windows and doors so that there are places to sit near the fire-place that are free of draughts; this is far from easy and requires great skill. For the places by the wall, which may in themselves be out of the line of the draught, are not free of draught because the warm air from the fire-place, which rises to the ceiling and is there diffused, drives the cold air downwards. It is altogether impossible to create areas which are entirely free of draughts in this way, most of all in small rooms.

148 Cavenham Hall

149 Cavenham Hall

In England, therefore, they have invented special armchairs that are closed in up to the top (Fig. 112) and resemble the beach chairs found at seaside resorts, to protect those seated therein from the draught. Thus this form of English chair, though not understood and usually a source of amusement in Germany, has its very natural justification. As has been said, it makes a difference in large rooms whether the main sources of draughts – the doors – are at a distance from the fire or very close to it. Since the obvious place for both the fire-place and the entrance-doors is the interior wall nearest to the centre of the house – obvious for the fire-place because several flues can easily be combined and the smoke vents are in a warm position, and obvious for the doors because access to the rooms is usually from a given central area or hall – it is here that the greatest difficulties arise. It is mainly for this reason that the fire-place in England is often on the external wall, despite the fact that the flue is in a cold position, which makes it more difficult for the smoke to escape. But then at least the door is a long way off, which gives some slight protection from the draught emanating from it. There is also the great advantage that the fire-place is well lit.

In the inconsiderable number of cases in which there is central-heating (on account of which the fire-place is never omitted), the draughtiness of the English room is substantially reduced. This is due in part to the fact that radiators under the windows absorb the draught from the window, in part because radiators in the passages mean that only pre-heated air enters the room, for the temperature throughout the house is fairly even.

Distribution and types

If we look more closely at the individual rooms of the English house we see the advantage of the great uniformity of the English habits of life in the fact that the notions of the individual types of room are most sharply delimited and the uses to which they are customarily put are the same in every kind of house throughout the country. It is rare for personal wishes to go to the length of changing anything in the main division of the house. The rooms of the English house are divided into two categories: sitting-rooms and bedrooms, and every room containing a bed is a bedroom, including the children's, governess's and visitors' rooms. This explains why bedrooms so strikingly out-number sitting-rooms in descriptions of houses in such things as advertisements of houses for sale or to let. In plans of English houses too all the rooms on the upper floors are usually described simply as bedrooms.

English residential needs are embodied most fully in the large country-house, which in every respect – both historically and in its continuing present-day significance – is the primal, basic form of English house. The small country-house is – not always to its advantage – a variation arrived at by reducing the large one, while the town house is a recasting of the country-house into a different form dictated by lack of space.

It would therefore seem appropriate to take the large country-house as the example of the general plan and basic components of the English house. The plan of the smaller house – though admittedly of far greater importance today – will then require only such explanations as concern its reductions and special developments; and the town house, both large and small, can likewise be discussed very briefly. At this point, however, we propose to deal only with the general plan and the problems of the individual rooms and to leave the artistic development of the rooms, in particular their furnishings and appointments, until later. In the case of kitchens and domestic offices only we shall deal with their internal arrangement at once.

A. The plan of the large country-house[17]

The house to fit in with surrounding nature

The curious traveller who imagines that by journeying across England he will be able to see the much celebrated English country-houses in their dozens will usually be in for a rude disappointment. The English country-house does not obtrude upon the gaze of the passer-by. It almost always lies hidden behind high walls or dense shrubbery and a person who knows the country well will only be made aware of its existence by an entirely inconspicuous entrance-gate and lodge. Special arrangements are necessary if one is to make its acquaintance, as well as good connections to break the spell of its privacy. In general one has the impression that the sequestered character of these houses is deliberate.

But he who penetrates into their preserves responds the more overwhelmingly to the beauty of the fairy-tale world that opens up before him. Here is marvellous, paradisian peace, here reigns a higher way of life, consummately cultivated. The house

[17] The necessities of the large English country-house are presented clearly, methodically and in great detail in an excellent book by Robert Kerr (*The gentleman's house, or, how to plan residences*, 1864; 2nd ed. 1865, 3rd ed. 1871). The book has, however, lost some of its value since it does not include certain more recent ideas, especially those concerning sanitation and others that have similarly changed.

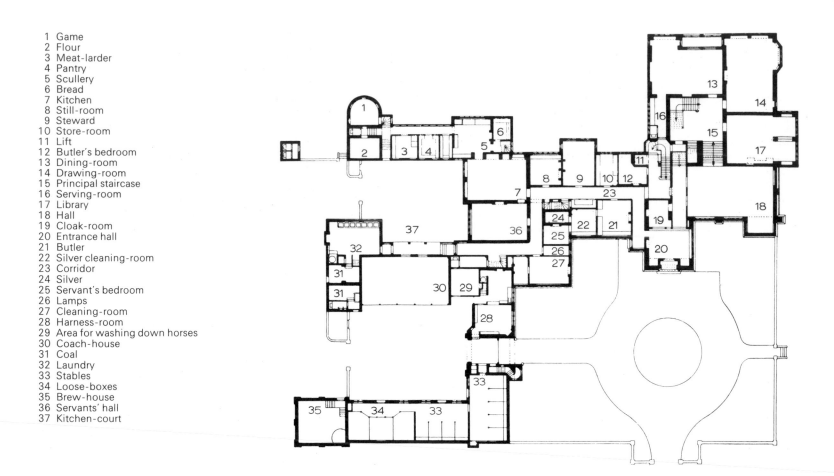

1 Game
2 Flour
3 Meat-larder
4 Pantry
5 Scullery
6 Bread
7 Kitchen
8 Still-room
9 Steward
10 Store-room
11 Lift
12 Butler's bedroom
13 Dining-room
14 Drawing-room
15 Principal staircase
16 Serving-room
17 Library
18 Hall
19 Cloak-room
20 Entrance hall
21 Butler
22 Silver cleaning-room
23 Corridor
24 Silver
25 Servant's bedroom
26 Lamps
27 Cleaning-room
28 Harness-room
29 Area for washing down horses
30 Coach-house
31 Coal
32 Laundry
33 Stables
34 Loose-boxes
35 Brew-house
36 Servants' hall
37 Kitchen-court

150–152 Cloverly Hall, Shropshire. By W. E. Nesfield. Above: Plan of ground floor. Right: Residential quarters. Plans of basement and first floor

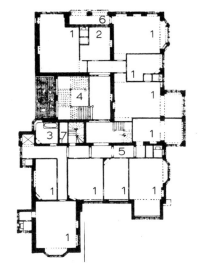

1 Bedroom
2 Dressing-room and WC
3 Bath
4 Principal staircase
5 Corridor
6 Balcony
7 Housemaid's room

appears before us, surrounded by a mass of flowers, wide lawns resplendent in the richest of greens extend before the downstairs rooms. Beyond them, pergolas, orchards, meadows and woods seem to stretch away into the distance. A perfect, secluded world of its own, a little paradise on earth. Here, if anywhere, is a surviving fragment of the old, placid way of life that stands, lonely as an island, in the brief transience of the modern world. Life here is lived far from the world, its dissipations apparently unpercieved. The owner of the house enjoys an idyllic existence in the bosom of nature, continually in touch with her powerful heart-beat that prevents his vitality from flagging; he is master of his land and of a widely ramifying body of dependants, for whom he cares with patriarchal solicitude. This is the life of the English nobleman and of the rich man joining the ranks of the nobility. He dwells thus for three-quarters of the year amid the solitude of nature; only in the spring does he move to the capital for a few months to devote himself to the life of society.

The problem facing the architect of a country-house in England is primarily that of suiting his design as closely as possible to the owner's need, decisive at every point, to live in the heart of nature. To choose the site with regard to the soil, to its position in relation to the surrounding country, to the sun, to the prevailing wind and weather; and having made the choice, so to build the house that it combines the most intimate relationship with nature with the highest standards of comfort, suitability and healthy accommodation – these are the several requirements of his commission.

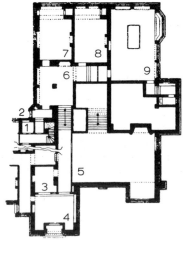

1 Lift
2 Entrance from garden
3 Cloak-room
4 Entrance-hall
5 Hall
6 Lower hall
7 Business-room
8 Morning-room
9 Billiard-room

Choice of site

Besides the considerations of the subsoil which we have already mentioned and which are particularly important in view of the damp English climate, questions about the lie of the land and its relationship to the influences of weather are the first and most important in choosing a site. A sunny position is in all circumstances the prerequisite for a good building site. But also, since the sun shines so rarely, it is important to take every advantage of it when it does so. A south-facing slope offers the best possibility here.

The prevailing damp necessitates as much movement of the air as possible; this is found at high altitudes, most of all on hillsides or near the tops of hills. Protection from raw north and north-easterly winds is also needed and a south to south-east-facing slope will provide this too. In the absence of a hillside, dense clumps of old trees lying to the north and east of the site can give protection from the wind. But it is considered essential in England that the house shall not be too near the trees since they would rob it of sunlight and in any case they always make the ground damp. Since rain comes from the west, a south-easterly orientation is certainly best in England.

The ideal site on which to build would therefore lie near the top of a hill that slopes gently away to the south-east and is sheltered from easterly winds by woods to the east.

Besides climatic considerations, considerations of the view play a part, if only a secondary one. The climate does not allow of this being the prime determinant, as it certainly is in continental countries more favoured by the sun. The ideal situation would be for the finest effects of the landscape to lie in the direction of the most favourable weather-conditions, i.e. to the south-east. But in England no one will lightly decide, for example, to orientate the whole house to the north for the sake of, say, a northerly outlook, nor for similar reasons would anyone build a house facing due west or due east. Furthermore, the position of a house in relation to a road or drive is unimportant. It is an inflexible rule in England that the climate and weather-conditions are considered first, followed by the view and other things.

This uncompromising preference for what is healthy and advantageous over so-called beauty may almost be regarded as the principal feature of the layout of the English house. And the progressive development of living-conditions will probably in time bring these attitudes to the forefront everywhere. Just as a plant growing on the north side of a wall is stunted, while the same plant growing on the south side flourishes in profusion, just as the foliage of every pot-plant grows firmly towards the light and sunshine, so, without doubt, people flourish best in rooms that face the sun. *Dove no va il sole va il medico* is an old Italian saying. And this belief comes not from a sunless land but originates with the people of a country where conditions necessitate protection from the sun rather than exposure to it.

House and dependencies

Once a sunny, airy, but sheltered position has been secured for the house, the next move will be to plan it and link it as befits its character with its whole environment of gardens, domestic outbuildings, stables, greenhouses, etc. Although these appendages must be considered from the beginning, their role is a secondary one. We shall examine them specifically at a later stage; at this point we shall consider only the proper plan for the house itself.

Division of the house

Every house falls naturally into two main parts: the residential quarters and the domestic offices. The residential quarters are the province of the gentry, the domestic offices that of the servants. As has already been said, they always constitute a sizeable complex in themselves (see Fig. 154). In the present-day English detached house, the domestic offices are always situated at the side of the house on the ground floor. In the larger country-house they are nearly always grouped round one, or – if the stables are there too – two special working courtyards (Fig. 150); they are rarely more than one, or at most two, storeys high and even externally they differ markedly from the residential quarter, which are more distinguished in treatment. The useful device of making one or two wings of the domestic buildings enclose a forecourt (see Figs. 146, 150, 154) has returned to favour recently.

1. Residential quarters

The rooms in the residential part of the house comprise reception rooms, bedrooms and children's rooms. Larger houses contain besides a number of other rooms for special purposes, such as a billiard-room, picture-gallery, library; and in very large ones (such as the houses of royalty) a number of other state apartments. One is struck, however, by the slight importance that is attached to such purely ceremonial apartments. Houses designed for quite large households (see Figs. 146, 150, 154, 159) contain, apart from a hall of variable size, no rooms that are not used for the purposes of every-day living. They have no ballroom, no banqueting-hall, none of the games rooms, etc. that would be found in a continental house of the same size.

The drawing-room. Its programme and position

The drawing-room is the most important of the reception rooms in the English house. It is difficult to find a German term for this room, for we have no room that is precisely equivalent to it. It was first used to describe the private room that split off from the great common hall of the English manor-house and was intended for the use of the gentry when they wished to withdraw (it was originally called a withdrawing-room). Later, as private rooms increased in number, it became the most important of these and was not even rendered superfluous by the Italian *salone* brought to England by Inigo Jones.

The drawing-room in the English house is the preserve of the lady of the house, though the English and German connotations differ here. The Englishwoman is the absolute mistress of the house, the pole round which its life revolves. The social side of life is entirely in her hands, she keeps an eye on all exchanges with the outer world, issues invitations and receives and entertains guests. The man of the house, who is assumed to be engrossed in his daily work, is himself to some extent her guest when at home. So the drawing-room, the mistress's throne-room, is the rallying-point of the whole life of the house, the room in which one talks, reads and spends idle hours, the room in which the occupants assemble before meals and amuse themselves afterwards with conversation and play. In this respect, therefore, it is the equivalent of our *Wohnzimmer* (living-room). In the afternoon the drawing-room belongs exclusively to the lady of the house, who also receives visits here, and to this extent it is the equivalent of our *Empfangszimmer* (reception-room) or 'gute Stube'. Thus, in our terms, the drawing-room combines the uses of the lady of the house's room, the 'living-room' and the 'reception-room'. It occurs in the smallest, as well as in the

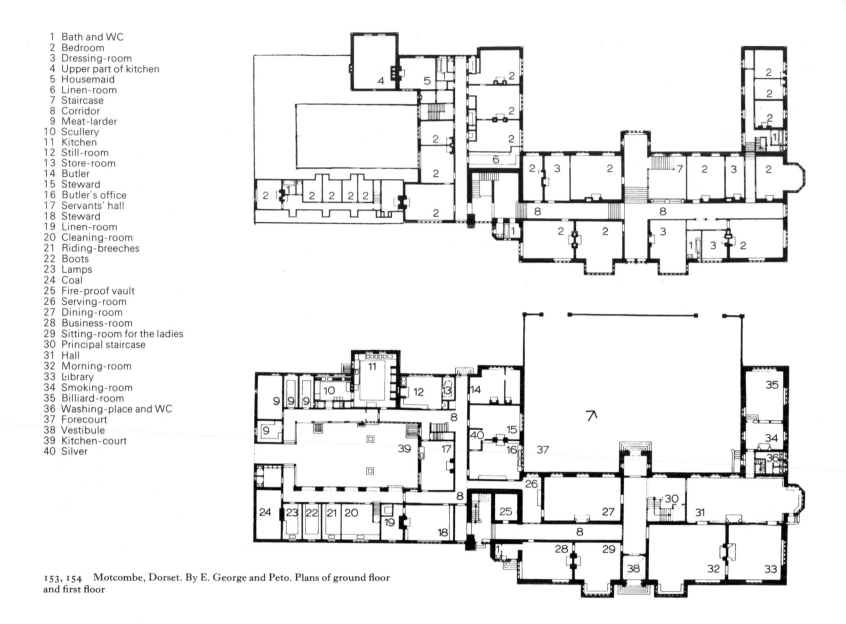

1 Bath and WC
2 Bedroom
3 Dressing-room
4 Upper part of kitchen
5 Housemaid
6 Linen-room
7 Staircase
8 Corridor
9 Meat-larder
10 Scullery
11 Kitchen
12 Still-room
13 Store-room
14 Butler
15 Steward
16 Butler's office
17 Servants' hall
18 Steward
19 Linen-room
20 Cleaning-room
21 Riding-breeches
22 Boots
23 Lamps
24 Coal
25 Fire-proof vault
26 Serving-room
27 Dining-room
28 Business-room
29 Sitting-room for the ladies
30 Principal staircase
31 Hall
32 Morning-room
33 Library
34 Smoking-room
35 Billiard-room
36 Washing-place and WC
37 Forecourt
38 Vestibule
39 Kitchen-court
40 Silver

153, 154   Motcombe, Dorset. By E. George and Peto. Plans of ground floor
and first floor

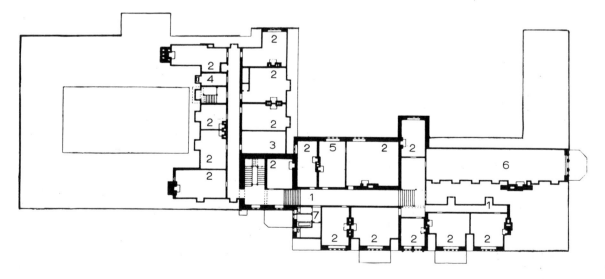

1 Corridor
2 Bedroom
3 Wardrobe
4 Maid's room
5 Dressing-room
6 Gallery
7 Bath and WC

155   Motcombe. Plan of attic floor

0   5   10   15 m
0 5   30   50 f

84

largest, houses, and its function is the same at every level of society.

Here I may perhaps be permitted a side-glance at the German house. Our 'reception-room' (*Salon, gute Stube*) is usually superfluous and the cost of its upkeep wholly unjustified. It nearly always looks dismal because it is not lived in and recalls the stiff 'model rooms' in furniture-shops. Ought we not to transform it into a combined living- and reception-room, or at least into a room in which the mistress of the house can receive and which she can have as her own? It is true that the need to maintain the drawing-room permanently in a fit state for receiving visitors has certain other small consequences. These include the rule that no one may smoke in the drawing-room, that the lady of the house sits in another room during the morning, that the nursery must be some way off and that, as is the custom in England, children are on the whole not allowed into the drawing-room except as visitors in their best clothes. But these circumstances notwithstanding, the system of room-usage in the English house is considerably simpler than ours.

Since it is the most important room in the house, the drawing-room must have the sunniest aspect; the room is expected to be bright, to produce a light, pleasing impression and a general air of *joie-de-vivre*. The favourite aspect is always south-east, not only because it is invariably the best in England, but also because, although the room must be very sunny, it must not be exposed to the direct light of the sun during the afternoon, when it is mainly used. A room with a south-easterly aspect gets its last sunshine at about two o'clock and the time for visiting begins in England at three o'clock.

Once a sunny aspect has been found for the drawing-room, the next thing is to relate it as advantageously as possible to the surrounding country, in other words to give it a fine view of the landscape. Since the room already enjoys the sunniest position, full advantage can, of course, only be taken if the view lies to the south-east. But there is at least a way of securing a glimpse of a view that lies in another direction and this is to introduce a bay window. Thus the deeply projecting English type of bay window gives a view to right or left even when the drawing-room occupies the centre of the front of the house. If it is a corner room, a bay window will even permit a view to the side opposite to the sunny side, i.e. to the north-west. The main reason why the drawing-room is nearly always given a large bay window is that it affords views that have had to be sacrificed on account of the rule, generally considered inflexible, that the room must face the sun. However, we might mention the well-known fact that a view seen against the sunlight is a second-best view. We like to see a landscape with the sun on it, which means that the sun must be behind us as we look. Thus landscapes to the north are most pleasing at mid-day and those to the east in the afternoon. The ideal view from a drawing-room would therefore be one stretching away to the east, which could still be enjoyed from the ordinary windows in the afternoon, but would be seen to best advantage from a bay window on the front elevation.

There is usually a door leading from the drawing-room on to a terrace, from which the flower-garden can be reached, or, if there is no flower-garden, the large lawn that is an invariable feature of an English garden. Or sometimes one steps straight out on to the lawn or into a flower-garden. In such cases all the windows are of the French type, extending down to floor-level, and the exit is through one of the windows; but there is never an exit in a bay window. The mildness of the climate makes it possible, where

156, 157 Motcombe: View. Below: Hall

necessary, for the door to open straight out into the open air, without a porch, and this is, in fact, what usually happens. It is naturally better if there is a small vestibule and this need is sometimes met by a little projecting garden-room, for which the term saloon, dating from the Palladian period, is still used. As regards the position of the drawing-room in the plan, it is desirable that the most important room in the house should be fairly naturally accessible to the visitor. So it invariably occupies the best position on the ground floor. Only in town houses, to which quite different conditions apply, is the drawing-room normally on the first floor.

Design of the drawing-room

The mutual positions of the fire-place, door and window are again the most important considerations in the specific design of the drawing-room and to meet every need would involve the planner in a web of difficulties from which even the most astute could only extricate himself with a compromise. One of the prime requirements is that the fire-place shall be well lit (from both sides), since the whole life of the room takes place in its vicinity. So it must be near the window. For the same reason it must be situated as centrally as possible, so that the middle of the room may be used. At the same time draughts must be avoided, which means placing the doors at least as far from the fire-place

85

158 Motcombe: Main staircase

as possible. Rooms of over 10 m. in length have two fire-places, situated on the two facing short walls or both on the inside long wall. Ground-plans of drawing-rooms vary enormously. Some are very long rooms, often they have a right-angled bend, i.e. are L-shaped, very often with a deeply projecting wall that forms an entirely flat bay window, but more usually with a suitably-sized bay window, in which several people can sit and enjoy the view as they talk or withdraw into a small, separate, more intimate group. As regards size, the drawing-room is always the largest room in the house.

A glance at Figs. 146, 150, 154, 159 will show how far our examples meet the various demands made of the drawing-room.

The dining-room. Its position

The next most important room is the dining-room. It is the only room in England over which opinions do not entirely agree on the question of the ideal aspect. Many people consider a south-easterly aspect best for the dining-room too, but others opt for a more northerly outlook, since the south-easterly position would catch the mid-day sun at one o'clock, the hour for luncheon. Places at table are immutably fixed and people do not want the sun in their eyes as they eat, but like to look out on a fine, sunlit landscape. Yet a westerly aspect is again impracticable. The main drawback here is that at dinner – the main meal that is served not later than seven o'clock – during the summer months the horizontal rays of the setting sun would make it impossible for anyone to sit facing the windows. The only sunlight that is welcome in the dining-room is that of the morning sun at breakfast. Thus all in all an easterly aspect is the most desirable. Yet one also sees many dining-rooms facing north (as at Motcombe), which becomes much more possible when breakfast

is served in a special breakfast-room. The most generally recognised position for the dining-room too is probably the south-easterly.

Regarding the position of the dining-room in the ground-plan, the general opinion is that it should be further to one side than the drawing-room, as, indeed, it must be, since it has to adjoin the kitchen department on one side. At the same time, the route from the drawing-room to the dining-room is considered very important. The occupants of the house assemble in the drawing-room before dinner, the men in tails, or at least in dinner-jackets,[18] even for ordinary family meals (tails in England are not gala attire, as they are with us, but ordinary evening-dress). The women, worthy partners to their menfolk, appear in evening-dress, which is usually *décolletée*. When they are summoned to table, usually by three muffled notes of a gong, the company in its ceremonial attire moves towards the dining-room two by two. This is everyday practice in England, whereas we regard it as appropriate only to a banquet. The daily procession to the dining-room must naturally have a ceremonial route along which to move. The company therefore usually passes through as imposing a room as possible, preferably the hall, if there is one. Thus it is an advantage if the doors of drawing-room and dining-room face one another on the same axis. This need is well catered for in the ground-plan of Cavenham Hall (Fig. 146). It is also important for the dining-room to communicate with the kitchen, a point that will be discussed more fully when we look at the kitchen and the rooms dependent upon it. In particular it is considered essential for the entrances to the dining-room for servants and gentry to be kept separate. If there is only one door for both purposes, which, of course, is only the case in modest households, access must in all circumstances be so arranged that the gentry approach the door from one direction and the servants from another. So much for the internal situation of the dining-room. Externally it does not usually open on to the large lawn, or the flower-garden or the terrace, all areas which can be reached from the drawing-room. Nor should it look on to the front-door in such a way that visitors can be seen arriving, for this would give them the uncomfortable feeling of being watched as they approached. This, indeed, applies to every room; but since the other rooms in English houses nearly always face the garden, in other words the side away from the front-door, the point seldom arises in their case, though it nearly always does in planning the dining-room.

Design of the dining-room

The dining-room is usually a long room, preferably with the windows on the long side. The obvious position for the fire-place is then on one of the short sides, with the sideboard taking its place on the opposite short side. The fire-place is not situated on the long side (unless, as in Fig. 146, an alcove is available) for the space occupied by the jutting hearth would reduce the effective width of the room. A point to note in connection with the size of the dining-room is that English dinner-tables are very wide (1.20 m.–1.80 m.), so that, even for those in modest circumstances, no dining-room can measure less than 4.80–5 m. The length naturally depends on the number of people to be seated, although, as we have said, the room is never larger than is necessary to accommodate the family circle. This means that even in houses of some size the dining-room never gives the impression of a room designed for great evening parties. It has

[18] The writer's experience at a hill station in the Himalayas typifies this English custom: it was during the quiet winter months and the only guest beside himself was an Englishman who had come to hunt bears; every evening the Englishman appeared in tails which he had carried with him up to these lonely heights.

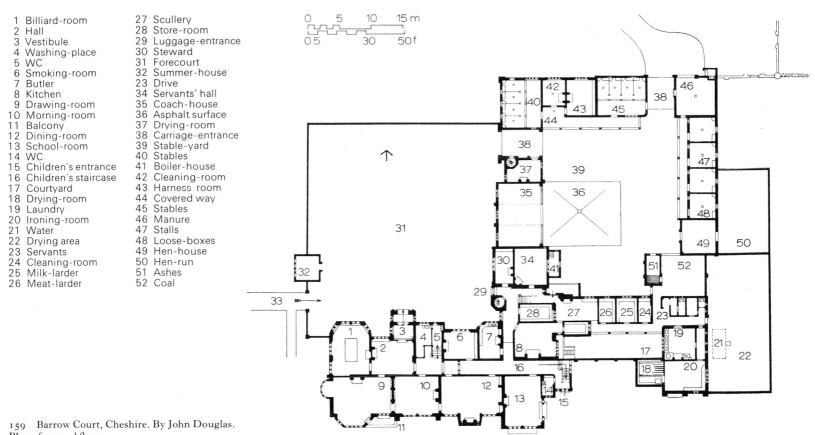

1 Billiard-room
2 Hall
3 Vestibule
4 Washing-place
5 WC
6 Smoking-room
7 Butler
8 Kitchen
9 Drawing-room
10 Morning-room
11 Balcony
12 Dining-room
13 School-room
14 WC
15 Children's entrance
16 Children's staircase
17 Courtyard
18 Drying-room
19 Laundry
20 Ironing-room
21 Water
22 Drying area
23 Servants
24 Cleaning-room
25 Milk-larder
26 Meat-larder

27 Scullery
28 Store-room
29 Luggage-entrance
30 Steward
31 Forecourt
32 Summer-house
23 Drive
34 Servants' hall
35 Coach-house
36 Asphalt surface
37 Drying-room
38 Carriage-entrance
39 Stable-yard
40 Stables
41 Boiler-house
42 Cleaning-room
43 Harness room
44 Covered way
45 Stables
46 Manure
47 Stalls
48 Loose-boxes
49 Hen-house
50 Hen-run
51 Ashes
52 Coal

159 Barrow Court, Cheshire. By John Douglas.
Plan of ground floor

become fashionable in some circles recently to dine at round tables, instead of at rectangular ones as hitherto. Vast circular tables to accommodate ten or fifteen people are being made; if the company exceeds this number, two tables are used. This fashion must presumably be regarded as the natural consequence of the widening of the dinner-table, for it had long since become impossible to converse with one's opposite neighbour. If the custom were to become more general, it would be bound in time to influence the shape of the dining-room. The service-door of the dining-room must give immediately on to the sideboard and must be hung so that the servant entering can reach the sideboard easily. It is also desirable for the inside of the door to open towards the table and fire-place. It is worth noting that many English houses, including large ones, manage without the serving-room preceding the dining-room that is usual in our houses, a circumstance that is connected with the manner of waiting at table. The old service-hatch through which dishes are brought in is still widely favoured despite the many attendant inconveniences.

The library as smoking-room and male preserve

Drawing-room and dining-room are the two pillars of the room-system of the English house. In smaller houses they are often the only true residential rooms and it strikes the continental observer as strange that there is no room for the men of the house, which we always find indispensable. Medium-sized and larger houses have such a room but here again it differs from ours. The room in question is called the library and has various uses, of which the first is equivalent to that of our *Herrenzimmer*. In fact the English house entirely lacks a room in which the man of the house may do his mental work. As a business-man, a civil-servant and even as an artist, scholar etc., he always has his place of work outside the

house and in principle he never brings work home, whither he returns only for peace and quiet. In any case he has much less mental work than his German cousin. During the working hours which he spends outside the house he labours intensively, using every available aid and labour-saving machine (in which he goes to far greater lengths than we do). But the idea of pursuing his professional work at home would be entirely alien to him. Hence the absence of a study for the man in the English house. Studies are, in fact, found only in vicarages, clergymen being the only men who are expected to work at home. The clergyman has a real study. The libraries found in other houses are merely used by the man of the house for writing letters, as a room to which he can retire to read and to rest. When there are no visitors he also smokes an after-dinner pipe or cigar in the library. When there are visitors, the men of the party smoke their cigars in some haste at the dinner-table after the women have retired to the drawing-room, which they always do before the men. The men then 'join the ladies', as the saying goes. As the drawing-room is in general the province of the women, so the library is that of the man or men. In many houses it is little more than a small smoking-room, but in large houses, especially when the man has literary leanings, it always contains a handsome collection of books.

Large collections of books are on the whole much more common in English houses than in German, a state of affairs that is due only to the greater wealth of the country. Special considerations relating to the care of books arise in rooms in which books are to be kept. The first requisite is that the walls shall be bone-dry and ventilation plentiful, since otherwise in that damp country the books would become fusty. A suitable place for work and reading must next be found. In England the best place for this is traditionally considered to be in a bay window, as in all university libraries. When several such places are required, short walls are built out from the window-piers towards the centre of the room. The sides can then be used for additional book-shelves and bays are formed in which tables may be placed (Fig. 160). An easterly aspect is considered best for a library, for here again sunlight is welcome; a northerly room would be too cheerless and humidity would tend to gather. The library is usually allocated a rather remote position in the plan of a house, often next-door to the dining-room, to which there is sometimes a communicating door. A true study is always put in a really isolated position, right out of reach of the comings and goings of visitors.

Morning-room and breakfast-room

Besides these three rooms, larger houses always, and medium-sized houses often, have at least one or two other residential rooms that require a word of explanation. The commonest is the morning-room. The room is best thought of as relieving the pressure on the drawing-room. The term drawing-room mainly implies a room for afternoon and evening use. The lady of the house occupies the morning-room during the morning. The morning-room is also used when for some reason it is desired not to use the drawing-room or when the size of the family is temporarily reduced. Then it assumes the character of the parlour, a room that invariably occurred in English houses of earlier times (in fact a room for talking in, but for centuries the word has meant no more than a living-room). Occasionally the family has breakfast, or even lunch, in the morning-room, or the children are given their meals there. At all events the room must have a sunny aspect, east or south-east being considered the best. Another room that is not uncommon is the breakfast-room, which should be thought of as relieving the pressure on the dining-room. Occasionally even it is found in smaller houses; here its name does not entirely correspond to its purpose, for it is rather a room, like the morning-room in other houses, that forms a useful complement and overflow to the main living-rooms. But in houses where there is a morning-room as well as a breakfast-room, the breakfast-room simply has the character of a second dining-room. It is used for breakfast and lunch, meals at which one appears in ordinary clothes and which are more hurried than dinner. Regarded thus as a second dining-room, this room too must face east, for nothing is more welcome at breakfast than a sunlit room – assuming the sun to be shining for once. (An English breakfast, one might add, is a complete meal consisting of fish, meat-dishes etc., which therefore takes longer to eat than our frugal breakfast).

The dining/sitting-room. The ingle-nook

The habit of regarding the drawing-room as a general living-room, and the main one at that, is a recent development. In earlier times lengthier family-gatherings usually took place in the dining-room, where members of the family often lingered after dinner. It is still the practice in smaller houses to use the dining-room as a general sitting-room after dinner, in winter probably often because, having been in use throughout the day, it is usually the warmest, perhaps the only warm, room in the house. This being the case, the dining-room is often arranged as a sitting-room, mainly by creating a comfortable sitting area round the fire. In dining-rooms of the usual shape with the fire-place on the short wall, the immediate surroundings of the fire-place are not particularly inviting. But with the new movement in house-building, during the past thirty years the ingle-nook, a feature of the vernacular architecture of earlier times, has been re-discovered, re-established and is much used, particularly in dining-rooms, to provide a snug and comfortable fire-place (cf. p. 16). The fire-place is situated in an alcove, the sides of which

are furnished with seats. It is important that the seats should have direct light, to enable people to sit and read there. An outside wall is therefore the only possible place for an ingle-nook, which is seen as a jutting extension, a very familiar motif in the external appearance of the English house. Inside, the alcove is always just high enough for a person to stand upright in it. It is the old form of domestic hearth as it existed in English farmhouses in the room in which the cooking was done and the family lived; and inasmuch as one derives most benefit from the warmth of the fire by sitting close to it, it is the exact equivalent of the old German tiled stove surrounded by stone seats. Most of the credit for having re-introduced the ingle-nook into the modern house must go to Nesfield and Norman Shaw; and probably the most attractive use of it is in Norman Shaw's house in Hampstead.[19] Few large dining-rooms today are without their ingle-nooks, as a glance at the accompanying plans will abundantly show. Current fashion not infrequently reduces this handsome feature to the most trivial imitation, so that one can now buy ingle-nooks all complete and ready to be installed in rooms as fittings. This has recently detracted from their popularity; and since it is also obvious that to situate a fire-place at the back of a deep alcove further increases the economic disadvantages inherent in fire-places by cutting the heat that reaches the actual room to an infinitesimal level, thoughts nowadays probably turn rather less freely to ingle-nooks.

Changed habits

The fact that the habit of using the dining-room to sit in for long periods after dinner is disappearing is probably further warrant for this. It used to be the custom in England to remove the table-cloth from the gleaming polished mahogany table even before the dessert; and after the meal the men embarked upon a drinking-bout that, as in the eighteenth century, often continued far into the night and not infrequently ended in the whole company being drunk. Sheridan has left us a picture of things as they used to be in *The School for Scandal*. Only very heavy wines (preferably port) were consumed and the company smoked and drank a great deal. During the nineteenth century men of better social standing gradually became more moderate in both respects (alcoholism is a problem among the lower classes only in England), so that drinking now plays no part in an English meal, even when there are visitors; and wines are even far less well understood. The English gentleman of today no longer drinks, and he smokes only very moderately. So there is no longer any reason for him to ensconce himself at the dinner-table for considerably longer than the women, whom, as we have said, he follows into the drawing-room after a speedily smoked cigar, and with whom he converses without smoking or drinking. He has in fact entirely departed from his former ways and has become 'fit for the drawing-room'.

The boudoir and the business-room

The characteristic of all the rooms that we have discussed so far is that they are general rooms, that is to say, they are used not only by all the members of the family but also by visitors. The man and woman of the house will therefore welcome a small private room to which they can retire from the comings and goings of the house and where they can devote themselves entirely to their personal affairs. In larger English houses the boudoir fulfils this function for the woman, as, to some extent, the business-room does for the man if he has no private sitting-room of his own. The boudoir does not as a rule correspond to what we in Germany understand by the word. The English boudoir is the exclusive preserve of the

[19] Published in the writer's *Die englische Baukunst der Gegenwart*.

160 New Place, Haslemere, Surrey. Built and designed throughout by
C. F. A. Voysey. Billiard-room

woman, into which no one penetrates except the house-keeper or
one of the upper female servants to whom she gives her orders. It
is therefore usually some distance away from the real living-
rooms of the house and often communicates with the master
bedroom (Fig. 147). The room chosen for this purpose is usually
of no more than moderate size and has a sunny, pleasant aspect
but it is furnished simply and unpretentiously. Besides this, the
true boudoir, one finds the same word sometimes used for a room
that is a sort of annexe to the drawing-room and in this case it
corresponds fairly closely to our boudoir. The man's business-
room is the room that we know by the same name
(*Geschäftszimmer*) in the German house: a simple room, near the
front-door, and so placed that the visitor who is received therein,
having no connection with the family, need not enter the inner
part of the house. It usually connects with the fire- and burglar-
proof safes in which valuables are kept. There is often a second
door to the room from the kitchen quarters, for the use of visitors
whose status takes them to the back door (Fig. 154).

Smoking-room

In larger houses it is not unusual to find a special smoking-room,
which relieves the library – to its advantage – or another room
that serves the same purpose and is known as the man's 'den'; it is
deliberately small and very snugly furnished.

Billiard-room

We have now come to the end of the real residential rooms. The
time has come to examine a number of rooms with special
functions, which are, however, much the same as those found in
large houses on the continent. First of all there is the billiard-
room. Billiards are now so popular in England that billiard-
rooms appear in quite small houses, in which the only residential
rooms are a dining-room and a drawing-room. Since a billiard-
room can be used for no other purpose and must also be a good-
sized room it is a very considerable luxury. The popularity of
billiards is probably largely attributable to the isolation of houses
in the country, because of which, on rainy days when the house is
full of people, billiards is the only cure for deadly boredom. So
that the billiard-room may be used for other purposes, billiard-
tables that can be lowered out of the way have been invented but
have not caught on. It is best if the billiard-room can be situated

next to a special entrance by which visitors may enter in the
evening and leave, possibly late at night, without coming into
contact with the rest of the household. The billiard-room often
has its own cloakroom and lavatory, for which the obvious
position is next to the special entrance, as at Cavenham Hall (Fig.
146). As regards the internal layout of the room, it is important to
allow ample space for non-players as well as to give the players
freedom to move round the table. The best means of providing
this is a very spacious ingle-nook, which is often built on a higher
level. Another solution is a deeply bowed bay window, also on a
slightly higher level than the room, to enable those seated there
to watch the players. When space permits, the room is built large
enough to take upholstered seats as much of the way round as
possible and these again will be at a higher level (Fig. 160). Since
billiard-rooms are nowadays ceasing to be the exclusive
preserves of men, all these extras are much to be desired and an
altogether more charming, less plain and solid interior is called
for. The first essential in planning the room is to allow for the
best possible lighting. Light must come from all sides, to prevent
shadows; top light is best. Where the inconveniences of top light
are unacceptable, small windows in continuous strips are placed
all round, or nearly all round, the room. Whether lit from above
or from all sides, the best form of billiard-room is a single-
storeyed annexe attached to the body of the house by one narrow
side or a corner only.

The billiard-table in the hall

To save space in smaller houses, room is made for the billiard-
table in the hall. But this measure is seldom satisfactory, for it
robs the hall of the very character that it ought to have, namely
that of a worthy area in which to welcome guests as they arrive. A
billiard-table gives it a rather trivial appearance. It also means
sacrificing much surrounding space in the hall when the hall rises
through two storeys. Billiard-rooms have occasionally been built
in attics, which does represent a saving of space, although with
serious loss of convenience. The attic offers an easy solution to
the problem of top light. Sometimes again, the billiard-room is in
the basement, if there is one. But since basements are exceptional
in country-houses – occurring, for example, when the house is
built on a slope – occasions for taking advantage of this otherwise
useful expedient are few.

The conservatory

A rudimentary form of conservatory is an almost invariable
feature of even quite small private houses in England. But large
constructions communicating with the living-rooms of the type
we have on the continent are none too common even in large
country-houses. A greenhouse in England is regarded as a
practical rather than as a beautiful object; also, contact with the
garden itself – which in the mild climate has its charms in all
seasons – is so close that there is no need for this substitute for
nature. Many people would object to having a conservatory
immediately adjacent to the house for fear that the damp air
might penetrate indoors. Moreover, there is usually no room
where it is needed because the living-rooms invariably face
south. So the only remaining possibility is to situate the
conservatory at the side of the house, beyond the main rooms, as
has been done at Cavenham Hall (Fig. 146), for example. There
is often an intervening area between the conservatory and the
living-room to keep the damp air out.

Larger country-houses do not usually have attached con-
servatories; instead there are separate greenhouses, in which all
kinds of plants are grown. There is not just one type, or even a
few, for they are extremely numerous and suited in form, size and

layout to the various purposes for which they are used. We shall return to them later.

The picture-gallery

Many English houses have special picture-galleries, for in general England has the richest and largest private collections in the world. In a country where centuries-old wealth has fostered the cultivation of the higher things of life, picture-galleries were bound to find their way into the houses. Later on in the houses of the Elizabethan period, when more systematic collecting had begun, the walls of the 'long gallery' proved the best place in which to hang the collection. In the Palladian houses, the saloon with its top light was the obvious place for an art-collection, for these houses were in fact well planned for display, much better, indeed, than for living. The large English house of today, the essence of which is its absolute adaptation to living with only a minimal desire to impress, does not offer much scope for hanging paintings to good advantage, especially since low rooms are preferred. Owners, therefore, who are lovers of works of art, plan special picture-galleries with top light, like that at Dawpool (Fig. 161), a country-house built by Norman Shaw, and also at the same architect's Cragside. In both cases he has made the gallery virtually the focal point of the plan, thereby typifying the owner's intense love of his art-treasures. At Dawpool the room opens very attractively off the broad passage which runs the full width of the house (see ground-plan, Fig. 35) and from which it is separated only, as it were symbolically, by a screen. There is a snug bay window for readers in one corner, with a little staircase leading from it to a point above the fire-place alcove, from which the whole room may be surveyed. The design and lighting of a room of this kind must obey museum principles. In such cases, however, Norman Shaw has always tried to avoid making the room look public and purely practical like a museum and has given it a comfortable appearance which fits in with the rest of the house. In both these instances he has succeeded triumphantly by means of a vast fire-place that dominates the whole room and occupies the entire narrow side.

The hall

The hall provides the best transition from the residential rooms to the set of connecting rooms and forms a kind of link between the two types of room. It is in any case one of the most prominent rooms in large houses and dominates the plan. It has been stressed that the nineteenth century saw an attempt to restore the hall to its former glory after the Palladian period had reduced its significance to that of a banal vestibule. None of the large country-houses that have been built during the past fifty years is without its hall. It was too worth-while a feature to be allowed to disappear – not to mention the love that was felt for old things. Thus Eden Nesfield, Norman Shaw, Ernest George and all other architects faced with a commission to build a large country-house have demonstrated their fondness for the hall. In certain cases, such as Norman Shaw's Adcote and Ernest George's Motcombe (Figs. 153–158) they created faithful imitations of medieval halls, including even minstrels' galleries. Such rooms surely reflect a large measure of backward-looking romanticism and archaeological amateurism, which forms a most striking contrast to the other qualities of the modern English house. The hall serves no real purpose. There is little occasion to use its great capacity, for it lies immediately inside the front-door and is therefore in the wrong position in the ground-plan to be used as a banqueting-hall or ball-room. All that remains, therefore, is to look upon it as an imposing area, the sole purpose of which is to create an aesthetic impression. A considerable amount of space is sacrificed to it, for a hall usually rises through two storeys. The

161 Dawpool, Cheshire. By R. Norman Shaw. (See Figs. 34 and 35.) Picture-gallery

musicians' gallery of earlier times now often serves as a passage-way on the floor above, whence passers-by may enjoy looking down at this area which exists simply for the sake of its beauty. It should be noted at once that, contrary to the prevailing belief in Germany, the stairs in England are not as a rule a built-in feature of the hall but are housed separately, as a glance at our plans will confirm. It would not be thought right to have the staircase in the hall, for it often gives a room a rather public air which detracts from its more intimate effect. A staircase in the hall is considered to be the mark of a public building rather than of a dwelling-house. A very conspicuous staircase in the hall would bring the floor on which the bedrooms lie into the general run of the house and the bedroom floor is regarded in England as absolutely private. It is, however, contrary to English ideas to make an architectural show-piece of a staircase which does not give access to the principle rooms. And finally, a staircase in the hall creates a draught – and there are plenty of these already.

Although instances of staircases in halls are rare in England, such examples as do exist were received so sympathetically in Germany that we have persuaded ourselves that the motif of the staircase rising in full view from the hall is the characteristic feature of the English hall.

Although the modern English hall, which is essentially an imitation of its medieval counterpart, is ornamental rather than useful, a room of so pleasing and impressive a form could not but attract some part of the life of the house to itself. In instances in which the hall lay comfortably within the plan of the house it often became not only the centre of all its traffic but also the occupants' favourite place in which to sit. Thus one sometimes finds that in country-houses, which are occupied mainly during the summer, the hall gets the most use of all the rooms in the house; for here the occupants read, play games, converse and assemble before meals. Some architects, seeing much more use being made of the hall, took this as a signal to them to help the process along and to restore the hall to a dominant position in the house. The step was taken at Motcombe (Fig. 153): the hall replaced the drawing-room and there is no drawing-room in the house. It was discovered, indeed, that once a hall has gained the favour of the occupants of a house, the drawing-room is doomed and often becomes an empty, unused room, like our *Salon*. At Motcombe it was therefore intended that all afternoon activities should take place in the hall. But two rooms were built on the east side specially for the women: a morning-room and a boudoir, the larger of which was entirely capable of replacing the non-existent drawing-room.

As we shall show later, an attempt has recently been made in smaller houses too to turn the hall into the main living-room of the house. The hall, reinstated originally largely out of romantic enthusiasm, is now in the process of acquiring a real importance. Thus the concept of the hall, the room that in the Middle Ages was almost the only room in the house, is still having its ups and downs; these recent experiments have made its significance less certain than ever. In some houses it is a dignified room of distinguished appearance in which the visitor receives his first welcome, in others an unused appendage, while in others again it is the focal point of family life.

Connecting-rooms. Passages, the central hall

In its capacity as a connecting room, the hall usually acts as the key to the whole plan of the house; it is the central room, off which all, or most, of the rooms open. In this way it is partly responsible for the fact that the need for passages, those necessary evils, is considerably reduced in the English house. Where they do exist, passages are often of imposing width, as at Dawpool (Fig. 35) – where there is no hall at all because the picture-gallery is the showpiece of the house – and are also known as galleries in memory of the long rooms of Elizabethan days. Those who reject the ideal of the Middle Ages, as the Neo-Classicists of the Neo-Inigo Jones School have done recently, plan a central area of purely practical design that serves simply as a centre for the comings and goings of the house and replaces the hall modelled on the medieval type. The area has top light and belongs to a type of ground-plan in which everything is condensed into rectangular form to which more recent movements are beginning to return.

Apart from connecting the ground-floor rooms, these central halls, ideal on plan, have to form the junction for the four cross-roads that carry the traffic of the house: that from outside, i.e. from the front-door, that to the interior of the house, i.e. to the private rooms (in other words, to the bedrooms, to which the stairs also give access), those to the kitchen-quarters and to the garden. It is true that there is usually a door from the drawing-room leading directly into the garden, but there is often another special way into the garden; or again, the garden is often reached through a special little garden-room.

Entrance-hall

Large country-houses always have a spacious, well-lit entrance-hall or vestibule inside the front-door, off which there is a cloakroom, which in turn opens into a washing-place and lavatory. Another door leads into the large hall and through this into the house proper. Norman Shaw, for example, has always designed extremely attractive entrance-halls that introduce the visitor at once to the atmosphere of the house; they have fire-places, often a bay window, their shape always makes one feel at home. There are often several steps to counteract any small variation of level and they are always low-ceilinged as a contrast to enhance the effect of the large hall that the visitor will enter next.

The open porch

There is invariably an open porch (debased form of the Latin *porticus*) in front of the front-door of an English house. It is a survival of the ancient antechamber that precedes the main chamber in both the ecclesiastical and the secular architecture of all countries and at all periods. There was always a porch before the entrance to the hall of the house in the medieval manor, where it sheltered the caller from wind and weather as he waited for the door to open. The Elizabethans liked to make it the special architectural show-piece of the house and it was usually surmounted by an oriel window rising through all the storeys; and even on otherwise absolutely plain houses it was adorned with columns, pilasters and coats-of-arms. During the period when Palladianism dominated domestic architecture in England the oriel was replaced by a columned portico. The same period saw the feature pass to small houses as well as great. Today all the minutest houses of the suburban developments have their porch, which is even found in the form of a columned portico looking very pretentious on workmen's cottages. In London every one of the dreary terrace-houses, the bare brick walls of which border the streets, has its columned portico in front of the front-door. The porch is as much part of the English house as the nose is of the face. In modern country-houses it usually takes the form of an elongated vestibule with a wide opening at the front and usually with windows at both sides, the floor of which is a step or two above ground-level. Oddly enough, it is rare for even large country-houses in England to have a covered forecourt where the carriages draw up. Perhaps the fact that the porch is so dominant has prevented the covered forecourt from coming into being. For a structure that projected beyond the porch would destroy its *raison d'être*. This lack is certainly a sign of backwardness in the English house.

Entrance-doors

Besides the front-door and the door into the garden, there is always another entrance for tradesmen, etc. leading into the kitchen-quarters. If we add to these the separate entrance to the billiard-room that we have already mentioned, the doors from the children's quarters, which we have yet to discuss, and possibly one from the parents' private quarters into the garden, it becomes clear that the English do not share our dislike of many entrances. There is yet another separate luggage-entrance, which again occurs in all large country-houses (Fig. 159). This door is not far from the front-door, so that when a visitor has been driven up and set down at the door, his carriage may move on to the luggage-entrance, where his trunk is handed over to the house-servants. The door lies on the dividing-line between the residential and the working parts of the house, very near the steward's room and not far from the back stairs that lead to the bedrooms and visitors' rooms.

The 'bedrooms'

The floors above the ground floor of the country-house are occupied by the rooms known by the general name of 'bedroom', a term used for any room that contains a bed. If one wishes to indicate that the room is also used for sitting, one uses the more precise term 'bed-sitting-room'. In discussing these rooms it will suffice to single out only real bedrooms and spare bedrooms, for there is nothing particularly remarkable about the others.

The bedroom

A south-easterly aspect is again considered best for the bedroom. The bedroom is a room in which we spend about one third of our lives, in continuous periods of between seven and nine hours. Consequently its position must be a particularly healthy one, which means, most importantly, that it must be sunny by day. Yet the afternoon sun in summer would make the room too warm. Since people like to salute the morning sun as they rise, an easterly aspect would seem to be indicated. But so that the room may continue to get the sun for several hours after the occupant

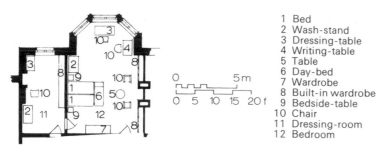

1 Bed
2 Wash-stand
3 Dressing-table
4 Writing-table
5 Table
6 Day-bed
7 Wardrobe
8 Built-in wardrobe
9 Bedside-table
10 Chair
11 Dressing-room
12 Bedroom

162　Lowther Lodge, Kensington, London. By R. Norman Shaw. (See Fig. 27.) Bedroom and dressing-room showing arrangement of furntiure. Plan

has left it, it is better that it should face south-east rather than due east. When designing the bedroom it is important to establish the position of the bed or beds (it is still usual in England to have a double bed in the conjugal bedroom) at the outset. The English bed always stands with the head against the wall and the long sides jutting into the room clear of the wall. It is also an acknowledged rule in England that the bed must be so placed that the occupant does not face the window, for he would find it extremely disagreeable to be dazzled on waking. Yet this rule, which must seem a matter of course for every bedroom in the world, is very often broken in England. In England there seems often to be no alternative to placing the bed with the foot towards the window, since one of the walls lying at right-angles to the window is taken up by the fire-place and the other by the door into the dressing-room. There is no great harm in this position if the windows are closed by light-proof shutters at night. Some people also prefer it for another reason: it is a certain guarantee that the occupant of the bed will not be exposed to the draught.

Yet there can be no doubt that the only proper position for the bed is with the head against a side wall and the plan of the room must without fail provide for this. This having been established, English opinion further requires the left side of the bed in double bedrooms to be near the window. The reason for this is that the conjugal bedroom in England is always used as a dressing-room by the woman and the furniture that she needs for her toilette, such as wash-stand, dressing-table and wardrobe, stand next to the window. As we shall see, the dressing-table, indeed, stands right in the window. The woman therefore takes the side of the bed nearest to her part of the room and since by ancient custom the woman sleeps on the man's left, the bed must stand with its left-hand half on the window side. The position of all the bedroom furniture and of the doors and windows is now firmly established. The door into the man's dressing-room is in the wall nearest to the right-hand side of the bed.

For the rest, the relative positions of the doors, windows and fire-place are subject to the general principles that we have already mentioned. A sharp lookout is kept, however, to ensure that the door opens with its back towards the bed and not the other way, for the desire to avoid embarrassing situations is specially apposite here. The modern English custom whereby a maid takes an early cup of tea to the couple's bedside before they rise makes the point clearly enough. The position of the doors in relation to the windows must be fixed in such a way that the bed is not in a draught, which means that a line drawn from the door to the fire-place must not touch the bed, or at least not the head end. And in general, in order to avoid draughts, the door should be as far from the fire as it is from the bed, and window and door should not be close to one another. Architects often try to give the master-bedroom an oriel window, in which the woman's

dressing-table can stand, thus giving her light on all sides as she dresses, as well as a pleasant outlook.

Good ventilation for the bedroom is considered the prime necessity. The English hankering for fresh air, which is shared by all classes and seems almost excessive to us, leads people fairly generally to sleep with the window partly or wholly open; even in winter they open sash-windows about an inch at the top and sometimes at the bottom too. Figures that one hears in England relating to amounts of fresh air which should enter the bedroom per hour tend to fluctuate. They vary between twenty-five and seventy cubic meters for each occupant. The wide flue is naturally a very satisfactory means of airing the room in this way when the difference between indoor and outdoor temperatures is great enough.

All the requirements of the bedroom in matters of convenience and hygiene assume a double importance and must be doubly stressed since every bedroom must on occasion do duty as a sick-room, when any inadequacy would be felt most keenly and might even be disastrous. The question of light must also be considered when siting the bed in the sick-room; the best position is with the windows on its left, since this is good for reading and administering to the patient.

Built-in cupboards

In old English houses each bedroom had one or more cupboards built into the wall; this was a great convenience, for it left the room less cluttered with furniture and the cupboards were usually much more convenient and capacious than free-standing pieces. There are fewer in the more modern houses, although in England careful architects still remember to plan for them. The projecting mantelpiece and chimney-breast, which is always very spacious and juts out a long way, favours the introduction of built-in cupboards in England. Those on outside walls should always have a small window, otherwise larger cupboards will be dark and their usefulness much diminished. Wooden cupboards fixed to the walls have recently become very popular for bedrooms and we shall discuss them in more detail later. But they are not as acceptable as the old-fashioned cupboard that formed a little clothes closet and was an organic part of the house.

The man's dressing-room

Whereas in England the conjugal bedroom is also used by the woman as a dressing-room, the man always dresses and undresses in an adjoining room. Thus, even in modest households, there is invariably a dressing-room for the man next-door to the bedroom. Only in the most primitive living-conditions do the man and woman dress in the same room and this – we need hardly labour the point – undoubtedly represents a great cultural advance. In English opinion the bedroom belongs essentially to the woman and it might almost be said that the man merely enters it as her guest, as we have seen him doing in the drawing-room, the main living-room of the house. No man, surely, will find fault with this state of affairs. The woman often remains in the bedroom for some time after she has risen, so she usually has a little desk in the room and the fire-place is comfortably appointed. If the house has no boudoir, the woman retires to the bedroom. The man's dressing-room must obviously communicate directly with the bedroom. It is usually only a small, modestly furnished room and it also houses all the man's clothes and underclothing. In smaller households the man uses the bathroom as a dressing-room, in which case it will be larger than usual and must have a fire-place.

Rooms ancillary to the bedroom

In very large English houses the bedroom is not only generously proportioned and luxuriously appointed but there is also a whole series of rooms dependent upon it. First of all, besides a dressing-room for the man as large as a handsome living-room, there is one for the woman. This room is more richly appointed than the man's and resembles an intimate living-room in character; it replaces the boudoir in which, as we have seen, the woman conducts her business and private affairs. Or there may be a second smaller dressing-room in addition to this room, which the woman uses only for her toilette. The lady's maid must be accommodated near the woman's dressing-room so as to be as close at hand as possible; but the idea that the man's personal servant should be housed close to the bedroom is unpopular and in the interests of complete tranquility it is preferred that the room should be some distance away and the servant rung for when needed. The bathroom and a lavatory communicate directly with the dressing-room, which means that the bathroom is not as convenient for the woman as for the man. Or else, and this is, of course, the ideal, there is a bathroom attached to each dressing-room – but this practice is not yet as widespread in England as it is in America.

Bathroom and lavatory

The lavatory naturally adjoins the bathroom. But we must stress the fact that in England a lavatory is never actually in the bathroom. Fifty years ago it may still have been permissible to put both in one room, but today it would be considered barbarous and is, we repeat, totally inadmissible. It is to be hoped that we in Germany will also soon begin to question the rightness of the custom. Even in its most splendid form, a lavatory is an appliance that one would prefer to keep out of sight as far as possible, primarily for aesthetic reasons. It is therefore also entirely out of place in the bathroom. Even there its presence evokes unpleasant associations of ideas, even assuming that the closet is entirely odourless, which can never be taken for granted. The bathroom, however, is a room that should be as agreeably appointed as possible, for bathing is pleasurable and not a necessary evil. Hand in hand with the increasing importance that is being attached to hygiene in our time, there has been a growing tendency to furnish the bathroom handsomely, as a room. But it should be axiomatic that even the slightest hint of anything dirty or evil-smelling is out of place in such a room, and that it should rather be an inviting place in which to linger, as befits its character of a room serving no purpose other than that of cleanliness.

It would hardly be necessary to underline such obvious matters if we did not daily see, even in the best houses in Germany, how lovingly and with what sang-froid the opportunity of combining the refreshing bath and that necessary evil known as the water-closet is seized. Apart from aesthetic considerations there are also practical disadvantages in combining the bath and the WC, for every time a bath is taken the WC is put out of action for a long-ish period, which might have awkward and inconvenient consequences.

Sets of living-rooms and bedrooms

In large English houses the parents' bedrooms and ancillary rooms are often connected with their private living-rooms, if there are any; this is contrived by situating them above these rooms and linking them by a private staircase. This is often no more than a small spiral staircase and frequently leads from the man's study to his dressing-room upstairs; but if the boudoir is also on the ground-floor, the convenience of the staircase can be increased by situating it in a special passage-way that separates the parents' private rooms from the rest of the house both upstairs and downstairs.

Spare-rooms

Very large mansions have similar private suites for distinguished visiting couples, but these are all on the first floor and are reached by the main staircase. They have an entrance-hall of their own as well as a bath and lavatory, like little hotel suites. The spare-room for single guests may also have an entrance-hall, bath and lavatory, but more often they are situated next-door to one another with several sharing a bath and lavatory. The bachelor bedrooms are in a different part of the house from those for female visitors and, besides the main access to the men's rooms, they are often accessible also from a back stairs, which gives them complete freedom to come and go. The favourite position for the rooms for lady-guests is next to the daughters' bedrooms. These are often grouped round a little hall of their own; there is a closet for their clothes as well as a bathroom and lavatory. There are seldom rooms for grown-up sons since they usually live away from the parental home and only appear occasionally as visitors.

As we have already said, visitors' rooms occupy much space in English country-houses, for visitors are a permanent phenomenon and are almost part and parcel of country life, which would be monotonous and lonely without them. Visitors make a change and, by sharing their hosts' enjoyment of the country round them, keep that continuing enjoyment alive. Weekends (i.e. Friday or Saturday until Monday) in the country are very popular in England and during the summer months every English country-house is full of visitors. They are cared for in a way that, as regards accommodation, food and, be it said, independence, is not dissimilar from that of a very good hotel, but with the addition of the kindly solicitude of the hostess who counts it a privilege to provide for her guests' every wish with the utmost attentiveness. The visitors' rooms occupy most of the first and second floors (Figs. 153, 155). In the larger establishments guests are expected to bring a servant and accommodation for visitors' servants is also provided, which considerably increases the amount of space required. But once it is clearly recognised that the house is as large as it is mainly for reasons of hospitality, it becomes evident that the same considerations influence the planning of a country-house as that of a first-class hotel in a summer resort.

The children's rooms

The nurseries are considered to be of extra special importance in every English house. The extent of the arrangements and routine devoted to looking after children is in the correct ratio to the high standard of their upbringing. The province of the small members of the family is always separate from the rest of the house, so that, for example, a stranger may visit the house without being in the least aware that there are children in it. They are strictly segregated geographically as well, as we have seen, as organisationally, for the nurseries are always in a remote part of the house (in a side wing or on the top floor) and the children and their nurses are looked after quite separately from the kitchen upwards. The children remain separate members of the household until adolescence.

Care is taken in planning the children's rooms to situate them so that they are readily accessible from the woman's private room (boudoir, dressing-room, or even the parents' bedroom) to make supervision as easy as possible. But since they must also be within easy reach of the kitchen-quarters, the obvious place for them is between the master-bedroom and its ancillary rooms and the kitchen-quarters. The rooms needed are a night-nursery, a day-nursery, for the small children in the day-time, and a schoolroom for the older children who receive lessons at home. Although smaller houses may have no schoolroom, it is considered essential for even the most modest houses to have both a day- and a night-nursery, since it is rightly believed that it must be possible to air the rooms for a period at least equivalent to the length of time they are in use. As regards the aspect of the nurseries, there can be no shadow of doubt that the sunniest position is best. If anyone needs a sunny, hygienic room it is the small children, whose whole later lives depend upon the conditions of their youth. South is therefore the ideal aspect. A slightly more easterly position may perhaps be chosen for the night-nursery, for this will catch the early morning sun and the room will not become excessively hot in high summer. The night-nursery is planned to accommodate two or three children's beds and a bed for the nurse. The requirements of an ordinary bedroom apply equally to the night-nursery, but with the further condition that there must be a particularly spacious and draught-free fire-place before which the very small children can be bathed and dressed. It is considered particularly important for the night-nursery to be of adequate size, for ample space is needed for underclothing, clothes, bath-tubs etc., which are best kept in built-in cupboards. The day-nursery is sometimes some way away from the night-nursery, often on the floor below. In planning this room, the most important consideration, after its aspect, is its size, which must be as large as possible to give the children plenty of room to play. It also has to be borne in mind that childrens' parties are regular events in England; they take place in this room only and hordes of children have to be accommodated. The children of visitors and house-guests are also taken at once to the children's quarters, where they stay for as long as their parents remain in those of the grown-ups. All this makes it essential for the room to be as large as possible. The furnishing of an English nursery is simple but as a rule extremely pleasant and attractive, as we shall see. The schoolroom in which the older children have their lessons is also the governess's sitting-room. It will usually be girls only who are taught at home, since the boys of well-placed families leave home at a tender age and are educated at one of the great schools of ancient repute (Eton, Harrow, etc.), in which they are excellently cared for both physically and educationally. But girls receive much, or possibly all, of their education at home and there is always an educated governess in the better homes. Of all the children's rooms the schoolroom is required to be nearest to the mother's room.

More pretentious houses contain certain ancillary rooms in addition to the actual children's rooms, the most important of these being a nursery scullery, a bathroom and a lavatory. The nurse also has a little room of her own, although she is expected to devote her whole time to the children, whose sides she may not leave by night or day.

Ceremonial rooms

Needless to say, provision must be made in the really great houses, those that are truly palatial in style, for suites of ceremonial and state-rooms in addition to the rooms we have mentioned. The planning of such rooms is subject to the same conditions as in the palaces of other countries and there is rarely anything specifically English about the ceremonial rooms in English houses, particularly since they are usually modelled on continental prototypes. It seems desirable, therefore, to exclude ceremonial rooms from this study altogether.

Cloakrooms

Certain important ancillary rooms require a word or two of explanation, however. The most important of these are the cloakrooms. They are used by men only in England and, as we have said, in medium-sized and large houses an obvious place is always found for them inside the front-door. Women never leave their cloaks at this point, so that even in large houses one will never find a cloakroom for women as a counterpart to that for the men. At evening parties the women leave their cloaks on the first floor, usually in the master-bedroom where the hostess places her dressing-table at their disposal, so that they may take a final glance at their appearance. On afternoon visits and even when invited to lunch, English women do not remove their coats, as, indeed, they keep their hats on during the day in all situations, even at their own weddings. In general, English ideas about removing the outer garments are quite different from ours. Men paying calls during the day appear in the drawing-room in their outdoor attire, stick and overcoat included, and, perhaps so as not to appear too pressing, they feel obliged to wait to be asked to remove them. The English public also goes to the theatre and to concerts in full outdoor attire and the large cloakrooms to which we are used are therefore non-existent. So in English houses a small room suffices for the men's coats and there is no special cloakroom for the women at all.

Washing-place and lavatory

The cloakroom by the front-door always communicates with a washing-place that is very well equipped by our standards, invariably having both hot and cold water. A lavatory adjoins this room. In houses of medium size, this lavatory is probably the only one on the ground-floor, though in larger houses there is another, which may be next to the billiard-room or the library. The main lavatory on the first floor is generally considered the preserve of the female members of the household and visitors. It is always very difficult to find the right position in the plan for the lavatory intended for the use of visitors and others and the English are particularly sensitive about this. A lavatory that opens directly out of a hall or landing is unacceptable, it must always be tucked away in an inconspicuous position and access must be through another room. But nor must it be too difficult to find. The prime requirement is that anyone should be able to slip in unobserved. For this reason, a lavatory communicating with a washing-place or cloakroom on the ground floor is always the most convenient and almost the obvious position. A suitable place for the lavatory on the upper floor is next to the bathroom or in a passage-way leading to a staircase or other thoroughfare.

Staircases

It is still a major concern in the English house that the paths of the servants and of the family and visitors shall never cross – a requirement that a designer does not always find it easy to meet. The proper solution depends largely on the position of the staircases, particularly on the upper floors. The main staircase is for the sole use of the occupants of the house and their guests. All other traffic, including that of the children to their rooms, uses a secondary staircase, unless a special 'internal house-staircase' is planned. If such a staircase exists, a service staircase for the sole use of the servants is still required. This is best situated in a position in which it can supplement the main staircase as usefully as possible. The service staircase extends right through from the cellar to the top floor, and one of its main uses is to provide access to the servants' bedrooms, which are in the attic.

Housemaid's room

On each of the upper floors there is a special room with water laid on to facilitate service to the bedrooms and cleaning; utensils are also kept there or left there temporarily. It is considered unacceptable to have exposed sinks and taps in the passages. Even medium-sized and smaller houses invariably have a room of this kind; it is often quite large and is an important aid to easy and regular work and contributes much to the achievement of that quality of a good house that the English call 'convenience' and value above all else in their domestic lives.

2. *Domestic quarters*

Size and ramifications of the domestic quarters in England

The most distinctive feature of any English house, even from the outside, is its domestic quarters. The continental observer may find that the residential quarters are not so very different from what he is used to, but the domestic quarters come as a total surprise. He knows the kitchen only from its insignificant status in the continental house and is now confronted by a full-grown domestic organism that amazes him not merely on account of its size but also of its comprehensiveness. Whereas on the continent the kitchen is the room in which every aspect of household management takes place, the room in which not only the cooking is done but in which the servants spend their time and take their meals and in which all the cleaning is done, in the domestic quarters of the English house the management of the household is broken down into a dozen different operations, for each of which a room is provided. The kitchen has a whole series of ancillary rooms, the larder is divided into storerooms for all the different provisions and there are various separate rooms for the various kinds of cleaning. And this does not apply only to large country mansions but also to medium-sized establishments. One may say that every size of house in England contains between twice and four times as many domestic rooms as the continental house. In the ground-plan the domestic quarters often appear considerably larger than the residential quarters, and even allowing for the fact that the residential quarters occupy several storeys, about a third of the whole area of the house is taken up by the domestic quarters. A glance at the plan of Motcombe (Fig. 154) will make this clear. English people who know continental houses find the small size of the kitchen and domestic quarters well-nigh incomprehensible and they never cease to wonder how the splendid banquets at which, perhaps, they have assisted and which contrast so strikingly with the simplicity of English hospitality could possibly have been prepared in such small kitchens. In nothing is the English house as exceptional as in the size of its domestic quarters.

Historical development

Part of the reason for this phenomenon lies in the historical development of the English house, which has largely developed out of the country farmhouse. In the Middle Ages the kitchen was always a separate building, usually centrally planned and standing on its own, whereas the store-rooms were directly adjacent to the end of the hall where the entrance was. It was not until the great social changes that took place in the fifteenth century that the kitchen was moved into the house, where it joined the other domestic quarters to form the domestic wing as it appears from then onwards. It always adjoined the end of the hall where the entrance was, while the private rooms were adjacent to the opposite end. When Inigo Jones brought the Palladian house to England and abolished all practical considerations at a stroke, the domestic quarters were moved into the basement, where they had to get along as best they could. Or else they were torn apart and set down arbitrarily in outbuildings attached to the main house by colonnades. This period saw a complete break in the development of the domestic offices. So that with the arrival of Romanticism, when the English house burst the bonds of Palladianism, they extended and spread themselves with all the greater freedom. They surfaced once more from the cellars and were from now on grouped to form a self-contained set of rooms on ground-level. Indeed, as though by way of compensation for long years of neglect, the generation that was now at the helm treated them with redoubled affection, and the main contribution of the nineteenth century to the development of the English house may almost be said to lie in its extremely ingenious development of the domestic offices.

High cultural standard of the English domestic quarters

If it be asked to what degree the modern English house is of value as a model, one must surely answer that it is primarily its domestic offices that make it so. One might say that it is here that the advanced cultural level of English life is most clearly recognisable. Just as in the eighteenth century society spent far longer powdering and rouging, while nowadays it is much more concerned with bathing and bodily hygiene, so here cultural progress is reflected in the greater cleanliness, orderliness and convenience of a domestic routine which forms the foundation of a healthy, well-regulated and comfortable life for the occupants. The stress is on the practical instead of on the superficially decorative side. And there is another determining circumstance here. English servants are accustomed to expect much more in the way of a becoming standard of life than those on the continent. They too expect to be people with rights as well as duties, leisure as well as work and they too expect certain standards of comfort and convenience which are as yet unknown on the continent. The upper servants have their own cosy, well-appointed room to which they repair in the free time to which they are entitled, the servants take their meals in a communal dining-room at a neatly laid table. But for their work in the house they expect arrangements to be absolutely suitable and sufficient. These circumstances – all marks of an advanced culture – raise the domestic offices of the English house to the exemplary level at which we find it today.

Domestic quarters on ground-level

The English have no doubt that the most important point about the general position of the domestic quarters in relation to the main house is that they must occupy one side of it and not the basement. The advantages of having these quarters to one side rather than below ground are, especially, that it facilitates service to the residential rooms (because there are no stairs), that kitchen smells, which are otherwise so apt to find their way upstairs, are more easily avoided, the fact that they can be extended or enlarged if necessary, and finally the fact that the position is healthier as regards both the living conditions of the servants who have to work there and the preparation and storage of food, which is more salubrious. As a rule only beer and wine are stored in vaults below the kitchen wing. All other stores, including wood and coal (because they are more accessible) are kept on the ground floor near the kitchen. The only disadvantage of having the domestic quarters on the ground floor is that it is more costly. But the sacrifice is no hardship when all the advantages are considered.

Position in relation to the residential quarters

Local circumstances alone can determine on which side of the main house the kitchen quarters shall lie. The first consideration will obviously be to situate the principal rooms of the house correctly. Once that has been done, the kitchen quarters must be linked on in such a way that they communicate as conveniently as possible with the dining-room. Any side of the house may turn out to be the most suitable for the kitchen wing. But the commonest and, in general, the most obvious is the north, or even the west, in short, the position that leaves the best aspects free for the residential part of the house. For the rest, the kitchen wing should be an independant domain, out of the way of all the occupants and inviting no one who has no business there to set foot therein. The size of the kitchen wing obviously depends on that of the household. The best yardstick with which to measure the household is the number of servants that are kept. Once this is accurately known, the size of the domestic quarters is established.

Rooms that make up the domestic quarters

Apart from the servants' bedrooms, the following rooms will regularly be found in the domestic quarters of sizeable English country houses: kitchen, scullery, a second kitchen known as a still-room, larders for dry stores, meat, game, milk and butter, store-rooms for wood, coal for the house and for the kitchen, cleaning-rooms and store-rooms for lamps, boots (Motcombe even has one for riding-breeches), a pantry and bedroom for the butler, with adjoining plate-room, a housekeeper's room with adjacent laundry-room and a communal dining-room for the servants (the servants' hall). Where a steward is employed there is also an office for him, as at Motcombe.

Communication with the dining-room

The position of the kitchen decides the relative positions of these rooms. Their position is also dependent on the dining-room, for service to it must be convenient. This does not mean, however, that the kitchen must be immediately adjacent to the dining-room; on the contrary, this should be avoided. English ground-plans as a rule show a much greater distance between kitchen and dining-room than would be acceptable to us. The route from kitchen to dining-room is not only often very long but also very complicated, with many bends. Most of the bends, however, are there by design and the kitchen is situated at some distance from the dining-room in order to minimise kitchen smells, about which the English are extraordinarily sensitive. But the route to the dining-room must never cross other service-routes; it is herein, and not in the close proximity of the various rooms, that the virtue of a plan is considered to lie. Dishes are covered to prevent their growing cold on their long journey. It is the general custom in England for all dishes to be brought to the dining-room with their covers on; every meat and vegetable dish that comes to the table has a cover; even joints have large, high-domed metal covers.

Rooms round the kitchen

Among the actual domestic offices the kitchen is not only the largest but it also forms the centre of the system with the other rooms communicating with it according to the degree of their relationship. Nearest to the kitchen and directly communicating with it is the scullery, while the tradesmen's entrance must not be too far away and the larders must be close at hand. In planning the other rooms care is taken to see that the area in which the female servants work is as far removed as possible from that of the men and that separate staircases lead from these areas to the bedrooms on the upper floors. The communal servants' hall lies at the point where the two zones meet. Motcombe (Fig. 154) is an example of a well thought-out plan of this kind. The domain of the maidservants lies in the south-west and north-west corners, that

of the menservants (cleaning rooms, butler's rooms, etc.) in the south-east and north-east and stairs lead from both to the upper floors. Only the housekeeper's room, which must be close to the main house, encroaches a little too far on the men's preserve. The servants' hall, however, quite properly forms a convenient meeting-place for the two sexes. Taking all these matters into consideration, the best solution is usually found to be to group all the rooms round a domestic courtyard. The internal connecting passage-way that runs round the courtyard is often an open loggia, which cannot come amiss in the English climate and has the great advantage that the openings can be situated opposite the larders etc. to promote through-draughts.

The kitchen

The first point to be made in considering the requirements of the kitchen is that the kitchen in England is used exclusively for the preparation of foods and that all forms of cleaning, etc. are rigorously excluded. Thus no English kitchen contains a sink and it would be regarded as a gross lapse to install one. The inviolability of the kitchen persists down to the smallest households and even in workmen's cottages the areas for cooking and washing-up are kept separate. Kitchen and living-room are often one and the same in these cottages, but no one would dream of combining the scullery with the kitchen, as we generally do on the continent. So even in the smallest cottage the English kitchen is unthinkable without its attendant scullery. In smaller houses the kitchen contains only the kitchen-range or ranges and a long, flat dresser with many shelves above, on which dishes, plates, cooking utensils, etc. are kept. The most important object is the cooking-stove and the layout and shape of the room is determined by and in relation to it. The cook, busy about the stove, needs light from the left. The heat engendered by the stove presupposes a cool, preferably northerly, aspect, while the fumes that emanate from it necessitate an adequate system of ventilation. The best position for the kitchen is therefore one in which, with the stove situated on the east wall, light and air enter from the north; and there should, as far as possible, be a broad, uninterrupted expanse of light; kitchens are also built as lofty as possible, so that the fumes can collect on the ceiling without worrying the cook. In large country-houses the kitchen is often made to rise through two storeys and is solidly vaulted, so that the condensation runs down the walls instead of dripping. In the best appointed kitchens the walls are tiled, as are the floors.

The functions of the stove

The most fundamental difference between the English and the continental ranges is that the former is always situated in an alcove. We definitely prefer a kitchen-stove to be free-standing, at least on two sides; indeed, we think the best form is entirely free-standing, accessible from all sides. The English, however, with unshakeable obduracy, cling to their practice of wedging it between walls, so that every French chef who comes to England declares that he cannot possibly prepare even the simplest sauce on such a medieval contraption. Historical development must again be accounted mainly responsible for the walled-in stove. The English stove has evolved out of the fire-place in the wall that was used for both cooking and heating and has not yet managed to rid itself of its fire-place-like appearance. So inseparably bound up with the English notion of an interior is it that they still want to create the impression of a fire-place in their kitchens. In the English view a fire-place is the one thing that gives life to the room and makes existence in it tolerable. So all English kitchen-ranges are to this very day designed to show an open fire. Since this is very unsatisfactory for boiling and for some other activities at the stove, devices have now been introduced which turn the open fire into an enclosed one by means of a cover that is pushed forward at an angle; nowadays there are even ranges in which the fire is entirely closed on top and is open only at the grate in front.

English cooking

But an open fire is still indispensable for several activities at the English stove. First among these is the toasting of bread that forms so important an element of the English breakfast; toast entirely replaces our continental breakfast bread and rolls. The English are also still very fond of roasting meat at an open fire, a method of preparation that undoubtedly has great advantages; for the juices remain in the meat and meat prepared in this way is tastier and more easily digested. It would not occur to the English to add any kind of sauce to roast meat; and indeed it needs none. At most they use one of the piquant sauces that can be bought ready-made, such as the famous Worcester sauce. Consequently an important aspect of the higher culinary art, the preparation of sauces, is practically non-existent in the English kitchen. If one adds to this the fact that vegetables are also simply boiled in water with nothing added and that all the dishes consisting of several ingredients combined and cooked together, in which our German cooking is so rich, are entirely unknown, it becomes obvious that English cooking is extremely simple, almost primitive.* English cooking is the most artless, most uncultivated cooking in the world. Any refinement in the way the food is prepared is alien to it, and is largely unwanted, for in eating, as in other matters, they endure, and indeed desire, the greatest monotony. They are content to eat roast beef and roast mutton alternately for their main meal throughout the year. Yet sweets with a farinaceous basis play a large part and no meal is complete without them; but they too are prepared very simply and in this respect differ greatly from our sweet dishes; they are content to empty the raw materials into a pan and to consign the whole thing to the stove. But all English dishes are made from the best raw materials. Nowhere will you find leg of mutton to equal that in England and their beef and vegetables are also excellent. Good materials make up for the lack of style; indeed, once one has become used to the artless English cooking, one has the feeling that embellishments would not find favour there; and once one has made its acquaintance, the sophisticated French cuisine seems rather spineless, almost insipid. Nevertheless it is customary in English houses of standing to employ French chefs. They do not reject the good aspects of English cooking (nor would their employers want them to do that) but simply add a style that is indispensable, especially on festive occasions. England has always depended on France for these higher refinements. The culture of their neighbours has for centuries met the few needs of the most exalted sections of the English population for a higher outward culture; yet they have not permanently influenced the English cultural scene, which has essentially always remained that of a countrified, rustic people.

The kitchen stove and the hot-water system

Another circumstance that determines the form of the English stove is that in every English house the cooking-range is combined with a heating-system that provides hot water for baths and the basins in the washing-places. This combination of hot-water system and cooking-range is found in the smallest five-roomed houses as well as in houses of twenty or thirty rooms. We shall discuss the installation later on and will content ourselves here with the preliminary comment that the hot-water system is often an abnormally heavy burden for the range and frequently

*Cf. the views of Muthesius's Viennese contemporary Adolf Loos. These have been collected in editions produced by Herold Verlag, Vienna, 1962– . [DS]

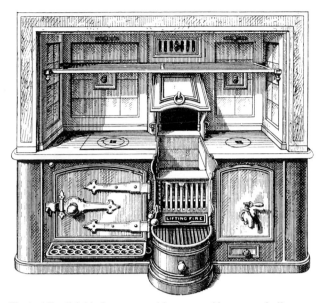

163 Typical English kitchen range with stove and hot-water boiler

results in great wastage of fuel. But thrift in the use of fuel is not the guiding principle for the English kitchen-range any more than it is for the English fire-place. Improvements continually come on to the market under pretext of economy, but the wastefulness lies in the uneasy double programme that the cooking-range is supposed to carry out alone and unaided. Although in view of these disadvantages the English stove cannot be recommended as a model, we shall nonetheless mention a few of its commonest forms.

The kitchen-range

There is a fundamental distinction between a range and a kitchener in that a range is immovably built in to the wall, whereas a kitchener is ready-made in iron and needs only to be connected with the flue. But there are no great differences in the general arrangement of the two forms. Figs. 163, 164 illustrate the commonest types of cooking-stove. In the centre is the open fire; this can be enclosed by pulling forwards and lowering the cover that is visible behind it; to the left of the fire is the oven, to the right the tank for the hot water for the house. The upper part of the stove is enclosed by side walls and a ceiling, even when the stove stands freely against a wall; for, quite unnecessarily, the old form based on the range has been adopted for the kitchener. There is always an iron rack a little way below the ceiling that forms a shelf for warming plates. In front of the stove is a fender some 15 cm. high, just like those before every fire-place in the rooms. Bread is toasted at the open fire on a special toasting-fork with a long handle, on which the cut slices are held. Meat too is hung on a special device in front of a glowing fire and the cook must naturally take care that each side is exposed to the heat equally. In ordinary households this is sometimes done simply by turning the joint continually, but in most houses there is a mechanical turning apparatus. At stoves of the type illustrated, the joint is hung in one of the well-known bottle-jacks, in the bottle-shaped part of which there is a clock-work mechanism that turns continuously (Fig. 165). The apparatus either hangs from a projecting iron bracket or is attached to a special stand, known as a meat-screen (Fig. 166) that stands in front of the fire with its open side facing it so that it also reflects the heat and makes better use of it. The hearths of earlier times were even more straightforwardly equipped for roasting on the spit, and these almost monumental mechanisms are found in large

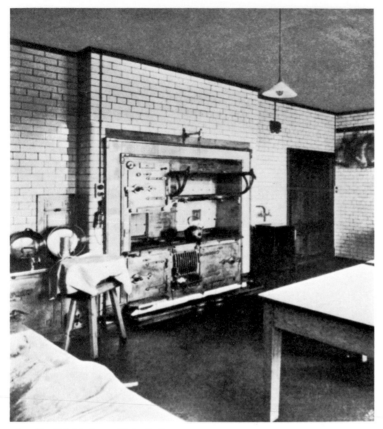

164 English kitchen with built-in stove

tally from ours in that it consists mainly of a large roasting oven in which the joint hangs freely from a hook in the oven-roof and roasts in the manner of meat roasted on the spit. The meat is roasted by gas-flames that burn all round it on the floor of the oven, so that it does not need turning.

Other kitchen furniture

Besides the main stove and the gas stove, larger kitchens have all sorts of ancillary stoves, warming-compartments, steamers, etc., though it would take too long to go into details here. In choosing these things and the particular kind of stove, the architect is usually guided by the cook, who looks for what he wants in the shops. To continue with the furnishing of the kitchen: the next item for consideration is the very solidly built kitchen-table with its surface of heavy oak planks. Since in England all the cooking appliances are situated round the walls, the table, with a measurement of between 3 and 4 m. in length by about 1.20 to 1.50 m. in width, always occupies the centre of the room. Part of the table is often topped with marble, or else there is a separate marble-topped table somewhere against the wall. In larger kitchens the dresser is also of some considerable length, often measuring up to 4 or 5 m. It is regarded in England as a fixture and is fastened to the wall. The space under the dresser may be open, in which case there is a shelf running its whole length at a height of 20 cm. to take the larger utensils, or closed in, like a cupboard. The upper part of the dresser consists of four or five shelves for dishes, with hooks on the front edge on which saucepans hang.

In general, the appearance of the English kitchen is never other than that of a working room. The English are not interested in arrays of copper vessels and fine crockery, or in show or comfort of any kind in the kitchen. In particular the kitchens of middle-class and lower middle-class houses contrast sharply with those of small and medium-sized houses in Germany, for the German housewife regards the kitchen as her concern and arranges it lovingly throughout, whereas in England, as we have said, even middle-class housewives never cross the threshold of the kitchen. The kitchen is therefore left to the cook, who, such is the casual relationship between employer and employee that exists today, sees no reason to do anything in particular to adorn it. This is why a German observer is usually disappointed by a glimpse into an English kitchen. The appearance of a present-day German kitchen must surely make a far better impression than that of an English one. Even the technical appliances, which have an antiquated air in England, are better in continental than in English kitchens. However, in its spaciousness and its ramifications the English kitchen-complex is so far in advance of the continental kitchen that there can be no question of our catching up at present.

The scullery

The scullery, the indispensable and immediate partner to every kitchen, is situated next-door to the kitchen in such a way that it can be reached with the greatest ease from the most used part of the kitchen, the space in front of the stove. It is entered by a door that opens inwards to the scullery, while another door leads out of it into the open air (for greater convenience during cleaning), but this must not also be the entrance-door to the domestic quarters. Store-rooms must not be accessible from the scullery. The scullery is used mainly for washing up dishes, but the preparations for roasting and boiling, such as cleaning the vegetables, dressing poultry, game and fish, are also done in the scullery. The scullery is often used as an overflow kitchen, in which the more minor processes, such as cooking the vegetables,

numbers in old English houses: in front of an immense brazier enclosed by iron rods, the spit with the meat on it turned on rods projecting on either side. The spit was sometimes turned not by spring-drives but by weight-driven clock-work, often by a tread-mill operated by a dog and sometimes again by a little windmill driven by the natural draught of the fire-place. The commonest form was the one with the weight mechanism. As with old clocks, the impulse was transmitted by a series of wheels, the driving-cord passed through the wall to the outside and the weight (a heavy stone) was out in the courtyard. An old spit of this type is still in use at Christ Church, Oxford, where it is shown to visitors. We find a survival of the earliest English hearth in the type of stove illustrated in Fig. 167, and intended for ancillary kitchens, combined kitchen-living-rooms etc.; even more space is reserved for the open fire in these than in the usual stoves of today. We can see that this stove still has the round, projecting trivet that the old stoves had in place of the hot-plates of today.

In larger kitchens the stove contains several more ovens, a grill, warming compartments, etc. This makes it far more versatile without fundamentally changing its form. No kitchen of any size will be without its grill, which is heated by charcoal but is for preference kept separate.

The gas stove

Despite very firm adherence to the old built-in stove in its alcove, with its many disadvantages, the much more rational gas stove has already won many devotees in the English kitchen. An English kitchen without a gas stove is unthinkable nowadays, though at present it is not much more than a makeshift or temporary expedient, since, while fully recognising the advantages of the newcomer, the public is unwilling to break finally with ancient custom. The English gas stove differs fundamen-

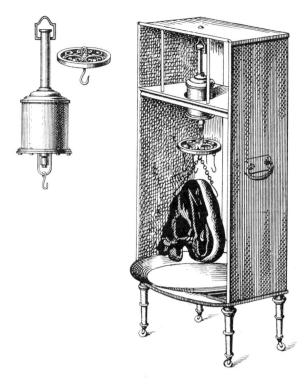

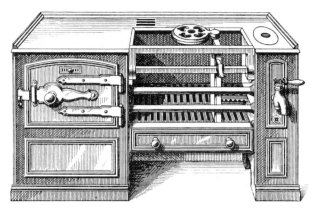

167   Small stove for ancillary rooms and domestic offices

165, 166   'Bottle-jack'. Clockwork mechanism for turning the joint and meat screen with 'bottle-jack' for use at an open fire

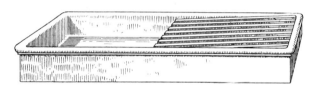

169   Kitchen sink in porcelain

168   Basic form of English gas cooker

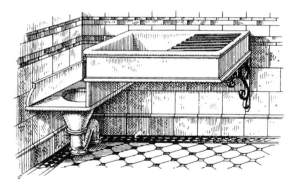

170   Slop-sink with connecting gulley

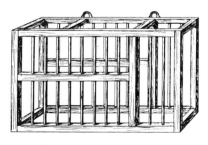

171   Plate-rack

172   Linen-cupboard

etc. are sometimes done when the main kitchen is overloaded. It therefore always contains a smaller cooking-stove, usually of the type illustrated in Fig. 167. Sometimes, as at Cavenham Hall (Fig. 146) and Adcote (p. 27), the baking-oven is also attached to the scullery, although this cannot be considered a good solution. Finally, especially in smaller households, it is also used as a wash-house. The main fixtures in the scullery are the appliances for washing-up dishes. For a large kitchen they consist of a row of sinks with hot and cold water usually situated immediately under a continuous strip of windows. Sinks used to be of stone and wood but now they are made exclusively of porcelain or earthenware. They consist of shallow, rectangular troughs some 30 cm. deep by 60 cm. wide and of varying length (Fig. 169); one side has a sloping grooved surface on which the dishes are laid. The draining board is made either of the same material as the sink or is a wooden grid or a corrugated vulcanite surface. The sinks are supported by iron brackets fixed to the wall or they may rest on brick or earthenware feet. Since, as we have seen, there are cleaning-rooms with slop-sinks on every floor in an English house, there is little need for an actual slop-sink to take dirty water carried in buckets. Nevertheless, to prevent the sinks being dirtied by having dirty water poured into them there is an arrangement like the one illustrated in Fig. 170, in which a separate slop-sink has been installed next to the sink. Above every English sink there is a plate-rack (Fig. 171), an extremely useful device that hangs on the wall like a book-shelf, in which washed plates are placed to drip. Besides the sink, larger sculleries contain troughs for washing vegetables, fish and other foods, as well as sets of small wooden box-like containers for the various types of vegetable, one or more cupboards like the kitchen-dresser, various coppers for boiling laundry and a wash-basin with hot and cold water where the kitchen-staff can wash their hands.

The cook's pantry and the meat-larder

Like the scullery, the various meat-larders and other store-rooms, in which the raw materials to be prepared in the kitchen are kept, may be regarded as directly dependent on the kitchen. First there is a small general larder, in which all stores except meat – i.e. butter, bread, milk, eggs etc. – are kept and which is known as the cook's pantry. It is distinguished from the meat-larder by its close proximity to the kitchen. It contains the essential fixture for all store-rooms: a table with drawers running round the room, with shelves above. The meat-larder, which is used only for keeping all uncooked meats, has marble or slate surfaces instead of the table and many devices for hanging meat in the shape of thick horizontal iron rods on which are moveable meat-hooks. There must be a refrigerated cupboard. One essential need is common to both kinds of store-room and this is means of creating a through-draught. They must have windows on two facing sides. The pantry has shutters of fine wire mesh that open outwards; windows that open inwards are fitted only during the cold season. Sometimes a meat-larder has no windows at all, only pierced zinc panes. The best position is one in which the window opens towards the north and the door facing it – the upper part of which is pierced – gives on to an open passage.

Other store-rooms

Every small house, down to the very smallest, has its larder and pantry. In large houses, however, the functions of these rooms are broken down into further subsidiary uses. First there is a separate pastry room, in which all the bread, cakes and flour are kept and where preparations for baking are made. The room must not, therefore, be too far from the baking-oven. There is often a separate store-room for flour, as at Cloverley Hall (Fig.

150). There is also a dairy for milk, butter and cheese, with the necessary appliances for keeping and treating milk and milk products. Besides the general larder for meat, there is a special one for game and another for fish, both of which are kept separate from the general larder on account of their ineradicable smell. For the same reason the game-larder (which again has plenty of hooks for hanging game) is preferably situated as far away as possible, often, as at Cavenham Hall (Fig. 146), in a little building of its own. In very large mansions there is also a separate larder for bacon and ham and another for salting meat and storing it when salted.

The cook's room

The domestic rooms discussed so far are directly dependent on the kitchen. They are part of the preserve of the cook, who supervises and looks after them. In large houses and everywhere where there is a male chef, there is another separate room for him next-door to the kitchen. It is, however, only a little day-room in which he can do his few reading and writing jobs (drawing up menus, consulting cookery-books, etc.). For the rest, the chef's bedroom is usually on an upper floor and he joins the upper servants (see p. 71) for his meals and free time.

The butler's domain

In addition to the cook's domain, we must consider those of the butler and housekeeper. We have already discussed the butler's duties (p. 71); not only is he one of the most important personages in the English house but his position is one of the oldest in the English household. He was originally the cup-bearer (who saw to the drinks, hence the name butler, from the same root as bottle); but nowadays he combines the duties of the old offices of cup-bearer and server. Where there is no steward, as is the case in the great majority of large English houses, the butler is responsible for the smooth running of the whole domestic machine. His narrower domain always comprises at least three rooms: the butler's pantry, his bedroom and the plate-room. A large part of his duties consists in keeping a careful watch over the household silver. His bedroom, therefore, as a glance at the plans of English houses will show, is always close to the fire- and burglar-proof plate-room, the doors of which often actually open into his bedroom. The cellars for wine and beer are also in his domain; he is responsible for the stocks and the proper treatment of the wine. His pantry is his base and it is of the greatest importance that his room shall be in the right position for his various activities. It must be as close as possible to the dining-room (because the butler serves at table), its position must be one from which he can observe the front-door of the house, so that he may attend to visitors the moment they arrive; it must be close to the owner's room, for he often needs the butler, the door to the wine-cellar must not be too far away, he must be able to keep an eye on the back-door and the luggage-entrance; and the housekeeper's room and, when there is one, the steward's room, must be nearby. The designer has his work cut out to meet all these requirements. The layout at Motcombe (Fig. 154) comes very close to an ideal solution.

The butler's pantry and the plate-room

The butler's pantry contains a large moveable table, cupboards for glasses and the daily table-linen, a large fire-place and two sinks with taps, one for hot water and the other for cold. They differ from the sinks in the scullery in that they are made of lead over a wooden base. They are used for cleaning the silver and are immediately under the window. The plate-room, which must not abut on any outside wall, contains built-in cupboards with baize-lined drawers for the various silver utensils. In houses in which large quantities of table-silver are used there is a special cleaning-room next to the butler's pantry; this is used by an under-butler, as at Cloverley Hall (Fig. 150), and in this case it is he who sleeps next to the plate-room.

Cleaning-rooms

As we have seen, every large house contains special cleaning-rooms for the heavier cleaning operations; first there is invariably a brush-room in which clothes are brushed and sometimes there are other separate rooms for cleaning boots and lamps. The room in which lamps are cleaned is also used to store lamps that are not in use. Many houses also have a drying-room for drying wet clothes, a most important room in view of the English climate and predilection for all kinds of open-air sports. Modern houses always have as well a special room in which bicycles are cleaned and kept, unless this is combined with the coach-house. It is naturally possible to combine the two only if the stables and coach-house are immediately next to the main house.

The housekeeper's domain

The third domain that we have to consider is that of the housekeeper. In houses where there is no steward it is her duty to see that the household has everything it needs and she also has charge of the household linen and stores. Her domain includes store-rooms for the more precious groceries, bottled fruit, sauces, biscuits, spices, etc., also the linen-rooms containing the appropriate cupboards (Fig. 172), china for the table, flower-vases, etc., and finally a secondary or tea kitchen reserved for her own use and called a still-room. She has besides her own large, comfortably furnished room, in which the upper servants also take their meals (see p. 71). This room should therefore be close to the kitchen. It is desirable to situate it close to the kitchen-quarters for another reason, namely that it is the housekeeper's duty to supervise all the female servants. And finally it is likely that her own still-room will be immediately adjacent to the main kitchen. These considerations have produced a suite of housekeeper's rooms which are very well put together and excellently situated within the overall plan of Cloverley Hall (Fig. 150). The only room that is lacking there is a laundry-room.

The still-room

Of these rooms, the housekeeper's own kitchen or still-room requires a further word of explanation. The origin of the room lies in the distant past and its existence today is incomprehensible without its past history. Still-room is a contraction of distilling-room and during the Middle Ages and later the room was used for preparing essences, scents and the finer liqueurs that in those days played an important part in the housewife's arts. Thereafter it remained the housewife's preserve until modern times, when the English housewife ceased to cross the threshold of the domestic quarters and it passed to the housekeeper. She uses it to prepare tea and coffee, to bake fancy cakes, bottle fruit, etc. As at Motcombe (Fig. 154), the housekeeper's store-room is very often accessible from the still-room. The still-room sometimes has its own scullery; or it may contain a sink with water laid on.

The steward's room

The duties of the butler and housekeeper are somewhat changed when a steward is employed. The steward replaces the butler as head of all the male servants and he, and not the housekeeper, has charge of all the household catering and the attendant accountancy and inventory-taking. His office is situated at the centre of the domestic activities, but as near to the tradesmen's entrance as to the main house. It is thus also used to settle much managerial business which would otherwise go to the owner's office. Its secondary role is that of dining-room for the upper servants, in which they take lunch and the evening meal, leaving only breakfast and tea to be taken in the housekeeper's room. Motcombe (Fig. 154) is one of the households in which a steward is kept. The housekeeper's room is therefore some way away from the kitchen while the steward's is close to it.

The servants' hall

Besides the domestic rooms already mentioned, all larger and even medium-sized houses in England have a servants' dining-room known as the servants' hall. It is a large, long room; it must be as near to the kitchen as possible but at the same time the butler and housekeeper must be able to keep an eye on it from their rooms. It is used not only as a dining-room but also as a communal sitting-room for the lower servants during their free time. It is never so situated that it can overlook the front-door to the house, to prevent visitors feeling that the servants' eyes are upon them as they arrive. It must, however, be in closest proximity to the tradesmen's entrance, since it also serves as a waiting-room and visitors' room for all visitors of the rank of the lower servants (the housekeeper's or steward's rooms fulfil the same function for the upper servants). Besides the long dinner-table and the chairs belonging to it, and a few comfortable chairs, the appointments of the servants' hall include provision for leaving coats and hats, washing facilities, if there are none in a vestibule, cupboards, sometimes with lockers for individual servants, and a book-shelf containing a certain amount of reading matter. In large houses the female servants have their own sitting-room, so that they only enter the servants' hall for meals. Where the domestic quarters are more restricted in size, however, the servants' hall serves various additional domestic purposes, becoming the ironing-room, cleaning-room (in which clothes are brushed), the room in which sporting equipment is kept and the drying-room for wet clothes.

The serving-room

The serving-room must be regarded as the connecting link between the domestic quarters and the main house and in a way belonging partly to each. We have already noted that ordinary houses in England normally have no such room, though large establishments like Motcombe (Fig. 154), Cloverley Hall (Fig. 150) and Cavenham Hall (Fig. 146), sometimes have one. In these cases it does not differ from the corresponding continental room, except that it is more meagre in size and appointments. In the traditional English view the kitchen is the place for preparing food and since, by comparison with the German kitchen, so many functions not actually connected with cooking have been removed from it, this view is understandable. The kitchen has the fixed dresser with its broad surface and many shelves, the name of which refers directly to this purpose (to dress, in the sense of preparing, food). It would appear, however, that the serving-room is becoming increasingly firmly established in newer houses, especially the larger ones.

The gun-room

The gun-room is again situated between the residential and domestic quarters of the house. It is a truly English development and has no German counterpart. It houses all the hunting equipment and fishing-tackle, together with the gear for all kinds of sports. Those who know how many different kinds of sport the English go in for will appreciate the importance such a room must have. All this equipment is in the butler's charge, so the gun-room must be close to his domain. Moreover it must be easily accessible to the occupants and at the same time near the front-door or at least near the luggage-entrance (see p. 91), which is itself near the front-door. It is inappropriate for the gun-room to look on to the garden since most of the sporting gear is used outside the premises. In smaller houses the gun-room is replaced by a largish cupboard, either in the servants' hall or in the butler's room, or the cloakroom.

The bake-house, brew-house, wash-house and engine-room

We have yet to mention the wash-house, brew-house and bake-house; these form part of the domestic offices but are usually detached from them. The bake-house, a necessity for isolated houses in the country, is frequently replaced by a smaller oven in one of the ancillary kitchens or in a special room. But there is often a baker's oven, even when bread can be obtained from outside, for there is much home-baking of cakes, fancy breads, etc. in the English house. A brew-house, when such still occurs (see Fig. 150), must be regarded as something of a special plaything. A wash-house, however, is always indispensable to every large country-house. As at Barrow Court (Fig. 159) and Cloverley Hall (Fig. 150), it often stands on its own in a building flanking a large service courtyard, so that the housekeeper can supervise the washing without too much ado. But if it is desired to dry the washing in the old way by hanging it on a line in the fresh air (and many people adhere firmly to this method), it is best to site the wash-house at one extreme so as not to disfigure the surroundings of the house with lines of washing. The size of the wash-house depends on the size of the house. It consists of the wash-house proper, an ironing and mangling room and a store-room for fuel. Fuel may be stored in the cellars and there may be a small drying-room under the roof.

There is no need to explain the technical workings of these installations in more detail, especially as there is nothing particularly remarkable in this sphere in England. Similarly it is unnecessary to go into details about the engine-house for the motors for the various technical systems in the house (electric light, water, ventilation, etc.).

3. Dependencies

Farming

All larger English country properties include a number of dependencies of specific types to suit the requirements of the house. There are naturally always stables, with all the attendant coach-houses, accommodation for the coachmen, etc. Most owners of country properties, however, do a little farming, which, though it may involve no more than cattle-rearing, requires a farmyard with cow-houses, pig-sties, a dairy, etc. Almost invariably too, there are enclosures for rearing poultry, which, should this be a particular hobby of the owner's, may assume considerable proportions. All these agricultural adjuncts have their own buildings, on which care is lavished in proportion as the owners regard farming as a hobby and the commercial viability of the enterprise is not the first consideration. To denote this type of farm attached to a large country property the English use the term model farm, which in itself indicates that all the details have been worked out with careful consideration and without stint. In fact these farms exist as show-places rather than as commercial undertakings. Their justification lies in the owner's desire to provide for all the needs of the household from his own land, and the pride he takes in doing so. Dairy-farms that produce only milk, butter and cheese are the commonest. The milk and cheese dairies are models of hygiene and are equipped with every modern appliance, which makes them a pleasure to

visit. A fountain splashes in the hall of the milk dairy and the floors and walls of the rooms are faced with marble. The sights that meet the eyes here surpass even the interiors of elegant butchers' or fishmongers' shops in the most expensive districts of the capital. But the cow-houses and sheep-sheds too are luxuriously appointed. Sheep are reared on a large scale on account of the acres of uncultivated pasture in England; and a flock of grazing sheep provides the figures in the landscape without which no English park would be conceivable. The foreigner is amazed to find that even Hyde Park in London has its flock of sheep. And the legs of mutton and the lamb-cutlets that surprise and delight the foreigner at an English table are evidence enough of the success with which sheep thrive on the rich English pasture-land.

Anyone who has visited a great English estate such as Eaton Hall, the Duke of Westminster's country-seat at Eccleston, near Chester, will know how considerable these incidental farming establishments can be. There are miles of them, scattered about the great park which in itself forms a whole rural district. Discussion in greater detail here would far exceed the scope of this book. Besides the farm-buildings many dwelling-houses for managers, servants and workmen are naturally required; but these do not differ much in plan from the small English house that we shall discuss later. It has recently become general practice to provide accommodation for the workmen as well and in the cases in which plans for these workmen's cottages have been entrusted to good architects, true model layouts have often resulted. At the Duke of Westminster's seat all these subsidiary buildings (dwelling-houses and farm-buildings) were carried out with great loving-care by John Douglas, the Chester architect (see p. 32) and are in themselves a sight very much worth seeing.

The stables and dependent rooms

Even in medium-sized and smaller country-houses the one really indispensable building among all these is the stables. With all the care that for centuries – though particularly in modern times – has been lavished on horse-breeding in England, it is hardly surprising that the best stabling for horses is found in England. Here again, however, it would take too long to go into details, especially since English architects themselves regard stables as a specialised field, in which, on the one hand, the owners' quite decided views and, on the other, the current views of experts, prescribe guide-lines for them.[20] So only a few general points of view that have an important influence on the construction of stables in England will be mentioned here.

Stables are situated either immediately adjacent to the domestic quarters, as at Cloverley Hall (Fig. 150) and Barrow Court (Fig. 159), or at varying distances from the main house. It is more usual nowadays to separate them, although in the interests of architectonic design many architects seek to improve the overall grouping of the building masses by bringing the stables in close to the main house. If they are attached to the main block, they are usually situated round a separate stable-yard, which is either inaccessible from the main drive or is reached by an underpass reserved for the owner's carriage. In the usual layout the stable buildings form one side of an architectonic outer court, following the celebrated monumental layout of the French palais. This

[20] Instructions for building stables will be found in the booklet Stable building and stable fitting, by Byng Giraud. All particulars of what is today regarded as the authoritative arrangement of stables will be found in the detailed and very well produced catalogues of firms engaged in building stables (e.g. Musgrave & Co., Belfast).

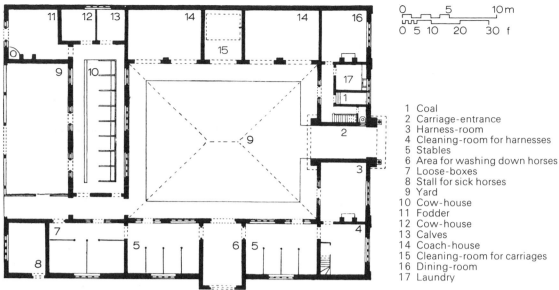

1 Coal
2 Carriage-entrance
3 Harness-room
4 Cleaning-room for harnesses
5 Stables
6 Area for washing down horses
7 Loose-boxes
8 Stall for sick horses
9 Yard
10 Cow-house
11 Fodder
12 Cow-house
13 Calves
14 Coach-house
15 Cleaning-room for carriages
16 Dining-room
17 Laundry

173   Bickley, Kent. By Ernest Newton. Plan of stable buildings

layout also became established for a time in England, during the period of French influence under the Stuarts, and the Palladian ground-plan with its elongated lateral wings adheres to the same basic idea.

When the stables are kept separate from the main building, the basic form of the English stable-complex may also be that of a group of buildings surrounding a courtyard (Fig. 173–175). But in this case, one side of the courtyard is enclosed by a wall and left free of buildings, to allow for proper ventilation (Fig. 175). Several other small buildings, such as chicken-houses, stalls for other animals, toolsheds and even the wash-house or brew-house are often included in the stable-complex, though care is taken to see that they do not open on to the stable-yard.

When there is complete freedom of choice in siting the stable-complex an airy, sunny position will be selected, if possible on rising ground, so that with first-class drainage the stalls can be kept dry, as is, of course, eminently desirable. It is also considered important for the doors into the stalls to be on the side away from the prevailing wind. This enables the stable doors to be left open occasionally without exposing the horses to draught. The English reckon that the stalls should measure at least 6 ft. (1.84 m.) in width by 9 ft. (2.75 m.) in length from the wall to the end-post of the wooden partition. It is always considered best for the stalls to occupy one side only of the gangway and only in the cramped conditions of the capital is it thought justifiable for them to lie on both sides. There is a general dislike of large stalls; instead, where many horses have to be accommodated, partitions

174   Cavenham Hall, Suffolk. By A. N. Prentice. (See also Figs. 146–149)
Stable buildings

1 Stall for sick horses
2 Stables
3 Harness-room
4 Fodder
5 Area for washing down horses
6 Loose-boxes
7 Covered area for washing carriages
8 Coach-house
9 Tools

0   5   10 m
0 5 10   20   30 f

175   Plan of model stable for twelve horses (after Musgrave)

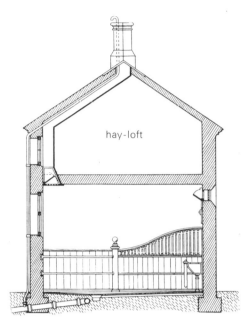

176   Ventilation and drainage of stable

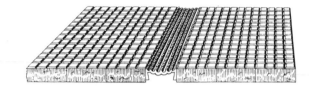

177   Stable-floor with drainage (after Musgrave)

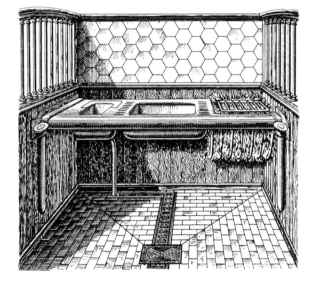

178   View of a modern stable (after Musgrave)

are constructed, dividing the area into sections to house between six and eight horses. The advantage of this arrangement is that the horses disturb one another less and they generate more warmth in the stalls. In these circumstances however, the several gangways are connected by sliding doors that open to almost the full width of the gangway. The width of the gangway equals the length of the stalls, i.e. 2.75 m. so that a stable with stalls on one side has a clear width of 5.50 m. Besides the ordinary stalls, there are loose-boxes measuring 12 ft. (3.67 m.) square, and medium-sized and larger stables always include a bay for sick horses, separated from the rest of the stable by solid walls. In the centre of the building is a washing-bay with water laid on for washing the horses. Elsewhere within easy reach of the stalls is the saddle and harness room with the necessary apparatus for hanging up the harnesses, saddles and bridles; next-door is the cleaning-room for the gear. There is a fire-place with an open fire in the harness-room, with a water-heater attached that both provides hot water for cleaning and centrally heats the coach-house. Larger stables, however, will also have a separate polishing-room with a fire-place, next to the coach-house. A store-room for the fodder will be found immediately next to the stalls, but as securely shut off from them as possible, consequently approached through a small sluice-room, as in Fig. 175. Hay is stored in a loft above the stalls. The ceiling of the stalls must therefore be solid, to exclude the air from them.

The English view is that stalls should measure at least 10 ft. (3.05 m.) in height, or 12 ft. (3.67 m.) in larger stables, but not much higher or warmth will be lost. The stalls are lit from the gangway side by iron windows which turn on a horizontal axis enabling the opening to be finely adjusted. To effect a continuous circulation of air there is another adjustable ventilator in the form of a small window that opens upwards on a horizontal axis fairly high in the wall above each horse's head (Fig. 176). On the opposite side of the stall there is an air-vent through which the foul air escapes by means of an air-shaft leading to an outlet on the roof. Stables are sometimes, though rarely, artificially heated, either by a warm-air system, by which warm air is piped in from the gangway wall or, in smaller stables, by warm-water heating supplied from a boiler in the harness-room.

Drainage is of prime importance in stables. The earlier method was to slope the floor downwards towards a channel running the length of the gangway. This method has now been abandoned because misgivings were rightly felt about the horse standing unevenly and causing uneven tension of the muscles. The current method of drainage is, therefore, to construct a channel in the centre of each stall running from the head-end towards the gangway. With this method the floor slopes only gently towards the centre of the long axis. The channel is covered by pierced iron plates small enough to be easily removable for cleaning. There is an outlet with trap either in the centre of each stall, or else liquids are conveyed to the channel in the gangway, where there are outlets serving several (up to five) stalls. The individual drainage-system is considered the better of the two. Loose-boxes always have a central outlet each. Recently there has been opposition to covered channels because they allow dirt to accumulate and encourage neglect in cleaning. Many stables therefore now have open channels with a specially designed cross-section which expedites drainage and does not interfere too much with the horse's gait (Fig. 177). Floors are generally of clinker bricks; they are usually set in a diagonal pattern in the gangways but in the stalls they form a special grooved surface. Walls are faced with wood up to the level of the manger, beyond which they are either plastered with cement plaster or tiled. In good stables all the woodwork is of teak, a very tough, firm wood. In the better English stables all the ironwork (with the possible exception of beams, posts and the coverings of gratings) is wrought iron. Mangers are of wrought iron throughout, hay-racks are nowadays almost always below the top of the manger, so that in fact they are not hay-racks but mangers for hay (Fig. 178), though loose-boxes still have racks of the old kind. Many mangers also have a drinking-trough with a waste-pipe to the drain in the stall. All these stable furnishings represent great luxury, which fortunately is expressed less in ornamental displays than in materials of excellent quality and the best workmanship. Thus, precisely because so-called art has been kept out, the stables look modern in the best sense and are a pleasure to see.

The largest stables have separate stalls for carriage-horses and riding-horses and occasionally for hunters too. There will also be a stall for strange horses. And loose-boxes are placed all together in a section of their own. The largest stables are princely in scale and magnificence. Stables such as these – there is an example at Welbeck Abbey, seat of the Duke of Portland – often have a sizeable covered riding-school. Welbeck Abbey has stalls for one-hundred horses most luxuriously appointed.

The prime requirement of the coach-house is a completely dry position, which depends mainly on its letting in the sunshine. There is often an open veranda in front of it or a deeply oversailing roof to ensure that cleaning operations may be done under cover. A properly appointed stable-yard always has a clock that is visible from a distance. It is placed above the entrance, which is usually surmounted by a tower-like structure. There is often a dove-cote in the tower.

Accommodation must be provided for the staff of the stable-complex. This will be situated either in a separate building, perhaps to one side of the entrance, or on an upper floor above the stables and coach-houses. In large establishments there is a separate kitchen and stable-boys' room for the lower staff. Coachmen are assumed to be married and to run households of their own.

The other dependencies of a country-house, such as gatekeepers' lodges, summer-houses and greenhouses, will be considered in the context of the garden, since they are an integral part of its layout.

B. The surroundings of the house
(Garden, drive, gate-lodge, boundaries, garden buildings, garden ornament)

Character and importance of the garden in England

House and garden have been inseparably linked at all periods of human civilisation. The garden has always brought joy to the house, love of the house is almost incomprehensible without love of the garden. A country-house without a garden would in itself be an unimaginable idea, for it is mainly for the sake of having a house in its natural environment, the garden, that people live far from the crowded conditions of the city. This is the only environment that renders the house worthy of its human occupants, this alone meets every human being's rightful claim to the ground that he treads with his feet and to which he belongs in all the circumstances of his life. Thus the garden is only a part of man's habitation, the wider dwelling-place wherein the smaller, the house itself, is situated.

The garden was bound to be extremely important to a people who value domestic and rural life as highly as do the English. Did not every single country-estate with its flower-beds round the house, its broad, green, meticulously tended lawns, its luxuriant shrubberies and plantations of trees that smilingly return our gaze like a fragment of paradise, confirm the fact, history would tell us of the importance the garden has had in England at all periods, for as long as there has been an English house. One need only turn the pages of the many old volumes with their views of the English country-houses of the sixteenth, seventeenth and eighteenth centuries to become convinced that the English garden has had a past of a brilliance equalled by the gardens of few other countries. It is true that the most important features of earlier garden design, as we find it in these books, was influenced by the continent. But they found hospitable ground in an England that was already rich and they continued to be fostered with the utmost assiduity.

England did not gain its real reputation in garden design until later, with the development of landscape-gardening in the eighteenth century, a fashion that replaced and destroyed the old tradition of gardening. Landscape-gardening prevailed for about a century. It was not until the general increase in activity that attended the new movement in art that the riches of the old gardening tradition were re-examined. A reaction set in, led mainly by architects, whose efforts, as they gained more and more ground, set the pattern for English gardening today. The ascendancy of the once-powerful English landscape-gardener is past, in his own country at least, and only the continental public is still dominated by his ideas. In England the garden that surrounds the house is no longer designed to imitate the fortuities and chaos of nature but is set out in an orderly and regular fashion. This at least is the case with all houses designed by architects and owned by persons who keep abreast of the latest ideas. The relative newness of the movement accounts for the fact that there are landscape-gardeners still at work. The following paragraphs deal only with the formal garden, the garden to which, as far as one can foresee, the future of English gardening will belong.

Gardens old and new

Although there has been a return to the principles of earlier gardening, this is not to say that the old garden should be revived just as it was. Conditions have changed in many ways. In the first place, the garden of the sixteenth to the eighteenth centuries, as we find it in the old gardening books and as it has survived in a

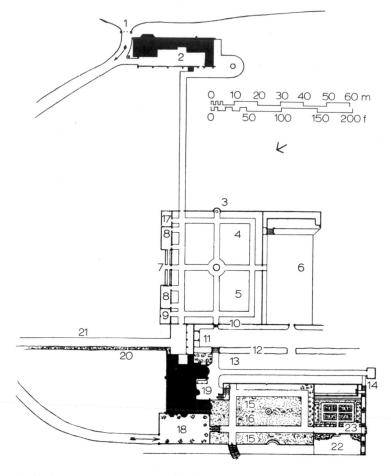

1 Carriage-entrance
2 Lodge-keeper, stables, coach-house
3 Statue
4 Vegetable-garden
5 Goldfish pond
6 Lawn-tennis court
7 Greenhouse for flowers
8 Vinery
9 Shed
10 Flower-bed
11 Grassed terrace
12 Slope
13 Flowering shrubs
14 Summer-house
15 Lawn
16 Sun-dial
17 Heating
18 Forecourt
19 Yard
20 Hedge
21 Back entrance
22 Rock-garden
23 Rose-garden

179 New Place, Haslemere, Surrey. By C. F. A. Voysey. (See also Fig. 160.) Plan of a garden

creation of the human hand and therefore a creation that has become absolutely natural, the garden has an inherent tectonic form, which in fact it had had at all periods until the false sentimentality of the eighteenth century wrought a change. The ordered human plan makes the curved straight, the sloping even, the irregular regular, it creates rhythm in place of inconsequence, calculated effect in place of the accidental. For men to decide to try to imitate, to concentrate and heighten the caprices of nature within the small framework of the garden is a wholly unnatural situation. Those in search of nature will find it in plenty outside the garden walls. The landscape-gardener pretends to compose landscape-pictures using natural objects as his means, but he forgets that this is work on the level of the waxwork dummy. He finds it unnatural to clip trees and hedges without reflecting that he himself mows the lawn to keep it short and tidy. He pretends to arrange the whole layout of his garden in the way that most favours the growth and display of the plants but forgets that he can do this just as well in the ordered garden as by imitating wild nature, nor that this need not be his only reason for calling himself an artist. It is true that during the last hundred years when the landscape-gardener has had the reins in his hand, great advances have been made in the cultivation of plants, to the benefit of the modern garden. The period of landscape-gardening marks a kind of realistic transitional phase of garden design that, like most realistic movements in art, meant a revision of technical means. But the end was bound to be the formal garden-plan, just as rhythm is the end of all art. With its interest in plant cultivation, landscape-gardening produced many sound results but also a number of unsound ones, such as the introduction and great predilection for innumerable exotic

few examples, was an aristocratic garden, over-pompous and ornate. The mighty avenues, broad walks, the convoluted patterns of the flower-beds are neither to our taste today nor are they a practical possibility in modern conditions. Love of nature which men, especially the English, have now cherished for a century and a half, demands plants in profusion and a mass of flowers rather than the empty beds filled with vari-coloured soils and the figures clipped from box of earlier times. Just as our attitude to nature has changed, so has our way of life. We spend less time on broad sunny terraces showing off the magnificence of our dress and the virtuosity of our court etiquette; we would rather enjoy the view from those terraces and take a healthy constitutional. As conditions have changed by comparison with the aristocratic age, so must the modern garden become a different garden from the old aristocratic one.

The formal garden

The feature of the old garden that modern designers, leap-frogging the art of the landscape-gardener, have felt bound to revive, is its ordered, that is to say, its formal, plan. As a natural

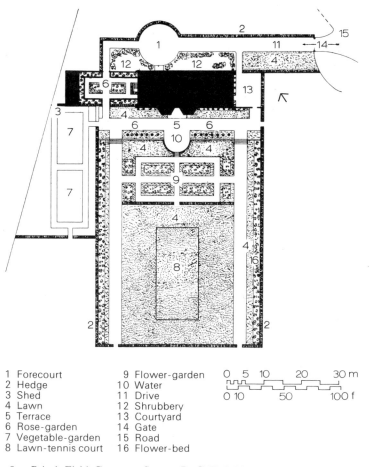

1 Forecourt
2 Hedge
3 Shed
4 Lawn
5 Terrace
6 Rose-garden
7 Vegetable-garden
8 Lawn-tennis court
9 Flower-garden
10 Water
11 Drive
12 Shrubbery
13 Courtyard
14 Gate
15 Road
16 Flower-bed

180 Prior's Field, Compton, Surrey. By C. F. A. Voysey. Plan of garden

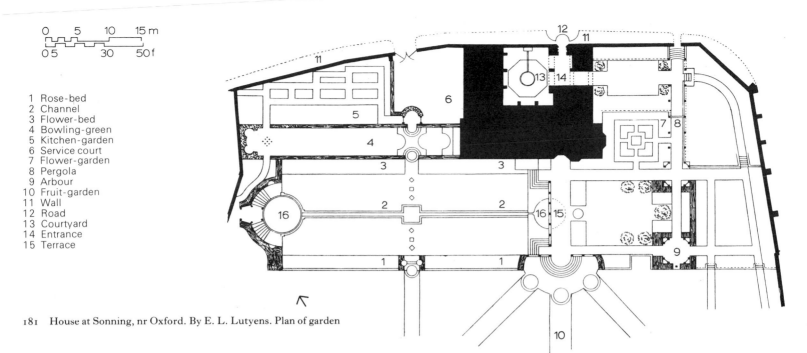

1 Rose-bed
2 Channel
3 Flower-bed
4 Bowling-green
5 Kitchen-garden
6 Service court
7 Flower-garden
8 Pergola
9 Arbour
10 Fruit-garden
11 Wall
12 Road
13 Courtyard
14 Entrance
15 Terrace

181 House at Sonning, nr Oxford. By E. L. Lutyens. Plan of garden

plants. It is precisely against these foreign intruders, among other things, that the modern English movement in gardening is aimed. The English wish to stock their gardens once more with native English plants, the quieter but more natural and, to us more congenial, charms of which had been overlooked and almost forgotten during the rule of the landscape-gardener.

Principles of the modern garden

The modern English view of the garden[21] is that the formal plan should be revived but that at the same time the utmost attention should be paid to the cultivation of flowers and plants, preferably indigenous ones. Little use is made of the decorative repertoire of the old aristocratic ornamental garden; but great care is lavished on flower-beds, lawns, fruit and vegetable gardens, which are all divided into sections in the manner of the old gardens and kept clearly separate from one another (Figs. 179–182). All the individual sections are horizontal and even, all the paths are straight, sloping ground is terraced, the boundaries of the several sections are clearly outlined by means of low walls or clipped hedges. Each part of the garden lies close to that part of the house to which it belongs, the kitchen-garden to the domestic wing, the flower-garden to the drawing-room, while the lawns lie facing the residential front of the house. The garden is seen as a continuation of the rooms of the house, almost a series of separate out-door rooms, each of which is self-contained and performs a separate function. Thus the garden extends the house into the midst of nature. At the same time it gives it a framework in nature, without which it would stand like a stranger in its surroundings. In aesthetic terms the ordered garden is to the house as the socle to the statue, the base on which it stands.

The position of the house in the garden

This means that the regularly laid-out garden must not extend merely to one side of the house, but all the way round it, so that the house appears from all angles to rest on an adequate base. When the residential front of the house faces south or south-east,

as it usually does, the non-utilitarian parts of the garden, i.e. the flower-garden and the ornamental garden, would adjoin it, facing the same way. If the domestic quarters are to the north-east, it is appropriate for the kitchen-garden to be situated beyond them in the same direction, while the area at the narrow end of the house could be used as lawns. And finally, the forecourt will be situated to the back of the house, where the drive leads in from the road. English opinion usually requires this side to be regarded as the back of the house since the whole development of the house is towards the garden side. Entry is from the north and the house faces and has its best rooms to the south. It follows automatically that as far as possible the house will be situated on the given site in such a way as to leave the largest area free for this south-facing development. This means that if the site is not large, the house will be built close to the northern boundary. The position of the house in relation to the road is entirely immaterial, since, as we have several times remarked, an English country-house has no relationship with the road, except one of complete dissociation.

The garden wall

An English estate with a house on it is always separated from the street by an impenetrable barrier, usually a high garden wall. This again reveals a peculiarity of the English, it is a way of keeping the house sacrosanct, protecting it from the common hustle and bustle of the street and making it a world of its own. This applies to all houses, even small ones. Indeed, the passer-by in the street, who sees none of the magnificence that lies behind the walls fares badly. But then what has a dwelling-house to do with passers-by in the street? And what good is it to the owner if his house can be seen by passers-by in the street? So, at least, the Englishman thinks, in contrast to many a proud owner of an estate on the continent whose one idea is to display his property and who believes that he is getting value for money only when it is a source of wonderment. Even in the densely built-up suburbs with their small houses, one does not, as in Germany, see the usual cheerless prospect of wire-netting fences through which glimmer wretched front gardens designed to be looked at – but by whom? And for what purpose? At all events the owner of the house gains nothing from them but the obligation to maintain them. And it is at least doubtful whether a street looks better with open front gardens than with walls or hedges. This is another

[21] The best book on the modern English understanding of the garden is T. H. Mawson's *The art and craft of garden making*, from which Figs. 182 and 211 are taken.*

*Mawson's book was first published in London in 1900. A small folio edition appeared in 1925, London and New York. [DS]

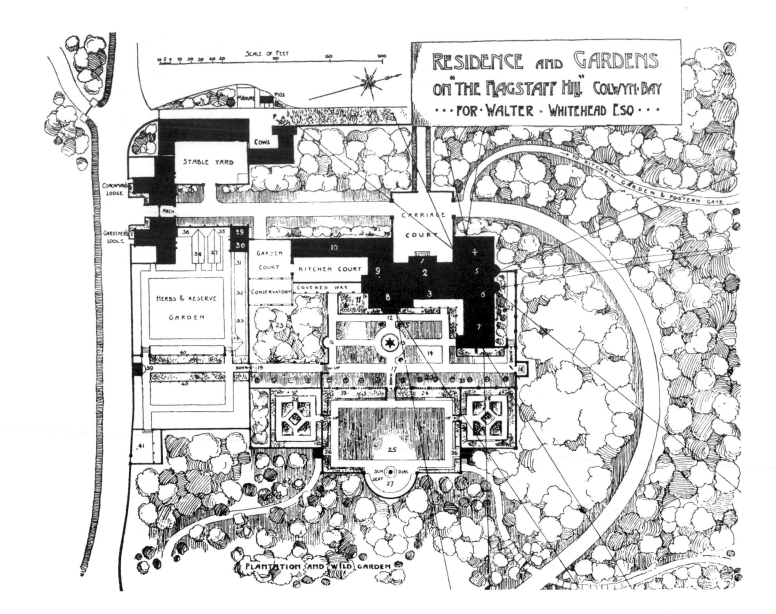

RESIDENCE AND GARDENS ON THE FLAGSTAFF HILL COLWYN-BAY ··· FOR WALTER WHITEHEAD ESQ ···

1 Entrance	21 Ornamental trees in tubs
2 Gallery	22 Lower terrace
3 Hall	23 Rock-garden
4 Billiard-room	24 Flower-beds on lower terrace
5 Staircase	25 Tennis court
6 Morning-room	26 Arbours
7 Drawing-room	27 Bay with seat and sun-dial
8 Dining-room	28 Flower-gardens
9 Butler	29/30 Potting sheds
10 Kitchen wing	31 Palm-house
11 Flower beds	32 Greenhouse for early grapes
12 Walk	33 Greenhouse for late grapes
13 Fountain	34 Greenhouse for flowers
14 Lawn	35 Greenhouse for early peaches
15 Clipped trees	36 Greenhouse for late peaches
16 Seat	37 Hothouse for flowers
17 Main terrace walk	38 Greenhouse for melons and cucumbers
18 Summer-house	39 Summer-house
19 Gate to reserve garden	40 Rose pergola
20 Grass border	41 Courtyard

182 Flagstaff Hill, Colwyn-Bay, Denbigh. Plan of garden by landscape gardener Thomas H. Mawson (from his book *The art and craft of garden making*)

example of the erroneous belief that the only way of making an effect is to reveal everything. The contrary is true. Flowering trees nodding over the garden-wall and one gable of the house emerging from a clump of trees is more exciting because it leaves far more to the imagination of the passer-by than a garden and façade as it were presented to him on a plate. Front gardens in England, where they exist, are separated by low walls, hedges or stout oak fences, so that, at least up to a certain height, the front garden is hidden from the gaze of the passer-by. Oak fences made of narrow split oaken planks, nailed vertically and so that they overlap slightly, to two wooden rails and finished off with a coping at the top, have become very popular since they were used by Norman Shaw at Bedford Park (see p. 32); indeed, because oak soon weathers to a beautiful silver-grey natural tone, it makes a pleasing and practical barrier. The entrance-gate will then be solidly constructed of wood, as in Figs. 183, 184. Apart from the rare streets that have front gardens, the favourite form of boundary for a garden in England is a high enclosing wall. And so strongly does the Englishman feel it to be his inborn right to shut himself away behind such a barrier that he would regard the remarkable ruling of the German surveyor's office that compels the householder to leave his ground open to the gaze of the passers-by as an almost unheard-of infringement of his rights.

183, 184 Garden gates in oak. Designed by C. H. B. Quennell

The garden gate

In the case of the large country-mansion it goes without saying that the land will be separated from the road by a wall. The entrance is marked by a gate, which, however, usually lacks the magnificence of the usual continental park gate with its precious wrought-ironwork. Of all the handicrafts, wrought-ironwork has always been the least cultivated and understood in England. During the Elizabethan period, when many of the decorative arts were practised to perfection, the smith produced nothing but the most primitive tracery. This situation continued until the time of Wren, who improved matters by bringing Jean Tijou, a French master ironworker, to England. Tijou remained in England and executed all the important ironwork of the time, such as gates at Hampton Court, Chatsworth, etc. Although the tradition he created persisted for a little while longer, ironwork in England did not remain at a high artistic level; it disappeared again after the middle of the eighteenth century and the English contented themselves once more with the work of mere craftsmen. Today, even on the gates of great estates, one sees none of those displays of decorative artistry that continental ideas would lead us to expect: the whole setting is modest and rustic. The craftsman's efforts seldom produce anything more than the simplest gate of iron bars; and even wooden gates of the kind recently re-introduced in imitation of the middle-class forms of the eighteenth century (Fig. 185) are considered adequate. The absence of any desire to impress is striking. Yet an attractive little gate-lodge usually stands beside the simple gateway.

The gate-lodge. Its history

There are excellent examples of lodges in English art of the earliest times. In the Gothic period, when notions of defence still clung to it, the lodge was a tall majestic building, which was

185 Entrance gate in oak. Designed by C. H. B. Quennell

186 Garden gate in oak. Designed by C. H. B. Quennell

lovingly decorated and adorned. Many such gatehouses over entrances to complexes of buildings surrounding courtyards survive in England, the best known being over the entrances to the ancient colleges of Oxford and Cambridge. In Elizabethan times, when the practice of building round a quadrangle began to disappear and a wall was usually the only boundary to the front of the quadrangle, a tall gatehouse over the entrance remained the sole survivor of the earlier complex of buildings. There are many such gatehouses, one example being the Elizabethan building at Stokesay in Shropshire (Fig. 187). Elsewhere the gatehouse had by now been shifted to the side of the entrance and symmetry now required twin buildings, as at Hardwick Hall. With the Palladian period the gatehouse either disappeared completely or was moved right away from the house to the farthest edge of the site, where it has remained ever since. Here was built a majestic park gate in the Italo-French style; it was often a brilliant structure with rich wrought-ironwork and great stone columns, beside which the gate-keeper's little house appeared somewhat dwarfed. With the advent of Neo-Classicism, under which the landscape-garden also replaced the formal garden, things changed again. The practice of making the entrance a feature of architectonic importance began to disappear and house-owners often contented themselves with a small wooden gate; but the necessity of housing the gate-keeper was often made the excuse to build a little Greek temple for the purpose, one of the exotic structures that now began to stud the garden. Such little, miniature, toy-like temples can still be seen at many park entrances in England, for they were also erected on estates where the house dates from an earlier period but where a landscape-

187 Stokesay Castle, Shropshire. Built in the 16th century. Gate-lodge

188 Gate-lodge on a Scottish estate. By R. S. Lorimer

gardener had been entrusted with remaking the gardens. With the Romantic movement came the replacement of the little temple by a, usually horrifyingly inaccurate, Gothic building. And it was not until Nesfield took the first step that lodges began to be built simply in the local vernacular style of the country revived for the purpose. Nesfield lavished special care on gate-lodges and in so doing has an almost pioneering influence on the revival of a more genuine middle-class architecture in general (p. 20).

The modern gate-lodge

Since Nesfield, the lodges of large English houses have developed most happily along the lines he laid down. These buildings are really delightful. The little house either stands detached behind the garden-wall or else one of its sides abuts on the wall. Its appearance is cheerful and attractive and some small exaggeration in its decoration and construction is countenanced and is, indeed, more commonly found in lodges than in the house itself (Figs. 188–190). Not infrequently the roof is thatched, to match what is perhaps the local village style. Few attempts have been made in England to combine the actual gate and the lodge. The idea that the lodge should be long and low – nowadays the desired form for all small English houses – would not favour the experiment. For this reason, lodges are usually single-storeyed, although they have spacious attics that can be converted into habitable rooms. The idea of the little lodge is so popular nowadays that a small building, serving, perhaps, as a gardener's cottage or as stables with accommodation for the coachman, as at New Place (Fig. 179), is often erected at the entrance even of small houses that could by their nature exist without a keeper at the gate, simply as an excuse for erecting a small building there.

The drive

The drive often still follows the pattern of the familiar twisting park track, but there is also a readiness to revive the grand straight approach of earlier days. However, the ideas of the landscape-gardener have on the whole remained intact and when architects try to persuade their clients to lay a straight drive they still encounter opposition; the winding approach road has been

189 Park-keepers' cottages, Leicester. By Edward Burgess

preserved more tenaciously than any other tradition. Early opinion always required a straight approach to the house. A fine road led from the boundary of the estate to the house, becoming under the influence of French garden-design a majestic tree-lined avenue. The visitor entering by the park gate could thus immediately see his goal, the entrance to the house (Fig. 192). Indeed, according to any naïve view this is the obvious and proper thing. The landscape idea in garden design was responsible for introducing the winding drive with the playful bends that leave the approaching visitor in the dark as to whither he is being led. Then, after he has enjoyed the impression of a primeval forest (no matter if it be a primeval forest with gravel paths) for a few minutes, the house looms up before him in one of those sudden surprise effects that are the whole pride of the landscape-gardener. This excludes every artistic idea, the idea of the proper aesthetic preparation for the impression of the house, the heightening of everyday experience into a significant experience, abolishing the idea of introduction, which is so important in works of art. One arrives without preparation, straight out of the wilderness. But although the recent revival of a formal layout for the surroundings of the house have not yet

1 WC
2 Larder
3 Courtyard
4 Coal
5 Bedroom
6 Kitchen
7 Living-room

190, 191 Norney, Godalming, Surrey. By C. F. A. Voysey. Gate-lodge and plan of ground floor

brought about the complete abolition of the much-loved drive, the course that these matters are taking in England suggests that it can only be a matter of time before it is replaced by the old straight approach. The idea can, of course, only be entertained when the site is level. If the house is on rising ground a winding drive is justified. In such cases, however, the architect may have recourse to the layout used by Norman Shaw at Leyes Wood (p. 21), in which a winding drive ends in a square architectonically designed area, where a straight approach-road begins.

A winding drive is far worse in a small house than in a large one. It is nothing short of comic here. One sees plans in which, with great difficulty, the house has been set back fifteen meters from the boundary-wall simply to make room for a winding drive.

Indeed, even the small suburban villa worth 1200 Mk. in rent often has a drive and must then have entrance and exit gates, without which the arrangement would not work. But this nonsense has fortunately now been abandoned, at least in the better type of small house. No architect nowadays would design a winding drive for houses below a certain size; the drive leads straight to the entrance and all that is needed there is space in which to turn.

The forecourt

Unlike the drive, the forecourt has generally been re-incorporated into the architectonic design. Every large and medium-sized house is provided with a rectangular courtyard on the entrance side (Figs. 179, 182, 193): it is surrounded by some

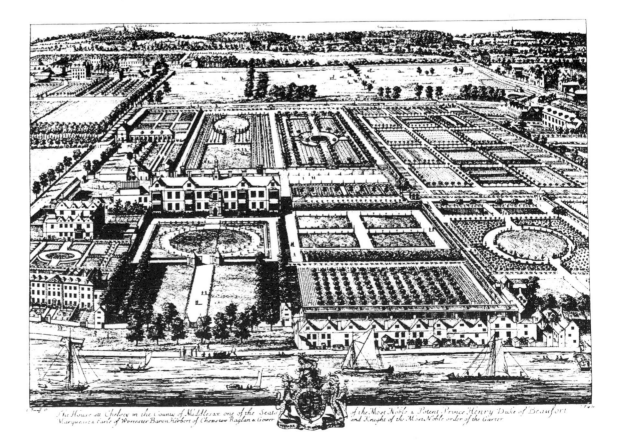

192 Plate from a book by Knyff: *Britannia Illustrata*, 1709, showing a country-house in Chelsea

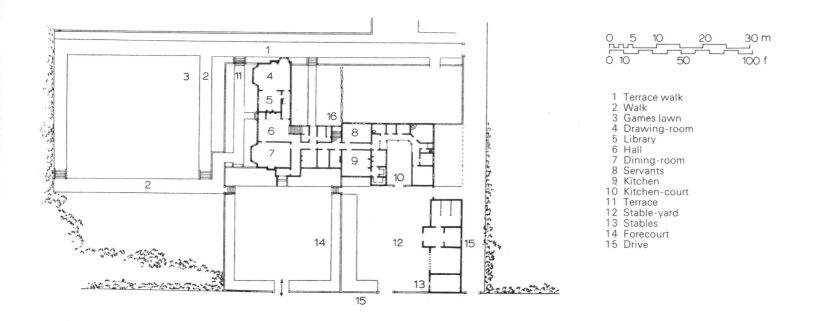

193, 194 The Close, Northallerton, Yorkshire. By W. H. Brierly. Site plan and view from forecourt

195 The Close. View with garden terrace

1 Terrace walk
2 Walk
3 Games lawn
4 Drawing-room
5 Library
6 Hall
7 Dining-room
8 Servants
9 Kitchen
10 Kitchen-court
11 Terrace
12 Stable-yard
13 Stables
14 Forecourt
15 Drive

sort of enclosure and either has an all-over gravel surface (Figs. 193, 194) or a circular lawn in the centre, or even a fountain, and has space for carriages to turn. The forecourt is usually separated from the entrance by iron railings. It is flanked on either one or two sides by wings of the house.

History

In this way a tiny fraction at least of the artistry with which the question of the approach was solved in old houses has been recovered. These houses always had not just one forecourt but often two or even three. The part of the courtyard (house-court) that lay immediately in front of the house was paved and raised a few steps above ground-level. It could be entered on foot only. It was bounded on the side of the second courtyard (forecourt) in front of it by an iron railing, before which carriages had to stop. The forecourt was a broad lawn, through which the approach road bordered by trees or plants in tubs led, usually in circular bends. It was again enclosed by iron railings or a wall and there were often elegant little houses at the corners. From the forecourt, always closely following the axis of the main entrance,

the approach road led directly to the garden entrance. A desire to be able to drive right up to the front-door in a carriage began to make itself felt in the eighteenth century. This spelled death to the house-court, which was replaced by the forecourt. Few of the old forecourt layouts have survived in their original form, but the old illustrations (Fig. 192) mentioned earlier tell us much about them. We find an astonishing variety of designs and plans for courtyards in every imaginable permutation and form. And the imaginativeness, the understanding of the artistic suitability and architectonic effectiveness in these solutions is truly remarkable; it really shows how impoverished our modern age has become when it can substitute the serpentine way beloved of the romantics for this well-considered order and obstruct the region of the front-door with miserable beds of rhododendrons.

Gardens. Elements of the old

In their treatment of the garden, designers already adhere much more closely to the old type of garden design than they have done in the matter of the approach. In particular the principles of the old art have been completely restored to their rightful place. To describe what English designers are trying to do it would in fact be necessary to begin by setting out at length the repertoire of old garden design, for the present situation is still one in which designers are drawing inspiration from the brimming fountain of earlier art and looking to see what they can turn to fresh account. Modern garden design is at the beginner's stage when the pupil is unable to use his material independently and is uncertain of its possibilities. It begins, just as the new architecture has begun, by imitating the old, and since there is a complete absence of any direct tradition, it cannot do better than, *faute de mieux*, start by re-learning the creative means of early garden design. Any one who looks with open eyes at the riches of early garden design must be both delighted and astonished at the lengths to which this art had evolved, with its multiplicity of motifs, such as terraces, flower-beds, greens, walks, belvederes, mazes, sunk gardens and hanging gardens, pergolas, ornate arbours, ponds, formal plantations, and the fine pavilions, architectonic bridges, sun-dials and decorative statuary. Most of the features of the English garden at the point of perfection that it had reached by about the beginning of the eighteenth century were, as we have said, of French or Dutch origin. Yet in the age of good garden design, English gardening in turn influenced France, most particularly in its treatment of lawns. Thus the bowling-green was adopted in France, name and all, and then in Germany, and was immediately further developed on the continent until it culminated in the open-air theatre with its grassy tiers and hedges for wings that became so popular during the eighteenth century.

The early gardens surrounded the house on all sides and the individual parts were distributed in a variety of different ways. The house formed only a small central point within the large area which lay at the designer's disposal to exercise his innate human delight in tectonic creativity and to form a garden. The domestic quarters were then usually grouped round the courtyard or else they lay immediately next to the courtyard round a yard of their own (known as a base-court). This architectural complex was then surrounded on all sides by the wide expanse of gardens, without which no country-house of the time was conceivable (Fig. 192).

Elements of the new garden

Present-day expectations are far more modest. Most gardens consist of no more than a formal layout of flower-gardens and lawns on the residential side of the house with a similarly formal kitchen-garden beyond it to one side, while the rest of the site is left in the state which the landscape-gardeners of earlier years had given the garden as a whole. With the progressive re-emergence of a more genuine artistic understanding, the formal garden is in the process of extending further and further into the landscape-garden and coming closer to the goal to which the modern English domestic architect aspires when he designs a garden: a formal layout within clearly visible boundaries, but beyond them wilderness, i.e. unspoiled nature in the form of wood, meadow, heathland, field or whatever it may be. Some garden-designers, such as Miss Jekyll, the celebrated writer on gardens, have a strong preference for the woodland garden altogether and restrict the formal layout to the immediate vicinity of the house. The wood is then cultivated as a wood, which means that natural woodland flowers are sown in great profusion in clumps, so that there is always a carpet of blooms to enjoy. The natural conditions of growth are everywhere improved upon and so nature is assisted, though in such a way as to avoid falsifying it by artificial scenery or settings. Woodland and meadow remain true to their natural state. Other garden-designers – these are mainly architects – extend the architectonic garden further outwards and are again treating the wider surroundings of the house formally, in the old way (Figs. 179–182, 196, 198).

Whichever style is chosen, every garden that is laid out today possesses at least three of the features that go to make up the formal garden: terrace, flower-beds and lawns. Of gardens with practical functions there are invariably fruit and vegetable gardens. Beyond this minimum of formal elements, designers of new gardens like to bring back all sorts of features from the old, although one cannot yet quote an established repertoire.

The terrace. Its significance

No English house, even a small one, lacks its terrace, the necessity for which was conceded even by the landscape-gardeners of the nineteenth century. An area raised above the surrounding ground, on to which one steps straight out of a room, is not as immensely important as it is merely on account of the view of the garden it affords; it is also important as regards the architectonic effect of the house. Thanks to the terrace, the house appears to rest on a stable base that sets it off to considerable effect. It also eliminates that feeling of insalubrity and damp that would be experienced if the residential rooms were to open straight on to the garden soil. The English consider it absolutely essential that the house should have a fitting and dignified entrance into the garden and they would never accept

196 Pressridge, Forrest Row, Sussex. Garden designed by Thomas H. Mawson

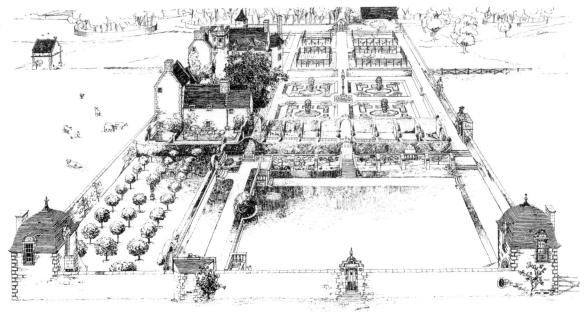

197　Earlshall, Fifeshire, Scotland.
Restored by R. S. Lorimer. New garden

the raised ground floor that is customary on the continent and from which a kind of chicken-ladder that is more of a barrier than a means of approach leads down into the garden. The practice of building the house without cellars derives in part from the urge for contact with the ground. English opinion is thus categorical in its conviction that the terrace is the indispensable link between the two almost equally important parts of the country-mansion, the house and the garden.

Raised walks

It is relatively easy to construct a terrace if the ground falls away on the residential side of the house, indeed it comes about almost of its own accord. But if this is not the case, if the ground is absolutely level, the architect is unlikely to adopt the obvious expedient of raising the house on stilts. He is more likely to construct an artificial terrace by excavating the ground in front of the chosen area by some 30 to 50 cm., thus creating a kind of sunk flower-garden. Sunk gardens, a favourite motif of the early garden-designers, have again acquired a certain popularity in the modern garden. The natural lie of the land frequently lends itself to this treatment and the soil that is removed is often very welcome elsewhere. The old garden-designers were fond of constructing raised walks round the flower-garden; they also liked to put a second terrace, a sort of counterpart to the main terrace, facing the house and giving not only a prospect back over the garden but providing an opportunity to enjoy a view of the house. This earth-bank also afforded a view over the garden-wall, for which purpose it was built higher than the house-terrace and the lateral walks. Modern architects design higher lateral walks and second terraces only when the ground in front of the house rises, in which case the solution suggests itself almost spontaneously.

Layout and construction of the terrace

The particular construction of house-terraces varies enormously and depends on circumstances. The terrace is bounded on the garden side either by a retaining wall with balustrade or a grassy slope with a clipped hedge on the upper edge. The wall is always preferred and, despite its not inconsiderable cost, is said to be cheaper in the long run than the grassy slope, for this involves the continuing expense of upkeep. In the case of very low terraces the wall rises only to the height of a seat (42 cm.) above ground-

level, but if it rises higher than that a proper parapet is required. This is always pierced so that it shall not block the view of the lower garden. Wherever possible the width of the terrace is generous, 25 ft. (7.60 m.) being considered the minimum. The terrace must be properly drained. This is done by sloping it slightly towards the garden. Where the ground rises widthways along the front of the house it will be necessary to slope the terrace more or less steeply in that direction, since if it were laid horizontally, the anterior line of the parapet would, by a well-known optical illusion, appear oblique. A terrace is often grassed over and plants in tubs are placed along its edges in summer, as at Avon Tyrell; some terraces even have flower-beds (Fig. 195). These are fairly small and symmetrical, while the paths, the total area of which must be sufficiently large to differentiate the terrace from the garden, are flagged or paved. This type of path is always preferred to gravel paths for terraces with flower-beds, and it has recently become fashionable to pave garden paths and forecourts with flagstones or bricks, doubtless because the appearance of such paths have a more marked architectonic and a more strictly formal appearance than the usual gravel paths.

The flower-garden. (Ornamental garden)

Steps lead down at suitable points into the garden below the terrace. According to circumstance this may be a flower-garden, lawns or even a second grassy terrace extending in front of the upper or promenade terrace. A garden with beds laid out in symmetrical figures, the modern form of the old parterre, usually lies at the foot of the terrace. If this is the case the designer will naturally omit the flower-beds on the terrace itself so as not to squander his means, and, indeed, this type of layout removes the flower-garden from its rightful position in front of the terrace on to the terrace itself. The old parterre with its flowers was the show-piece of garden-design, for indeed the earliest gardens were always first and foremost flower-gardens. The Elizabethan garden was a flower-garden of the most highly evolved kind, in which the favourite flowers of the day, especially the pink, were fittingly displayed. But at this period too beds were laid out in fantastic shapes or box borders were used to divide a large bed into a geometrical pattern, forming the extremely intricate so-called knot-garden, of which old gardening books are full. The Elizabethan garden was replaced by the French parterre, the main purpose of which had been from the beginning to divide up

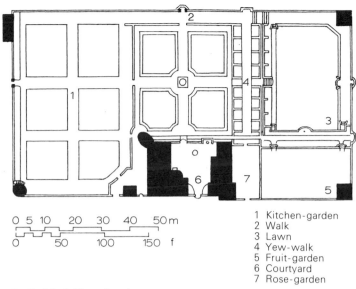

1 Kitchen-garden
2 Walk
3 Lawn
4 Yew-walk
5 Fruit-garden
6 Courtyard
7 Rose-garden

198   Earlshall. Plan of garden

199   Earlshall. Flower-garden

a large area into exact rectangular and geometric compartments. Desire for formal effect so far outweighed notions of plant cultivation and flower growing that the individual compartments were often merely filled with coloured soils. This marked the beginning of the over-refinement of the flower-garden that in its final form was one of the main reasons why the architectonic garden in general gave way to the landscape-garden.

As we have said, the modern flower-garden has restored flowers and plants to their rightful position. But this is not to say that its character as ornamental garden has suffered. The flowers that are needed for the house, in particular those used to decorate the dinner-table, are grown not here but in the kitchen-garden. The commonest way of parcelling out the flower-garden is the old traditional manner of the French garden; that is to say, it has a central walk and two, four or six large squares which are in turn sub-divided into geometric figures, usually introducing diagonals and circles (Figs. 200, 201). The flower-beds have borders of wood or terracotta and often follow the old style in being banked up to a considerable height above the path. Paths are usually gravelled. But sometimes they are paved with flints (Fig. 199) or bricks to produce a patterned effect. Flower-beds are not the only motifs in these ornamental gardens; there are also lawns and such shrubs as are particularly suitable on account of their basically geometric form. Fountains, statuary and every kind of garden ornament belonging to the old tradition of the French ornamental garden may be found here. If the site lends itself the flower-garden may comprise several terraces. If it lies at a higher level than the main part of the garden it is known as a hanging-garden.

Specialised flower-gardens

One result of the love of flowers that has now become so very keenly developed again is that individual species of flower are planted together in segregated beds so that they may be cultivated specially. In accordance with the basic ideas of modern garden layout, these beds are clearly marked off and surrounded by hedges or other borders, within which they in turn are laid out symmetrically. The commonest of these specialised gardens, and one to be found nowadays in almost every garden, is the rose-garden. It is often laid out as a sunk garden and usually consists of rose-bushes planted in beds in a

lawn. There are also lily-gardens, rock or alpine gardens, so-called American gardens (containing plants native to America) and, a recent development, gardens containing historical collections of flowers, such as a Shakespeare garden (containing flowers of Shakespeare's time) and a Tennyson garden, with the flowers loved and celebrated by the poet. Fig. 199 illustrates a garden of this kind. Another type of specialised garden is the so-called wild garden that one encounters here and there. Flowers of meadow and forest are allowed to grow there in random confusion and shrubs and mountain plants are introduced. Wild gardens existed in Bacon's time and he mentions them as forming a large part of his ideal garden. They must, of course, be enclosed within sharply drawn limits and architectonically separated.

The lawn

The most indispensable part of an English garden has always been the lawn. The English climate particularly favours the growing of lawns, which flourish there more luxuriantly than in any continental country. They retain the same lush freshness throughout the year during the mild winter and moderate summer, and are so indestructible that even in crowded municipal parks the public is allowed to tread on them at will.
The idea that in order to preserve lawns people must be kept off them is entirely unknown in England. At most the edges are protected in public gardens by small hoops placed at short intervals over the edges and little notices warn: 'Please keep off the grass-edge'.

The bowling-green

It was only to be expected that such a heaven-sent gift of bounteous nature as the English lawn would be likely to be made one of the special beauties of the garden. In England in the old days, furthermore, games were often played in the open air and, since nothing could have been more inviting than the lawns, special care was taken to see that they were smooth, level and meticulously tended. Thus, from the sixteenth century onwards, we find the bowling-green appearing regularly in the English garden as a hedged area for a certain game, much played formerly, with wooden balls, or woods, which have an eccentric lead weight to make them run a curved course. The bowling-green occurs in ground-plans of the most varied types. But it always has a smooth grassy surface, surrounded by a walk raised

200 North Cliff, Filey, Yorkshire. By W. H. Brierley. Flower-garden

Games pitches

Later, when the landscape-gardener remodelled the large English gardens, most of the bowling-greens and formal lawns fell victim to his innovatory zeal. He introduced artificially undulating ground and the only quality the lawn was permitted to retain was that of 'background' to the pictorial effects of his clumps of trees. But the English fondness for sport and activity in the open-air, for which a level, rectangular pitch was essential, told against him. Rectangular, level lawns had to be laid out in all gardens, for lawn-tennis, croquet, cricket, etc., and even in the otherwise most thoroughgoing landscape-gardens they always form a kind of architectonic backbone. The result has been that the lawn, the most characteristic feature of the English garden, has at all times been the chief adornment of the immediate surroundings of the house. Today it is still valued almost more highly than the ornamental flower-garden and, where space is limited and there is no room for both, a broad green lawn is laid immediately below the terrace; and as we stand at one of the front windows and allow our eyes to roam we have that impression of precious peace and that sense of quietude and composure that surrounds one on an English country-estate. If the drawing-room is situated on a corner the designer will prefer to lay out the flower-garden in front of the windows on the narrow side of the house so as to keep the residential side for the grassy terraces. Where there is ample space it is probably better to site the games-lawns some distance away, perhaps in a lateral direction, instead of sacrificing the main lawn in front of the house to the sportsmen.

The commonest of these games-lawns is the lawn-tennis-court. In English terms it measures 50 ft. by 100 ft. (15.25 by 30.50 m.), added to which, whenever possible, a space of at least 7 ft. (2.14 m.) wide should be left all round. It is considered essential for all lawns to have a proper depth of soil beneath them and to be properly drained, but more especially is this important for lawns on which games are played, for they are required to dry out as quickly as possible, even after downpours of rain.

Ponds and fountains

Of the elements of early garden-design that have been revived,

some 75 cm. above the level of the green and bounded towards the lower level by a slope, and usually broadening out at the narrow ends into semi-circles. The walk was intended for the spectators. The whole is enclosed by a dense, close-clipped fairly high hedge with bays at regular intervals for seats or groups of seats and tables. Until the eighteenth century the bowling-green was one of the most welcoming adornments of the English garden and has recently been revived and become very popular (see Fig. 181), although usually in the form of a croquet-lawn. As we have said, it was the first and most important borrowing from England on the part of the continent. And with it appreciation and cultivation of the lawn as an artistic motif in the garden in itself passed to the continent. When Le Nôtre formulated the laws of the French garden he was already familiar with a *parterre à l'anglaise*, i.e. one in which the beds are simply lawns. And from then onwards grassy slopes, etc. became a permanent part of the reperfoire of the French gardener as well as the English.

201 House near Bedford.
By C. E. Mallows and Grocock.
Flower-garden

202 New Place, Haslemere, Surrey. By C. F. A. Voysey
(See also Figs. 160, 179.) View from lawn

203 New Place. View from flower-terrace

least use has probably been made of water. It is true that ponds and ornamental fountains have never been particularly popular in England, probably because of the damp climate. There is enough moisture in the air without collecting more on the ground. Early country-mansions always had a fish-pond which would be divided into several compartments to suit the needs of the various fish. It served the practical purpose of providing fish for the table. This pond later developed into an ornamental pond, which, like the fish-pond, was naturally a formal structure. Under French influence, fine ornamental waters were laid on in England too, as is shown by the surviving examples in the gardens at Hampton Court. The landscape-gardener transformed the formal pond into his apparently fortuitous lake. While this may have been permissible in a large park, the cement-lined puddle that simulates the Lake of Lucerne in cartographic reduction in every tiny villa garden has become one of the greatest absurdities of his art.

Modern garden-designers are once again making use of the formal pond, occasionally in the shape of a lily-pond, or they may run a long narrow canal down the length of the lawn, as in Fig. 181. A fountain sometimes forms the central feature of a flower-garden, a vegetable-garden is never without its well, or even a fountain, which here serve primarily practical purposes. Yet the fact remains that all these features are used sparingly in the English garden.

Arbours. Pergolas

By contrast, the arbour, a favourite motif of the early English garden, is once again being used with considerable frequency. In early times arbours of all kinds were known as bowers, but a distinction was later drawn between the leafy walk, which then became known as a bower, or, especially later on, a pergola, and the arbour. The arbour was one of the principal features of the old Gothic garden and acquired many sentimental attributes which appear with great frequency in medieval verse. Especially in the form of a covered walk, it persisted into later times as an important shade-giving element. Bacon devotes particular attention to the pergola in his essay on gardens. Pergolas, either as central walks or walks running parallel to the garden-walls, were a constant feature of the garden before French influence began to make itself felt. Later they became rather less common. But valuable examples still survive in old gardens. Nowadays

arbours and pergolas are constructed in wrought-iron, which, harking back to the French-influenced art of the eighteenth century, has become popular again and has seen some charming developments (Figs. 204, 205)[22].

Clipped hedges and trees

The most typical features of the old garden, clipped hedges and trees, have also been used to a considerable extent in the newer garden. A strange inclination towards the bizarre, taking the form of a fondness for all kinds of curious figures, is apparent in old garden-design, particularly in England. A few gardens of this kind have survived, one example being the remarkable garden at Levens Hall, Westmorland, where the strangest configurations, such as cubes, spheres, mushrooms, moss-huts and lanterns have been clipped from yew; they are irregularly dotted about the garden and give the whole thing a rather childish, almost idiotic appearance. These extravaganzas are ascribed to Dutch influence, though with what justification is not entirely clear. Examples like Levens Hall are important today in that they enable us to understand why it was precisely in England that the old geometrical garden was to be thrown to the winds. It was here that the new landscape movement began. Yet even in the old garden such excesses found only very limited approval; thus Bacon in his essay on gardens writes drily 'I do not like images to be cut out of Juniper or other garden stuff; they be for children'. The fact that modern garden-designers will have nothing to do with creations such as those at Levens Hall scarcely needs stressing. The point about topiary work is its ordered architectonic form, which the artist, taking the material that is to hand – in this case bushes – uses and applies just as he would any other material and to other architectonic ends. Clipped hedges are the walls by means of which the garden-designer delimits his areas. They also lend themselves to rhythmic repetition, as with certain crowning-pieces, indentations and box-like configurations, just as clipped trees, by repetition of the same geometric form,

[22] Much credit must go to the manufacturer John P. White in Bedford (the Pyghtle Works) for his improvements to all kinds of garden-furniture, as well as garden-gates, fences, etc. His practice of commissioning the best artists to design for him and of issuing tasteful catalogues (from which Figs. 204, 205 and 216–220 are taken) to make known and disseminate his artistically outstanding pieces may be described as exemplary. This, of course, assumes a certain standard of taste on the part of the public. John P. White's commercial success shows, however, that his confidence has not been misplaced.

204 Pergola in lattice-work. Designed by W. A. Forsyth

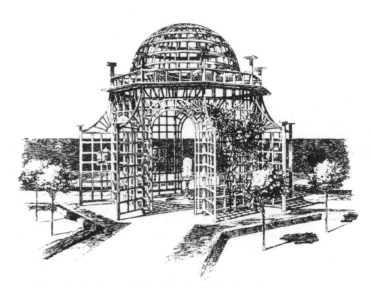

205 Arbour in lattice-work. Designed by W. A. Forsyth

establish certain points in the geometric composition of the garden. Thus topiary work is one of the principal elements of garden-design in general, the indispensable means of establishing form. Such are the considerations that led to the use of topiary work in the good examples of early garden-design, of which Figs. 206–208 provide some idea. More recent garden-designers use clipped hedges and trees with the same intention.

In yew, holly, box and many other plants the English flora produces the best bushes for evergreen hedges. Certain trees grow naturally in a fairly regular form well suited to ornamental gardens. Yet forms that are exactly clipped to shape are essential to the formal garden. A favourite way of making a hedge a decorative feature is to give it a rounded contour, either concave or convex, at the top (Figs. 196, 201). The angle formed by two hedges meeting at right-angles may be crowned with a pyramidal form. Other free finials are popular, most particularly the topiary peacock, a borrowing from early garden-design. Another very popular decorative motif is a semi-circular archway placed at regular intervals across a path. These are formed by training two bushes to grow together over a constructed wooden framework. Another favourite ploy is to create bays along a hedge by means of buttress-like walls; this produces a fine festive effect, as in the walk at Earlshall, which, incidentally, was planted quite recently. In addition to their architectonic purpose, hedges in English gardens very often serve the practical purpose of a protective fence. In the old days a suitably high and well-grown hedge was considered the best type of enclosure because it was unscalable. Land is still today fenced with hedges; a favourite practice is to plant them behind the iron railings of the garden in front of the house, where they provide something the railings cannot offer: seclusion.

Bordered walks

Modern English designers use the old tree-lined avenues, of which the French were so proud, but sparingly. They were too purely majestic in intention and seem unsuitable in modern eyes if they do not actually lead to an imposing termination. Yet designers do not, of course, despise the splendid perspectival effect that can be achieved by a walk with some kind of border on both sides. They lay out long walks between hedges with lawns to

right and left, or sometimes the walk itself is grassy and leads to a summer-house or other focal point (Fig. 206). In the fruit- or vegetable-garden espaliers may line a path on both sides to provide a suitable border.

The kitchen-garden

The kitchen-garden is one of the few parts of the garden that has retained its old geometrical form unchanged through the shifts in taste that have taken place during the last centuries, simply because it was never thought to have any connection with art. As in the case of a few other utilitarian objects which have escaped the attempts at over-refinement of the past century, we see in the kitchen-garden a fragment of ancient culture that has remained unfalsified. The landscape-gardener scornfully dismissed the kitchen-garden and thus enabled it to survive. In many old country-mansions today, therefore, the kitchen-garden is the only part of the garden that can be viewed with satisfaction. Not, however, in every respect, for it is nowadays usually fringed by greenhouses that are not exactly things of beauty in their modern form.

Present-day efforts are directed towards re-incorporating the kitchen-garden and fruit-garden into the general garden and making them as inviting to enter as the other parts of the garden.

206 Old Place, Lindfield, Sussex. Clipped hedges

The vegetable-garden is laid out as a rectangle with the long axis running from east to west. The main requirement is for a fertile and sunny position. It is usually enclosed on all sides with walls which provide space for training espalier fruit-trees. The south wall is lower than the others to allow full sunshine into the garden (Fig. 212). The area is usually divided by two broad paths crossing one another at right-angles in the centre, and there are also narrower paths running parallel to the enclosing walls and leaving narrow beds between themselves and the walls. To one side of the central paths is a narrow border of flowers and behind it a low trellis for growing dwarf fruit. At the point of intersection of the paths there will be a well or at least a pond (Fig. 179).

Greenhouses. The garden courtyard and buildings

The north side of the vegetable-garden is usually occupied by greenhouses. The English country-house is extraordinarily rich in greenhouses of every variety. Not only are all sorts of rare flowers cultivated, but grapes, peaches and vegetables are grown in greenhouses because these delicacies should always be eaten fresh and undamaged by transport, which also usually robs them of some of their aroma. Even small country-houses will have two different greenhouses for grapes (early and late-ripening), one for flowers and palms and one or even two for (early and late) peaches. On large country-estates not only are all these greenhouses large, but there are additional houses for muscat-grapes, melons and cucumbers, mushrooms, bananas and pineapples, figs and nectarines, cherries and plums; also for ferns, azaleas, hyacinths, orchids and innumerable other horticultural hobbies. It would be hard to imagine a more splendid set of greenhouses than those at Welbeck Abbey, the Duke of Portland's seat, where, in addition to numerous other houses for flowers, there is one long greenhouse devoted exclusively to the cultivation of a certain species of carnation. The kitchen-garden at Welbeck Abbey with its exceptionally extensive greenhouse complex covers an area of thirteen hectares.

In average-sized schemes consisting, as we have said, of a plant-house and a few sections for grapes and peaches, these parts are so arranged that the plant-house forms the centre and projects like a bay window (Fig. 210). Owners prefer a self-contained scheme because it simplifies and reduces the cost of heating. Attached to the plant-houses there is always a suitably large area

207 Above left: Meslington Hall, Yorkshire. Terrace with mature clipped trees (after *Country Life*)
208 Above: Brickwall, Sussex. Clipped yew-trees (after *Country Life*)
209 Below: Terrace with entrance to kitchen garden. By Thomas H. Mawson

210 Typical greenhouse complex

for re-potting plants; and the vegetable-garden must have a tool-shed, space for compost-heaps and the hotbed frames. Larger schemes also contain areas for storing fruit, one for seeds, one for root-vegetables, space for fuel and an office for the head gardener, etc. These parts of the complex are usually situated round a little garden courtyard so as not to spoil the pleasant appearance of the garden itself. The gardener's residence is also situated in this courtyard. Fig. 211 illustrates a good average example of a layout of this kind.

Although the ice-house does not actually belong with the garden, it usually forms one of the elements of the buildings of the kitchen-garden. In England, where our hot summers are unknown, it plays a less important part than it does on the continent or in America. The average English household can go the whole summer through without ice, especially as the English are not as fond of iced drinks as the Americans. In fact the custom of chilling drinks is unknown in England. Yet the larger country-mansions need ice for keeping food and therefore always have an ice-house. The gardener usually has charge of it and superintends it, together with the other buildings in his care.[23]

The commonest greenhouses are still factory-made and are often hideous to behold. Yet the realisation is gradually dawning that even in greenhouses practical considerations may be combined with beauty; and hand in hand with endeavours to re-incorporate the kitchen-garden into the general garden go attempts on the part of architects to give greenhouses a more agreeable appearance (Fig. 210). That this is not impossible is proved by the greenhouses of the eighteenth century, the ancestor of which was the old orangery.

[23] For information on the layout of these buildings see F. A. Fawkes: *Horticultural buildings*, 1881.

1 Hothouse
2 Orchids
3 Peaches
4 Uncovered walk
5 Flowers
6 Vinery
7 Office
8 Greenhouse
9 Vinery
10 Peaches
11 Cold-frame
12 Gardener's cottage
13 Frames
14 To fruit-garden
15 Turning-space for vehicles
16 Shed
17 Heating
18 Potting-shed
19 Stores
20/21 Kitchen-garden

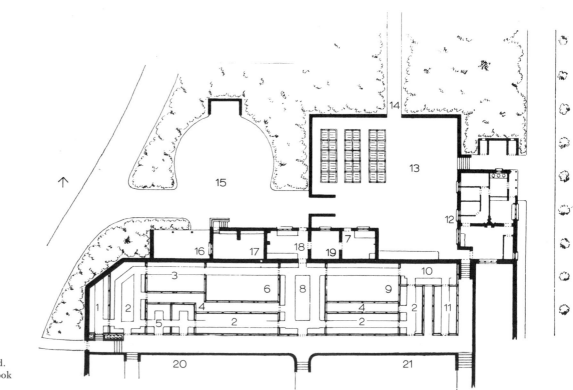

211 Holhird, Windermere, Westmorland.
By Thomas H. Mawson. Plan (from his book
The art and craft of garden-making)

212 The Orchards, nr Godalming, Surrey. By E. L. Lutyens.
(See also Figs. 121–125.) South end of kitchen-garden

The fruit-garden

As with the kitchen-garden, so with the fruit-garden, architects are again giving it its own individual layout and making it a pleasure to enter. It is obvious that this can be done easily with a little organisation and care. In the smaller house the main emphasis is in fact on the vegetable- and fruit-gardens and architects try to combine these utilitarian gardens with the lawn and terrace to form a pleasing whole.

The smaller garden of earlier times was undoubtedly planned in this way and in country districts it can still be found in its unaltered form. Perhaps the old parsonage garden shows most clearly what the gardens round our houses were like originally. It was not until the nineteenth century with all its artificiality – in which the landscape-gardener with his artificial nature played his full part – that undulating lawns scattered with rhododendron bushes, serpentine paths bordered with geraniums aimlessly wandering through them, absurd imitation rocks looking as though someone had mislaid a waggon-load of stones, began to be seen as something nobler than these truly natural, perfectly sound creations of the human gardener's hand and of human industry.

Gazebos. Architectonic ornament

Few of the architectonic embellishments that adorned the gardens of the past have so far been revived in modern times. The movement is probably still too young to have reached this advanced stage of development. One of the principal adornments of the early gardens was the gazebo. It usually stood on the raised second terrace and therefore at the end of the garden and was a two-storeyed building of which the ground-floor was accessible from the garden and the upper floor from the terrace. The windows of the upper floor were above the garden-wall and commanded an uninterrupted view over the countryside. Where there was a view-point in the form of one of the popular rounded hillocks or 'mounts' the gazebo stood at its summit. Many fewer of these garden-houses have survived in England than in Germany because the English landscape-gardener of the turn of the eighteenth-nineteenth centuries was almost universally given a free hand to destroy the beauties of the old garden. Exotic rarities, such as Chinese pagodas, Greek temples or Gothic ruins were put in their place. The nineteenth century saw the emergence of those miserable log-built, 'picturesque' summer-houses that were set down at random on the lawns. They were the

final step backwards and mark the sad level of garden-appointments that prevails today in many German gardens, where they are common.

Summer-houses in more recent English gardens are still fairly primitive in construction but are architectonically more rational. As yet no real use for them has evolved such as existed in the eighteenth century, when people liked to retire into a summer-house and, indeed, conducted part of their social lives there. Present-day owners are content with little wooden huts containing a bench and table or with diminutive rustic chalets with thatched roofs like those at Voysey's New Place (Figs. 213, 215). And there is as yet no sign in the new gardens of the architectonic bridges, monumental staircases, grottos and other such favourite features of the old gardens.

Sun-dials

But there is one old motif that has been revived with enthusiasm: this is the sun-dial. Probably no garden laid out in England today lacks its sun-dial; the science of its construction has been wholly recovered and there are experts who specialise in setting them up. The base is usually made of stone, the dial itself of cast bronze. The whole thing is a small architectonic ornament that forms the centre-piece of one of the gardens, such as the rose-garden, flower-garden, the lawn or terrace, and is usually situated at the crossing of two or more paths (Figs. 200, 201, 202, 214, 216). Excellent prototypes for this favourite feature of the garden occur in almost inexhaustible variety in early garden-design.

Statues and other decorations in lead

Statues and other three-dimensional decorations, in which the French garden is so rich, have always been of minor importance in England, where there was virtually no visual art before the eighteenth century. Then, in the gardens of the eighteenth century, statues and other decorations made their appearance in a most singular form, namely cast lead. Lead existed in quantity in England and was therefore a readily available material. A native industry grew up that was conversant with methods of counteracting the disadvantages of the material and means of inhibiting the pliancy of the statues – despite which one sees lead statues in old gardens that bow lower and lower as the years pass, often with extraordinarily comic effect. The statues first cast in lead were usually copies from the antique. During the early eighteenth century most of the better examples of the art of lead-casting were made at the celebrated lead-works of the Dutchman John van Nost in Piccadilly in London. He was probably responsible also for the elaborate vases, urns, etc. decorated in the French and Italian styles which appeared from that time onwards in English gardens; and perhaps also for the shepherds and shepherdesses in eighteenth-century dress, some of them extremely well modelled, which, considering the state of English art at the time, can hardly be regarded as native designs. It is well known that lead offers excellent resistance to the weather and takes on a pleasant pale grey patina, so that these lead statues and urns, of which old English gardens are still full, constitute a very good form of garden decoration. Besides these ornaments, lead was much used in English gardens for large cisterns, the sides of which are handsomely decorated in relief. The ornament is usually genuinely English and they almost always carry the date of manufacture.

The dove-cote

The dove-cote is another object that often appears in modern gardens (Fig. 218). By its nature it should really appear in the

213 New Place, Haslemere, Surrey. By C. F. A. Voysey. (See also Figs. 160, 179, 202, 203.) Summer-house

214 North Cliff, Filey, Yorkshire. By W. H. Brierley. (See also Fig. 200.) Sundial

215 New Place, Haslemere, Surrey. By C. F. A. Voysey. (See also Figs. 160, 179, 202, 203, 213.) Summer-house

domestic yard but its agreeable contours also make it a suitable ornament for a garden; and in fact dove-cotes used to occur in old gardens either on their own or in the upper part of a small building, of which the rest was used for other purposes, such as an aviary, tool-shed or even a gazebo.

Garden-furniture

Great attention has also been paid recently to furniture for the garden, especially garden seats and tables. Designers have returned with happy results to the wooden forms of the eighteenth century, which have been adapted to present needs and to some extent modernised, thus giving them new life (Figs. 217, 219). This wooden furniture is replacing the iron objects – the forms of which were sometimes inconvenient and always inhospitable and alien to the character of the garden – which used to fill the gardens of the past. The wooden furniture is painted white, or sometimes green or yet again left in its natural state. Old forms have also been revived, with most fortunate results, for the tubs which contain the shrubs for the terrace (Fig. 220).

Thus we note in the English art of garden-design, as in all the arts of living, a new departure, an effort to reverse the absence of art and culture that had overtaken the world with the new social conditions of the nineteenth century. Here too an eager attempt to recover the remains of the old tradition that had disappeared in the eighteenth century, here too a longing for the culture of our ancestors with its formal certainties and full-bloodedness that seemed to exist as a matter of course. And this in a country in which the aristocracy did not founder on the revolutionary wave of the end of the eighteenth century but rode out the storm, a country in which there was no break but a peaceful transformation. As a result of this peaceful march of events, England has also been the first country to be able to consider what it owes to itself; and in both house-building and garden-design she has for several decades now been seeking to return to a steadier course, in both cases through a revival of local tradition.

As has happened with house-building, these circumstances will entirely of their own accord produce something new in the way of garden-design. In England they do not fret to produce something new, they do not seek to wring a new style out of the present; on the contrary, they live in amity with the old. The ever-present undercurrent of sound commonsense and the catalyst of new conditions produce innovations quite automatically, they come of their own accord.

The old garden, from which the English are now eagerly learning, was the product of a different society and a different philosophy. The new garden will quite naturally become something different. We cannot tell from the present phase of development what the end-product will be. But one thing is certain: it will be formal and orderly, its future will lie in rhythmic form and its principles will not be those of the contemporary landscape-garden but those of the old regular garden plan.

We may certainly envy the English, from whom the errors in which we ourselves are still wholly entangled originally sprang, for the fact that this is the firm conviction of all who are educated in matters of art.

216 Sun-dial. Designed by W. A. Forsyth

217 Garden-furniture in white painted wood. Designed by C. H. B. Quennell

219 Garden seat in white painted wood. Designed by C. H. B. Quennell

218 Dove-cote. Designed by W. A. Forsyth

220 Plant tub. Designed by W. A. Forsyth

C. The smaller country-house

Great boom in house-building

The great majority of the houses eligible for consideration as works of art that are being built today are smaller country-houses containing between two and four reception rooms and between four and ten bedrooms and ancillary rooms and costing from 20,000 M to 100,000 M.* Most English architects are employed in building this sort of house; their houses are springing up in areas of fine scenery throughout the country, and especially in the more outlying environs of London, in Kent and Surrey and on the south and east coasts they are thick on the ground. Not only do they represent the best in contemporary English architectural practice but they contain what is probably the best in modern English art as a whole. If one thinks of all the branches of modern English art one comes to the conclusion that the best and most attractive work is to be found in the small country-house.

Rise of the middle-class country-house

The fact that these country-houses are being built in large numbers is due in great part to the new attitude to the country and to nature that has been made possible by modern conditions of communication, particularly the railways. The large country-houses of the past were inhabited continuously, if not throughout the year, at least for most of it.† The small houses in the country, however, were only the homes of the resident rural population and differed from the urban home as radically as the rural population differed from the city dwellers. In England from the 1860s onwards, however, members of the middle-class

*Between £1000 and £5000 at the time. [DS]
†See the two recent studies by Mark Girouard: *The Victorian Country House*, London, 1971, and *Life in the English Country House*, London, 1978. [DS]

urban population began to move further out into the country surrounding the city, taking advantage of the facilities of the railways. The first to flee the city were not the worst elements; indeed, some had artistic interests and expected their houses to be something more than mere roofs over their heads. Morris's house at Bexley Heath (p. 17) was the first house of this kind to claim artistic and individual quality. Besides Morris's architect Philip Webb, the others who applied good design to the middle-class country-house were, as we have seen, Nesfield and Shaw; and Shaw in particular exerted an immense influence with his houses in Bedford Park, which showed the man of modest means that he too could own a tasteful house (p. 30ff.).

The weekend house

Yet that movement did not produce quite the boom that is affecting the smaller country-house at the present time. Despite the fact that they lay further out of town and had a character of their own, these houses were still a form of suburban house. There were two circumstances that opened up yet another new opportunity for the smaller country-house to spread right across the country and to increase enormously in numbers: the recent growth of prosperity among the middle classes, and the great wave of new enthusiasm for nature and the rural life which has been noticeable in England in recent decades (p. 60). The result was the 'weekend house', in which the weekend, i.e. the period from Friday to Monday, is regularly spent. A weekend house may lie further out, for the journey to it is a weekly rather than a daily one. At the same time it obviates the necessity for special arrangements for summer holidays, for the family lives there throughout the fine season (only the man with his business in the city spends the mid-week days there). In fact the fashion for owning a weekend house stems in large part from the custom of visiting summer resorts. So universal has the habit become with

1 WC	10 Kitchen	19 Washing-place
2 Meat-larder	11 Chef	20 Dining-room
3 Cupboard	12 Scullery	21 Front-hall
4 Ice	13 Still-room	22 Library
5 Silver	14 Cleaning-room	23 Hall
6 Larder	15 Servant	24 Drawing-room
7 Lift	16 Steward	25 Bicycles
8 Coal	17 Corridor	26 Entry
9 Courtyard	18 Pantry	27 Servants' hall

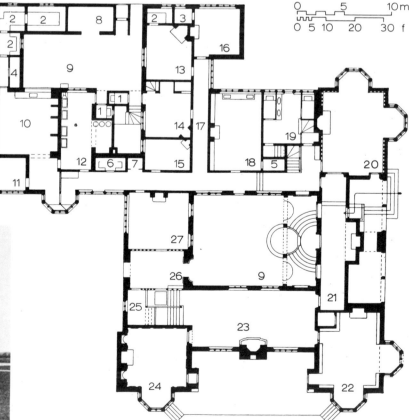

221, 222 Overstrand Hall, Cromer, Norfolk. By E. L. Lutyens. View from garden and plan of ground floor

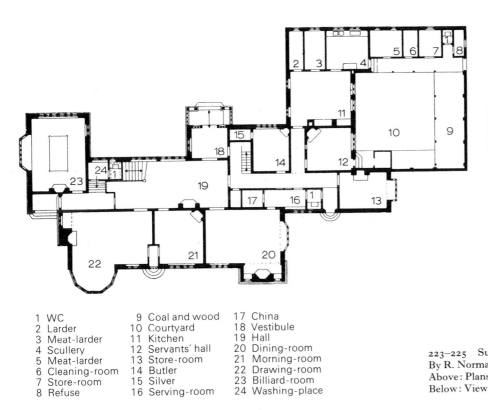

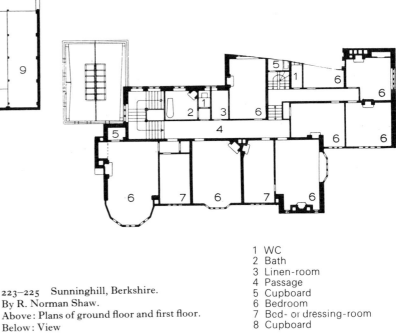

1 WC	9 Coal and wood	17 China	
2 Larder	10 Courtyard	18 Vestibule	
3 Meat-larder	11 Kitchen	19 Hall	
4 Scullery	12 Servants' hall	20 Dining-room	
5 Meat-larder	13 Store-room	21 Morning-room	
6 Cleaning-room	14 Butler	22 Drawing-room	
7 Store-room	15 Silver	23 Billiard-room	
8 Refuse	16 Serving-room	24 Washing-place	

223–225 Sunninghill, Berkshire.
By R. Norman Shaw.
Above: Plans of ground floor and first floor.
Below: View

1 WC	
2 Bath	
3 Linen-room	
4 Passage	
5 Cupboard	
6 Bedroom	
7 Bed- or dressing-room	
8 Cupboard	

the English of spending time in the country during the summer holidays that living conditions have become difficult in the most popular spots and in particular houses have become extremely expensive. Many people have therefore decided to buy or rent a farm-house on a permanent basis while others have built themselves small houses.

So weekend houses are now to be seen all over the country, on the coasts, in the hills and at beauty-spots. Families that once lived in large houses in town or in the inner suburbs now prefer to divide their households and to install themselves in smaller houses in town, or even in one of the new small flats, and to have a second home in their weekend house. Neither household is as large as it

would be were it their sole place of residence, but in one of them there is at least the recompense of the natural life, which is so much the rage, the chance of gardening in the open air, of pursuing sports and games to the heart's content. If he is his own master, the man so arranges things that he is already off to the country by midday on Friday and returns to town on Monday evening or Tuesday. Thus he spends roughly half the week in the country. The English railways cater for this régime by issuing special return tickets, known as weekend tickets, valid from Friday until Tuesday, with which one can return from Sunday onwards, for the price of a single journey. The habit of regarding Saturday as a half-holiday has long been entirely universal in England. All shops shut at one o'clock, business-men go to their

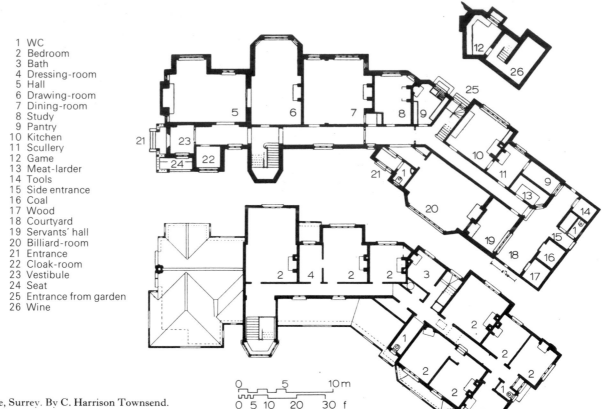

1 WC
2 Bedroom
3 Bath
4 Dressing-room
5 Hall
6 Drawing-room
7 Dining-room
8 Study
9 Pantry
10 Kitchen
11 Scullery
12 Game
13 Meat-larder
14 Tools
15 Side entrance
16 Coal
17 Wood
18 Courtyard
19 Servants' hall
20 Billiard-room
21 Entrance
22 Cloak-room
23 Vestibule
24 Seat
25 Entrance from garden
26 Wine

226–227 Dickhurst, nr Haslemere, Surrey. By C. Harrison Townsend. Plans of ground floor and first floor

offices for no more than a brief stint on Saturday mornings to see to urgent matters, but no business is done; tradesmen and workmen work only until midday and Saturday is a whole holiday in the schools. Thus it will not take much to eliminate Saturday completely as a working day and the English are already well on the way to doing so. Already everyone feels that they have the right to leave for the country after work on Friday and to return on Monday morning.

Obviously only a rich country can afford the luxury of this short working week and it is also clear that to keep two households going instead of one presupposes a high annual expenditure. However, it must be admitted that in using his income in this way the better-off Englishman spends his money wisely. The pleasures of country life are basically of a modest character and demand a large measure of renunciation, which our city-dwellers, proud as they are of their culture, are not so readily inclined to make. The English forgo the theatre, concerts, dinner-parties, the races, at-homes and much else that goes by the name of pleasure for the sake of breathing simple, fresh country air and enjoying their gardens and the countryside. Not everyone would tolerate this, solitude presupposes great mental resources. This irresistible desire for the simplicity of nature reveals admirable qualities in the English. Anyone who has become acquainted with them has gained an insight into the soul of the English people and has beheld one of the most precious of all its treasures.

Types of small country-house. Difference between them and the large ones

The houses that will be considered in this chapter comprise detached houses in the more outlying suburbs, weekend houses and, of course, houses for those who live permanently in the country, whether because their profession allows them to do so or because they have retired from gainful employment. The main

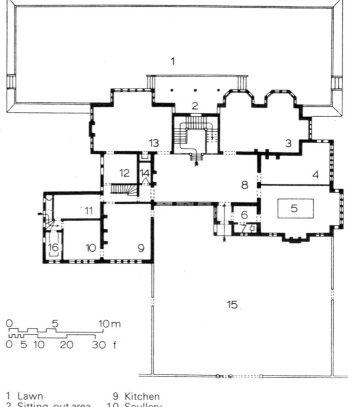

1 Lawn
2 Sitting-out area
3 Drawing-room
4 Library
5 Billiard-room
6 Cloak-room
7 WC
8 Hall
9 Kitchen
10 Scullery
11 Servants' hall
12 Pantry
13 Dining-room
14 Silver
15 Forecourt
16 Larder

228 Westover, Milford, Surrey. By Arnold Mitchell. Plan of ground floor

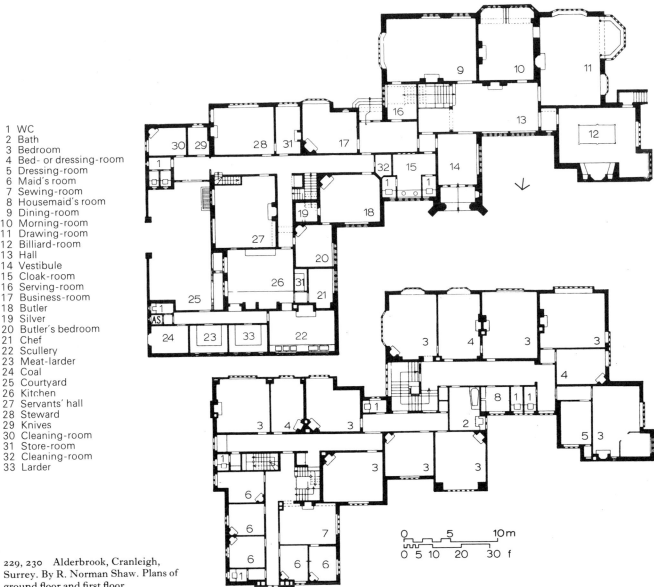

1 WC
2 Bath
3 Bedroom
4 Bed- or dressing-room
5 Dressing-room
6 Maid's room
7 Sewing-room
8 Housemaid's room
9 Dining-room
10 Morning-room
11 Drawing-room
12 Billiard-room
13 Hall
14 Vestibule
15 Cloak-room
16 Serving-room
17 Business-room
18 Butler
19 Silver
20 Butler's bedroom
21 Chef
22 Scullery
23 Meat-larder
24 Coal
25 Courtyard
26 Kitchen
27 Servants' hall
28 Steward
29 Knives
30 Cleaning-room
31 Store-room
32 Cleaning-room
33 Larder

229, 230 Alderbrook, Cranleigh, Surrey. By R. Norman Shaw. Plans of ground floor and first floor

difference between them and the large country-houses is that the plan is smaller and less spacious, though there may not be so much difference in numbers of actual reception rooms, for these may be the same in the smaller house that costs, say, 75,000 M to build as in the large one that costs 500,000 M.* For even the large house has no real state rooms. But it does possess something that the smaller house does not: a certain air that shows that no expense has been spared; it has everything that pertains to a complete country-house of the old style; in particular the garden, dependencies and surrounding grounds are of generous size, the domestic quarters are very extensive and are designed to accommodate a large staff, there are many spare-rooms and all the rooms, but especially the communal reception rooms, are large. The smaller country-house, however, is designed to provide only the essentials. In every case, only the real requirements of the family are catered for and building costs will usually have been restricted in an attempt to avoid all inessentials.

Characteristics of the small country-house

There is little difference between the three basic forms of the small country-house except that the weekend house resembles a

*English value at the time £3750 and £25,000. [DS]

summer residence more than the others, i.e. it makes provision for sitting out in the open air. The small country-house differs from the detached town house in the fact that the domestic offices and all the reception rooms are on the ground floor, which at once gives it a long, low appearance in contrast to the taller town house. Even town houses that lie further from the centre are nowadays expected to have their domestic offices on the ground floor. The servant question becomes much more difficult in England the moment a house has its kitchen in the basement. Even in town houses the addition of the words 'no basement' is one of the most powerful inducements in seeking servants and no opportunity is missed of stressing so palpable an advantage when it is available.

The layout of small country-houses differs from that of large ones in that it is a reduction rather than a fundamentally altered programme. The rules governing the aspect of the house in relation to the sun and the surrounding grounds are the same for both, except that the site of the small house will impose more restrictions and so entail more concessions than that of the large house. Whereas the large country-house is surrounded by grounds so extensive that the position of the site in relation to the road is unimportant, in the case of the small house, especially the

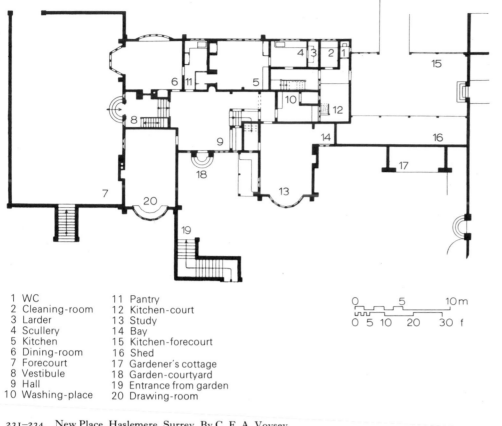

1 Wine
2 Beer
3 Heating
4 Coal
5 Meat-larder
6 Billiard-room
7 Bedroom
8 Dressing-room
9 Room
10 Bath
11 Housemaid's room

1 WC	11 Pantry
2 Cleaning-room	12 Kitchen-court
3 Larder	13 Study
4 Scullery	14 Bay
5 Kitchen	15 Kitchen-forecourt
6 Dining-room	16 Shed
7 Forecourt	17 Gardener's cottage
8 Vestibule	18 Garden-courtyard
9 Hall	19 Entrance from garden
10 Washing-place	20 Drawing-room

231–234 New Place, Haslemere, Surrey. By C. F. A. Voysey.
(See also Figs. 160, 179, 202, 203, 213, 215.) Above: Plan of ground floor.
Right: Plans of cellar and first floor. Below: View from forecourt

suburban house, the road may have an extremely important bearing on the matter; it is easy to imagine a case in which a moderately sized house lies to the north of a west-east road; here the rooms, if they are to have the sunniest aspect, must either look straight out on to the street (to which the English will not readily consent) or else access to the house must be through the whole length of the garden. These are problems that come very close to those that govern the town house, where it has almost ceased to be possible to pay any attention at all to the house's aspect in relation to the sun. In houses other than suburban houses the architect will still have a fairly free hand and even with a suburban house he will try his best to keep the aspect of the house in mind, at least for the most important rooms. This

consideration will affect, first, the drawing-room or dining-room, depending on which is used as the main reception room, then the bedrooms and the nursery. The nursery has the greatest need of a south aspect. The drawing-room faces south or south-east, if necessary even south-west, or, if this is impossible, it will at least have a spacious bay window that faces in that direction. The bedrooms should face east or south. The kitchen always lies to the north, a requirement that is not hard to meet since there is usually sufficient space available on the north side of the house. In many smaller houses the old idea of using the dining-room as the main sitting-room still prevails (p. 88). In such cases it properly takes priority over the drawing-room, in both size and position. However, the custom of living in the dining-room is dying out and only persists among the 'old-fashioned' people of the old school.

Garden and drive

The layout of the gardens of these houses will differ according to whether they lie in the suburbs or outside the town in the open country, and according to whether the owners are particularly fond of gardens or not. But there will always be a terrace in front of the main rooms of the house and below it a flower-garden or a broad lawn (Figs. 228, 235). In particular, a house will never lack a kitchen-garden. As has already been said, the present trend is to ensure that the kitchen-garden and the fruit-garden as a whole have first priority in the garden of the small house. The question of the approach to these houses is beset with very considerable difficulties, since an appropriate drive up to the front-door usually entails the sacrifice of a large amount of space. But, wherever possible, people like to be able to enter their carriages from the hall without getting their feet wet and will forgo this convenience only where hilly ground makes it impracticable. All the better architects now try to provide even small houses with a small enclosed forecourt (Fig. 228).

Layout of the garden

In its general layout the small house does not aim at the same effect as the large country-house, in which the main block is reserved for the family and the domestic offices are removed to a lower ancillary block. The main reason for this is that the domestic department is not large enough to be treated separately in this way. It is therefore usually treated as one with the rooms of the main house, though in such a way as, first, not to infringe the English principle of keeping the family's quarters separate from those of the staff and, secondly, not to situate rooms over the kitchen. The first of these principles should not be regarded as springing from arrogant class-consciousness but rather from the opposite: consideration for the servants. Their right to a world of their own is fully admitted and an effort is therefore made to give them the privacy that is so highly prized by the family. Rooms are not built over the kitchen because the English kitchen, with its colossal coal-fire burning continuously (see p. 96) would make the room above it unbearably hot in summer. Consequently this type of country-house consists of a main block with a wing adjoining either axially or at right-angles. Sometimes the plan is angular and encloses a courtyard on two sides (Fig. 235). Or it may be very obtusely angled (Fig. 226) to enable the architect to exploit certain peculiarities of the site to the full, but also to express symbolically a modest aversion of the gaze on the part of the domestic wing, which is by definition in a subservient position, just as a groom rides beside and a little behind his master. Certain architects, especially E. L. Lutyens, have recently revived the idea of the plan in which the buildings surround a courtyard for small houses as well as large (see Figs. 221, 222), the plan that Norman Shaw first used with such success at Leyes Wood (p. 21). There is no denying that it holds great romantic interest and provides an opportunity for architectonic effects that cannot be achieved by other means. But it is very extravagant in wall-masses and, especially as the plan inevitably involves some coercion, it comes within an ace of looking artificial, not to say forced.

Basic forms with four, three and two reception rooms

As we have said, the residential quarters of the small house often differ from those of the large only in that the rooms are smaller. It is quite impossible to draw a sharp distinction of any kind between the small and the large country-house, for there are a whole host of gradations. But as a guide-line, we shall state at the outset that no house containing more than four reception rooms in addition to the hall will be included in our hypothetical category. Norman Shaw's houses at Sunninghill (Figs. 223–225) and Alderbrook (Figs. 229, 230), Townsend's house Dickhurst (Figs. 226, 227), A. Mitchell's Westover at Milford (Figs. 228) and Voysey's New Place at Haslemere (Figs. 231–234) fall within this limit. At New Place one of the rooms is in the basement.

The four rooms concerned are the drawing-room, dining-room, billiard-room and library. The library may occasionally be replaced by a morning-room or breakfast-room. In such cases the books must be housed in the dining-room or hall. A billiard-room is very rarely omitted since, in the country when there are visitors, it is a highly important adjunct. Larger-sized houses with four reception rooms and spacious staff quarters as well, such as Norman Shaw's Alderbrook and his house at Sunninghill, form as it were a bridge between the large and small country-house.

Houses with only three rooms in addition to the hall are much more common. The drawing-room and the dining-room will ac-

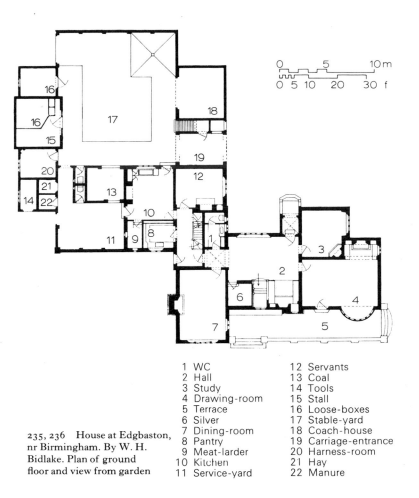

235, 236   House at Edgbaston, nr Birmingham. By W. H. Bidlake. Plan of ground floor and view from garden

1 WC	12 Servants
2 Hall	13 Coal
3 Study	14 Tools
4 Drawing-room	15 Stall
5 Terrace	16 Loose-boxes
6 Silver	17 Stable-yard
7 Dining-room	18 Coach-house
8 Pantry	19 Carriage-entrance
9 Meat-larder	20 Harness-room
10 Kitchen	21 Hay
11 Service-yard	22 Manure

count for two of the rooms, the third will be either a library or a billiard-room, usually a library, or occasionally a breakfast-room. This category includes Bidlake's house at Edgbaston (Figs. 235, 236), Baillie Scott's houses at Cobham (Figs. 237, 238) and Helensburgh (Figs. 239–241), Seth Smith's house at Esher (Figs. 242, 243) and Prior's house with the remarkable plan, The Barn at Exmouth (Figs. 244–246).

This category of house is only one step removed from the maximum reduction in reception rooms conceivable for a house of any sort of comfort, the house containing a hall, drawing-room and dining-room. This house has few possibilities outside the lower middle-classes, unless the individual dimensions of the

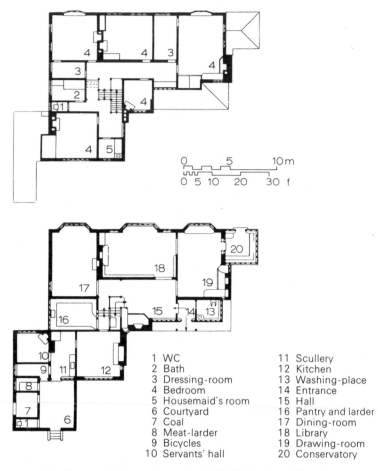

0 5 10m
0 5 10 20 30 f

1 WC	11 Scullery
2 Bath	12 Kitchen
3 Dressing-room	13 Washing-place
4 Bedroom	14 Entrance
5 Housemaid's room	15 Hall
6 Courtyard	16 Pantry and larder
7 Coal	17 Dining-room
8 Meat-larder	18 Library
9 Bicycles	19 Drawing-room
10 Servants' hall	20 Conservatory

237, 238　House at Cobham, Surrey. By M. H. Baillie Scott. View from forecourt

house are so large that it almost becomes a large country-house, as is the case with Baillie Scott's Blackwell (Figs. 103–108). In a house of only two rooms and hall the hall must necessarily become a residential room. It will be large enough to be used also as a billiard-room or else it will be planned for use as the main living-room of the house, in which the family eat and spend their leisure-time (Fig. 248); this will leave another special room in which the men can smoke (library, study, smoking-room). Some of the younger architects, in particular Baillie Scott and Voysey, have achieved excellent results with this type of small house. Whereas Voysey has actually chosen the inexpensive small house as his object of study and all his work tends towards the idea of the greatest economy compatible with the greatest possible comfort, Baillie Scott is a poet who embodies ravishing ideas of spatial organisation in a layout in which every single room, down to the smallest corner, is thought out as a place to be lived in.

Aping the large house

The contemporary school of architecture is seeking to break the spell of the impersonal, stereotyped small house, the essence of which is that it is a reduced version of the large house. This point must be discussed in rather more detail. It has become characteristic of the lower middle classes in England that they have no mode of life of their own but style their lives on an imitation of the *mores* of the rich. This peculiarity, which has been described by everyone who has observed English life, does not rest solely on the aspiration of the individual to a more prosperous class of society, to which it is usually attributed, but especially also in the absolute predominance of the prosperous elements in the population who therefore quite automatically

determine the customs and institutions of the country. Thus nearly all the public institutions in England, be they hotels, restaurants, the theatre or concerts, are designed for the rich. There are also, of course, appropriate opportunities for those without means, but these are attuned to working-class tastes, omitting the middle-classes – so outstandingly well catered for in Germany – who accordingly go short. The situation is exactly similar in residential accommodation. The average small house of today, as mass-produced by the developer, has all the constituents of the larger house – a hall, drawing-room, dining-room and perhaps a smoking-room or breakfast-room as well – but the rooms have all become so small and are usually also cluttered up with useless household effects to such an extent that it is difficult to move, let alone to live, in them. Anyone in England who wants a house with a few large rooms will find that such houses no longer exist among ordinary houses; only those who are fortunate enough to be able to acquire an old house will be able to find what they want. Rooms of an agreeable – though to our eyes still a modest – size, measuring, say, 5 to $5\frac{1}{2}$ m., will be found only in houses of at least twelve reception rooms and bedrooms. Not only does the small house have tiny little rooms but these are also firmly shut off from one another, like the large rooms of the larger house (see p. 79ff.), thus presenting a row of comfortless little cages.

Attempts to find a better form

This being so, it is understandable that sensible architects are offering resistance to the prim little house of today and are doing their utmost to find a better solution. But when one realises that, even in England, of a hundred houses that are built, barely five come into the hands of architects, one understands how difficult it is to make a beginning, quite apart from the fact that the small man, philistine that he is, actually wants and likes this palace of woes with which the developer presents him. Much of the ground towards a tolerable small house has already been covered, either by making one fair-sized room do duty for two or by linking two rooms by means of a wide arch.

The old English farmhouse contained – and still contains in the country, where many have survived – a large all-purpose room, the spacious kitchen- living-room, the vernacular variant of the hall of the gentleman's house, into which one stepped straight from the road. Here in earlier days burned the great fire at which

239　The White House, Helensburgh, nr Glasgow. By M. H. Baillie Scott. View from garden

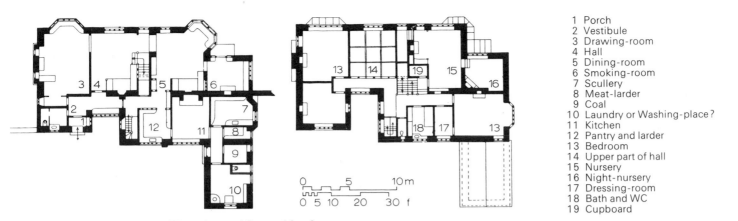

240, 241   The White House. Plans of ground floor and first floor

the meat was roasted on a spit, here stood the large kitchen dresser with its pots and pans and here the family ate at a central table and smoked while comfortably seated round the fire after meals. It seemed an obvious move to reintroduce this splendid room into the small house. As we have seen, one attempt to do so took the form of the hall-living-room, which also serves as a dining-room (Fig. 248). So that the table may be laid without creating a disturbance Baillie Scott has proposed a dining recess (Fig. 251), which can be shut off by a curtain. Another attempt has also been mentioned earlier; it consisted in restoring to the dining-room the character of the old middle-class living-room of the eighteenth century, the parlour, i.e. a combined living-room and dining-room. For this reason the dining-room is sometimes L-shaped, so that the table stands in the main arm while the shorter arm serves as an area in which to sit. Finally, Baillie Scott has no hesitation in adopting the device of joining the rooms by means of wide archways, as at the rectory of St Mary's at Wantage (Figs. 252, 253). In this way he creates some elbow-room at least in what would otherwise be very cramped conditions. But he is virtually alone in adopting the device of joining the rooms together and presumably also encounters stubborn English prejudice against so doing, for it is seen as detrimental to privacy (p. 79). Many other attempts are being made to solve the problem of the small house but all is still in a state of flux. And perhaps no fixed form will emerge in the near future. Those who have their houses built by architects certainly

all have their special wishes and predilections in matters of taste. At most, therefore, one may hope that independent solutions undertaken by architects and art-lovers will cut more and more ground from under the feet of the actual, existing fixed form of the small house, the miserable houses of the developer.

The hall in the small house

As with the large country-house (see p. 90) so with the small, the real uncertainty of the programme lies in the hall. While we saw that even in that context the hall is a room in which expenditure is unmatched by practical usefulness, this peculiarity must give rise to special misgivings in the small house, in which economic considerations are of first importance. Most of the more recent attempts that we have mentioned in the small house also aim to give the hall the enclosed character of a living-room, especially by entirely removing the staircase from it, as in the house of the architect Collcutt (Fig. 56) and in Townsend's house Dickhurst (Fig. 226). But this leaves nothing much of the hall except the name, for it has in fact become a room. In Collcutt's house it does indeed retain the quality of being the central room, out of which all the other rooms in the house open, but at Dickhurst this too has ceased to be the case. Other architects try to get round the uselessness of the hall by making it a mere extension of the staircase, as Walter Cave has done at Eventyde (Figs. 254, 255) and also at Belgaum (Fig. 82). Others again substitute a long, passage-like room, which, if the space is

242   The Gables, Esher, Surrey. By Seth Smith. View from forecourt

243   The Gables. Plan of ground floor

131

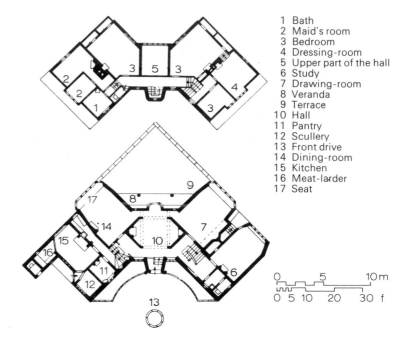

1 Bath
2 Maid's room
3 Bedroom
4 Dressing-room
5 Upper part of the hall
6 Study
7 Drawing-room
8 Veranda
9 Terrace
10 Hall
11 Pantry
12 Scullery
13 Front drive
14 Dining-room
15 Kitchen
16 Meat-larder
17 Seat

244–246   The Barn, Exmouth, Devon. By Edward S. Prior. Front view and plans of ground floor and first floor

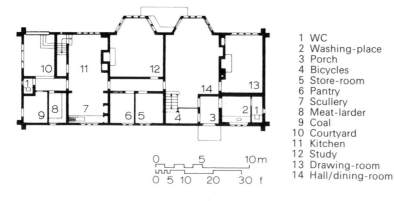

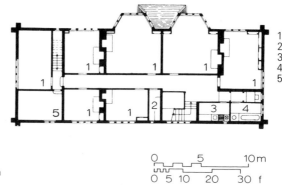

1 WC
2 Washing-place
3 Porch
4 Bicycles
5 Store-room
6 Pantry
7 Scullery
8 Meat-larder
9 Coal
10 Courtyard
11 Kitchen
12 Study
13 Drawing-room
14 Hall/dining-room

1 Bedroom
2 Linen-room
3 Housemaid's room
4 Bath and WC
5 Wardrobe

247, 248   Prior's Field, Compton, Surrey. By C. F. A. Voysey. Front view and plan of ground floor

249, 250   Prior's Field. View from garden and plan of first floor. (See Fig. 180 for plan of garden)

132

1 Study
2 Bay
3 Dining-room
4 Kitchen
5 Scullery
6 Coal
7 WC
8 Pantry
9 Vestibule
10 Washing-place
11 Business-room
12 Hall and living-room

251 An architect's house with hall-living-room. By M. H. Baillie Scott. Plan of ground floor

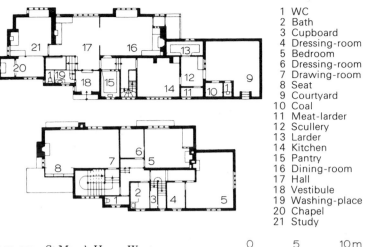

1 WC
2 Bath
3 Cupboard
4 Dressing-room
5 Bedroom
6 Dressing-room
7 Drawing-room
8 Seat
9 Courtyard
10 Coal
11 Meat-larder
12 Scullery
13 Larder
14 Kitchen
15 Pantry
16 Dining-room
17 Hall
18 Vestibule
19 Washing-place
20 Chapel
21 Study

252, 253 St Mary's Home, Wantage, Berkshire. By M. H. Baillie Scott. Plans of ground floor and first floor

treated correctly, creates an effect which leaves nothing to be desired (Figs. 70, 110). When the stairway is retained in the hall, no architect will allow more than a few steps to enter the hall, it is never permitted to appear there in its entirety. This obviates the necessity of making the hall rise through two storeys, which happens very seldom in the small house. In England, where ceilings are very low, the result would anyway not be the ugly, well-like impression that is so often made on the continent by halls that are small in area and also rise through two storeys. On the whole the trend in England is towards either making the hall in the smaller house an ordinary, usable room or else suppressing it altogether.

The smallest country-house

The smallest form of country-house, as we find it in, say, Quennell's house, Gallop's Homestead (Figs. 256–258), has only two rooms including a habitable hall. This type of house may justifiably be called a cottage, though nowadays it is the fashion to extend the name to include even houses containing many comforts, admittedly on grounds that have more to do with appearance than with layout.

First-floor rooms

The first floor of the small country-house is always occupied by the main bedrooms, nurseries and spare-rooms. The attic rooms are occupied by the staff, unless they are used as additional spare-rooms and a play-room for the children. The nature of these rooms has been discussed in detail in the section on the large country-house (p. 51ff.) and the smaller house has little to show that is different. It is extremely unusual to find living-rooms on the first floor in the manner of Baillie Scott's rectory of St Mary's, Wantage (Fig. 253), where the drawing-room is upstairs. The main staircase does not usually ascend beyond the first floor, but there will be a second that rises right through from bottom to top. It will also be used by the children, so it must be convenient and safe to use. Even the smallest house will always have a dressing-room for the man next to the parents' bedroom. There will also always be a housemaid's room on the first floor, with a slop-sink to facilitate service. The water-closet is never in the bathroom, as is the custom in Germany. In addition to the water-closet on the first floor there is usually one on the ground-floor near the front-door, which can be reached through the cloakroom.

The domestic quarters

The greatest differences between the smaller country-house and the larger are to be found in the domestic quarters. One thing in particular is clear: the families are very often of the same size in both houses but the staff is not, being on the whole many times

1 WC
2 Washing-place
3 Cupboard
4 Porch
5 Loggia
6 Drawing-room
7 Forecourt
8 Hall
9 Dining-room
10 Terrace
11 Pantry
12 Serving-room
13 Wine
14 Servants' hall
15 Store-room
16 Coal
17 Fence
18 Courtyard
19 Wood
20 Cleaning-room
21 Meat-larder
22 Scullery
23 Kitchen

254, 255 Eventyde, Woking, Surrey. By Walter Cave. Entrance front and plan of ground floor

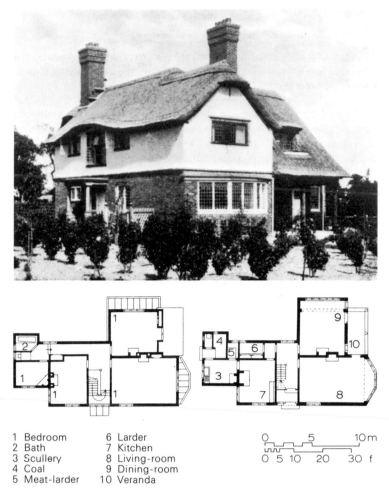

259 House in Maltman's Green, Gerrards Cross, nr London. Converted by W. A. S. Benson. Conservatory

1	Bedroom	6	Larder
2	Bath	7	Kitchen
3	Scullery	8	Living-room
4	Coal	9	Dining-room
5	Meat-larder	10	Veranda

0   5   10m
0 5 10   20   30 f

256–258 Gallop's Homestead, Sussex. By C. H. B. Quennell. View and plans of ground floor and first floor

larger in the large house than in the small. Bearing in mind the enormous area and the ramifications of the domestic quarters in the large mansion, we find these radically reduced in the smaller house, which brings it considerably closer to the continental house. Menservants are not usually kept in smaller houses, where maids are usually expected to do the work. A butler is still seen occasionally. When a horse and carriage are kept there must obviously be a coachman and groom and a gardener for the larger garden, but they are accommodated outside the house, the gardener usually in a little gate-lodge and the coachman either above or next to the stables. In order to simplify the running of the house, the one thing that is avoided in the matter of servants is the mixing of the sexes. The usual smaller house, where between two and five maids are kept, has only one servants' dining-room by way of accommodation in the staff quarters, a room that is not readily omitted when, say, four servants are kept. The domestic offices comprise a kitchen, scullery, one or more larders and a pantry. But these four rooms are present in every house, down to the smallest. The English find them indispensable, although on the continent their place is taken by two rooms: kitchen and larder. The kitchen and scullery have been discussed in detail in the chapter on the large country-mansion (p. 96ff.); on the smaller scale the kitchen contains only a simple stove, a dresser and a table; there is a second stove and a sink in the scullery. Where there are two larders (as there almost always are), one is designed for meat and milk and the other for dry stores, bread, groceries and preserves. But in smaller establishments dry goods are always kept in the pantry.

As one of the peculiar features of the smaller English house, the pantry requires a word of explanation, the more so because the name gives rise to misinterpretation. Despite its name, the pantry has nothing to do with the bread store but is nowadays a room in which crockery – that is, tea-things – glasses, knives and forks and silver, etc. are kept and washed-up. The things are usually kept in a built-in cupboard that occupies the long side of the room and has solid doors below and glass doors above; the sink for washing-up, with hot and cold water laid on and in this case always lined with lead, is directly under the window. The other sides of the room are occupied by shelves on which to rest the crockery. There will often be a fire-proof and burglar-proof recess in a solid wall in which the silver is kept. The room is thus a simplified form of the butler's pantry as we found it in the large country-house (p. 100); its uses also cover those of the plate-room and the china-cupboard and, in simplified form, even those of the housekeeper's store-room. But it is primarily the room in which the finer china is washed and kept and as such is the province of the parlour-maid. It will therefore be found fairly close to the entrance so that the maid can attend to the front-door from it. The natural desire for the room also to be close to the dining-room will usually point to a position between the family's quarters, which end with the dining-room, and the domestic quarters; this position often corresponds with that of our serving-room; but it is not a serving-room because, as has already been explained, food in England is not dished up here but is prepared in the kitchen right up to the state in which it appears in the dining-room.

In addition to these absolutely essential domestic offices, there are almost always two or three cleaning-rooms (for lamps, boots and knives). And a frequent and most useful addition is a small workshop with a joiner's bench; this room is becoming increasingly common as a result of the cultivation of handicrafts in England. Not only can the boys of the house occupy themselves here but the owner can also do simple repairs etc. himself. Finally, the house must, of course, have the necessary store-rooms for fuel and, indeed, there will usually be special compartments for fuel for the house and kitchen respectively. A dust-bin will be essential.

As in the larger house, the cellars only occupy a small area just large enough to store wine and beer. A cupboard for wine and beer under the staircase with its floor dropped a little below ground level will often be found adequate.

The service courtyard

If the house has stabling or possibly a wash-house of its own (washing is usually sent out to be done) this is often taken as an opportunity to place all these domestic offices round a small courtyard, as in Figs. 223, 235. In any case there will often be a small, separate service courtyard, usually adjoining the kitchen quarters and surrounded by a wall. The back entrance is through this courtyard and the bicycle-house, which has recently become ubiquitous, communicates with it, while a small covered shed is often constructed along the length of one wall; it may communicate with the coal-cellar and can also be used for the gardener's tools, if he has no special sheds for them.

Greenhouse and garden

Usually, however, there will be provision of this sort, since every small country-house has its greenhouse and therefore a group of garden buildings, which will include a tool-shed, potting-shed, etc. As we have noted in the case of the large country-house, the greenhouse adjoins the kitchen-garden and its size and equipment naturally depends on the horticultural proclivities of the owner. If he does not run to a special building in the garden, he will at least have a little conservatory attached to the house; these are made of wood and countless shops supply them ready-made in all sizes. This type of conservatory is heated by hot water piped from the kitchen stove. There can be scarcely a house in England, down to the tiniest cottage, that does not have some kind of arrangement for forcing plants (Fig. 259). For, apart from the many flowers that are needed in the house – the dining table, for example, being decorated with flowers daily – the Englishman is so deeply attached to nature and all that she produces that he has to give himself the pleasure of growing plants and flowers in winter as well as summer.

A garden and all that goes with it is therefore the necessary complement to the country-house in all its forms. Indeed, the garden often gains the upper hand to such an extent that one has the impression that the garden is not there because of the house but rather the house because of the garden. Yet the urge to leave the cities, which is observable nowadays throughout the urban population of England, is in a very real sense a flight into nature, a reaction against the sapping and destructive effect of the gigantic massing of people herded together in the cities.

The country-houses of the great have shown us clearly enough that a certain fraction of the English people has not allowed itself to be diverted from its adherence to the more natural life of the country, despite the development of the cities. But the smaller country-houses that are springing up everywhere like mush-rooms are eloquent witness of the fact that even the middle classes are now beginning to leave the cities and return to the country. Similar movements are now beginning to appear everywhere. In Germany, America and even in France the desire is stirring among city-dwellers to flee from the din of the streets into open country; having had their fill of the turmoil of the great cities, people are beginning to turn to nature. And since in social and economic matters England has of recent years always been ahead of developments on the continent, especially in Germany, we have here a clue to the direction in which we ourselves will move. There can be little doubt that we are heading for the day when the houses of the great cities will be abandoned by all who have anything approaching the means to do so for a house in rural surroundings, however modest and small it may be.

D. The urban dwelling-house

Importance and character of the town house

Moving from a consideration of the country-house to the town house in England, we see that it means two rather different things there and on the continent. On the continent it is the urban home that is the important one, the one that has been, almost exclusively, the subject of the development of the house during the last hundred years. All the burning questions about housing have centred in the town house, all the ingenuity in the development of the ground-plan and the layout of the dwelling-house has been directed towards the urban dwelling-house. The situation is quite different in England. In England the urban home always takes second place to the country-house. This does not mean that the problem of city-dwelling is not an important social question in England too, but no one doubts for a single moment that city-dwelling can never be more than a mere makeshift, an enforced substite for the ideal of the freehold, free-standing country-house. The only science, therefore, is that of the layout of the country-house, the layout of the town house being a variant and reduction of that of the country-house that has arisen out of sheer necessity.

Since the motive cause of the reduction is the cost of land, the decisive difference between town house and country-house is apparent from the outset in that the town house develops vertically and the country-house horizontally. The elements of the town house stand one above the other, those of the country-house side by side. The domestic quarters of the town house are in the basement and the reception rooms on the ground floor and first floor, while in the country-house all these rooms lie side by side on the ground floor.

Prejudice against houses with shops attached

The town house has developed along different lines in England and on the continent. In the old basic form of the London tradesman's house the business premises were on the ground floor while the family lived on the upper floors. But this type of house had vanished without trace by the first half of the nineteenth century. The idea that business and private life are better kept apart soon crept in. The tradesmen left the houses in which their businesses were carried on and went to live in the more select western quarter of the city. If one had a shop (the word in English has a disparaging secondary meaning), one wanted, at least as far as social life was concerned, to be as far away from the neighbourhood as possible.

This, moreover, is why combined business premises and homes have almost entirely ceased to exist in London and all over England. No self-respecting family lives in a house that has a shop below it. Sometimes, if the business does not occupy all the floors of a house, people regarded as slightly disreputable or socially unacceptable – women who let rooms or small business-people struggling for existence – may live on the upper floors; but these usually contain offices. Shops in London houses nearly always extend over the ground floor, basement and first floor, which are linked by handsome staircases. The feeling against houses containing shops extends to the new blocks of flats, where the flats are extraordinarily difficult to let whenever there is a shop downstairs. Not even the most resourceful developer would cheerfully risk such a combination, although in many districts in which blocks of flats are going up the idea would seem a most natural one.

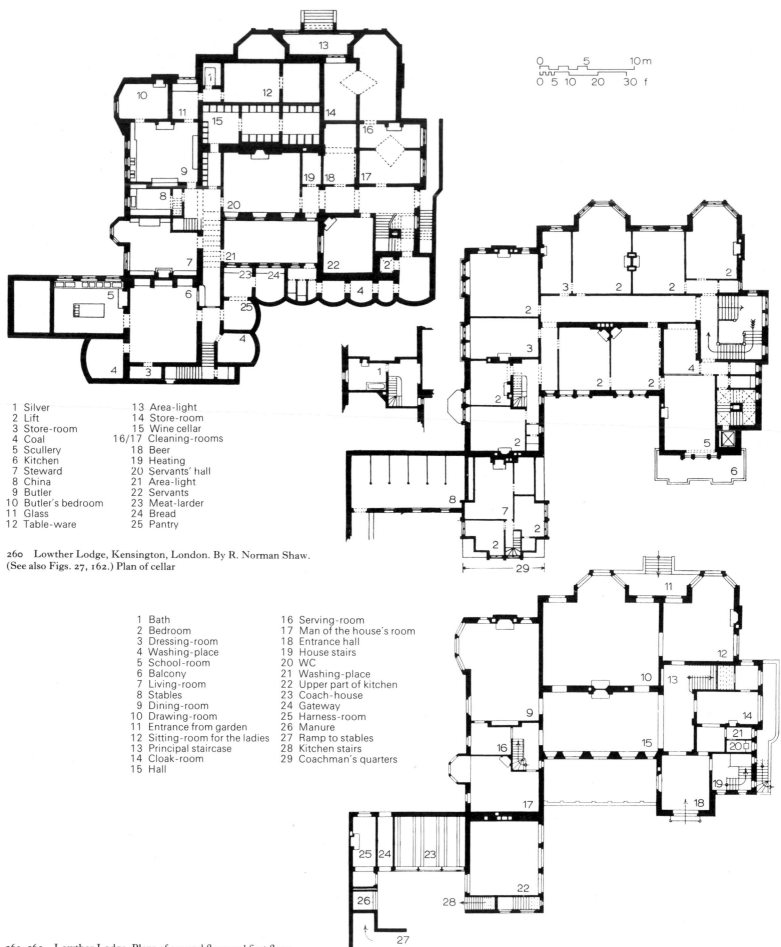

1 Silver	13 Area-light
2 Lift	14 Store-room
3 Store-room	15 Wine cellar
4 Coal	16/17 Cleaning-rooms
5 Scullery	18 Beer
6 Kitchen	19 Heating
7 Steward	20 Servants' hall
8 China	21 Area-light
9 Butler	22 Servants
10 Butler's bedroom	23 Meat-larder
11 Glass	24 Bread
12 Table-ware	25 Pantry

260   Lowther Lodge, Kensington, London. By R. Norman Shaw.
(See also Figs. 27, 162.) Plan of cellar

1 Bath	16 Serving-room
2 Bedroom	17 Man of the house's room
3 Dressing-room	18 Entrance hall
4 Washing-place	19 House stairs
5 School-room	20 WC
6 Balcony	21 Washing-place
7 Living-room	22 Upper part of kitchen
8 Stables	23 Coach-house
9 Dining-room	24 Gateway
10 Drawing-room	25 Harness-room
11 Entrance from garden	26 Manure
12 Sitting-room for the ladies	27 Ramp to stables
13 Principal staircase	28 Kitchen stairs
14 Cloak-room	29 Coachman's quarters
15 Hall	

261, 262   Lowther Lodge. Plans of ground floor and first floor

Leasehold and street planning

Besides these social considerations, other circumstances, in particular the laws of land-tenure (p. 71ff.), have had a determining effect on the building of town houses. When the cities began to spread, the great landowners repossessed their land and withdrew it from the free market. This artificially retarded the whole development of the several districts for the term of the lease and only when this fell in was there a sudden burst of activity and the landlord was showered with riches fleeced from the population. For reasons connected with the leasehold, whole quarters of the city were laid out at a time, subsequently coming under the authority of the owner of the land; the outcome has been that the municipal authorities in England have never concerned themselves with the idea that the laying-out of streets was in fact their responsibility. As we said earlier (p. 75), each developer in England lays out the streets for himself. The planning of the whole city is thus handed over to the lowest order of intelligence. The result has been the English cities of today, the sorriest product that English culture has to show.

It is in the nature of things that the town house, which is dependent upon drastic measures and arbitrary conditions, cannot be a natural end-product of the development of the house. Its merit is limited and it is far inferior in importance to the freely evolved country-house.

Types

As regards the form of individual town houses, we have to distinguish between various types: the large, free-standing mansion, the house in a row in all its gradations from the grandest detached house to the little suburban one, the semi-detached suburban house and the block of flats. By far the most important of all these sub-varieties is the larger urban terrace-house.

1. The larger free-standing town house

International character

With the free-standing town house we are, of course, concerned with the residence of the very richest class of the population, who are able to acquire not only a large freehold house in town but also enough ground to allow it to stand grandly isolated from its surroundings. There are many such houses in London, especially in the districts bordering on Hyde Park and Green Park. These are the millionaires' houses. Many of them are known to wider circles because they contain magnificent art-treasures, which the owners are prepared to show to those who make special application. The most celebrated of these houses, among those that have been built more recently, are Dorchester House, Stafford House and Bridgewater House. These houses differ little from the private palaces of Paris, Berlin and St Petersburg; both plans and architecture are international. Many of their interiors abound in gilt decoration, but they rarely strike a more homely note nor do they even reflect a specifically English feeling. Even among the more recent palaces of this kind there are few which it would be profitable to discuss more fully in the present context. We shall single out two only of the few that have come the way of architects of modern feeling: Lowther Lodge in Kensington built by Norman Shaw in 1874 and the house built in 1896 by F. B. Wade in Mount Street, near Hyde Park, for Lord Windsor.

Lowther Lodge by Norman Shaw

We have already discussed the importance of Lowther Lodge in terms of the history of art; it nearly caused a riot, for it was an example of a really distinguished house being built of brick, which had been considered commonplace until then. The house does not abut on the street but lies back from it, the L-shape of the building enclosing a forecourt. A large garden stretches in front of the main (south) side. For a view of the house see Fig. 27. The ground-plan (Figs. 260–262) shows the characteristic feature of all town houses: it has an extensive basement in which the space is exploited with the utmost care to accommodate all domestic activities. The architect has tried to compress into the basement everything to which the owner of such a house would have been accustomed in his country-house (which he always regards as his normal home). Broad light-wells have been sunk on the courtyard side to bring adequate light into the basement. But on the south side the terrace blocks the light, so dark store-rooms have been sited there. Stables adjoin the house and in the basement below them is the scullery, while above it on the ground floor is the coach-house; the stables, reached by a ramp, are on the first floor. The kitchen rises through the height of the first floor with the coachman's flat above it. There is a fine hall on the ground floor, from which the main staircase ascends in full view; on the first floor are the principal bedrooms and a schoolroom for the children; the rooms in the attic provide more bedrooms, children's rooms and rooms for the domestics. There was enough land to make it unnecessary to put some of the reception rooms on the first floor, as is usually done in town houses; the house is therefore a border-line case between the country-house and the town house.

Lord Windsor's house by Wade

Lord Windsor's house in Mount Street is in this respect a more characteristic example of this palatial type of town house. A complete series of plans is reproduced in Figs. 265–269. The house occupies a corner site; one side abuts on the next-door house and, by purchasing the adjacent property, the owner has been able to keep the third side free. This has made it possible to lay a courtyard bounded by a stone balustrade on the street side. In the basement, cellars have been constructed under the whole of the courtyard and are used for domestic purposes. As is usual in London houses, an area surrounds the house on all sides to a width of between 2.10 m. and 2.80 m. between house and pavement and is enclosed by handsome iron railings. Areas are characteristic of all English town houses; they occur not only on the street side but often on the garden side of the houses as well and ensure that the basement receives a certain amount of air and light. We have already (p. 75f.) examined the legal regulations governing the dimensions, drainage etc. of areas, together with their size in relation to the depth of the basement floor. It has long been the practice to run cellars under the pavement on the side of the area facing the house and to use them for the house, thus obtaining considerably more cellar space. The cellars under the pavement are mostly used to store fuel. There are round openings in the pavement with thick glass covers through which coals are tipped. The coal-cellars are closed by doors on the area side. In the present instance the pavement provided so much space that it has been possible to put store-rooms below it. Thus this basement has produced a usable floor-space two and a quarter times as large as that of the storeys above it. A glance at Fig. 268 will illustrate the way in which it has been used for the domestic activities of the house. Not only is there a magnificent kitchen measuring 6 m. × 9 m. but also nearly all the rooms that a country-house of similar size would have. Indeed, there are even

263 Lord Windsor's house, Mount Street, London. By F. B. Wade

more servants' rooms than is usually the case; e.g., besides the servants' dining-room, there is a cook's room and a sitting-room each for the male and female staff. When one considers that over and above this the attic contains bedrooms for the servants, the domestic and servants' quarters of the house will be seen to occupy an area as large as, or even a little larger than, the family's quarters. The family's quarters are divided between the three main storeys, the reception rooms being on the ground floor and first floor and the bedrooms on the second floor. The main staircase – or rather the grand staircase, for it is very elaborate –

264 Stoneleigh Hall. (See also Figs. 270, 271)

ascends only as far as the first floor. Immediately next to it is the house or ancillary staircase, in the well of which is a lift. The main staircase is lit from above. A large light-well above it lights the adjacent areas. Both for its plan and for the admirable way in which it has been realised, this house can be regarded as one of the best examples of this type of grand house.

A house in Glasgow

The house Stoneleigh in Kelvinside, Glasgow, built by the Glasgow architect H. E. Clifford (Figs. 264, 270–271) is a smaller example of a free-standing town house. The spatial conditions here were, however, extremely convenient, so that it has been possible to site even the kitchen on the ground floor. The remaining rooms of the domestic quarters are in the basement. The plan of the ground floor is outstanding for its most delightful hall (Figs. 264, 271), from the central axis of which a long flight of stairs ascends to the first floor. It is lit by two bay windows that project in a flat rectangle giving on to a terrace in front of the house; there are window-seats inside. The staircase landing is cleverly used as the connecting link between the domestic quarters, which lie to the side of the hall, and the dining-room. A large sliding door is used to connect two of the ground-floor rooms – one of the Scottish ideas which resemble the German in many respects. The bedrooms with their dependent dressing-rooms and bathrooms are on the first floor. The servants' rooms are on the floor above.

In its whole layout the house differs very little from the type* of the country-house. This whole class of house is certainly among the exceptions in the development of urban housing. It must, however, be said that it has been on these houses – since they have been built by good architects – that some skill has been bestowed. This has unfortunately not been the case with the great majority of houses that cover the various districts of London and other English cities.

2. The urban terrace-house

Importance and character

The normal town house, the house that occurs all over England, is the terrace-house. Its street frontage measures between 6 and 9 m. and it is usually built in long, uniform rows, the effect of which is in most cases dreary in the extreme. This is true even of the best quarters in which people who keep horses and a carriage live. These houses are mass-produced by absolutely untrained labour, like the tenement houses in continental cities, and neither the ground-plan nor the building and its appointments can have much call on our attention. Nevertheless, one will find few of the excesses of jerry-building and tastelessness that we know so well from the tenement houses of Berlin; and, indeed, the total absence of any display of forms, which can lead to such fearful results in incompetent hands, is almost comforting and partly reconciles one to the lack of intelligence apparent elsewhere. This type of terrace-house covers mile upon mile of land in London. Large areas of the city were developed during the second half of the eighteenth century and houses with the characteristic bare brick façades – of which Gower Street is an example – were built. A second wave of building followed round about the 1820s, when houses with stuccoed façades were built in Regent's Street and the environs of Regent's Park. From then until the 1870s plaster remained the usual finish. But this period

*See introduction by the Editor for a discussion of 'Type' as referred to by Muthesius. See also Posener, J. 'Hermann Muthesius' in *Architects' Year Book*, 10, 1962. pp. 45–51. [DS]

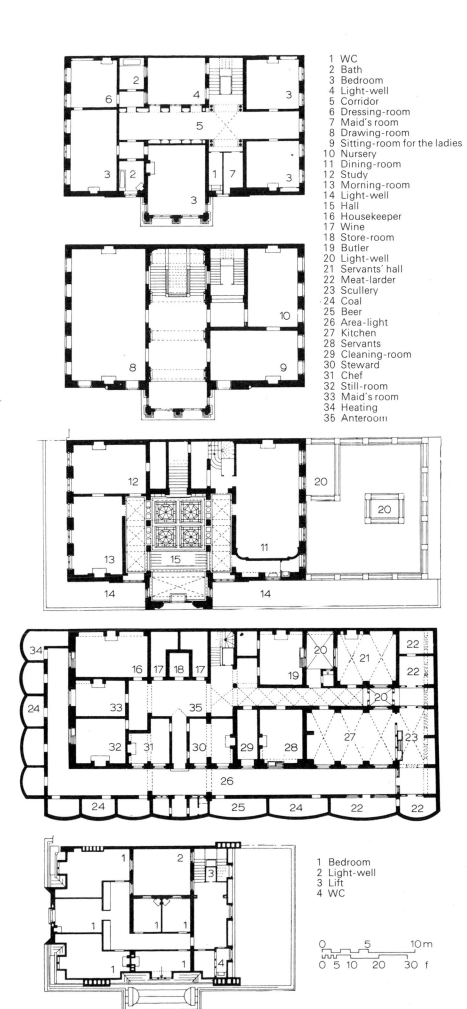

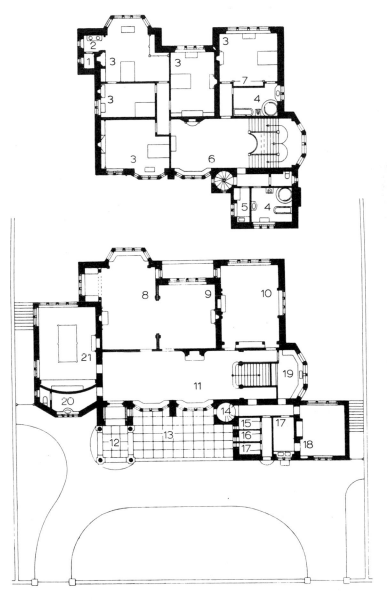

1 WC	
2 Bath	
3 Bedroom	
4 Light-well	
5 Corridor	
6 Dressing-room	
7 Maid's room	
8 Drawing-room	
9 Sitting-room for the ladies	
10 Nursery	
11 Dining-room	
12 Study	
13 Morning-room	
14 Light-well	
15 Hall	
16 Housekeeper	
17 Wine	
18 Store-room	
19 Butler	
20 Light-well	
21 Servants' hall	
22 Meat-larder	
23 Scullery	
24 Coal	
25 Beer	
26 Area-light	
27 Kitchen	
28 Servants	
29 Cleaning-room	
30 Steward	
31 Chef	
32 Still-room	
33 Maid's room	
34 Heating	
35 Anteroom	

265–269 Left: Lord Windsor's house. Plans of cellar, ground floor, first and second floors. Bottom: Plan of attic floor. (See also Fig. 263)

1 Bedroom
2 Light-well
3 Lift
4 WC

1 Wardrobe	12 Porch
2 Wash-stand	13 Terrace
3 Bedroom	14 Back stairs
4 Bath and WC	15 Larder
5 Housemaid's room	16 Meat-larder
6 Upper hall	17 Scullery
7 Cupboard	18 Kitchen
8 Drawing-room	19 Serving-room
9 Library	20 Cloak-room
10 Dining-room	21 Billiard-room
11 Hall	

270, 271 Stoneleigh, Kelvinside, Glasgow. By H. E. Clifford. Plans of ground floor and first floor

0   5   10m

0 5 10   20   30 f

saw a further increase in the use of brick, in which the eighteenth-century developers had also worked. During the last decades, mostly in the western districts of London, in the area south of the South Kensington Museum, whole new residential quarters of this kind have grown up. The basic form of the house has remained constant for a hundred and fifty years; it is a six-storeyed, extremely narrow-fronted terrace-house entirely lacking in individuality. The architecture of the exterior does not usually vary between one house and the next, their façades run on with the same features to the point at which the developer has staked the limit of his plot.

Streets badly laid out

Since, as we have noted, streets are laid out by the ground landlord (nearly all these houses stand on leasehold land) or the developer, these residential streets criss-cross one another in wild confusion, without any kind of guiding principle. Only the initiate can find his way through this remarkable system. A few thoroughfares that were formerly the old high roads provide the only guide. These soon become overloaded with traffic, a condition that is typical of the narrow old streets of London. The traffic cannot be diverted into a parallel side-street because none exists. Having once left the main street behind, one is in a maze. Should one have to make one's way forward in the direction of the main street in a quarter that lies between two such streets, the only possible course is usually to emerge into the main street, to walk on until one is level with the point aimed at and then to turn back into the labyrinth. Probably no area today provides a better idea of the medieval city than the network of streets in which the Englishman of the twentieth century lives. The cheerfulness with which he submits to the intelligence of the speculative builder in this matter is amazing.

Trees growing in the squares

Nevertheless, there are many features in the layout of the residential districts of London that merit attention. Most important are the numerous squares surrounding these houses at back and front, all planted with trees. The whole of London is dotted with squares like this and their fresh green and well-tended flower-beds and lawns not only help considerably to make living in these quarters endurable but sometimes almost give the area the appearance of a garden-city; this is the case especially when there are as many of them as are to be found in the districts north of Hyde Park and south of the South Kensington Museum. These squares with their horticultural embellishments serve as communal gardens for the inhabitants. If the square is in the centre with the fronts of the houses round it, it will be surrounded by iron railings and entered by a gate to which each householder has a key; if it is behind the house, the backs of the houses give directly on to the garden. There are also half-squares which belong to the houses that back on to it and have iron railings on the street side; the gardens at the bottom right of Fig. 272 are of this type. Or there may be a communal garden so arranged that it lies between the backs of two rows of houses while the third and fourth sides of the garden are left open. In this system of unbuilt-up garden-squares the layout of London's residential quarter may almost be described as exemplary and what is lost in the way of long vistas down the streets is regained in this immense benefit to health. One glance at the map of London speaks volumes here and, especially when it is compared with the map of Berlin, shows up the short-sighted policy pursued in the German capital, where the few green squares that exist are still being sold off as building-land.

272 Detail from map of London: South Kensington

Mews

A second noteworthy feature of these residential districts is the existence of little separate streets of stables. These streets, or mews, are lined on both sides by stables which form the rear buildings of the large houses. The stable buildings contain the coach-house and stalls on the ground-floor with the coachman's accommodation above; sometimes the stalls too are on the first floor. Mews are not open to public traffic but are a sort of private road, which also serves as a stable-yard for all the adjacent stables, since coaches and horses and other cleaning is done here. Each stable has a container for manure enclosed by iron bars that leans against the wall and projects a very short distance into the street. Fig. 272 which illustrates part of the area of London south of South Kensington shows the layout of the mews.

Distribution of rooms in the house

The ground-plans of the urban terrace-houses differ slightly according to the depth of the blocks, but on the whole, especially in regard to the distribution of rooms on the various floors, there is a basic, unchanging form. The domestic offices in the basement occupy every inch of available space, which, as we have seen, extends to the cellars under the pavement and the whole of the courtyard, including even the stables, if such there be. Since the English see it as the butler's place to sleep beside his pantry so that he may guard the silver (p. 100), his room is in the basement. The dining-room and library are on the ground floor, as, in large houses, are the billiard-room and perhaps a morning-room; there is always a cloak-room and a men's lavatory as well. The drawing-room is on the first floor; in accordance with an old tradition it is a 'double drawing-room', i.e. either two rooms one behind the other joined by a wide archway, or a large room of some other shape, such as an L-shape. A large house will probably have another room for the women of the house on this floor, as well as a bedroom with communicating dressing-room and bath for visitors. The second floor is the main bedroom floor. The main staircase ascends to this floor, if as is sometimes the case, it has not terminated at the first floor. The third floor is reserved for the children: there will be a large day-nursery (facing south if possible), two or three bedrooms, a bath, lavatory, store-room, linen-cupboard, etc. The fourth floor is occupied by servants' bedrooms and possibly spare-rooms; here also is the storage tank for the house and a fire-exit.

Old ground-plan

The ground-plan of the old houses of the end of the eighteenth and beginning of the nineteenth centuries had a wing extending back from the side of the front block, as in the present-day block of flats in Berlin. This layout not only produced the inevitable 'Berlin room' but meant also that, to reach the stairs at the end of the wing and the lavatory that was also there, the adjacent rooms in the side wing also had to be used as a passageway. The staircase lay in the centre of the front block and was lit solely by top-light.

Modern ground-plan

This form of house has now been completely abandoned. With all its faults it had the advantage that the rooms followed on from one another without a break, an arrangement which, as has been said elsewhere (p. 79), both old English and present-day continental opinion agree in preferring. But since English ideas have changed radically on this point and rooms, instead of communicating, are shut off from one another, the separation of the back from the front rooms is no longer an obstacle. Thus the characteristic ground-plan of the larger English terrace-house has evolved and the sequence of rooms is broken in the centre by

the introduction of a light-well, by means of which light and air are brought into the centre of the house; it also provides an opportunity of lighting the main and the service staircases, both of which adjoin the light-well. All the ancillary rooms, such as lavatories, bathrooms, cloakrooms etc. are grouped round the light-well, thus enabling them to be fitted comfortably into the ground-plan. There is usually no side-wing, especially as the plan never has much depth, as Fig. 272 shows.

The regulations of the Surveyor's Office concerning the light-well, the empty space behind the house and other rules that influence the houses have been discussed elsewhere (p. 75f.). The regulation that governs the angle of inclination that must be observed in the construction of the back of the house (cf. Fig. 144) suits the case of the London dwelling-house in so far as it actually is stepped in this way: the floor-area of each successive storey is smaller than the one below it. The current regulations mean that newly developed districts escape the worst excesses of the high-density building of earlier days, but they cannot alter the situation to any extent since the whole of London has already been developed in the old way, often with deplorable results as regards supplies of light and air.

Ground-plans of architect-built houses

In more recent years several eminent architects have been at pains to build homelier and more convenient houses on the ground-plan of the London terrace-house. Best known among them are Norman Shaw and Ernest George who, with others, have had the opportunity during the last decades of working on the rebuilding of the district south of the South Kensington Museum. Norman Shaw in particular has again shown himself to be an inspired master of planning (as in houses in Queen's Gate, Cadogan Square (Figs. 273–277) and Chelsea, London); and in the block of houses in Cadogan Gardens, London has to thank Ernest George's devoted absorption in his task for one of the finest layouts of this kind ever created.[24] The usual heedless

[24] Nearly all the London houses of this type that are of outstanding artistic quality have been published in full, some with plans of every floor, in the writer's *Die englische Baukunst der Gegenwart*, from which Figs. 273–277 are taken.

1 Light-well
2 Bedroom
3 Light-well
4 Dressing-room
5 Light-well
6 Fire-place
7 Play-room
8 Bath
9 Drawing-room
10 Man of the house's room
11 Dining-room
12 Entrance-hall
13 Porch
14 Cellar
15 Area-light
16 Butler
17 Steward
18 Cupboard
19 Wine
20 Kitchen
21 Scullery
22 Yard
23 Servants' hall
24 Silver
25 Larder

273–277 Terrace-house,
68 Cadogan Square, London.
by R. Norman Shaw.
Plans: cellar to third floor

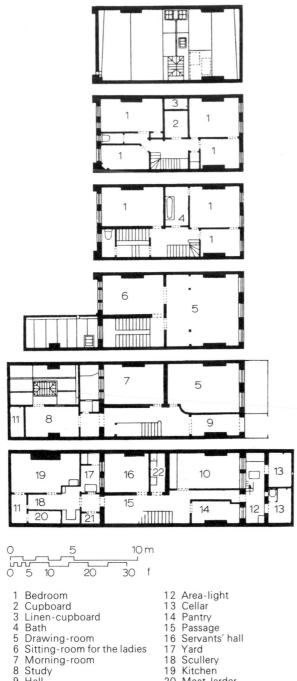

1 Bedroom
2 Cupboard
3 Linen-cupboard
4 Bath
5 Drawing-room
6 Sitting-room for the ladies
7 Morning-room
8 Study
9 Hall
10 Housekeeper
11 Light-well

12 Area-light
13 Cellar
14 Pantry
15 Passage
16 Servants' hall
17 Yard
18 Scullery
19 Kitchen
20 Meat-larder
21 Cupboard
22 Larder

278–283 Typical London terrace-house with 6,10 m frontage. Complete plans

284   Terrace-house in Chelsea, London. By R. Norman Shaw

division into absolutely equal blocks has gone and has been replaced by a flexible distribution. The houses are not all flush with one another, one here and there lies a little back from the others and sometimes they are arranged in pairs so that they flank a forecourt on the street side. It goes without saying that the plans are also treated individually.

The typical London house

As regards the layout of the urban terrace-house with the more rigid plan, one may draw a radical distinction between the house that extends only to a front block two rooms deep and those that, by the use of light-wells, extend more deeply into the site. Figs.

278–283 illustrate an early example of the shallower kind of house with a street-frontage of 6.10 m. (20 ft.). It gives a good idea of a type of house that extends for mile after mile across London. This house is unsatisfactory in many ways and would no longer be permitted under the current regulations of the Surveyor's Office. In the better districts of London it represents a rental value of some 6000–7000 M and requires four servants to run it. The accompanying plans speak for themselves; we may note only that not merely does the basement extend over the whole available space but that even on the ground floor a small additional study (or smoking-room) projects into the narrow courtyard, so closely has every inch of space been turned to account. The study forms a little side-wing on its own.

Form of house with side-wing and light-well

When the site is deeper and perhaps slightly wider, the side-wing becomes more pronounced, as in the example by Norman Shaw illustrated in Figs. 284–286. The wings extend up to the upper floors. Norman Shaw has introduced a small ground floor with entrance-lobby and cloak-room (not illustrated), which is unusual. If the site is deeper still it has to be lit by a light-well and this creates the plan which is usual nowadays and of which Figs. 287, 288 illustrate an example. In a house with this ground-plan and a width of 7.63 m. (25 ft.) one steps from the street through a

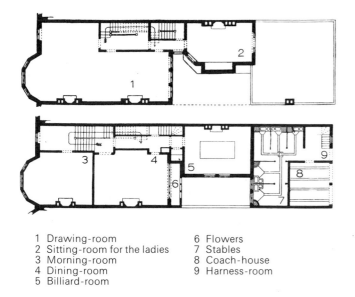

1 Drawing-room
2 Sitting-room for the ladies
3 Morning-room
4 Dining-room
5 Billiard-room
6 Flowers
7 Stables
8 Coach-house
9 Harness-room

285, 286   Terrace-house in Chelsea. By R. Norman Shaw.
Plans of ground floor and first floor

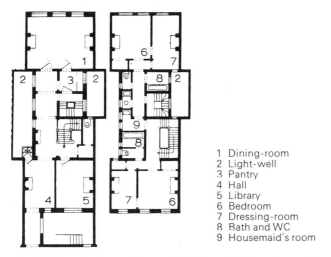

1 Dining-room
2 Light-well
3 Pantry
4 Hall
5 Library
6 Bedroom
7 Dressing-room
8 Bath and WC
9 Housemaid's room

287, 288   London terrace-house with light-well. Plans of ground floor and
second floor

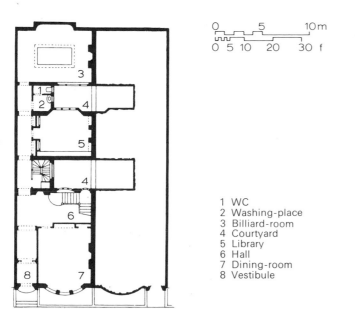

1 WC
2 Washing-place
3 Billiard-room
4 Courtyard
5 Library
6 Hall
7 Dining-room
8 Vestibule

289   London terrace-house with two light-wells. Plan of ground floor

small lobby first into a small outer hall and out of this into an inner hall, which is lit by a small light-well. The inner hall is much favoured nowadays. It always has a fire-place and is appointed in as homely a way as possible; it can provide very useful space for parties and the like. A washing-place and water-closet are accessible from it, the main staircase leads out of it (the staircase always has top-light) and a door opens off it on to the service stairs. To avoid all disturbance to the inner hall, the architect looks for a suitable means of giving the servants access to the front-door without having to cross the hall. A smallish library lies at the front of the house, behind it the larger dining-room. On the first floor (not illustrated) the drawing-room is at the front with the billiard-room behind it. The main staircase ends at the next floor; this is the main bedroom floor on which there are two bedrooms, each with dressing-room, wall-cupboards, bath and lavatory. There are more bedrooms on the upper floors. The whole organisation of this building shows great ingenuity, as for example, in the use of a common light-well for the two adjoining houses. A glance at the detail from the plan of London (Fig. 272), which shows a whole street of houses with tiny light-wells on the same side of the house, shows that this obvious device is anything but general.

Form of house with two light-wells

An even deeper site brings us to the point at which two light-wells, one behind the other, are employed. This has the effect of dividing the usable floor-space into three separate sections, as in Fig. 289. Obviously even the principal rooms have now to derive their light from these meagre wells. The second well could, of course, be at the back, between the main house and the stables, but this would not greatly improve the situation. Yet the example illustrated has one important advantage, which is that the main staircase is well lit. However, in any country but England, the fact that the rooms are ruthlessly separated might well be an obstacle in the way of using this type of house and, as we have said, it is possible here only because the idea of communicating rooms is out of favour for the moment.

Appointments and the running of the house

Obviously the better houses of this kind will be the most comfortably appointed, with a food lift from the kitchen, telephone between the various floors and a service-lift from the kitchen to the roof. Naturally too there are always hotwater pipes all over the house and on all the upper floors there are housemaids' rooms with slop-sinks and water laid on. Despite all this there is a tremendous amount of work for the servants in such a house. The stairs alone make great demands on physical strength, to say nothing of the effort expended on keeping clean the innumerable lobbies, passage-ways and ancillary rooms, areas that are repeated on each floor and arise out of the extremely irrational format of these houses. This clearly represents a great squandering of energy, which must be described, economically speaking, as a deplorable state of affairs.

And herein, quite certainly, lies one of the reasons why the idea of living in flats has had such an appeal during the last decades, despite the fact that it is contrary to the English notion of living to its inmost core. The separate house has limitations. Once a man has decided to live among the masses that gather in our great cities today, there is no great point in clinging to the separate house through thick and thin. The whole of life in the great cities is artificial, so why should not living-conditions be artificial too? By avoiding the artificiality of flat-life a man merely condemns himself to what is perhaps the greater artificiality of running one of the cramped, six-storeyed London terrace-houses.

3. The block of flats

Reasons why flat-dwelling has become popular

There are various reasons why flats have recently begun to appeal to the English. Although the tiresome servant-question may be a factor that contributes to the shrinking of the household, the more desultory, hastier life of today is beginning to loosen the ties even of the closed circle of English home-life; many circumstances peculiar to modern times automatically create the conditions for a less rigid way of living. For about the last twenty-five years all kinds of foreign influences have found their way into England. The insular seclusion of the happy isle with its very independent and secure culture has been breached at many points. New phenomena have emerged to bring confusion into the old cultural scene. The modern English-woman has a strong American bias; instead of the patriarchal family life of earlier times, many English families nowadays favour variety, freedom from encumbrances, liberty of move-ment, social distractions. It is for this section of modern England that flats exist. It is small, but because it floats on the surface it obtrudes itself upon even the superficial observer of London life.

Dwellers in large houses in the country who habitually come to London in the spring, where they used to maintain or rent a house, now occasionally take a mere flat. This gives them greater flexibility of movement and the advantage that they need leave nobody in charge of the house when they return to the country or depart on their travels, nor have they the responsibility for the cost of keeping up a whole house, with roof and street-frontage. Again, young married couples take flats for as long as their means are limited and they have to economise. For them the flat has the advantage that they need reckon on only half the expenditure of a household and in particular they require fewer servants. They live a kind of interim life which at the same time leaves them free of the domestic duties that will ultimately be theirs. Or again, bachelors or unmarried ladies take small flats in blocks that are specially designed for their needs. Here we must bear in mind the odd fact that there are virtually no furnished rooms in England. For many families whose resources are somewhat limited, a flat has become a means whereby they can at least live in a good neighbourhood and still pay less for their accommodation. The prime advantage for which flats are celebrated, however, is that they require fewer servants.

Extent of flat-dwelling

As we have seen, the Scots, like the continentals, are accustomed to living in flats. But virtually none of the English cities outside London has taken to blocks of flats. About forty-five years ago a few developers tried unsuccessfully to introduce them into London. It was not until the 1880s that they began to be built in larger numbers.

Opinion is deeply divided as to whether there is a future for flat-dwelling in England. Whether it will really seriously endanger the relationship of the English with their houses is an important question and one on which those who have penetrated the soul of the English people most deeply will perhaps pronounce most cautiously. At the moment there is undoubtedly a certain need for them and every year dozens of new blocks, most of them very large, are going up, especially in the good residential districts. During the last decade it seems in a way to have become fashionable in a certain section of London society to prefer flats, a phenomenon that has been reflected in an unusually large increase in rents for flats, while that for houses has remained approximately the same.

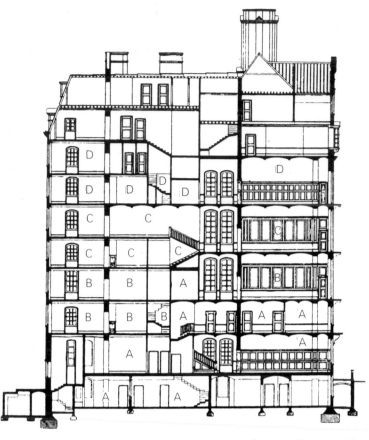

290, 291   Albert Hall Mansions, London. By R. Norman Shaw. West corner of building. Section and view

The situation today

The current situation in regard to flat-building in England presents as yet no coherent or complete picture. England is still in an experimental phase, in which there are naturally attempts to profit by the experiences gained in flat-building in Paris, Berlin and Vienna. The form of the flat has not yet been established, nor have the requirements of the public using the flats been definitively formulated. Naturally the extensive domestic offices of the English house cannot be reproduced in the flat, where there is a high price on every square foot of space. The

1 Lift
2 WC
3 Bedroom
4 Dressing-room
5 Vestibule
6 Courtyard
7 Hall
8 Dining-room
9 Drawing-room
10 Principal staircase
11 Entrance
12 Bath
13 Side entrance
14 Porter
15 Balcony

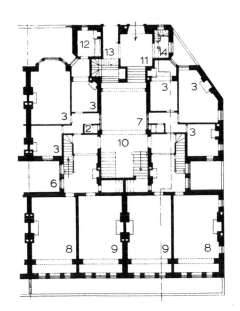

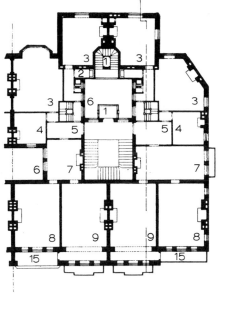

292, 293 Albert Hall Mansions. Plans of ground floor and first floor

English, therefore, are trying out the small continental kitchen without ancillary rooms, occasionally even going so far as to make the maid's room a wide recess off the kitchen, which has no light of its own. But everyone in England recognises that these are unjustifiable outrages. They are accepted since, for the time being, no one looks upon the flat as his permanent home. There is a firm belief all round that it is out of the question for a family with children to live in a flat. A flat always puts an Englishman in mind of an hotel.

Rooms too small

Another general fault is that the reception rooms in the new blocks of flats are far too small. This is an unjustified example of reproducing a peculiarity of the small house in the flat. For there can be no doubt either that smaller, lower rooms are valid in the house or that the flat requires large, tall rooms. The house brings its inmates into much closer contact with nature and allows them to move freely into the open air, whereas the flat-dweller must find his whole world behind the front-door of his home. Furthermore, in the fresh, healthy air of the countryside the volume of air can be smaller and ceiling heights therefore lower, than in the contaminated air of the city. It is instructive to note that in England, where heights of rooms and storeys have evolved in the country-house, these characteristics have been carried over into the flat in the same misguided way as in Germany, where flat-dwelling has been the norm, the very large, tall rooms of the flat have been reproduced in the smaller country-house. The larger form of room will in time make its appearance in the London flat, just as in Germany the smaller, lower room will be ever more generally adopted in the house, as soon as these basic forms of the home have gained their independence.

Views on layout

Although it is as yet scarcely possible to present rigidly defined forms for the English block of flats, it is nevertheless instructive to trace the opinions about the layout of flats that are current and may soon crystallise. As regards the general form of the ground-plan, when large sites are being developed there is really no alternative to the acceptance of a large central courtyard. But large sites are very often not available and narrow irregular plots, for which there are as well dozens of restrictions resulting from rights of light and ventilation, have to suffice. In such cases the

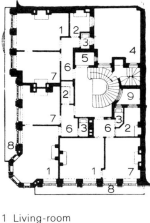

1 Living-room
2 Store-room
3 WC
4 Courtyard
5 Lift
6 Passage
7 Bedroom
8 Balcony
9 Light-well

1 Scullery
2 Kitchen
3 Bedroom
4 Dressing-room
5 Bath
6 Library
7 Drawing-room
8 Dining-room
9 Hall
10 Lift

294 Alliance Assurance House, Pall Mall, London. By R. Norman Shaw. Bachelor's suite. Plan

295 Block of flats, Sloane Gardens, London. By E. T. Hall. Plan of an upper floor

sin of building to too high a density has frequently been committed. Only recently has it become clear that flats built to too high a density are a poor investment of capital since the flats have to be let at lower rents. Rooms that give access to other rooms (or 'Berlin' rooms) are found totally unacceptable in England. A flat containing such a room would simply not find a tenant. The planner must therefore think of something else. Another peculiarity is the dislike of back stairs. People prefer to avoid them altogether and to replace them by an outside lift at the back of the block, by which goods etc. are hoisted up from the courtyard to the various floors. The kitchens have small balconies from which the service is operated. The dislike of back stairs stems from the feeling that they provide a means of entry for all sorts of people who cannot be checked. There is also the desire to limit the coming and going and the tittle-tattle of the maids between one flat and another – both reflect a concern to protect the privacy of the home. A service staircase is in general only considered admissible when it lies close to the main stairs. Blocks of flats always have passenger-lifts. It is always found necessary to provide a large, well-appointed hall, an idea that has been borrowed from the hotel. But instead of being appointed in the continental fashion with obtrusive luxury it has a more homely air. This is achieved by wood panelling, a fire-place and a restful finish to walls and ceiling. Solid ceilings are becoming increasingly common nowadays. Iron girders are laid at intervals of some 60 cm. and the spaces filled with clinker concrete on laths. The filling extends to between 3 and 5 cm. below the underside of the girder, so that the girder itself is embedded. Parquet flooring is laid in asphalt on the concrete floor, or in a few cases linoleum has been laid on smooth levelled cement. But the drawback of these solid floors is that they are not sound-proof. In the better built blocks, therefore, the lower ceiling is suspended in the old English manner. The over-all ground-plan of a block of flats is often U-shaped with the uprights towards the street to form an unobstructed courtyard. This shape gives many front rooms and increases the value of the flats, for it must be remembered that the flats are not at present occupied by a public that would be content with homes that look on to a courtyard.

Examples. Albert Hall Mansions

Perhaps the most successful and most stimulating of the very large blocks of flats to have been built is Norman Shaw's Albert Hall Mansions of 1881, next to the Albert Hall in Kensington. (Blocks of flats are regularly given the pretentious name of mansion, though in fact the word denotes a very large country-house.) Although it is already over twenty-five years old, there has been scarcely a single building erected since that has surpassed it, either in general layout or in distinguished architecture (Fig. 291). The building covers a whole street-frontage. The front, which has a view across to Hyde Park is divided into three equal sections, of which Figs. 290–293 illustrate the north-west corner. Each section has two flats on each floor, with reception rooms facing the park and bedrooms and domestic offices behind. In order to give the front rooms sufficient height without wasting unnecessary height on the back rooms, Shaw hit on the device of making the storeys at the front of the building taller than those at the back. There are interior stairs to compensate for the difference. This most ingeniously achieves the result that for each one of the three main storeys in the front there are two at the back, which at the same time very effectively meets the need for extensive ancillary accommodation. In the vertical section (Fig. 290) the rooms belonging to each flat are all given the same letter. Among more recent blocks of flats we illustrate The Mansions in Sloane Gardens (Fig. 295). The best-known and most distinguished of these giant blocks is Whitehall Court, which towers above its surroundings on Victoria Embankment, not far from Charing Cross in London. It was built by the architects Archer and Green.

Flats with communal dining-room

Since, as we have remarked, the English could already see little difference between life in a flat and hotel-life there seemed nothing odd to them about bringing flat-life a further step or two closer to hotel-life. This is the situation in blocks where the flats have no kitchens and food is served to all the inmates from a communal kitchen, usually sited on the attic floor; unless, that is, there are actual communal dining-rooms, as in a hotel. In such houses the difficult servant-problem automatically solves itself in the simplest way. Many regard these flats as the homes of the future. There are other blocks that contain small bachelor's suites consisting of two rooms, a servant's room, bath and lavatory (Fig. 294); sometimes there is no servant's accommodation and the inmates are looked after communally, as in an hotel. There are also similar houses for women, which have proved their worth and have met a universal need. There are several other intermediate stages between the kinds of flat that we have described. The present state of affairs leaves nothing to be desired in the matter of variety but it is not yet possible to deduce rigid types that can be presented as such.

4. The small suburban house

Dreariness of the English suburbs

Like the suburbs of the great English industrial centres, the inner suburbs of London, most particularly those lying to the east and south, are covered by endless expanses of small houses, all exactly alike. The deadening uniformity that we noted in the terrace-houses of the city reaches its peak in the suburbs and anyone approaching London above the roofs of these little houses has only to glance at this sea of dwellings to feel something of the misery that seems to prevail here. The commercially-minded ruthlessness of the developer reigns triumphant and whereas at least fairly large gardens and garden-squares bring some variety into the sea of houses in the corresponding districts for the rich in London and make life there endurable, in these districts for the less well-to-do there is nothing but houses and streets. The streets have been laid out with dull-witted indifference, with no higher aim than that of naked gain; there are no bends, no variety, no squares, no grouping to relieve the unease that anyone who strays into these parts must feel. 'All hope abandon, ye who enter here' would be an appropriate injunction.

Type of building and layout

And yet these little houses fulfil their purpose. It is questionable whether their occupants would be housed in a manner more fit for human beings in tenement-houses. Here they have at least a measure of independence and quiet, they are nearer to the soil and in a home that is easily reached from the street, they cultivate their gardens and, best of all, know that they are masters in their own houses. The basic form of these houses is immutably fixed, as a mass-produced article, and in every respect they are built so cheaply that, in return for a low rent, the lessee or owner lives in a relatively comfortable and sound house which would not be available to him in any other way. The mild English climate permits a certain lightness of construction that would be out of the question here. Moreover, it does not seem entirely unreasonable that these houses are as cheaply and as lightly built as their purpose allows. Who knows how long the houses will stand and whether a few decades will not so greatly change the character of the district and conditions in general that they will have to make way for a different type of building? In as fast-moving an age as ours it would perhaps be irrational to issue regulations compelling the builder to build every cottage for eternity, when in fact it will be pulled down in ten years' time.[25]

Houses of 16 ft. width

These suburban terrace-houses vary in size according to the allotted space, from the terrace-house with a width of 4.88 m. (16 ft.) to the semi-detached house occupying a site of between 10 and 12 m. in width. Building costs vary accordingly (costs for the

[25] The method of building these little houses has been carefully described in word and diagram in Oscar Delisle's concise but thorough study in the *Zentralblatt der Bauverwaltung* of 17 November 1900, to which I must refer the reader.

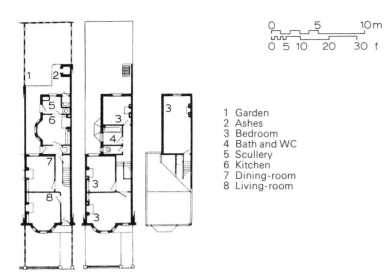

1 Garden
2 Ashes
3 Bedroom
4 Bath and WC
5 Scullery
6 Kitchen
7 Dining-room
8 Living-room

296–298 Terrace-house with 4,8 m frontage, Hornsey, nr London. By Rowland Plumbe. Complete plans

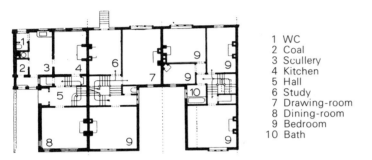

1 WC
2 Coal
3 Scullery
4 Kitchen
5 Hall
6 Study
7 Drawing-room
8 Dining-room
9 Bedroom
10 Bath

299–301 Terrace-house with 7,63 m frontage. Designed by H. V. Lanchester. Complete plans

1 Meat-larder
2 Coal
3 Scullery
4 Kitchen
5 Hall
6 Dining-room
7 Bedroom
8 Drawing-room
9 Bath and WC

302–304 A pair of semi-detached houses on two plot of 7,63 m width each. Designed by H. V. Lanchester. Complete plans

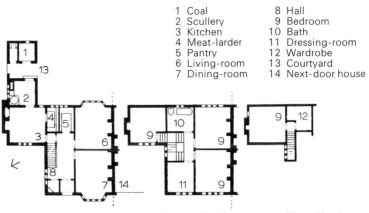

1 Coal
2 Scullery
3 Kitchen
4 Meat-larder
5 Pantry
6 Living-room
7 Dining-room
8 Hall
9 Bedroom
10 Bath
11 Dressing-room
12 Wardrobe
13 Courtyard
14 Next-door house

305–307 A pair of semi-detached houses with identical plan, Kings Heath, Worcestershire. By Bateman and Bateman. Complete plans

same house vary considerably from district to district) between 8000 and 20,000 M. The narrowest plot on which a house of this kind can be built is reckoned to be one measuring 16 ft. wide. The usual ground-plan will then be as illustrated in Figs. 296–298. Clearly all the measurements are extremely small and, considering the room-sizes that we usually expect on the continent, one cannot but be uneasy at the sight of these little rooms measuring 2.75 × 2.96 m. But these people know at least what a complete house is, even if it is in miniature; they have their drawing-room, their dining-room and a number of bedrooms, their bath with hot water piped from the kitchen-stove, in short, a real house, as befits those known in England as 'respectable people'. Whether one large room on the ground floor instead of two small ones would make for greater comfort is another question. The power

of prejudice demands its sacrifice, nothing in the world would persuade these people to forgo a drawing-room such as real 'well-to-do people' have. The heights of the rooms in these houses are usually round about the permitted minimum, perhaps 9 ft. (2.75 m.) for the ground floor, 8½ ft. (2.59 m.) for the first floor and 8 ft. (2.44 m.) for the attic. The floor-level of the rear part is always a little lower than at the front of the house. Of recent years none of these houses has been built with cellars and all the domestic offices are on the ground floor, which signals a great advance on the earlier method of building. The entrance-hall only has a cellar below it which is used to store fuel; this can be tipped straight in through an opening in front of the front steps.

Houses of 20–25 ft. width

Houses on slightly wider plots have the same ground-plan as the examples cited, although the rooms are a little larger and there will probably be a second storey with three additional bedrooms (in place of the attic rooms in the previous example). The commonest are houses with a street-frontage of 20 ft. (6.10 m.), although some have a frontage of 25 ft. (7.63 m.). On wider sites, however, the houses will often be grouped in some way or will be built to one side of the site. Figs. 299–301 illustrate an example of the grouped type; here again the front and back rooms of the house are on different levels and there are two reception rooms at the back, looking on to the garden. This house costs between 15,000 and 17,000 M. to build in London and already has many more comforts than the first example.

The semi-detached house

The same advantages as these can, however, also be achieved on a plot with a frontage as narrow as 7.63 m. by building semi-detached houses. They have a separate entrance to the kitchen, thereby relieving the front-door of all the domestic traffic; there is also a path to the garden which greatly facilitates gardening. The two adjacent houses are usually built as complete mirror-images and their exteriors are all in one or identical, although present-day architects try to vary them slightly (but, of course, architects seldom figure in such commissions). Both the houses illustrated in Figs. 302–304 could be built for between 12,000 and 13,000 M.

A plot even some 40 ft. (12.20 m.) wide will give greater freedom of movement for the semi-detached house. One can already look for a more convenient ground-plan, one can within limits plan a pleasantly shaped entrance-hall and site the kitchen rather further away from the rest of the house, which is important in excluding kitchen smells. Figs. 305–307 illustrate two houses that have been planned with these points in mind; both cost 15,000 M to build; these and the following example are the work of the architects Bateman and Bateman in Birmingham, who deserve special credit for their small houses.

In designing semi-detached houses the question arises as to whether to build the individual units exactly alike or to vary them. The usual practice is to build them exactly alike for reasons of economy: two precisely similar houses are cheaper to build than two different ones. This is in particular the point of view of the developer, who reigns supreme over the realm of the small house. But one can see at once that any fairly well developed sense of individuality will be bound to oppose it, especially when, as is usually the case, the two houses are architecturally continuous and thus appear to be one. As in the case of the urban terrace-houses, which were earlier built in similar form, each owner hastens to express his sense of individuality by having his house painted a different colour. This, however, completely destroys the developer's 'architectonic' idea.

So discerning architects soon began to build their semi-detached houses in a way that showed that they were two houses and not one and to give the two houses different ground-plans (Figs. 308–310). These houses immediately began to resemble the small country-houses discussed in an earlier chapter. With the first move towards varying the ground-plans the advantage of cheap building is largely or wholly lost. The only practical factor in the semi-detached house now is that each house, standing as it does on the boundary of its plot, has a more continuous garden than it would have were it completely detached. The further advantage that the houses are warmer because one of the main walls is not exposed to the elements carries less weight in England, where the climate is mild, than with us. Against this, however, the English object to noise that carries from one house to the other. To prevent this, hollow blocks are often introduced into the division wall but this has not entirely removed the dislike many people have of wall-to-wall living. The Englishman's strong sense of independence asserts itself here: whenever he can possibly manage it, he likes to stand on his own two feet. Despite the fact that the English have therefore made many experiments with the semi-detached house and the English authorities do not restrict the building of such houses, but rather welcome it by allowing the division wall (see p. 76), the general view in England today is that it is preferable to build the house on a site with a street-frontage of 40–50 ft. (12.20–15.25 m.) as a detached house and have done with it. There is nothing against this because England has no regulations governing the space permitted between buildings or other restrictions.

Heedless design of the small house

The whole field of small houses rests almost exclusively in the hands of the developer. This explains why the stereotype prevails and why the ground-plans show very little variety and, in general, little intelligence. This applies right from the layout of the site to the way in which the house is placed on it. It is only with difficulty that the rooms of a terrace-house can be made to face the right way in relation to the sun; but this is rarely done even when the desired effect could be achieved by siting the main rooms at the back instead of at the front. The developer in his unthinking way sites these rooms to overlook the street even when there is, for example, open country at the back with a distant view, to say nothing of designing the ground-plan individually to suit the needs of the purchaser. So the only stimulus in favour of this class of house lies in the economics of

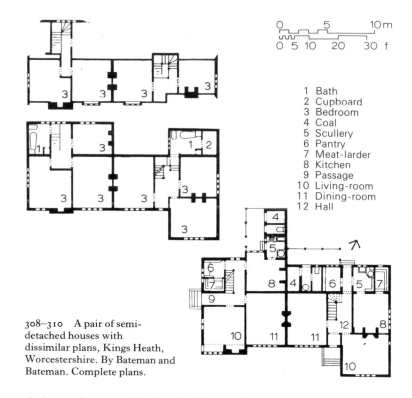

1	Bath
2	Cupboard
3	Bedroom
4	Coal
5	Scullery
6	Pantry
7	Meat-larder
8	Kitchen
9	Passage
10	Living-room
11	Dining-room
12	Hall

308–310 A pair of semi-detached houses with dissimilar plans, Kings Heath, Worcestershire. By Bateman and Bateman. Complete plans.

their production. But in the little colony of Bedford Park (p. 30ff.), Norman Shaw showed a good thirty years ago that economy could be combined with artistic, or at least with rational and practical, ideas. The suburban developers have derived little stimulus from it, nor are they in general in any position to do so. But the influence of the Bedford Park colony has been long-lasting and extremely happy in two other fields; one of these is the smaller country-house, whose heyday dates from that moment, and the other the workman's cottage; here certain great landowners have taken the matter in hand during the past twenty years and, helped by competent artists, have acquitted themselves with distinction (p. 58ff.).

The workman's cottage

A new chapter in house-building has opened in the last decades as it has become necessary for cities, authorities and large industrial concerns to build houses for workmen. It is a chapter for which England, where industrial development first reached its climax, had already done much preliminary work. But this is not the place to seek to treat the subject as it deserves. The programme of the workman's residence is too primitive and is dictated by external circumstances to too great an extent for there to be any possibility of its providing a fruitful stimulus to the building of houses in a general sense. The construction of workmen's houses is a special discipline and would have to be treated in a specialised study. Strong socio-political considerations clash with the most stringent economic conditions and produce solutions which in themselves – precisely, of course, because of their iron necessity – are of the greatest interest, but which barely come into consideration for the house-building public who has greater freedom and wider scope for its houses. We shall therefore refrain from discussing the workman's house. It must be left to the expert to refer to the copious specialised literature in this important field.[26]

[26] Since this was written Walter Lehwess has studied the English workman's house in his little book *Englische Arbeiterwohnhäuser* (Berlin 1904). He had access to the material relating to workmen's houses that I had gathered in connection with the first edition of this book, so that his book may be regarded as complementary to what has been said here.

Conclusion

Advantages in terms of hygiene

The most obvious virtues of the English house lie in its strong emphasis on what is beneficial to health, so that, come what may, the rooms must face the right way in relation to the sun and the climatic peculiarities of the site; in the determining consideration given to ensuring a healthy mode of life for the occupants in the development of the plan and the distribution of the rooms; in the highly evolved attitudes reflected in the sanitary and technical installations of the house. And as the guiding principle in all this has been physical health, it is merely for the sake of some sort of spiritual health that the English house always maintains that intimate communion with nature that is expressed in its relationship to its site, the gardens that surround it and in its withdrawal from the bustle of the streets.

Relative comfort

Opinions about what is comfortable and agreeable in a house vary greatly between individuals and – especially if he is of another nationality – it is idle to dispute about whether a man's house is uncomfortable and unsuitable, as long as it meets the wishes of the occupant.[27] A non-English occupant will undoubtedly find a number of discomforts in the English house, in particular the fact that the individual rooms are cut off from one another, that the house is inadequately heated and that it is generally draughty. But the occupant for whom it has been built likes it as it is and would not dream of exchanging it for a house which embodies continental ideas about ground-plans. Thus it suits him and therefore it is comfortable.

High level of culture in the domestic quarters

But quite apart from such qualified merits, one cannot help recognising a high level of culture in certain individual features of the English house, especially the uncommonly large number of rooms allocated to domestic purposes. This is, of course, a situation that assumes the existence of armies of servants and has something strongly patriarchal about it; it is also one that permits one to doubt whether future social development will

[27] In this opinion I find myself at variance with those English writers who declare every non-English plan, constructed on other than English ideas about living, to be, in the familiar insular view, 'bad' (one such is Statham, in his otherwise good book, *Modern architecture*, London 1897).

allow it to continue for much longer. It is also remarkable how a kindly, considerate attitude towards servants is reflected everywhere, even in the layout of the house, in the way that they are given every comfort – in particular complete privacy, that amenity that is so highly prized in England.

Practicality

However, the genuinely and decisively valuable feature of the English house is its absolute practicality. Whatever it is, it is a house in which people want to live. There is nothing extravagant, no desire to impress about its conception, no flights of fancy in ornament and jumbles of forms; it does not give itself airs or try to be artistic, there is no pretentiousness, nor even any 'architecture'. It stands there, not magnificent, unembellished, with that self-evident decency that, however obvious it may seem, has become so rare in our modern culture. And combined with it is a quality that constitutes a precious part of the English character: an unassuming naturalness. The English have long outgrown the cultural level of wanting to pretend to others, to impress them. Indeed (however pronounced the desire to do so may be in our modern German culture), they are inclined rather to wish to remain inconspicuous. To the Englishman, to parade whatever advantages of position or breeding he may have smacks immediately of the parvenu.

Thus the richer a man is, the more restrained his behaviour, the more modest and inconspicuous he is. And this is expressed so clearly in the English houses of today, so unusually pleasantly for anyone who has recognised their character, that it is a delight to make their acquaintance. Fancifulness, originality (the self-conscious kind!), display, architectonic window-dressing, decorative forms – the English find them as little in place in the house as in the dress of the man who inhabits it. What serious-minded man today would think of wearing bizarre clothes? Even artists in England are careful to avoid making themselves look different from others by the way their hair is cut or their choice of tie.

And so, to an architect who presented him with a bizarre plan overladen with architectonic forms, an Englishman about to build a house would simply repeat the short sentence with which three-hundred years ago Bacon began his little essay on the building of houses: houses are built to live in, not to look at.

Part III: The interior

Part III: The interior

The interior in the nineteenth century

1. Up to William Morris's artistic reformation

The new period

The bells that rang in the nineteenth century sounded the knell of an era in social life and hence in the field of artistic handicafts. A complete overturning of existing circumstances gave rise to new conditions of work, which in turn produced new results. But, as every embryonic beginning must evolve stage by stage and improve itself, the change from the old to the new was extremely gradual. The generation that was involved in the transformation was probably hardly aware that it was happening. Furthermore, since, in the development of tectonic art-forms, the results of new conditions always take shape first through a metamorphosis of old forms that are made to drag on, it was many decades before the new forms became visible. The old forms persisted as mere masks that grew ever more vitiated and hideous as vital energy drained away. They ended up as fearful caricatures – for no other interpretation of the furniture of the period of historicism in the late nineteenth century is possible.

The Empire fashion marks the beginning of the decline

Nowhere can this development be observed with such clarity as in England. The graceful, aristocratically reserved, sensitive furniture of Sheraton had already given place to a hotch-potch of high-flown motifs drawn from all sorts of sources that brought disorder into the fine totality of the picture. This active borrowing of foreign elements was new. English furniture was influenced only in a much attenuated way by the swift succession of fashions to which French furniture had been subjected during the last decades of the old century. Although in his later designs Sheraton was an assiduous imitator of the French, neither the inlays of Sèvres porcelain or of Wedgwood, nor Japanese lacquer-work, which followed one another in quick succession in French furniture found their way into England. Only the white-painted Marie-Antoinette furniture was palely reflected in similar white-painted furniture, known as Chelsea furniture, but

312   Chair of c. 1820

there does not seem to have been any great quantity of this. One of the greatest merits of English furniture was that it did thus remain unchanged through many decades. So much the more must one regret the breaching of the dam of the native idiom by the French Empire style in the first quarter of the new century. An entirely new spirit inspires Thomas Hope's *Household furniture and decoration* of 1807 and George Smith's *A collection of designs for household furniture and decoration* of 1808. Both proclaim the French Empire as the new gospel (Fig. 311). No matter if the association of ideas that had evoked the new forms in France, if the memories of liberty and Roman republicanism that were sought in the fasces, the Phrygian caps and the crossed swords meant nothing in England. All was imitated.

The most striking changes were in chairs. They now assumed the form, imitated from the Greek, that was to characterise them between the years 1800 and 1830: backboards were bowed and splayed legs curved to front and back (Fig. 312). There were also armchairs with rams' heads, arms in the shape of sphinxes and claw-feet. Egyptian and Assyrian motifs mingled with the antique; so-called Chinese and Gothic furniture form a class on their own. A pylon-like form, tapering towards the top, appears in pedestals and cabinets. A wine-cooler standing under a serving table assumes the shape of a Roman sarcophagus, two crossed swords form the frame of a table. This was plainly a worthy prelude to that nineteenth-century art in which it was to be considered the ultimate triumph to construct a clock in the shape of a hound that wags its tail with the swing of the pendulum and has the face incised on its flank. All the absurd rubbish for which the generation of the nineteenth century felt so pleased with itself, all the thoughtlessness in artistic matters, the total collapse of taste, all are foreshadowed here. Yet the furniture that was actually made during the first three decades of the new century was not as bad as the designs in the pattern-

311   Interior from a book on furniture by Thomas Hope, 1807

books. The old furniture-books always depict the aims of their period in exaggerated, tendentious form blended with the author's personal whims and desires. The public smooths down and generalises. It is certainly obvious from the actual furniture of the time that Sheraton's delicate forms have been forsaken and replaced by a growing heaviness all round and a high-flown pomposity, but it is also clear that the good traditions of handicraft from former times could not be negated at a stroke. Furniture is still solidly made, well proportioned and, while violating good taste, still maintains a certain air of distinction. This effect was sought in particular by the house of Gillow, which followed the new stylistic trend more thoughtfully than others. As regards decoration, the wood inlays of the Sheraton period gave place to applied brass ornament or florid carving in a Greek ornamental style of sorts. By the beginning of the 1820s columns were appearing on the fronts of commodes, cabinets acquired fantastic crestings, cupboards became pompous, unarticulated monstrosities with clumsy round columns; legs of furniture assumed the form that would be characteristic of the mid-century: they were turned, with fasces-like flutings, terminating at the top in carved capitals, the carved decorations breaking into bombastic acanthus foliage. It is hard to say what these forms were thought to signify but presumably a vague idea that they belonged to the Louis XIV style lay behind them. When, with the July Revolution of 1830 in France, Empire in turn was declared outmoded and allegiance reverted to the Louis XV style, England followed suit, welcoming the change of front the more readily as its own creative forces were already fully spent.

Stylistic historicism in furniture

Nothing is more striking in all the imitation of styles that began at this time than the entire blindness to the character of the styles selected for imitation. We of today can detect next to no connection between the imitation and the original style. On the title-page of his *The cabinet-maker's and upholsterer's treasury of designs* of 1847 H. Whitaker promises designs in the Greek, 'Italian', Renaissance, Louis XIV, Gothic and Elizabethan styles. And the caption to each of the pieces illustrated faithfully ascribes it to one of these styles. But with the best will in the world it is impossible to understand what particular grounds there were for doing to. A piece of furniture described as Italian might equally well have been classified as Louis XIV or Elizabethan. All the designs show a terrible hotch-potch of every kind of misunderstood motif roughly thrown together and flattened and watered down in the process. This is combined with a vulgar mania for display contrived with the cheapest effects. The ideal is ostentation at any price. The sideboard acquires a back with a mirror, the mirror over the fire-place is set in a heavy gilt frame. Not only that, but parts of the glass were painted in oils to represent naturalistic flowers. Naturalistic flowers modelled in wax and placed under a glass bell were a popular form of room-decoration. A gilt clock stood resplendent beneath a glass bell on the mantelpiece. Walls were faced with whole panels of glass, while another favourite ploy was to use glass backed with folded red material for the panels of cabinet doors. Antimacassars gleamed white on the backs of horsehair-filled chairs and sofas. The effect achieved by all these devices was that of a fair-ground booth.

Wall and ceiling. Fashion for wallpapers

Treatment of walls and ceilings tended in the same direction, but as it remained in the hands of trained architects it did not descend quite to the level of the furniture, all of which was now supplied by 'shops'. With the extinction of the art of Robert Adam treatment of wall-surfaces had gradually been forced into the ways of the Italian Renaissance; its forms were churned out with no great interest, while the same muddled aims of 'grandeur' and 'magnificence' were pursued with the same total neglect of the requirements of good taste and tectonic propriety which had wrought such havoc with furniture. It was an age which almost set a premium on imitation. Papier mâché that looked like metal, stucco almost indistinguishable from stone in appearance, wallpapers that gave the illusion of marble facings, oil-painting that deceptively imitated woodgrain – such were the things that interested and excited admiration at the time. The principal study of indoor painters was marbling and the imitation of woodgrain, printers of wallpaper bent all their energies towards producing the illusion of textiles and even of wood and stone. Cornices were removed from the walls, together with any wood panelling that might still have existed below it, in order to achieve more 'grandeur'. Walls were papered all over, papering being considered more refined than panelling, so that, for example, in old houses where the wooden panelling had survived, the panelling was ripped out of the best rooms and the walls were papered. Even Carlyle did as much in his London house, where to this day the walls of the smaller eighteenth-century rooms are decorated with large wooden panels, whereas the drawing-room was 'renovated' in the 1850s by papering the walls. Wallpapers now began to be produced in large quantities. Even ceilings were papered, for to the eyes of that generation the artificial, imitative paper surface appeared to be the ideal. The fact that we have inherited the preference for wallpapers from those days is perhaps still the clearest reminder of those ideas, for the modern world in general has by no means turned its back on these aberrations, most especially not in Germany; one could almost take the rooms of the average well-to-do German citizen as a telling example of the taste of that 'Early Victorian' period that is regarded in England nowadays as the embodiment of every kind of error.

Early Victorian textile patterns

Yet not everything in the Early Victorian period was equally bad. Among the textile patterns of the time, especially the printed materials, there were some very attractive, unaffected, cheerful and pleasing designs. England was at the time beginning to develop a brilliant textile weaving and printing industry, which was to become one of her most productive sources of income. The youth of this branch of industry – in previous centuries it too had been entirely dependent on foreign countries – was attended by a certain measure of fresh life. Patterns were made out of naturalistic flowers, usually in the form of a semis, still at first very specifically following the study from the life that had been done in the Rococo period, which has bequeathed us such a delightful repertoire of flat plant patterns. By that time also there were already designs showing Indian influence. There were naturalistic flowers available for wallpapers too, though vertical columns were preferred here. Wallpapers with very bright grounds that gave the room a cheerful, joyous air were favoured. Bright, strong colours were also popular and no particular attention was paid to whether or not they harmonised. As long as there was a neutral (usually white) ground, little harm was done. But disaster loomed over the colours and forms of carpets: the same gaudy flower patterns were introduced, but now set closer together and greatly magnified and bordered by golden-yellow scrolling motifs borrowed from metalwork, all producing the most horrifying results that have ever been devised in the way of floor-coverings.

Carpets apart, there are many good ideas in the patterns for textiles and hangings in the Victorian era and they undoubtedly represent the best of anything that the period achieved in the way of handicrafts.

The state of industry at the Great Exhibition of 1851

The first great world exhibition in London in 1851 provided a survey of the achievements of the time. It also marks a break in the development of things that was of great consequence in that certain lessons were learned from it that led to understanding and change and finally resulted in an all-embracing reform. Those who wish to gain an idea of the handicrafts of the time can find their information in the illustrated catalogue of the exhibition, published by the *Art Journal*. The furniture is the result of experiments with forms tentatively borrowed from all four quarters of the globe; it is inconsistent and lacking in style and is pompous and florid into the bargain. It meanders helplessly without the slightest awareness of the relevant criteria in design and without any conscience in the matter of the values of material and construction. The good tradition that had been preserved by the guilds for centuries had entirely disappeared and with it the backing that it had given the old craftsmen. The personal, inner stability of the individual artist, based on philosophical and artistic discernment, had not yet emerged, nor could it yet be expected, for a feeling for it had not yet become part of an artist's training. Historical styles had been exploited wholly superficially and in a dilettante manner and the period was inextricably caught up in false ideals of display and illusion. Had one of the periods of art, the forms of which had been chosen for imitation, been thoroughly examined and its underlying drives, rather than its external formal effects, been studied, there would at least have been a chance of achieving greater understanding. But this could only have been expected of a dominant artistic mind and not of the furniture-manufacturer into whose hands the execution of artistic handicrafts had fallen. It is typical of the situation at the time that, apart from the exception about to be mentioned, there were no longer any architects who cared about the contents of the house. The architect considered this to be beneath his dignity, a feeling reinforced by the belief that he should aspire to more 'ideal' goals, and he indulged at length in fantasies about a high Italian or Greek universal art. This 'ideal' conception that during the eighteenth century had been the sole prerogative and to some extent the right of the small, select Society of Dilettanti, had now become more general – especially in breadth of interpretation. For every speculative builder now felt called upon to pay homage to this idealism and in his attempt to realise his notion of grandeur and nobility created chaos with the maddest substitutes. The public was even more at a loss than the practising builders. It simply followed the fashion set by the manufacturers. The shop-boy acted as mentor in matters of taste to the woman who purchased the furnishings for the house. For in the rush of making a living in business, which was developing rapidly now, the man no longer had time to spare. As long as a carpet, a sideboard, a set of glasses were of the very latest design this was enough. And for commercial, if for no other, reasons, the very latest design changed every year. The contents of the house were now subject to the dictates of unthinking modishness, which was determined by incompetent persons guided simply by commercial considerations. And anyhow it was considered so unimportant that people were not even aware of the disaster. The situation remained the same until the later decades of the nineteenth century. The whole wretched state of the arts during the recent past is attributable to these circumstances.

Struggle against artistic decline. The Gothicists

It was natural that the more seriously minded would one day have to set their faces against this abuse. And it is to England's credit that resistance not only began but was also most radical and urgent there, that a number of men of genius made it their lives' work to combat the monster of artistic degradation. The Gothicists went to work enthusiastically and, whatever the end-result, theirs must be the credit of having been the first to put their finger on the sore place. With immense energy and the greatest self-sacrifice they looked for ways of alleviating the disease. For decades in England the Goths performed the task of watch-dog, barking at artistic corruption. Thus the corruption at least became publicly recognised. Herein, rather than in its actual successes, lay the importance of the Gothic Revival in England. From Pugin onwards it was the belief of the whole Gothic camp that salvation must come from the Middle Ages. Ruskin and Morris shared their belief. By directing attention back to the flourishing state of handicrafts in the Middle Ages, to the solid and workman-like quality, proficiency and even genius of the old hand-made products, they believed themselves to be pointing to the right road to improvement. If one compared this earlier art with what their contemporaries were producing, the idea certainly seemed a good one, but they forgot that the social and economic conditions of the two eras were totally different. In the enthusiasm that they felt for the Middle Ages, primarily in its artistic aspects and then in a general sense, they overlooked these two foundations of all human productivity.

But their enthusiasm was also essential if a real beginning was to be made. Contemplation in philosophical repose, a clear recognition of the likelihood that after all nothing would be achieved by the medieval recipe would have nipped in the bud the power of men like Pugin, Ruskin and Morris, that great power of conviction, the suggestive force that was conveyed to their contemporaries through their works. The shortsightedness that accompanied their inspiration was essential if they were to storm their way forwards, to sweep others along with them, it was essential simply to start the ball rolling.

Once the movement had gathered momentum, another way out emerged: the way of modern art. The essential means towards it had been the ethical values preached by those apostles on the basis of medieval art, the sincerity, faithfulness, the pleasure taken by the workmen in their work, in general; the good workmanship, genuine materials and sound construction, in particular. The medieval forms that the apostles had advocated as indispensable concomitants of these values disappeared at last and out of the ashes rose the phoenix of modern art.

Pugin and the interior of the Houses of Parliament

If one looks at the work of the forerunners of modern art one sees that Carlyle and Ruskin (see p. 13) were as prominent on the literary side as that group of powerful characters on the side of the practising artists, the chief warriors in the Gothic camp. The most inspired of the Goths was Pugin, who had ample opportunity to exercise his talent on interiors. When the Houses of Parliament were being built, the government, to its credit, decided that the interior should embody the best that the age could offer in the way of handicrafts. The intention was to improve the standard of art and handicraft by allowing them free rein in the Houses of Parliament. This had been the decision of a government commission which met in 1840–41 to recommend ways of raising the standard of artistic craftsmanship. Pugin was made responsible for the design of the interior of the Houses of Parliament and no more suitable person could have been found.

Gothic furniture in the style of the fifteenth century of 1835 (see Fig. 313), which contains numerous and varied designs. Similar designs appear in his books for artist-craftsmen *Designs for iron and brass work* and *Designs for gold and silversmiths* (see Fig. 314), both of 1836. The book for silversmiths is the best of the three, that for iron and brass the next best. In both instances the Middle Ages provided actual prototypes on which Pugin could build.

Looking back today at the achievements of the Gothicists in the field of artistic handicrafts, one can have no doubt that Pugin's work stands supreme. Not only did he create the whole repertoire in which the next generation of Gothicists worked but also put into it the best of anything that was ever done. His flat patterns remained the order of the day, nothing could surpass his glass and metal, his furniture was either imitated or replaced by other, inferior, furniture. The whole Gothicist tradition that was available in the nineteenth century had been evolved and established by him throughout its whole range. Such shops for church furnishings as exist are today still living on the stock-in-trade created by him and have his influence to thank for their very existence. None of the Gothicists after Pugin ever again surpassed him in the so-called Gothic interior; anything that this interior could achieve reached the peak of its development at once.

The other Gothicists

The generation of Gothicists after Pugin did what they could in the way of interiors. Their field was in any case mainly that of church art, but they used far too much patterning, coloured ornament and carving. Sounder ideas, giving due weight to undecorated form and the value of materials, did not emerge until decades later; the first sign of them is to be observed in the churches that are being built in England now, and then only in the best of them. In the secular interior and in furniture, work continued in the ways adumbrated by Pugin whenever there was an opportunity to work in the Gothic style. The public did not like this style, finding it too stiff, sharp-edged and stark. And the public was right in this, although in other respects one cannot attach overmuch weight to its judgment in matters of taste. Gothicists who proceeded on more independent lines in interior design included Butterfield, Bodley, B. J. Talbert, Eastlake, Godwin, Burges and Sedding. Through his *Hints on household taste* of 1868, Eastlake had a powerful influence on his period. Sedding forms a direct transition to the moderns, to whom the trammels of style are now unknown. Of those mentioned, the most fanciful of the artists of the interior was probably William Burges. There was something of Pugin's genius in the versatility of his talent, his mastery of the whole range of art and artistic handicrafts. He designed vessels, jewellery in gold and silver, metalware, furniture, wall paintings,

Even today a stroll through the House will convince any one that, considering his period, he executed the commission brilliantly. Pugin was entirely in his element with decorative work; he combined inexhaustible imaginative power with a thorough knowledge of the medieval repertoire of forms, so that it was child's play to him to find forms for every sort of commission. It stands to reason that it was usually necessary to invent them afresh, for the forms handed down from the Middle Ages furnished little more than a guide-line or two, especially where secular interiors were concerned. Thus it is also evident that he worked most successfully where this medieval inheritance was still to some extent capable of guiding him, as in coloured glass for windows and metal objects, whereas his freshly imagined sallies into the medieval mode are often extremely questionable. Where there are no paintings on the walls, they are covered with painted patterns derived from medieval materials, almost always with the aid of an abundant use of heraldic devices. The effect of the patterns is hard and sharp-edged. The roofs of the halls are traditional wooden ones, which require few additions, except perhaps some painting; there are boldly carved wooden beams in the chambers and some of the infills are painted. The floor-tiles are as excellent as the glass, in both of which medieval ornament is used with great skill; furthermore, in the case of the glass windows, Pugin has struck an entirely new, extremely happy note by choosing a very light over-all effect that would let in plenty of daylight. The main objection today would perhaps be levelled against the furniture. Here the only prototypes were ecclesiastical. Pugin applied Gothic architecture over the whole surface of the furniture, and in doing so brought an error into the world, in which all the Goths followed him. Here we can immediately recognise the impossibility of trying to take over the art of a past cultural period in a period of more advanced culture and totally different social conditions. Most of the things we use today did not exist then and this applies to the whole use of Gothic in houses. It had, therefore to be imagined, using as guide-lines the art that was available in a developed form at the time. This was ecclesiastical art. Pugin's motifs for furniture are borrowed largely from richly carved medieval choir-stalls. The best impression of his furniture can be gained from his book

314 Silver vessels from Pugin's book *Designs for Gold and Silversmiths*, 1836

figural friezes. He tended towards luxury and magnificence rather than that primitive plainness and simplicity of life, on which the Goths, with Ruskin at their head broadening their outlook, insisted. In the late 1870s, after a successful career, he built a house for himself at 9 Melbury Road, London, in which he tried to embody all his ideals. The exterior was simple enough: it was built in plain brick and had a stair-case turret (otherwise unknown in England). The interior made up for it in richness. The tone was set at once by the front-door, which was made of bronze inlaid with silver. The walls of the dining-room were faced with marble, above which was a tall painted frieze representing scenes from Chaucer; the drawing-room was a state-room with the richest figural and coloured decoration; there was stained glass in all the windows. The fire-places were made of marble and the chimney-pieces above, modelled on French prototypes, were richly decorated with figures in the round by the best sculptors. The wall paintings were by Leighton, Burne-Jones, Albert Moore and others; the carpets, furniture, table-ware and even the bibelots, down to the smallest trinket, were designed for the house; in short, it was an artist's house in the fullest sense of the word. A monograph by R. P. Pullan with forty photographic illustrations shows the house as Burges left it when he died shortly after completing it (1881). This house was perhaps the most highly developed Gothic house to have been built in the nineteenth century. It was also the last to be built in England. It coincides in date with Street's Law Courts and it closes the chapter of domestic building in the Gothic style as do the Law Courts of public building. Bearing in mind the fortunate circumstances under which it was built, one would expect a consummate achievement. Burges was the most talented Gothicist of his day, he was building for himself, he was rich and means were unimportant. Nevertheless the result is distressing; it may be described in a word: non-culture. Everything is solid, hard, sharp-edged, overladen. The good ideas about spatial design, articulation of walls, about colour-schemes and, indeed, about ornament are all obliterated in the archaeological attempt to build genuinely in the spirit of thirteenth-century Gothic, for Burges gave his allegiance to this precise phase of Gothic. Worst of all, perhaps, is the furniture. Some of it is in the earlier manner overlaid with three-dimensional ornamented articulations, some of it is box-like in form and painted all over. Fig. 315 shows a painted desk. This style with polychrome painted motifs had now become fashionable among the medievalists, though with what historical justification (for no motif was thinkable without such a justification) it is not easy to say.

Yet not everything that was produced by the Gothic movement at that time was of the same questionable kind. The simpler designs found in, for example, B. J. Talbert's books, *Gothic forms applied to furniture, metal work, etc.* (1877) and *Examples of ancient and modern furniture, etc.*, are less objectionable. Talbert is probably the first architect to have resumed responsibility for the whole interior; he gives many views of interiors in which walls, ceilings and furnishings are all treated consistently. Nor is he any longer a dyed-in-the-wool Gothic purist but allows Renaissance and other motifs into his furniture designs. Everywhere there is much more rationality and down-to-earth and artistic sensibility than in the work of the contemporary Gothicist architects. No wonder, then, that from the 1860s until his death in 1881 he was regarded as the leading designer of interiors.

Japanese, Indian, Persian influences

Like Talbert, E. W. Godwin* pursued practical aims and was responsive to rational progress. The furniture he designed for W.

315 'Gothic' writing-desk by William Burges, 1880

Watt's shop and which Watt published in 1877 does in fact show a great advance: lightness and elegance have replaced the deliberate heaviness of the earlier Gothic. Foreshadowing the idea of the modern interpretation which was soon to follow, Godwin was wide open to the Japanese influence that was circulating at the time and even produced 'Anglo-Japanese furniture'. This furniture is rather wildly picturesque but elements are slender and the desired effect is one of elegance (Figs. 316, 317). In fact it is the exact counterpart of the remarkable furniture which was later – indeed almost up to the present day – sold in the shops of German and French dealers as 'English' furniture. It is possible that these forms were copied on the continent from Godwin's designs at the time.

In fact we must see in this mixture of Japanese and Gothic one of the influences that have helped to shape the new art of the interior in England. The springs which finally became the mainstream of this art flowed from various different directions. Morris was incontestably the most powerful of these tributaries, yet he had nothing at all to do with Japan. But other influences came from all quarters of the globe, including India, Persia and Italy. In this connection, particularly as regards the opening-up of the Eastern world, Owen Jones's splendid book of 1856, *The Grammar of Ornament*, must be considered as of paramount importance. A book that presents the ornamental art of foreign lands in such perfect form, so well drawn, so appropriately coloured and excellently printed, so that it is a treasure in itself, could not fail to exert a lasting influence. Owen Jones was fond of

*Godwin's work is still not properly documented but the essay by D. Harbron 'Edward Godwin' in Service, A. (Ed.) *Edwardian Architecture and its Origins*, London, 1975, is a useful short study. pp. 56–67. [DS]

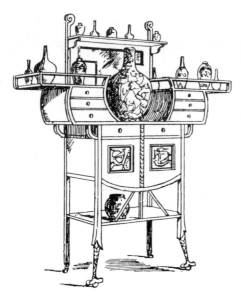

316 Small cupboard by E. W. Godwin, 1877, showing Japanese influence

317 Writing-table by E. W. Godwin, 1877, showing Japanese influence

introducing oriental motifs into his own designs, and Indian and Persian motifs are unmistakable in the newer English textile designs. Persian influence contributed much, particularly to the naturalism which again began to play a part in flat pattern round about the 1860s and 1870s. Yet a contribution as large as, if not larger than, the Persian came from Japan, whose art was celebrated in a long book by Dresser in 1881. Both Godwin and Dresser designed many wallpapers that closely followed Japanese art. The combination of Gothic and oriental influence must be held responsible for the characteristic ornament that prevailed in England generally around the 1870s and 1880s and that always appears on, for example, the title-pages of books of those years. It is a rather spiky flat pattern made up partly of geometric, and partly of naturalistic flower-motifs and was the precursor of the later entirely modern stylised flat plant ornament.

Italian influence

Yet all these influences should not lead us to overlook the existence of that fundamental influence that was at the same time affecting the state of affairs in Germany. I mean that of Italy. It too was strongly represented and, from about 1850 until 1870, was even the prevailing influence, at least in the activities of the South Kensington schools and the work of at least half of the practising architects. The refreshment rooms at the South Kensington Museum furnish the best example of the aims of interior design at the end of the 1860s. The central area was designed by the South Kensington school in the most elaborate Renaissance forms applied in an entirely academic manner. Next

to this is the grill-room, the commission for which went to Poynter, later for many years President of the Royal Academy but then a struggling young talent; independently conceived as it was, this room nowadays offers a much more interesting picture than the one by the school. On the other side of the central area lies the celebrated green dining-room. Executed by the firm of Morris, Marshall and Faulkner, it is already historically important as an interesting early example of Morris's art. It shows how extremely independent Morris's thought already was and how far he was from becoming involved – like the architects – in the entanglements of Gothic formalism.

Alfred Stevens

Little came of the cultivation of Italian Renaissance forms in England, but one may perhaps agree that it had a certain clarifying influence that was useful later when English artists began to follow their own paths. The most notable of the artists who used and fostered this Italianising ornament was the brilliant painter and sculptor Alfred Stevens (1818–1875), who for want of better opportunities worked primarily in the field of artistic handicrafts. His figural designs, and especially his studies of the nude, revealed a daring, energy and a surpassing artistry hitherto unknown in England and he also handled Italian ornamental and tectonic forms in a masterly fashion. In this way he exerted a powerful influence on his period. His best work is scattered among private houses and it has not yet been possible to form a coherent and comprehensive view of his œuvre. Younger artists in the field include Lewis F. Day, equally talented as a writer and designer, Owen Davis and Jouquet. But all that remains predominant in these more modern artists are the Italian predilections and Italian sensibility. Even they have long since ceased to believe in the dogma of archaeological correctness. Fetters have been burst asunder everywhere and hearts opened to every influence. The battle of the styles is over and the battle-field is now only of historical interest. And as regards the object of the struggle, it is becoming ever clearer that in waging war over styles, the combatants were tilting at windmills.

2. William Morris. *The development through him and beside him*

William Morris the reformer

Again and again during the nineteenth century reorganisations were effected not by qualified professionals but by people who came in from outside. This was particularly true of the industrial arts and it seems to be quite inevitable today in all the artistic handicrafts. To the English art of the interior, which the most varied influences had passed by without bearing fruit and in which even the Gothic Revival, powerful movement though it was, had produced no satisfactory results, salvation came from an outsider who was actually a poet by profession and whose assistants were not architects but painters. The man was William Morris. We see the same thing happening with the revival of the German Renaissance in Germany during the 1870s and the new departures in handicrafts in the mid-1890s, both of which were brought about in spite of architects rather than because of them.

Rossetti's circle

Morris's artistic environment was Rossetti's circle, which at that time was still a small clique largely unknown to the public, although Ruskin, with his far-reaching literary influence, had lost no opportunity of trying to make it known. Already at Oxford, Morris (1834–96) and his friend Burne-Jones (1833–98) had felt strongly drawn to Rossetti (1828–82), who was their senior by a few years, and later in London became his admiring friends. Ford Madox Brown (1827–93), Rossetti's friend and in a certain sense his mentor, naturally belonged to the circle. Philip Webb (b. 1830), the architect, then the senior draughtsman in Street's architects' office, had become a close friend of Morris during the nine months Morris had spent with Street trying to become an architect and had joined his circle as a result. Webb was the only architect among painters. But he was an architect in an entirely different sense from most of his colleagues; he was an introspective, deeply-feeling artistic nature, in the broadest sense of the word equally remote from the professional dealings of his contemporaries and sincerely indifferent to the pastiches that represented the aims of the architectural confraternity, from whom he held aloof throughout his life. Having embarked with Webb's assistance on building his house (see p. 17), Morris had to find furnishings, for those available on the market he considered entirely unsuitable. What more obvious than for Morris to decide to design the furnishings himself and to call in his friends? They had long been fostering in their midst revolutionary ideas about the household furniture of the time. In choosing his furniture Rossetti had taken refuge in a return to eighteenth-century art and was the first to bring Chippendale chairs back into fashion. At the same time he started that vogue for the blue-and-white Chinese porcelain that became so popular in England in the following decades that nearly all the good pieces of this ware found their way to England. Brown had not only designed furniture and utensils before but had tried to exhibit them at the Hogarth Club, a small body devoted to the encouragement of individual artists. But they were rejected as 'not works of art'. All the friends helped to furnish Morris's house, he was full of enthusiasm, entertained the whole group every Sunday and fired the others with his boisterous conviction that the creation of furnishings for houses was a worthy aim for artists. Everything was made specially, created from the rough. Wallpapers were not allowed; they proposed to have wall hangings, for which the women embroidered patterns on to plain material. Webb designed the furniture, which consisted of simple box-like forms with wrought-iron bands (see Fig. 9) and large panels intended to take paintings. They meant to paint them gradually: some were done, some were left unfinished and it is impossible to say which of the group were responsible for them.

The firm of Morris, Marshall, Faulkner & Co. founded

Out of the zeal with which this work was carried through sprang the idea of making the friends' common ideals available to a wider public. They founded a firm to decorate interiors and dispatched prospectuses in 1861. The text, which was probably written by Rossetti, said that a number of historical artists had come together to produce work in a way that was at once wholly artistic and inexpensive and had decided to use their leisure-hours to create all kinds of pieces of artistic handicraft. It is clear from the emphasis laid on the fact that the artists involved were 'historical' that they not only intended to work on the lines of historical art but even found it necessary to lay special stress on the point; and in fact the first distinction won by the firm at an exhibition was awarded for 'exact imitation of Gothic art'. But it must not be forgotten that no one at that time yet wished their work to be independent, to deny historical art, least of all Morris – and this goes for his whole life's work. They saw the perfecting of old art, in this case medieval, as their sole aim. The prospectus was signed by eight members: Rossetti, Brown, Burne-Jones, Morris, Webb, Arthur Hughes (the well-known painter; he left immediately afterwards), Faulkner and Marshall. All those members who, unlike Rossetti and Brown, had not yet made their names later became world-renowned artists, except for Faulkner, who was a civil servant connected with building, and

318   Stanmore Hall, nr London. Room with frieze by William Morris

Marshall, an Oxford don, both of whom were friends of Morris. But they were members on the strength of their work as designers of handicrafts, for all of them were anxiously concerned to exclude the purely commercial element. The enterprise began on the most modest scale with each member holding one one-pound share; the registered name of the firm was Morris, Marshall, Faulkner & Co. and the premises Morris's former studio in Red Lion Square; the first commissions, guaranteed in advance, were for decorating churches and had been placed by the well-known architects Street and Bodley.

Growing influence

This was the beginning of the new art. The enterprise, which had been initiated in the first instance partly to enable the members to execute the furnishings they had designed, was soon occupying Morris's whole talent and energy, while as time went on the other partners withdrew more and more. From about 1865 it began to be more generally known; by about 1870 every connoisseur recognised it as the only source to which he could turn for really artistic articles of interior design of all kinds. The name of Morris, who was highly regarded as a poet and certainly accounted one of the best of his period, helped the reputation of the decorating business very considerably. From the 1870s onwards Morris completely renovated the interiors of several houses, including Old Swan House in Chelsea, Lord Carlisle's London house (Figs. 10, 11) and executed the celebrated interior of Stanmore Hall in the country north of London. Fig. 318 gives an idea of the character of Morris's early decoration, in which his love of ornament is very much to the fore. It was also for Stanmore Hall that Morris executed his most famous – and never surpassed – tapestry hangings depicting the legend of King Arthur (Figs. 319, 320). Burne-Jones worked with him on all these interiors. Philip Webb too remained in constant touch. In addition to designing the furniture, he drew the animals that appeared in the designs, as Burne-Jones always drew the figures and Morris the plants.

Meanwhile, true to his maxim that nothing should be made in his studios that he could not execute with his own hands, Morris had learned one handicraft after another. In 1877 the firm moved to 449 Oxford Street. The enterprise that had begun hesitantly fifteen years earlier, at a time when no one seemed to care about the arts of everyday life and nothing short of academic painting was recognised as art, the enterprise that had had to wage unceasing war against the obtuseness and distaste of the public, had now achieved a fame that was all the more auspicious for having something mysterious about it, something that many people still cannot fully understand. But all could dimly perceive that from here, from the studios of artists of the first rank, whose names were established in high art, qualities of a special kind must come. Thus this line of thought further contributed to the re-awakening of that interest in handicrafts that had been dormant since the beginning of the century. It also helped to circle, with its aroma of mysticism and its appeal to minds versed advancing: English aestheticism.

The period of aestheticism

This phenomenon grew during the 1870s, reached its peak in the 1880s and its influence has continued to be powerful up to the present day. Ruskin's writings had reached all levels of the English population; hearts were ready and waiting for a new artistic culture. The cult of Rossetti, confined hitherto to a very small community, became general after the founding of the Grosvenor Gallery in 1877, when the intense art of Rossetti's circle, with its aroma of mysticism and its appeal to minds versed in its romantic and literary terms of reference, became accessible to the general public. Burne-Jones became famous with Rossetti; and Albert Moore, G. F. Watts and Walter Crane spoke to the public in similar tones. They were the new great ones whom the public took to their hearts. Rossetti became the idol of the people, Burne-Jones with his mood of sentimentality meant almost more. At the same time a wider public became acquainted with the complex of ideas comprehended in the catchword 'Queen Anne'. This formed the complement in terms of the house to the visual and literary art of Rossetti and his circle. Bedford Park was built and was talked about (see p. 31). People in general suddenly began to feel that they were living in a hideous environment. Ruskin and Morris had been preaching

319 Stanmore Hall. Wall-hanging by William Morris

this for decades, though mostly to deaf ears, and now at last the seed was beginning to germinate. People looked about them for help. The call for art was heard. Names of all kinds of household appointments now began to be prefixed by the word art – art-furniture, art-fabrics, art-colours – a form that still survives. In order to be entirely artistic even the phrase high art was created; it is still used by shop-assistants to extol articles reputed to be artistic and appears so mysterious and cultivated to the English philistine. Simultaneously with the paintings of Rossetti and Burne-Jones, the Italian masters of the Early Renaissance came into vogue; Botticelli has remained the favourite with the English public. Reproductions of his works, most especially the *Primavera*, began to adorn the walls of every English house with any pretention to being furnished 'artistically'; they were accompanied by Rossetti's paintings, the *Annunciation*, *Beata Beatrix* and his Dante paintings, Burne-Jones's languorous

320 Stanmore Hall. Wall-hanging by William Morris

canvasses, Albert Moore's joyous, quiet existential paintings and Watts's melancholy allegories.

The apparatus of aestheticism

In their enthusiasm for these favourite painters the public copied the characteristics they saw in the paintings. The loose, diaphanous garments of the Early Renaissance were the inspiration for a new feminine fashion, a trend met and promoted by the firm of Liberty with the introduction of its softly falling materials in the most delicate, muted colours. Societies were formed for the new feminine attire with leading artists at their head, periodicals were founded to introduce the new costume and lectures were held – exactly as happened in Germany with the latest trend in clothing. The long-stemmed lilies and the sunflowers beloved of Rossetti became society's favourite flowers, they were never absent from the tables of artistic homes. Instead of the bouquet of earlier times, ladies now carried a single lily in their hands. Rossetti's favourite green and Burne-Jones's greenish-blue were introduced into interiors, art-green became the colour of the day and the blue and green peacock's feather became a favourite decorative motif. And as at first Rossetti had been alone in collecting blue-and-white Chinese porcelain, now the whole world did so and no house was complete without its pieces on the green-painted mantelpiece or shelf above the green wooden panelling. Japan contributed largely to the decorative ideals of the time, Japanese fans, screens, utensils and curiosities of every sort were imported in quantity and, like Chinese objects a hundred years before, every art-lover wished to own them. Japanese colour-woodcuts had a very special significance: they revealed to the England of the day a new world of grace and colour-harmonies and in both respects exerted the most powerful influence on the new, emerging ideas about art.

Changed ideas in furniture

Most importantly, there now came a revival of taste for the old furniture of the eighteenth century. The delicate art of Chippendale and Sheraton was rediscovered at this time. The graceful little cabinets and little tables with spidery legs were brought out of store and were found to fit the present mood excellently, for they were as slender, delicate and light as anyone could wish. All the old Sheraton furniture that could be laid hands on was collected avidly. Most of it came from small houses and from the villages to which it had been scattered when the original owners grew tired of it and exchanged it for pompous Victorian furniture. And almost at a stroke the factories that still supplied furniture for everyday needs mainly in the Victorian tradition ceased to do so. Imitation Chippendale and Sheraton furniture was manufactured instead and it has again become the universal furniture of the English house of today. Incidentally, this was not the first time it had been revived in the nineteenth century. Attempts to reintroduce Sheraton furniture had already been made in the 1860s by the large furnishing firm of Gillow. Gillow deserves great credit for upholding at least moderately good taste during the battle of the styles in the nineteenth century. Compared with the present broad swing, however, Gillow's attempts were insignificant, they were no more than a phase in the rapidly changing fashions of those decades.

Morris's later furniture

The first thing to be said is that Morris's furniture had nothing to do with the newly awakened taste for the eighteenth century. It was based on Gothic ideas and has remained true to these ideas right through to its current continuation in the Arts and Crafts furniture of London. Only Morris was much too modern a man to lose his way among the archaeological imitations of Gothic architecture to which the architects descended in their furniture. He soon abandoned the cumbrous box-like furniture with painted panels, as well as unpolished oak in the case of better rooms. He had begun to make rather more refined mahogany furniture. He could not avoid similarities with the furniture of Chippendale at least, although, with his feeling for greater solidity, he was unable to enthuse over the slender lines of Sheraton's pieces. In general Morris's furniture was not particularly successful, nor was it of obvious excellence. One has the feeling that he was not really at home with it and in fact he never prepared his furniture designs on his own, but delegated them to Philip Webb, Lethaby and Benson and, in his late years, to George Jack, Webb's pupil. His true element remained flat pattern.

Morris's flat patterns

So great was his importance here, however, that he dominated the whole field. The flat pattern he used for wallpapers, tiles, printed and woven materials soon developed out of the slightly feeble powdered, or at least broadly spaced, naturalistic patterns of his early period into the fullest, most luxuriant richness of form and colour. Everywhere he copied the Middle Ages, though never slavishly and always only in general feeling, a feeling that he took for medieval. Yet his line always remained rhythmic, his individual forms stylised in the medieval spirit. But his designs always depend closely on nature; one could say that new life flowed continually into the medieval forms from the fountain-head of nature. And so one result was absolutely inevitable: whether he liked it or not his flat pattern bore the stamp of his personality more markedly than that of the Middle Ages. Morris's flat pattern is probably the most important phenomenon that the English Arts and Crafts movement produced. Large, serious and commanding unqualified respect, it towers above the average work of the movement, its stature never equalled by any other achievement. The flat patterns of the great industrial manufacturers have reached an extremely high standard in England for the past twenty-five years and have been strongly inspired by Morris's work. Morris's flat pattern was, however, always of a special, personal kind and so did not in any case become general, it was on too high an artistic level for that.

English flat pattern in general

The English commercial flat patterns of the last phase of Arts and Crafts are the products of the South Kensington schools, an entirely general, popular artistic achievement, the result of a long process which has been subject to various influences. It has been built up on the study of nature as its actual foundation and a certain characteristic use of line as its ideal foundation. The study of nature means, very largely, the study of plants, which form the typical basic motif of these patterns. The characteristic line became what it is today quite distinctly under the spell of aestheticism, more precisely, under the influence of Rossetti's art. There is a certain affectation in the linear construction of Rossetti's paintings. The rigidity of the straight lines in his figures combines with the flow of the curves to create a line that is full of emotive atmosphere and distinctive elegance, a line that has something strangely affected and yet seductive about it; the slender lily with the pendent flowers that he is so fond of introducing into his paintings, the long, swan-like necks of his female figures, the broad treatment of the full garments, the meditative, calm, dreamy expression of the faces, the eyelids drooping with sentimentality – all breathe a style of a very particular kind, a style that is not without affectation and is yet the opposite of trivial, a style full of linear attraction and yet of a frail and feminine nature. Rossetti's line transposed into plant ornament produced the modern English flat pattern.

Rossetti's line with its languorous affectation set the whole tone for this entire movement in art. And the aesthetes' adherents did not always manage to avoid the familiar step from the sublime to the ridiculous, which never failed to unleash the jeers of the crowd. *Punch* during the 1880s made aestheticism the butt of innumerable witticisms and sarcastic drawings (many of them by the celebrated draughtsman Du Maurier); and the operetta *Patience* by Gilbert and Sullivan, a skit on aestheticism, was an enormous box-office success in its time. It is still fashionable among the public at large to joke at the expense of aestheticism and, just as the Victorian period is characterised as the era of the ultimate in bad taste, the aestheticism of the early 1880s is regarded as a comic excess in the opposite direction.

Significance of aestheticism in domestic culture

Nothing, however, would be more perverse than to underrate the cultural importance of this period. Its influence on the house at least was enormous. While it was certainly a great thing in itself that the wave of fashion that so often tends to express itself in the most absurd excesses made the domestic interior its objective and influenced it for good in the artistic sense, the positive results that remained when the wave had ebbed have also been of the most far-reaching importance. The house emerged from the process greatly improved. The public had been through an intensive course in taste, the results of which could not be expunged so rapidly. The furnishings, such as wallpapers, materials and furniture, which the artists had devised and which previously had been appreciated and wanted by a small circle, had now become the common property of all cultivated people. The very fact that the manufacturers had revived Sheraton furniture must be accounted a gain.

The most important point was that the attention of the public had been guided back to the appreciation of the interior as a work of art. This was the season of the flood-tide of books on 'taste in the house'. They were written mainly by women and there was not much profit to be made out of them. But the books show that these questions had by now become burning ones. A few books of the kind had been written before, in particular Eastman's influential *Hints on household taste*, mentioned earlier, which originally appeared in 1868 and was the first to refer in concrete form to the distortion of taste prevalent at the time. But Eastman still looks almost exclusively to the Gothic for salvation and the Gothic furniture recommended in his illustrations, although very moderate in form, is still not immune from the familiar architectural disease. The Gothic dream was virtually over by the 1880s. True, the Arts and Crafts circle that clustered round Morris in particular tried to adhere to the Gothic tradition in furniture too, but it did so in quite a different way, holding to the spirit of Gothic design and not to the repertoire of forms that had previously been regarded as Gothic. Thus one may say that the terrible architectural furniture that had for decades tried to be Gothic and was, through many decades, the delusion of the nineteenth century, had finally vanished from the scene.

Such was the general situation in the 1880s. The flood-tide of that movement has ebbed again with time, but good taste has spread continuously and without fuss in England since then. The two movements that developed separately until the 1880s, the reform of domestic architecture embodied in the name of Norman Shaw and the reform of the interior in that of William Morris now united in the pupils of both men to form a single broad stream. The house-building activity of this younger generation has been described already (see p. 37). The next section will show in greater detail how the modern English interior took shape in the hands of the present generation.

The achievement of the nineteenth century in the development of domestic furnishing

If one tries to describe what the development of the interior during the nineteenth century added in the way of actual innovation to what already existed, one finds that despite the boom in art of the past fifty years, it is not in fact to be sought on the aesthetic side. The English interior under Adam and Sheraton had reached a level of artistic perfection that has not yet been equalled in general today, despite all the good work of the new art. Nor, as regards the variety of furniture, was the nineteenth century able to add much to what already existed. The only real and important advances have been made in the fields of comfort and sanitation. And so here too we have to look for the real cultural achievement of the nineteenth century in work of a scientific character.

Advances in comfort

The scientific spirit of the age addressed itself first to developing furniture in forms that perfectly suit the body and provide the maximum of comfort. Despite all the distortions of taste in the Victorian age, this must be recognised as one of its goals. All furniture became more spacious, tables became larger, chairs deeper. It is significant that this period saw the foundation of the many clubs, in the furnishing of which – since they were for men only – considerations of etiquette could increasingly give way to ideas of comfort, a trend that was in any case in keeping with the tendency of the day. Everything in the clubs was massive, ponderous, extremely solidly made, but comfortable-looking. In particular, deep arm-chairs that allowed one to lounge in a half sitting, half lying posture, were developed. In their absolute comfort they represent the culmination of the evolution of the chair, which developed steadily from a wooden to an upholstered structure. The use of the fully upholstered chair and the comfortable low-seated form of the leather chairs in the clubs was copied in the chairs in houses, except that woollen material or chintz was used instead of leather. A similar move towards greater comfort is reflected in the deep and softly upholstered sofas of modern times. Dining-tables and dining-room chairs also became more comfortable, dining-tables in particular became almost monstrous objects.

Advances in sanitation. Water-closet

More important even than the question of comfort in the process of the transformation of the house during the nineteenth century was the question of sanitation. The work that was done in this field is perhaps seen in the clearest and most concentrated form in the concept of the water-closet. Coming under the heading of necessary, rather than aesthetic, elements in the house, this object is the most outstanding evidence of domestic improvement in the nineteenth century. And England, as the country of its birth, has every reason to be proud of it. The development of all the devices connected with health and cleanliness forms no inconsiderable part of the fame that England has earned in the design of the interior.

Bedroom and bath

Certain radical changes affecting the bedroom formed another important part of these advances in hygiene. Four-poster beds were abandoned around the mid-century when it was recognised that air that was trapped between curtains was wrong from the point of view of hygiene. The great world exhibition of 1851 brought metal bedsteads into general fashion. The wash-stand grew into a sizeable piece of furniture and was equipped with a large wash-basin and a whole range of washing-gear. The Victorian love of marble came into its own here, the back and top of the wash-stand being made of the solid stone. The love of marble now found other favourable ground in the bathroom, which was now becoming increasingly important, and in the various other washing facilities that were scattered throughout the house and which developed in quite novel ways with the use of this and related solid materials. Houses now became veritable networks of pipes, supply-pipes and waste-pipes, pipes of every kind, for hot water, heating, electric light, for the news service, so that they resembled complex organisms with arteries, veins and nerves like the human body. The most important consequence was that the aesthetic beauty of the earlier ideals was necessarily relegated to the background. But in time perhaps it will be replaced by an entirely new type of beauty, that of a spiritualised practical intention. There are signs of this in those parts of the house that have to do with hygiene. But as the whole area of hygiene in the human habitation is still in its infancy, one cannot as yet predict what form the house will assume in time to come.

Like the result of any development, the house of today is a compromise between tradition and new conditions gradually making themselves felt.

The contemporary interior

A. Wall, ceiling and floor

1. The wall

Space as a combination of wall, ceiling and floor

When Ruskin says that the wall means to the architect what the blank canvas means to the painter, his words can make no real sense to the interior-designer unless the concept of the wall is extended to include the floor and ceiling. But the dividing line between wall and ceiling is blurred anyway, as in vaulted rooms. The interior is a whole, the essence of which lies, in fact, in its totality, in its quality as space. In conceiving the interior as a work of art, therefore, the artist must first think of it as a space, that is, as the over-all form and the interrelationship of the space-enclosing surfaces.

Space in our dwelling-houses can, of course, almost invariably be assumed at the outset to consist of enclosed rectangular spaces. And when it comes to giving the room artistic form the wall is the determining factor among the enclosing surfaces. Since for practical reasons the rooms are all built to the same height, this means that their proportions, especially that of floor-area to height, are laid down beforehand. Architects are commonly reluctant to lower ceilings to correspond with smaller rooms. Yet there were precedents for doing so in the Palladian period in England: the ideas behind the design of the façades necessitated building exaggeratedly tall rooms, so ceilings were usually hung between half a meter and two meters below the ceiling joists in order to give the rooms a tolerable height. Ceilings cannot be hung nowadays for the simple reason that heights of storeys have been reduced to a minimum in England. Today they are suited to small rooms, whereas in Palladian times they suited large ones.

Homely rooms

If one is looking for homeliness and comfort, there can be no doubt that a low ceiling at once conduces to this ideal. It is often their very lowness that gives old rooms their agreeable homely air. By contrast, every interior-designer knows that it is uncommonly difficult to create a more intimate, pleasanter general spatial effect of any kind in tall rooms. Everything always tends towards magnificence, theatricality, pomposity and the designer has to use every kind of artifice to counteract this unwanted impression; such a room must to some extent be treated against its nature. The naturally comfortable room is a low room. Thus all English architects nowadays prefer very low rooms 2.50–3 m., or at most 3.50 m. in height, and such heights apply even in houses that we should describe as aristocratic, to use a fine word. The whole treatment of the interior aims at making the most of the character of intimacy and homeliness indicated by the proportions.

Design of the modern English room

The English movement in art cannot be too highly praised for having evolved this new type of room. The successful new departures and new results achieved by the continental movement during the past fifteen years have been built on the foundations established in England. As we have seen, it first began in England as long ago as the 1860s. But even there it was not until some twenty to twenty-five years ago that a new and in

any way clarified form of dwelling-room could be observed. The architects of the Queen Anne movement, headed by Norman Shaw, certainly created interiors that were very much their own, but they were still too backward-looking, too antiquarian in outlook to work in complete freedom. Morris pursued his own, wholly personal, ways but was, perhaps, too fond of ornament. The truly modern interior made its first appearance with the next generation, the men who now constitute the Arts and Crafts movement. The process was the same in this as in all new creations: those who discovered the idea groped their way forwards with their feet still firmly planted in the old world; but the younger generation immediately drew the full consequences from what had been mere hints and, with their new experience, proceeded to the full solutions.

Field of application in England

We shall examine this type of interior in particular. Despite all the different views of the leading individual architects today, one can discern a consistent movement that is clear about its aims. Most of the younger generation and the leading firms of decorators subscribe to it. But there are, of course, several other views. Thus some of the aristocracy, and with them the newly rich financiers, adhere to the French concept. These people want gilt furniture, silk damask wall-coverings or, indeed, wallpapers simulating brocade, and they love the gilt stucco ceilings of ancient memory. Some sections of middle-class society still like to bask in the reflection of this aristocratic ostentation. Needless to say, there are sources of supply from which they can obtain the necessary articles. There is also a special sort of fashion followed mainly by women. At the moment it can find no wall-covering to equal the glaring Victorian floral patterns on calendered chintz, and the windows of all the wallpaper shops are full of displays of this material. There is another fashion for imitation Chinese Chippendale. And finally the Neo-Palladians among English architects fancy their literal imitations of the bleak rooms of the

321   Blackwell on Lake Windermere, Westmorland. By M. H. Baillie Scott. (See also Figs. 103–108). Hall

eighteenth and early nineteenth centuries. They restore columns to the drawing-room, divide wall heights according to the classical orders and the ceiling into large fields of stucco decoration on the lines of the Late Renaissance. We must pass over all these vogues here, for they do not represent cultural achievements but are imitations and therefore either incorrect forms or variations on what once existed. Only independent artistic achievement can claim our attention and the only one of these, besides the interiors of the Adam and Sheraton period, that comes into question in the history of English interior design is the result of the modern movement in art. When the first edition of this book appeared I was able to report discoveries. Since then the principles of the new English interior design have also become universal currency in Germany, where in a certain sense the English beginnings have been taken up and carried forward. Nevertheless, it may still be worth considering English room decoration systematically.

Technical considerations

Before entering into details of the artistic treatment of the wall, a few words may be said about the technical and structural bases of the interior, making particular mention of those constructions in which English building practice differs from the German.

Wooden partitions

Solid interior walls are not as common in the English house as in the German; instead, the widest use is made of wooden partitions, but the walls of plaster reinforced with wire that are so popular in Germany have been relatively unknown until recently. The wooden walls do not serve merely to separate rooms but also carry the joists. There are no building regulations of any kind in England to say that joist-bearing walls must be solid and of a certain thickness. If the wooden wall has only itself to support and it stands on a good floor it is constructed simply of thin studs between 5 and 10 cm thick and between 30 and 45 cm apart inserted into a sill at the base and a plate at the top. There is a single rail half-way up. If adequate support from below is lacking, the wall will be trussed and will rest on two stone supports inserted into the load-bearing walls and jutting out from them like brackets. If the partition has to carry joists the trusses perform a greater structural function and two are

sometimes placed one above the other with the upper one beginning above the lintel. The intervening space is only occasionally filled with bricknogging; usually it is filled with coke breeze, mineral wool or other similar material as a means of preventing sound passing from one room to another and also to make the walls warmer. In very simple structures the space is left empty. These wooden walls are plastered in the same way that ceilings are plastered, as we shall see.

Interior stud-work

The partition wall, which is almost universally constructed of wood, also has a part to play in the artistic treatment of the interior, since interior stud-work forming a frieze or occupying larger areas has become a favourite decorative motif in rooms. The spaces between the always very strong studs are then plastered white (Figs. 321, 322).

Plaster-work

There have been considerable changes in the technique of plastering interior walls in England in recent times, owing to the introduction of plastering cements. The old traditional English wall plaster consists of three coats, two of mortar mixed with calf-hair and a final one of fine lime mortar. Simple buildings are given two coats only. But in order to speed up the whole process of plastering, new, quicker-setting plasters have been produced recently. An attempt was made to accelerate the drying process by adding gypsum, but this was found unsatisfactory because the plaster cracked. A synthetic product known as Keene's cement has been put on the market and this sets moderately quickly, at the same time giving a surface that can be painted at once. This was followed by a synthetic cement introduced under the name of Parian cement. This material has been completely successful and has meant that the process of plastering in England has been entirely transformed within the past fifteen years. Using this plaster it is possible to apply the three successive coats within a few days and to paint straight on top of the third coat (so that they shall dry out better, walls in England are distempered and left for a year and only then, if at all, are they papered). Besides these two plasters, the composition of which is kept secret but which are supposed to consist essentially of an admixture of alum in the case of Keene's and of borax in that of Parian cement, there are a

322   The architect's house. Four Oaks, nr Birmingham. By W. H. Bidlake. Hall

323   The White House, Helensburgh, nr Glasgow. By M. H. Baillie Scott. (See also Figs. 239–241). Drawing-room

whole series of similar substances, the best known of which is Martin's cement. These plasters are used universally in England, in particular for buildings where much depends upon speed of construction. To simplify the process of plastering even further there are now plaster slabs on the market; these are screwed to the wall and plastered very thinly.

Corners

English plasterers take extreme care over corners. Keene's white cement is invariably used because it dries hard and produces a sharp corner which it is almost impossible to damage. But for even greater security, corners are often rounded or a convex moulding applied. Iron or other reinforcements for plastered corners are not used in England.

Artistic treatment of the wall

Artistically speaking it has been important for the treatment of walls during more recent years that the artistic movement was instigated by painters. Their first move was to look at the wall as a surface. They immediately felt the urge to treat the wall in the noblest way a flat surface can be treated, by covering it with paintings. Burne-Jones at once set to work on a frieze for the drawing-room of Morris's house (Fig. 9) and in the later houses that Morris decorated, particularly those of Lord Carlisle (Figs. 10, 11), and of Arthur Balfour in Carlton House Terrace in London, the plan of the wall paintings was drawn up at the outset.

Wall tapestries

Apart from wall painting, Morris considered wall-hangings to be the most dignified form of decoraton for walls. As everyone knows, one of his greatest services is to have reintroduced genuinely artistic tapestry-weaving. He believed that for northern Europe tapestry hangings were the natural substitute for the frescos of the south. Some of his finest tapestries are those in the chapel of Exeter College, Oxford, representing the Adoration of the Magi, and the five hangings for Stanmore Hall depicting scenes from the life of King Arthur (Fig. 319). In these tapestries Morris achieves a seriousness and depth of artistic effect which rivals the tapestries of the Gothic period and contrasts sharply with the character expressed in modern French tapestries.

Painting

As Morris always went for the monumental and only the best was good enough for him in decoration, so he preferred hand-painting where others were prepared to make do with stencilled or printed patterned papers. Many of the ornamental friezes and especially many ceilings in his houses are hand-painted from beginning to end. But nowadays such decorations can never be regarded as anything but great exceptions, although such exceptions are necessary in order always to hold up the highest ideal to a world that so easily lapses into triviality.

Division of the wall

From the outset the artists of the modern movement restored the division of the wall according to fixed artistic principles to its rightful position. In place of the Victorian papered wall that ran from floor to ceiling, they revived the dado (from the Italian, *il dado* = pedestal) of earlier times. It became so important in the aestheticism of the 1880s as to be found almost indispensable to an artistic room. No less importance was attached to the frieze.

The frieze has always been invested with a special sentimental value in the history of interior decoration. The area of the wall below the ceiling has always been the favourite position for some of the best decoration, not only in our European culture but also in eastern countries. A youthful movement like the one in England at that time was bound to revert to it. The revival of the dado and the frieze at once made three wall areas available. But this was decidedly too much and English wall decoration took a long time to rid itself of the excess. In the refreshment rooms in the South Kensington Museum (see p. 158) decorated by Morris in 1866, a fourth area, a frieze above the panelled dado with small painted infills, was actually introduced. This was one of Morris's favourite motifs and he used it again in Lord Carlisle's dining-room, except that there it extends all the way up to the painted frieze (Fig. 11). It was finally recognised that a limitation was called for and that there must be a choice between dado and frieze. The frieze was preferred and the wall was divided into a shallow area at the top and a deeper one below. The dividing-line was marked by a cornice at the level of the lintel of the door, which is also meant for hanging pictures. There is always a cornice, even when the frieze is restricted to a very small strip of wall below the ceiling.

The frieze and the lower wall

When a wall is divided in two by a frieze and a dado, the dado is kept fairly plain if the frieze is highly decorated and if the dado is decorated the frieze will be plain, possibly entirely undecorated. The dado may be panelled in wood, papered or covered with leather or matting or even plain plaster, with or without stencilled patterning, stucco, Japanese leather hangings, any kind of relief facing in pasteboard or – an extremely popular motif – half-timbering with plain infills. Tapestries are sometimes placed in the frieze, which then becomes the main decoration in the room and may perhaps be deeper accordingly.

Dado and upper wall

However, when tapestry hangings are desired, they will usually occupy most of the wall except for a dado, as do Morris's tapestries at Stanmore Hall. This then becomes the second category of wall division, consisting of a dado and upper wall. The dado is usually the height of a chair-back and is topped by a moulding. This is the old classicising form. But to give the division greater charm the height of the dado is often increased a little. Good proportions will often be obtained by raising the dado to just under half the height of the wall (Fig. 323). Dados are usually wood-panelled or a wooden framework is constructed and infilled with Japanese matting, or it may be covered with some material or a special dado paper with or without relief; or again the dado may be left in coloured plaster with only a skirting-board and capping above. Skirting-boards in England are always of a fair height, at least 20 cm. and often as high as 36 cm., when they consist of two parts. The wall above the dado is usually papered, or it may be plastered, either colour-washed or with a stencilled pattern. Large rooms may have another, smaller, frieze at the top, which then belongs rather to the ceiling and is separated from the main part of the wall by the picture-rail. In the absence of such a frieze the picture-rail lies immediately below the ceiling.

It need hardly be said that there are also walls that are not subdivided, as in the speculative houses built by developers. Such walls will be papered all over, as with us. Or – and this is a specifically English case – a wall may be panelled in wood from floor to ceiling. This treatment is very popular in the best-appointed houses and lends the room a comfortable appearance and a general atmosphere of luxury, comfort and extreme homeliness, which is not so easily achieved by other means.

Wood-panelled walls

Wood-panelled walls are more popular in England than in almost any other country. This was already true of the old houses: as we have said, vernacular English houses invariably had panelled walls until far into the eighteenth century. It is almost as if the inmates looked to this warm, comfortable interior motif to compensate for inhospitable nature outside. One of the first and most important steps taken by the modern movement in art was to revive wood-panelling on the widest scale. With proper appreciation of the value of 'flatness', designers returned to the Elizabethan form with its little rectangular infills covering the whole wall like a pattern. Designers have remained true to this form to this day and it has been by far the commonest, as a glance at the illustrations in this book will show. There are as well, of course, numerous variants, from simple cladding with tongued-and-grooved timbers (Fig. 326) to the most ambitious architectural effects in wood (Fig. 329). Individual artists favour particular forms, such as very tall and narrow continuous panels or heavy mouldings. However, in this matter of moulding there has been a striking desire for simplicity, so that today there is, for example, usually no moulding to effect the transition between frame and panel, nor is the panel sunk. By far the commonest material today is unpolished oak; cedar-wood, American conifer woods and walnut (this more rarely) are also used in their natural state. Of the various types of oakwood available, English oak is considered to be unquestionably the best; oak is the only wood still grown in England, but for this too they have already had to rely heavily on foreign (German) wood. Another wood that is much used is mahogany; it is occasionally employed to panel dining-rooms in dwelling-houses but its commonest use is in business houses, for the interiors of which it is the universal wood in England. It is always polished. In addition to these luxury woods, commoner or softer woods such as fir or pine (jointly known as deal in England) are used to face walls. The wood is then given a coat of paint, the favourite colour being white, most particularly for the drawing-room and the bedrooms. In its simplest form, the white consists of three coats of oil-paint; a lacquer-like, finer paint is used in better decorated houses, a glossy finish being avoided by rubbing the paint down when dry, as with Japanese lacquer. The result is a fine, matt surface like egg-shell, which is durable and from which dirty marks can very easily be removed. Besides white paint, pine panels stained green enjoy some favour. It has to be recognised, of course, that the parts exposed to the light will fade. A coat of lacquer will preserve the green for a little longer. For those who want the green colour to be more permanent there is green oil-paint, which is, in fact, used very often. The English nowadays do not want their woodwork painted in any other colour; the popular colours are natural-colour, white and green, in that order.

If the wood-panelling extends to just above head height it will terminate in a shelf on which decorative porcelain, pictures, etc. may be stood. In this case the hanging of pictures causes some perplexity, since it is difficult to determine whether they should hang on the panelling or the frieze. The frieze is the proper place in tall rooms, in lower rooms there will only be small pictures and these will be hung on the panelling.

Cupboards built in to the panelling

Wooden panelling provides an excellent means of building the necessary cupboards into the wall, thereby freeing the room of some of its furniture. This device is popular and is frequently used in England, especially in libraries and bedrooms. But in dining-rooms too the sideboard is often constructed in one with the panelling, being built into a niche formed by two wall-cupboards projecting on either side. In such cases all the panelling of the wall will encroach to a cupboard's depth into the room. But in an English house, where there are always large chimney-breasts, there is also ample room for built-in cupboards on either side of the fire-place (Fig. 330), if the architect has not already provided for these by adjusting the position of the partition walls. If the panelling is high the panels of the doors are made to match the panelling of the walls so that they shall not interrupt the continuous pattern, as the main artistic effect of wall-panelling, most particularly when treated in the English way, is to give the room a restful unity.

Papering the walls

The papering of walls, or, if the walls are sub-divided into sections, the main areas of walls, has been scarcely less common in England during the past century than on the continent. During the last decades England has actually been ahead of other

324 Motcombe, Dorset. By E. George and Peto. (See also Figs. 153–158). Dining-room

325 Fernleigh, Nottingham. By Arthur Marshall. Hall

326 Prior's Field, Compton, Surrey. By C. F. A. Voysey.
(See also Figs. 180, 247–250) Hall

The characteristic feature of this style is that it is invariably based on stylised plants, from which it always blossoms into a bold, rich display. In both respects Morris pointed the way. But whereas, thanks to his unusually subtle sense of colour, Morris always moved within this powerful range of forms and colours with complete mastery, many English pattern designers lapsed into crudity and harshness. Despite the undoubted beauty of the patterns in themselves, this is the failing of the English wallpapers as wall-coverings. One cannot discuss them without first stressing the questionableness of their quality. The harshness of the patterns may be one of the reasons why designers of interiors are becoming increasingly reluctant to use wallpapers.

History of wallpaper

Wallpaper was originally a substitute for textile wall-hangings. The concept of hanging has clearly persisted in the English language, in which, though in fact pasted, wallpaper is said to be 'hung'. The first wallpapers (which can still be seen at Hampton Court) were deliberate imitations of material: the paper is coated with glue and wool or silk dust is blown on to it to give it the appearance of stuff. The next stage, to produce a pattern by gluing only a part of the paper, followed automatically. These papers, the equivalent of our velours papers, were still popular in Victorian times and were known as flock papers. They were extremely expensively made and cost up to 75 M a roll. Silk could have been bought for that price, but imitations were the triumph of the age. The first papers with wider artistic aims were designed by Pugin; they were mostly of the kind known in England as diaper, i.e. the motifs were rectangular or otherwise

countries in the use of wallpaper because it was the first to strike out in new directions and develop a characteristic flat pattern. It is not only Morris's own papers that reach such a high level, but the generation that followed him in the Arts and Crafts movement continues to work along Morris's lines with excellent taste; with a light but sure touch they are creating the new kind of pattern that one can almost regard as the English national style.

327 Westover, Milford, Surrey. By Arnold Mitchell. (See also Fig. 228) Hall

328 Windyhill, Kilmacolm, nr Glasgow.
By C. R. Mackintosh. (See also Figs. 109, 110). Staircase

329 Motcombe, Dorset. By E. George and Peto. (See also Figs. 153–158, 324) Morning-room

330 House in Chelsea, London. By C. R. Ashbee. Dining-room

geometric. The Gothicists after Pugin used much geometric ornament for wallpapers, although the public seems not really to have liked them.

Morris's wallpapers

The father of modern wallpaper is Morris. He devoted much of his energy to wallpaper and it was certainly through his wallpapers that he became most widely known to the English people. Because he hated all modern manufacturing techniques, his wallpapers were printed not by machine but by hand – and it must be said at once that, exceptionally, he did not print them himself but had them done by the well-known firm of Jeffrey & Co. Hand-printed articles are, of course, fairly expensive. But the demand for really good quality is always so great in England that no one need shrink from producing expensive goods. Morris's wallpapers became known far and wide. One finds houses in England today which are almost exclusively papered with Morris's papers, although their owners have very little to do with art. Seldom before in the history of artistic handicrafts has the public favoured the same article over so long a period. Some of Morris's papers, such as the celebrated 'Daisy pattern' and particularly the 'Pomegranate pattern' (Fig. 331), are as popular with the public today as they were forty-five years ago, when they first appeared on the market; indeed, in the past ten years particularly, the demand has risen steeply because the desire for art is becoming ever more general. Since the wallpapers are hand-printed they can be reprinted at any time and in any quantity, whereas, as is well known, machine printing requires very expensive and time-consuming preparations, which accounts for the manufacturer's unwillingness to make arrangements for a new impression of an old pattern. He has greater expectations of the public's hankering for novelty. Herein obviously lies the advantage of the hand-printed paper, for it is better suited to a continuing small demand. But the artistic quality of the paper itself is also greatly superior, because hand-printing gives the pattern a sharpness and at the same time a smoothness which cannot be obtained with machine-printing, by which the whole roll is printed with all the colours simultaneously. For this reason hand-printed papers, of which every wallpaper manufacturer has a wide selection, are used in all the better decorated interiors in England. A roll of hand-printed paper costs anything from 6 M upwards. But it must be said at

once that the English roll of wallpaper is considerably larger than the German, measuring 53 cm. wide by 10.91 m. long (21 in. × 36 ft.).

As has already been remarked, Morris's early papers have a more naturalistic, looser but always entrancingly attractive and poetical pattern. There is no wallpaper to compare with the pomegranate pattern (Fig. 331). Its effect is bright yet the colour is deep, at once bold and light and at the same time wonderfully poetical in feeling, it has rightly become the favourite wallpaper of every art-lover in England. In both his wallpapers and his materials Morris later worked his way through to the flat pattern that was to remain his own for the rest of his life. This pattern is rich and scintillating with life and vigour and each time it is seen its freshness surprises; it will stand for all time as one of the brilliant achievements of human artistry.

Morris analysed his thoughts on textile patterns in a few shortish essays. He requires a pattern to be balanced and rich, i.e. the line must be meticulously exact and the spread of the pattern luxuriant. He was master of both. His basic lines always have an incomparable roundness and his patterns are always big with a fullness of life. He is very fond of a secondary pattern behind the main pattern so that one plant-system develops over the other. The two are on quite different scales. He further requires a pattern to contain something 'mysterious'. By this he presumably means the personal, inexplicable attraction inherent in every artefact of the highest order. If any flat pattern has achieved this, it is Morris's. He finally insists that pattern must have a narrative quality. Every true art until now, he says, has meant something, it was quite unthinkable for naïve periods of art to produce a meaningless work of art, a mere picture, a mere pattern, every good art of the past was a narrative art. Pattern should tell us about nature, about the beauties with which it is filled, it should convey a reflection of the enjoyment that we experience out-of-doors in the midst of nature. In this he found himself at odds with some of his contemporaries and, had he experienced it, he would have been almost fanatically opposed to the doctrine of 'non-representational ornament' that was introduced on the continent a few years after his death.

Anyone who looks closely at the artistic phenomena of the world

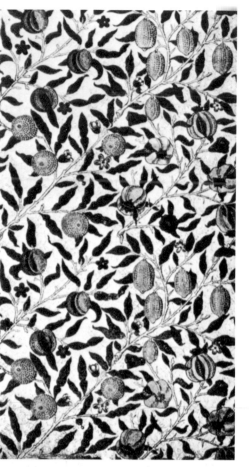

Left: Wallpaper Pomegranate design by William Morris. Below: Wallpaper Wine and Willow design by William Morris (from working drawing, reduced). Right: Honeysuckle design for printed linen by William Morris (from working drawing, reduced)

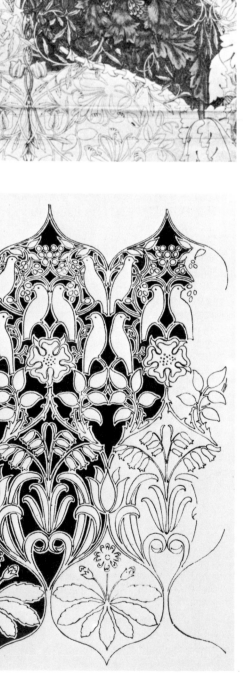

334–336   Left: Wallpaper Acanthus design by William Morris. Above: Textile design by C. F. A. Voysey. Right: Design for a wallpaper by C. F. A. Voysey

170

337 Wallpaper Rhododendron design by Heywood Sumner

338 Wallpaper Peacock design with matching frieze by Walter Crane

will scarcely feel inclined to attach too much importance to claims of this sort advanced by individual artists. But one can only stand before a phenomenon such as Morris with the deepest respect and, mindful of his inspiring works, gladly agree with all his propositions. Any artist who enraptures us may put forward as many propositions as he likes, he has every right to do so.

The celebrated wallpaper and material designs, Vine and Willow (Fig. 332), Bird and Vine, Dove and Rose, Anemone, Honeysuckle (Fig. 333), Wandle, Kennet, Lily and Pomegranate, Acanthus (Fig. 334), Pimpernel, African Marigold, Rose, Norwich, Trent and many others which have become a national heritage of the English people and the names of which are known to every art-lover, date from Morris's best period. Most of the patterns depend in form on medieval brocades, for which Morris felt unbounded admiration; plants always form the theme, sometimes with the addition of birds and other beasts. Although one can say that these materials and wallpapers would have looked very well in a medieval room, they certainly do not prompt medieval associations of ideas. Without wishing to be so, they are modern in the best sense of the word, an ornament in every decorative scheme. They stand alone, far above any stylistic consideration. As in form, so in colour their effect is incomparable. Only a master of the first order could harmonise such powerful combinations of colour to achieve such euphony, only Morris would have ventured always to wade knee-deep, as it were, into these original, rich deep colours. He is the best counter-argument to a sensitive decadence that dare express itself only in grey and pale lilac. His is strong, primal, rustic colour heightened to the loftiest artistic effect.

Wallpaper patterns after Morris

The excellence of Morris's work had a repressive effect on his contemporaries and successors. Of these, Walter Crane and C. F. A. Voysey have remained to this day the best and most prolific designers of patterns for wallpapers and materials. Their work in this field has been spurred on mainly by a number of manufacturers who turned to the best artists to raise the standard of their products. England was the first country to recognise the truth that industry cannot live on the intellectual nourishment of a low category of pattern-designer. Success has shown that this brings up not only an artistic but also an economic question, for the increase in exports reported by England during the past twenty years is due entirely to their high artistic quality. Both Walter Crane and C. F. A. Voysey, together with Lewis F. Day, Heywood Sumner, Aymer Vallance, Allan F. Vigers, Arthur Silver, Brophy, Mawson and others have produced designs for all the important textile manufacturers and have thus done much to raise the standard of the industry. Walter Crane with his characteristic versatility introduces new motifs, especially figural and animal, into wallpaper (Fig. 338), borrows freely, now from the antique repertoire of forms, now from the medieval, uses his own individual lines and colours and is almost inexhaustible in the imaginativeness of his design. Voysey adheres more closely to Morris's more primitive plant designs and likes to combine birds with plant forms (Figs. 335, 336). His colours are deeper and richer than Crane's and altogether one can say that he is the one who has best continued Morris's great tradition.

Textile patterns

Textile pattern has gone hand in hand with wallpaper pattern everywhere in England during the past twenty-five years. Here again it was Morris who set the high standard almost on his own. His printed cottons and woven woollen and silk materials are on the same superlative level as his wallpapers. These materials too are much used as wall coverings, simply replacing wallpaper in the better decorated interiors. But they are most commonly used for covers for furniture and for curtains. For the rustic style of the more modern English interior silk-covered walls have something too soft, too suggestive of the salon about them to have been much used.

Materials for wall coverings

But other kinds of material for covering walls have become extremely popular, most of all unbleached linen, also a large selection of untreated cottons. Japanese or Indian matting is also sometimes used. Plain-coloured wall coverings are either undecorated (especially when there is a richly decorated or painted frieze above the wall) or carry a printed or stencilled

339 House at Weybridge, Surrey. Designed by George Walton. Dining-room

340 Painted frieze by Arthur Gwatkin

pattern. Stencilling in particular has been revived most successfully for the decoration of wall coverings. The best interior designers, such as B. Walton and Mackintosh, use nothing else. Stencilling always lends the wall an individual appearance for it is in fact hand-painting though applied mechanically because it has to be repeated. Thus it raises the decoration of the wall to what the highest aspirations would have it: an individual decoration, for which it is naturally assumed that a special design will be prepared for each interior.

Leather wallpapers

Japanese leather wallpapers are not often used, though they do appear occasionally in friezes. The genuine Spanish leather hangings that were not unknown in Elizabethan interiors are sometimes used in very luxuriously appointed rooms especially when pieces of the old material are available, but it is mostly found nowadays in the form of panels in screens.

Relief wallpapers

Relief wallpapers form a chapter to themselves in England; they exist in the trade under all sorts of names and are apparently widely used. Remarkably enough, Morris in his early period liked to use them and there is one in the room at South Kensington that we have already discussed. Did this perhaps give a boost to the manufacture of these papers? The commonest are products sold under the names of Cordelova, Anaglypta and Lincrusta-Walton; Tyne Castle Canvas and Lignomur are similar papers. Relief papers are unfortunately meant to evoke ideas of genuine tooled and painted leather hangings; on dados they even simulate wood-panelling or tile facings, a procedure which carries its own condemnation.

Decoration of the frieze

There is perhaps rather more justification for using relief papers on friezes when the means for real stucco are lacking, though they are better not used here either. We shall discuss stucco and stucco substitute in more detail when we deal with ceilings. If the frieze is not decorated with a special figural or other painted decoration (Fig. 351) a stencilled pattern will probably be improvised, for these are extremely popular in the more modern interior design (Figs. 339, 341). Rich, deeply luxuriant, flowing patterns derived from plant forms are also popular (Figs. 340, 342). A vast selection of special papers for friezes is available in England as substitutes for stencilled patterns; they are often designed specially for the paper on the lower part of the walls, which they are intended to complement. Walter Crane and all the other wallpaper artists have designed matching wall and frieze papers (Fig. 338) and some also have special papers for the dado. Yet it is clear that, artistically speaking, there is a certain danger in this notion: it is easy to decorate and patternise to excess.

341 House at Dunblane, Scotland. By George Walton. Hall

342 The architect's house, Gullane, nr Edinburgh. By Sidney Mitchell. (See also Fig. 140) Hall

In fact, things have gone too far with patterned wallpaper in England. It is true that Morris with his unquenchable love of ornament pointed the way down this slippery slope. In the rooms that he decorated he often covered not only all the walls, the frieze and the inside of the fireplace with pattern but he also painted patterns on to the beams in the ceiling and the spaces between them (see Fig. 318). But his subtle sense of colour enabled him to weld it all into a whole. The commercial decorator, however, who begins by sticking a dado pattern – possibly even in the form of a relief paper – to the dado, then covers the wall with one of the boldly patterned English papers and finally glues a no less loud paper to the frieze, can produce simply appalling results.

343   Design for a frieze by M. H. Baillie Scott

2. *The ceiling*

Dependence on the Elizabethan ceiling

Since the primary aim of the new movement in house-building was to revive the methods of the old popular handicrafts, it was inevitable that when it came to decorating the ceiling artists should return to the period of the greatest triumphs of the national art, namely the Elizabethan. Two forms of ceiling were re-introduced, one timbered with the beams left exposed, the other stuccoed and covered with a flat pattern. This meant that the whole period of French and Italian influence expressed during the past two and a half centuries in ceilings with architectonic sub-divisions, which achieved high artistic perfection in the graceful confections of the Adam brothers, was simply skipped over. The old, genuinely English ideas of ceiling decoration whereby embellishments were simply applied to the flat surface with no architectonic articulation was now revived. This goes only for those ceilings that were decorated. Obviously, considering the great tendency to simplify that pervades the English house, absolutely plain, undecorated ceilings occur frequently.

Structural considerations

As we touch briefly on the question of technique it becomes clear that the English method of constructing ceilings differs radically from the German. As in the English roof, very thin plank-like beams are laid side by side with little space between them.

English ceiling beams are only some $5-7\frac{1}{2}$ cm. (usually 5 cm.) wide by some 20–25 cm. high and lie between 30 and 38 cm. apart from centre to centre (Fig. 344). These thin, tall beams are used to span lengths of up to 5 m. It is interesting to note that the German ceiling with its thicker beams placed farther apart has almost exactly the same wood content as the English; one could think of the English ceiling as taking each of our ceiling beams and sawing it into three planks, which are then distributed over the area spanned by the German beam.

It must be admitted that the English construction has the advantage of spreading the weight of the ceiling more evenly over the wall and this might even be thought to be one of the reasons why the English in general manage with thinner walls than we do. Another factor that helps to distribute the weight evenly is the universal use of a wall-plate. But it is considered advisable to embed it in the wall only if it is made of iron, a practice that is common nowadays (Fig. 345). Wooden wall-plates are now usually laid in front of the wall on either stone or iron brackets embedded in the wall at intervals of 90 cm. (Fig. 346). Care is always taken with beams that lock into the wall to see that the masonry does not touch the wood, space being left on all four sides of the end of the beam for air to circulate (Fig. 347). Extreme precautions are taken in timber constructions of this sort in England to protect the wood from rotting, since, as it is, the damp climate favours the growth of fungus. Herring-bone strutting diagonally crossing the spaces between the beams and repeated every $1\frac{1}{4}-1\frac{3}{4}$ m. prevents the tall thin ceiling timbers from being deflected sideways (Fig. 348).

Sound-proofing

In all better built houses steps are taken to prevent sound from passing from room to room by covering the spaces between the beams with an 8 cm. layer of mineral wool or specially shaped slabs made of a material known as satin gypsum. But on the whole this infill cannot be expected to have much effect and it is not used at all in the small, cheap suburban houses. However, in better built houses so-called double ceilings are a more effective way of insulating against sound. As has already been noted, this type of ceiling was introduced during the period when rooms were exaggeratedly tall for reasons connected with the form of the façade. It was found that if the lower ceiling were constructed

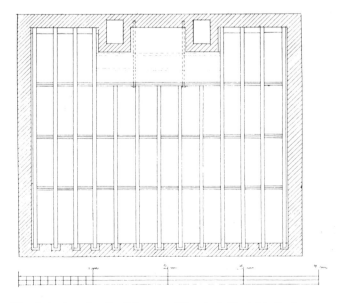

344   The timbering of an English room. (The plank-like joists lie close together and are reinforced by cross-strutting)

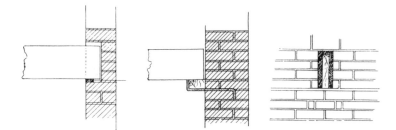

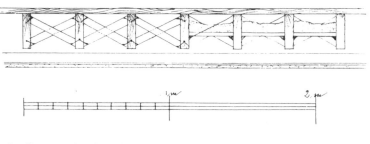

345–347　Joist on an iron wall-anchor. Projecting wall-plate on bracket.
Joist-head allowing space for air to circulate.

348　Cross-section through timbering and cross-strutting

entirely independently of the upper, floor-bearing ceiling, sound did not pass from room to room. Ceilings of this kind are still sometimes constructed in this way in the interests of sound-insulation. But in order to save height, the two ceilings are pushed as close together as possible without touching at any point. This method has given rise to the shortened form of double ceiling that is much used today: special small laths (between 5 and 8 cm. thick) placed at intervals of between 30 and 38 cm. to take the plaster of the ceiling are attached to joist-bearing girders. In order to prevent the passage of sound, a layer of good thick felt is laid between all the surfaces of contact of the upper halves of the ceiling. The laths to which the plaster of the ceiling is applied are laid on battens which are nailed to the girder so that they lie flush with its lower edge (Fig. 349).

Plastering the ceiling

The ceiling is plastered in the same way as timber-framed partition walls by nailing small thin laths to form a surface for the plaster, which is applied directly to them. A small cleft, about 1 cm wide, is left between the laths, into which the plaster penetrates (Fig. 349). This forms a small thickening behind the laths at each cleft, which prevents the plaster on it from falling off. Wire mesh is sometimes used nowadays as a surface for plaster. If a ceiling with exposed beams is wanted, the beams mentioned in connection with the double ceiling are usually used in the form of complete beams. In this case they will be thicker and made of better wood and the plaster will lie between them instead of on their under-surfaces.

More modern ceiling structures, especially solid ceilings, have so far found little place in the English house. Even the sill below the ground floor, which stands some 50–80 cm. above the soil, consists of a timber-beamed structure. Admittedly, plastered, or occasionally iron, girders are used instead of wooden ones. But although in theory hollow spaces in wooden ceilings are now condemned, the only buildings in which solid ceilings have been adopted are the blocks of flats that are now going up in numbers in London; and their construction has nothing in common with that of the detached house but rather resembles that of public buildings.

Artistic treatment of the ceiling

One thing that strikes a German as most typical as he looks at the various ways in which the modern English ceiling is decorated is that there is nothing even remotely reminiscent of the 'painted ceiling', executed by the room-painter, that is so popular with us. This type of painting is never taught at the schools of arts and crafts or the technical training colleges. Nor are mass-produced stucco motifs for decorating centres and cornices always available, as they are in Germany. Both these forms of so-called decoration have disappeared entirely from the modern English

room. With the best of intentions it would be impossible to decorate a room in England in the manner that is so popular in Berlin, where it is known as the 'aristocratic' manner, with these devices, except by obtaining them from Germany. The fact that they are neither available nor desired can only be regarded as a mark of the high level of public taste in England.

Papering the ceiling

Simple rooms in England have smooth, plastered ceilings with no 'rosette' and no stucco moulding; the ceiling is either plain white or papered. Papering is very popular; in simple houses especially the drawing-room ceiling is usually papered since this is considered superior to a plain white finish. A large choice of special ceiling papers is available. They differ from wallpapers in that instead of vertical patterns they have non-directional powdered patterns, usually with some sort of star or rosette as motif. They are also always very clear and pale in colour. The effect of papered ceilings is most agreeable; while the pattern gives them variety they yet look refined and are unobtrusive and reticent.

Morris's painted ceilings

Rather than paper them, Morris painted the ceilings of his better decorated houses by hand. He embellished the different compartments of the ceiling with a pattern painted in pale tones, always in a regular star-pattern similar to the one on his ceiling papers (see Figs. 10, 11). As has already been said, he was particularly fond of covering the dividing beams with painted patterns.

Division of the ceiling

Where richer decoration is desired the ceiling will be divided into compartments instead of being left entirely flat. If there are beams they themselves will form the framework and additional dummy beams may be introduced at right-angles to them, as Baillie-Scott has done at Blackwell (Fig. 106), also Sidney Mitchell in his house at Gullane (Fig. 342). In the compartments that are thus formed, either the closely laid smaller ceiling beams will be visible or the large main compartments will be

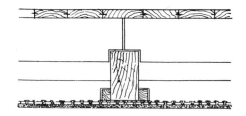

349　Shortened form of double ceiling used for sound-proofing

350 House at Four Oaks, nr Birmingham. By W. R. Lethaby. Drawing-room

351 Frieze in gesso: Music and Dance, by R. Anning Bell

subdivided, possibly by wooden ribs, behind which the whole ceiling will be lined with wood exposed to view, as in Norman Shaw's example at Cragside (Fig. 26), a ceiling that has an exceptionally homely air.

Timbered ceilings

This form of ceiling is, however, relatively rare, clearly because it is basically non-structural. Plain timbered ceilings in which the beams are left exposed are much more common and are a very popular construction in England. The small, elegant timbers are always laid close together. The older architects, such as Norman Shaw and Ernest George, were fond of applying bold mouldings to the beams, in the Gothic form that was still the established manner in Elizabethan times. But nowadays they are always kept plainly rectangular. The exposed beams are treated in a great variety of other ways. In drawing-rooms they will probably be meticulously painted with white oil-paint; they are sometimes stained dark but nowadays the wood is far more often left in its natural state. Oak is the most popular on account of the fine natural patina it acquires with time. Many architects like to leave the timbers unplaned so that one can trace the marks of the saw, if not the axe-blows (Fig. 321). Characteristic of England nowadays is a general desire to recover the old romantic methods of work. But since this does not prevent their disappearing, the English try to express their love by holding fast at least to their visible trappings – rather as Faust snatches at Helen's garment as she is spirited away.

The areas between the beams of the timbered ceiling will either be plainly plastered, or plastered and painted in a plain colour, or boarded in. Mouldings effecting the transition to these areas are rarely seen nowadays, they simply abut at right-angles.

Grid ceilings

Another type of ceiling has a flat surface simply sub-divided by a grid of flat wooden, only slightly projecting, battens (Fig. 350). The battens are painted white like the ceiling or the wood may sometimes even be left in its natural state (Fig. 355). This type of ceiling marks the transition to the reintroduction of the unmistakably English grid ceiling of Elizabethan times. The ridges form small rectangular, lozenge-shaped or polygonal panels or sometimes a mixture of all three, but the resulting pattern spreads uniformly over the whole ceiling so that the effect is definitely that of a flat pattern.

Fibrous plaster

As in the Elizabethan period, so now the wooden fillets were soon replaced by plaster ones. But whereas in the earlier period the plaster fillets were always applied to the ceiling itself, a way of simplifying the work was soon discovered whereby the motifs formed by the fillets were produced singly by machine to be attached to the ceiling in a finished state. A substance known as fibrous plaster is now used universally for the purpose. Thin pieces are formed by pressing a paper-like material into a matrix and these are then screwed to the ceiling. As in the case of relief papers (see p. 172), there are several products on the market (Anaglypta, Salamander, Cordelova, Lincrusta, etc.), for which the most varied qualities are claimed, including resistance to fire, though there is not much to choose between them. The material contains various constituents, of which asbestos and fibres are presumably always present, and the base is usually canvas. Although very light and thin, the pieces are stiff enough to retain their shape. There is a large choice of patterns, the best being the quite simple all-over ones of which the motifs are outlined in ribs (Figs. 352, 353). Here again machine-production unfortunately leads to an excess of ornament, of which the pattern-books give examples in plenty. As soon as plant-ornament or the like is introduced on these pressed pieces, the effect is usually unattractive, for the ornament becomes ordinary, like all machine produced decoration. The pieces are made in sizes varying between 53 and 75 cm. and the joins are arranged so that they come at inconspicuous points, such as to the side of a rosette. Since the pieces are flexible they can also be used to cover vaulted ceilings. They are not cheap; prices range from 4 M per square meter upwards, the useful patterns being unlikely to cost less than from 6 to 8 M. Despite the high price, fibrous plaster is in fact used with wearisome frequency today, usually, in the hands of the developers, in its over-elaborate form. But it does offer architects a very convenient means of having their own designs executed by the factories, which the latter are always prepared to do as the pieces are largely produced by hand. All reputable architects do this for their interiors and, used in this way, there can be little objection to fibrous plaster. For as long as it is confined to patterns that have to be repeated many times over, mechanical production is the obvious answer. As well as the grid patterns composed entirely of ribs, other grounds decorated in relief were made of fibrous plaster and used for both ceiling patterns and friezes. Baillie-Scott's ceiling to the drawing-room at Blackwell (Fig. 108) is a very handsome example of the use of architect-designed pieces, in which the plant-motif stated in the frieze is echoed in the panels of the ceiling. The pattern in these panels changes.

Fibrous plaster has the advantage that it can be prepared in advance and applied quickly without bringing damp into the house. Moreover it can be painted any colour if a coloured treatment is required.

352, 353   Fibrous plaster for ceiling (Cordelova Comp).

354   Pressed ceiling paper (Cordelova Comp)

Relief ceiling papers

Midway between ceiling papers and fibrous plaster comes a type of pressed ceiling paper (Fig. 354) patterned in relief of varying heights similar to those that have been mentioned in connection with walls. They may be used to cover whole ceilings or the compartments of sub-divided ceilings (see Fig. 327), but they are rarely of any artistic interest.

Free-hand stucco-work

In addition to the grid-like style of stucco decoration for ceilings, another form of stucco decoration which was also extremely popular in the Elizabethan period has recently been revived: it is applied free-hand and embodies a unified composition. This technique was freely used by Norman Shaw, one of whose best examples is illustrated in Fig. 34. Ernest George's morning-room at Motcombe (Fig. 329) has a similar ceiling. This type of stucco, when used, is always kept quite flat and is usually decorated with the strap-work motifs of the German Renaissance. It is applied free-hand in one of the quick-setting mortars currently favoured for plastering, or in Portland cement. It is extremely costly and examples of its use are therefore relatively infrequent.

Inset stucco

But another type of stucco that again goes back to the Elizabethan tradition has been much used in the last few years; in particular the Elizabethan practice of inserting ready-cast sections into the wet plaster of the ceiling is widely followed. Credit for having introduced this technique must go to the Bromsgrove Guild of Handicraft, one of whose members, the architect G. P. Bankart has already designed and executed a large number of very good ceilings. This type of stucco is modelled on examples in old English vernacular buildings, especially the elaborate specimens dating from the seventeenth and eighteenth centuries that still survive in the environs of Banbury. The initial idea of reviving it came from the architect Lethaby (see p. 39), who made lavish use of stucco at Avon Tyrell (see Figs. 63, 64), a country-mansion built by him near Salisbury. The basic motifs of the decoration are simple vegetal ones modelled in a primitive style, obviously by hand, deliberately avoiding any refinement and with a preference for unsharp, slightly blurred outlines. Casts are taken from the original model and inserted into the wet surface of the plaster. This means that the stucco appears only at certain points, in powdered patterns, bands or friezes. Artistically the advantage is that the effect is truly decorative, for the ornament forms a contrast with broad undecorated surfaces. There is something refreshing about the primitive quality of the foliage, flowers and fruit and it accords well with the rustic feeling that nowadays pervades the English house as a whole. This stucco certainly represents one of the most attractive means of decoration at the disposal of the modern English interior-designer (see Figs. 355, 132).

Coloured relief. Gesso

In none of the forms in which the old stucco decoration had been revived had anyone ventured to use colour, of which there are such fine examples in the art of earlier times. This has been attempted only in extremely isolated cases and modern stucco is in general uniformly white. But there is a new type of stucco that is lavish in its use of colour, indeed it is virtually based on colour. This is the polychrome relief first re-introduced by the painter G. E. Moira and the sculptor F. Lynn Jenkins. The plastic element is restricted to a low and fairly flat relief, usually in the form of a figural composition. This is then treated with tempera, the paint being applied in a sort of rubbing technique, so that it appears fuller and deeper in the sunk than on the raised parts. This produces a fine, interesting effect, in fact suggesting a heightened form of painting rather than sculpture. Artists of considerable reputation, in particular Walter Crane and Anning Bell, have taken to coloured stucco-work, which had previously been used only in figural compositions: it now forms almost a department on its own among the very numerous techniques practised by the Arts and Crafts group in London. Walter Crane has used it in an ambitious figural frieze in a dining-room at Paddockhurst; the relief here is fairly high and bold. In a few other instances where he has been entrusted with the decoration of ceilings and friezes in living-rooms, e.g. at A. Ionides's house at 1 Holland Park Road and especially at Combe Bank, a house at Sevenoaks, Crane has used another decorative means which has since also won an honourable place for itself in English artistic practice. This is a form of relief executed in a semi-liquid substance applied with a brush, for which, following Italian precedent, the term gesso has been adopted. But its character makes gesso mainly suitable for decorating small objects such as furniture and caskets. Like his wallpapers and materials, Walter Crane's coloured relief decorations are primarily figural and are strongly reminiscent of Italian classical art, though they always bear the stamp of his personal style. Anning Bell's friezes (Fig. 351), like his paintings, are always unusually pleasing, light and vibrant; his favourite subjects are women with wind-blown hair and fluttering, billowing drapery.

The figural friezes of the Glasgow school

The fanciful figural panels of the Glasgow group, Mackintosh, Macdonald and McNair, are totally dissimilar from other relief decoration. These compositions, which arouse so much hostility for the novelty of their conception, are purely linear fantasies, in which the figures serve merely as a pretext. They appear in the widest variety of styles and all possible techniques – embossing, gesso, glass mosaic, enamel – and are always executed by the artists themselves.

Vaulted and other ceilings

Although flat ceilings are naturally the rule, vaulted ceilings are found occasionally (Fig. 357), especially barrel-vaults that span an area with a light segmental arch. This form is particularly effective in long rooms, which is where Norman Shaw liked to use it; his segmental-arched barrel-vaults are always lined with stucco, to which the vaulted surface, subject as it is to a changing play of light, seems so particularly well suited. Niches and other extensions of the room also often have arched ceilings (Figs. 356, 358). It is, in fact, a very popular means of organising space in an interesting and welcoming way, indeed it seems to be made for the purpose. As we have noted repeatedly, timbered roofs with exposed framework have remained a favourite feature in halls to this day. Since the attics of English houses are also always habitable, they present a specific type of irregular ceiling, which virtually invites unusual treatment and the forms of which suggest all sorts of ways in which space may be handled artistically.

Conclusion

If one looks for the basic features that the current ways of treating walls and ceilings in the modern English interior have in common, one can say with certainty that architecture in the sense of the orders and architectonic articulation of surfaces in the generally accepted meaning has gone. Walls and ceilings are treated rather as absolutely flat areas. Even wood panelling, when present, has no architectonic purpose but becomes a flat

355   Brahan, Perth, Scotland. By Bedford and Kitson. Hall

356   House at Edgbaston, nr Birmingham. By W. H. Bidlake.
(See also Figs. 235, 236) Upper landing

357   St Mary's Home, Wantage, Berkshire. By M. M. Baillie Scott.
(See also Figs. 252, 253)

358　House at Dunblane, Scotland. By George Walton. (See also Fig. 341) Dining-room

pattern; and the same goes for stucco decoration on ceilings. Great emphasis is laid on friezes, which are usually fairly deep and are considered necessary links between walls and ceiling. The wall is sub-divided into two. The whole interior demands to be recognised as an independent art, different from the architecture of the exterior, in which the primary goal is calm and restraint. This calm and restraint, indispensable to an intimate and homely effect, is achieved largely by substituting the idea of the surface for the architectural idea. This is the exemplary element in the English treatment of the interior.

3. The floor

Carpets

A carpet extending over the whole floor has been the generally accepted floor-covering in England for more than fifty years. The carpet has been fitted exactly to reach into every recess and window bay. It is nailed down and the floor underneath it is only an ordinary rough floor.

The first opposition to this practice, which had persisted since the eighteenth century, came only recently and when it came it was for reasons of hygiene. People no longer want carpets to be nailed down, for they wish to be sure of being able to have them cleaned regularly and often. Consequently carpets are laid so that a strip of floor all round the wall remains visible. In this way it may also be possible to move a carpet intended for one room into another since it is not so serious a matter if the strip of uncarpeted floor varies slightly in width. This arrangement has, however, necessitated the use of a better type of floor. Once the carpet had ceased to be fastened to the floor, people soon also took a liking to the good wooden floors of the continental type. So ideas about floors are now in process of changing: parquet floors with loose rugs laid over them are becoming increasingly popular.

Wooden floors

In ordinary rooms rough flooring is generally replaced nowadays by good planed flooring, the narrow boards of which are grooved and tongued or secret nailed in the continental manner. Parquet floors are laid on the rough wood floor in better rooms; parquet

may be solid, i.e. 2½–3 cm. thick, or, more often, ¼ inch (6 mm.) thick. The parquet that consists of veneered pieces on frames, which we use, is only just coming in (it is known as parquet-de-luxe) and will perhaps in time prove a suitable replacement for the very thin parquet that is at present used almost universally. When a parquet floor is laid in an old house, the old unsatisfactory floor is simply treated as a rough floor.

Wooden floors laid on a solid base

A wooden floor laid on a solid base, as in the ground floors of town houses and on solid ceilings, represents a major difference from our method of construction. In this case the parquetry pieces or blocks are laid directly on top of the level concrete surface, with the aid of a thin bed of an asphalt mixture. This substance penetrates into dovetail-shaped grooves on the underside of the blocks, thus holding the floor firm. The reason for this method of construction lies in the dislike that is felt for any kind of cavity. Cavities, it is believed, can only serve as hiding-places for vermin and pockets of dirt.

History of the floor carpet

Considering the ubiquity of carpets in the modern home and the fact that it goes so far in England that even servants' bedrooms, indeed even the farmhouse living-room in the remotest hamlet, are unthinkable without their carpets, it comes as a surprise to discover how relatively new the idea of the carpet is. There was no question of carpets during the whole of the Middle Ages; those oriental carpets that existed were costly treasures and were hardly ever used as floor-coverings. Until the seventeenth century the only carpets known in Europe were imported oriental ones brought to the western world in the Middle Ages by the crusaders, the Moors in Spain and later, as the import trade developed, the Venetians. Indigenous carpet-weaving began in France with the flowering of the arts under Louis XIV and in England at the end of the seventeenth century following the arrival of the Huguenots bringing the technique with them. The settlement of French weavers at Wilton at first worked on a small scale but guild rights were granted as early as 1706. Wilton carpets, a plush-like carpet with cut pile, is still one of the most used of English woven carpets. From 1735 onwards a different type of carpet-weaving became established at Kidderminster, a small Worcestershire village. The name Kidderminster, designating a certain kind of carpet, also exists to this day, although the carpets are now made differently. In 1740 the so-called Brussels weave was introduced into Wilton. It is not clear why this name was adopted, but the particular kind of long carpets with short, uncut velvety pile, which began to be produced then, are still universally known by the same name. Finally the Wilton concern, which had already developed into a respectable industry, absorbed the special type of plush carpet with long cut pile that had originally been produced at Axminster in Devonshire and when the factory there went bankrupt, the Axminster manufacture was removed to Wilton. These names cover the main native types of carpet used in England today. In the mid-eighteenth century the Earl of Pembroke, whose seat was the celebrated Wilton House at Wilton, did a great deal to stimulate the Wilton carpet-industry and towards the end of the century the place was already employing 900 weavers. The nineteenth century saw the introduction of many mechanical improvements in weaving, the most important of which, the Jacquard loom, had a revolutionary impact on carpet-weaving. In 1825 the Scottish triple-cloth carpet and in 1832 the so-called Halifax carpet were invented. A vast English carpet-trade now developed to become one of the triumphs of nineteenth-century English weaving activity and to supply a large part of the world market. In England itself, particularly after the first great world exhibition in 1851, carpets were seen in every house down to the most modest. In the 1860s and 1870s, with the opening up of the east to native products, real oriental carpets began to appear in quantity, pouring in in countless ship-loads. Besides these, genuine French Aubussons were still the thing for the drawing-rooms of good houses.

Carpet patterns

The development of the pattern of English carpets is no less interesting than the history of the carpet industry. The carpets made in the eighteenth century still depended entirely on France for their patterns; Adam was the first to prepare his own designs. In the nineteenth century, just as the English industry was becoming immensely strong in the technical and economic fields, there was a falling-off in artistic respects, including that of carpet-design. The horrors of Victorian carpets with their strident flower-patterns, their naturalistic animals and landscapes, their imitations of Rococo gilt borders and other monstrosities, have become legendary in England. The introduction of Persian carpets had a favourable impact on indigenous design in that manufacturers now sought to imitate eastern pattern. But it was inevitable that the fresh charm of the oriental pattern, which lay in its very originality and irregularity, should be lost and that all that there would be to show for this trouble would be an artistic falsification. In the 1870s, however, a real improvement in pattern came from another source and has proved long-lived and sustained. The general upswing of flat pattern in England, which in its broad effect was largely the fruit of the training in the South Kensington schools, affected carpets in particular. Like the manufacturers of materials, carpet-manufacturers had recognised that they must enlist the aid of artists if they were to improve the artistic standard of their products. Walter Crane, Lewis F. Day and Voysey designed a large selection of carpets for the English industry. As with all his techniques, however, Morris entered the field only as a hand-worker. Under the name of Hammersmith carpets he executed hand-knotted carpets which are, indeed, not without a certain charm but which cannot compare with his materials and wallpapers (Fig. 359). Voysey's carpets use the same motifs as those employed in his materials (Figs. 360, 361). But he also designed some quite different carpets, some having, for example, leafy scrolls resembling a family tree, others designed for children's nurseries with all sorts of realistic representations of fairy-tale characters, etc. George Walton has designed many excellent carpets in his distinguished, limpid yet ornament-loving style. All these carpets carry stylised plant and floral ornament. Brangwyn is the only artist who has designed really modern carpets in the present-day continental sense (Fig. 362). His patterns have a mysterious ambiguity which is extremely attractive, but the really excellent thing about his carpets is the colour, which is fresh without being startling, lush without becoming brutal. In so far as it is new, pattern in general at the moment is gentle and pleasing, but taste is sure and no foot is put wrong. Especially among the cheaper, non-velvety woollen carpets one finds extremely satisfactory designs in plenty. Among the more expensive carpets, in particular the Axminsters, imitation of oriental styles is still rife. Yet among these too one can find perfectly satisfactory patterns in every colour one could wish for, especially as the choice is uncommonly large.

English carpets, Axminster, Brussels, Wilton, Kidderminster, etc., were until recently, and usually still are, made in widths of 68 cm. The widths are sewn together and edged with borders 35–50 cm. wide to form carpets of any size. Recently, however, manufacturers have also begun to make large carpets in one piece or at least to put the separate widths together on the loom. This means that the carpet need not be cut to waste, as would otherwise be necessary to make the patterns match.

Modern oriental carpets

Besides English carpets, modern Turkish carpets in particular, made of thick thread with cherry-red grounds intermixed with sparse green patterns, are frequently used nowadays in English houses, especially in dining-rooms. They are made specially for the European market and can now be had in any desired size. Large Persian carpets, as well as Indian and various other types

359 Knotted carpet by William Morris (so-called Hammersmith carpet)

360 Design for a carpet by C. F. A. Voysey

361 Design for a woven carpet with matching border by C. F. A. Voysey

362 Knotted carpet by Frank Brangwyn

of oriental carpet, still enjoy great favour, everywhere now the orient is meeting European demands for exceptionally large carpets. And finally, these carpets have the advantage that they are produced for prices that would be unimaginable for a European hand-knotted product; an English hand-knotted carpet would cost double.

Strips of bare floor round the carpet, carpets for passages and staircases

The bare strip of floor between carpet and wall is treated separately. It will either be painted or the thin parquet that we have already mentioned will be laid, or else the border will be covered with felt, linoleum or matting. If parquet is chosen, its thickness will make it stand out a little above the floor on which the carpet is laid, so that the carpet will be sunk. The carpet itself is laid over felt, felt paper or ordinary strong paper. In the better houses, where hard wear is not anticipated, plain deep-coloured carpets are still always laid in passages, halls, staircases, etc. These carpets are fixed, but with special sprung eyelets so that they can be taken up easily. Every English house has a stair-carpet of one of the better velvety or plush-like carpetings.

Floor-coverings made of felt or matting

There are various other kinds of floor-covering besides carpet. Where there is no parquet, the whole floor may be covered with felt or with Japanese or Indian matting. Both materials are frequently used in England. From the purely artistic point of view, felt, which is available in all colours and is of excellent quality (we are, of course, thinking only of the plain material, not of the hideous felt with printed patterns), makes an excellent floor; its softness and unassuming reticence forms the best possible foundation for the decoration of the room. But there are practical difficulties because it shows every mark, even water-stains, and becomes dirty very easily. Matting is a very popular floor-covering for rooms in which a bright, airy – one might say healthy – impression is desired (Fig. 342). The clean, neat Japanese matting is used for all rooms but most often for bedrooms. Like felt, matting covers the whole floor and it is assumed that small decorative rugs will be laid at chosen points.

Linoleum and cheaper floor-coverings

Linoleum floor-coverings have found their way into English houses, though not in such quantities as the excellent qualities of the material might have led one to expect. Certainly one sees it on the floor of the occasional bedroom and of course it appears in purely utilitarian rooms such as bathrooms, lavatories and also in some of the superior domestic offices. But it is as yet hardly ever used for actual reception rooms. There is reluctance to use it even in billiard-rooms and smoking-rooms; in English eyes the material smacks somewhat of the business office, which precludes any feeling of homeliness. The nursery is the only room in which it is almost always found. It is widely replaced in the simplest houses by the related, but much cheaper, oilcloth, which is not nearly as thick and is backed by a coarsely woven material. It is used in workmen's cottages and in the cheaper suburban houses of the lower middle-classes as a floor-covering for landings, staircases, kitchens and sometimes even reception-rooms. The patterns selected for this material are usually of the most commonplace kind, which in itself rules it out for better houses, even for their meanest rooms. For simpler houses there is also a wide selection of good and very inexpensive materials for floor-coverings which can even make some small claim to beauty; some are called 'Roman', others 'Dutch' carpeting.

Stone floors

Stone flooring of some kind is popular for halls. Certain architects have recently returned to the old floor of large stone flags, which always have such a patriarchal air. Marble slabs of different colours, preferably black and white, are sometimes used to form a simple pattern (Fig. 363).

363 Scottish mansion. By R. S. Lorimer. Hall

The hearth-rug

In front of the fire in every English room, forming an indispensable part of the furnishings, lies the hearth-rug. This is a small rug of the exact width of the fender, or a little wider; it is of special quality and may be called the show-piece of the floor. It is even found in rooms that are carpeted all over, provided that the carpet is such that another rug can be laid upon it; but it is always found in rooms in which the floors are covered with felt, matting, linoleum or pile-less carpet. Its place is sometimes taken by a valuable animal-skin. It lies close to the fender and maintains its superior position as the natural consequence of the great importance that attaches in England to the fire-place in general, and the hearth in particular, as the focal point of the room, the rallying-point of the family and the embodiment of domestic and family life.

B. Openings in the wall

1. Fire-places

Ethical significance of the fire-place

If one takes the idea of the room as a whole, one must look upon the openings in the wall, essential as they are on grounds of utility, simply as necessary evils. But since the human spirit can always make a virtue of necessity, they can be made to lend a special charm, indeed they can be accepted as points of departure for certain creative ideas without which the room would not assume its individual appearance. As far as the English interior is concerned, this applies with special force to the fire-place.

To an Englishman the idea of a room without a fire-place is quite simply unthinkable. All ideas of domestic comfort, of family happiness, of inward-looking personal life, of spiritual wellbeing centre round the fire-place. The fire as the symbol of home is to the Englishman the central idea both of the living-room and of the whole house; the fire-place is the domestic altar before which, daily and hourly, he sacrifices to the household gods.

This is why the English have never thought, and will never think, of relinquishing the fire-place, however irrational it is, however much trouble it causes and however doubtful its practical value. To the English, to remove the fire-place from the home would be like removing the soul from the body. Out of love for the fire-place they overlook all its faults, indeed so great is their love that they are unaware of these faults. And even those who are capable of proving its faults mathematically have not the least intention of concluding from the proof that the fire-place should be scrapped in favour of a better means of heating. In England the fire-place remains and always will remain.

For its justification lies almost exclusively in ethical values. And when one recognises these, one can even go so far as to admit that a country whose climatic conditions permit of fires is to be envied. The fire-place performs its function as a means of providing adequate heat throughout the greater part of the year. Should there actually be a few very cold days in winter, one can be sure that they will soon give place to the usual moderately cold but mostly wet winter weather, during the rigours of which the radiant, drying, warming fire in the fire-place is so greatly appreciated. What luxury to sit before an open fire!

In addition to its comfortable side, the fire-place has a purely artistic significance which places it well to the fore among all the elements of the English house. As in the use of the room by the household, so artistically it is the rallying-point in which the whole essence of the room is concentrated, the central point of its whole development. It is always by far the most important part of the room; even in the poorest house it is the part on which a little money is spent, the part for which a sacrifice is willingly made. It is the soul of the decoration of the room.

Renewed appreciation of the fire-place today

The fire-place occupied the same position in early times in all the countries of western civilisation, but nowhere has the idea remained so much alive until this very day as in England. Indeed, the enormous appreciation of the fire-place as an artistic motif has only just reasserted itself in its full force with the modern movement in art. The tremendous regard in which the fire-place was held in the Elizabethan period has been revived. It was as if by redoubling their affection for it designers wanted to make up for the neglect suffered by the motif during the period of the domination of Italian and French art. Philip Webb, Eden Nesfield and Norman Shaw have made the fire-place the principal motif of their interiors. But whereas in the Elizabethan period the fire-place had been before all else a show-piece on which artists lavished their virtuosity in costly carving and ornamental fantasies, it now became a place which they sought to develop to the utmost in the way of cosiness and comfort. Especially when combined with the old rustic motif of the inglenook, the fire-place became a room within a room, a house in miniature. More has been achieved in the last half-century in the development of the fire-place in England than in all the previous centuries put together. And means have been so many and various as to have been almost unlimited. A book could be written on the English fire-place alone.

Structural details

Before we discuss the artistic development of the fire-place, a few facts concerning its construction would seem to be in order, especially since on the continent fire-places are often incorrectly installed. In England the thickness of the walls, the foundation, the measurements of chimney-breasts, the way in which the opening is arched over and many other details of the fire-place and the chimney are determined by the building regulations. Among other things, these insist that the floor in front of the hearth shall be built solid to a width of 45 cm., that the fireback shall be one brick thick (Fig. 364) and that the chimney shall be plastered inside and out. Following an old tradition, the interior is plastered with mortar made of one part lime to three parts cow-dung; ordinary plaster would crack. A better way of

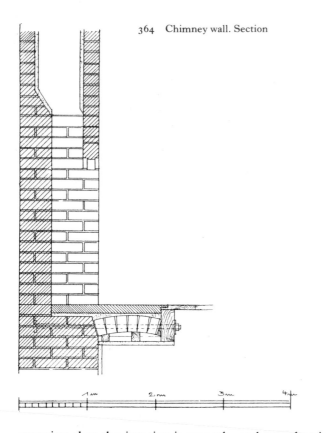

364 Chimney wall. Section

grate reached the climax of its artistic perfection during the eighteenth century in the hands of Adam. The surviving grates of that period, usually made of polished steel most sumptuously embellished with brass or gilt are real models of artistry and good taste. But at the same period a change came about and the fire was entirely surrounded by iron plates. This narrow iron fire-place with its rather high grate and ash-pan open at the bottom remained largely unchanged throughout the nineteenth century. Not until recently was there any attempt to curtail the excessive squandering of fuel, a drawback inherent in this construction, and a whole series of improvements specially aimed at a more rational form of heating have been introduced. Skimming through a modern catalogue of grates, the number of these constructions purporting to incorporate such improvements is legion: whole pages are filled with the makers' promises. But one must be clear about the fact that, viewed as a source of heat, a fire-place will always be a senseless device and it matters little whether its utilisation of fuel be increased from 14% to 18% or 20%. We know, after all, that all such new ideas, with which every branch of the building market is flooded nowadays, have to be treated with circumspection. If one glances at a builder's handbook of twenty or even ten years ago, one usually finds whole series of such innovations that were considered important at the time but have now disappeared without trace. They have vanished as swiftly as they came.

Recent technical improvements

All the devices introduced recently to improve the fire-place aim in particular to improve the rate of fuel-consumption by making the fire burn more slowly (hence the name slow-combustion stove for most of these fire-places). The fire can be regulated and the iron jacket is replaced by one made of fireclay, which, when heated, supplements the direct radiation of the fire by giving out an even warmth over a longer period, so having the effect of a stove. To increase this effect still further, the sloping sides of the fire-place between the opening and the jambs, which was formerly made of iron, is now faced with tiles and the whole hearth as far as the fender is faced with the same material; indeed the fender itself, once made of metal, is now replaced by a low surround of glazed bricks or marble. The trend of the time is thus definitely towards abandoning the iron fire-place in favour of the fireclay type. In order to prevent the fire from burning too quickly, the up-draught from below the ash-pan is restricted by placing the fire very near the ground and having an ash-pan like a drawer with an enclosed front under the grate. The pan also serves to regulate the draught, which is increased when it is pulled out and reduced when closed. What is more, the radiation is carefully directed by constructing the fire-proof surround in the shape of a half-hexagon behind the fire (Fig. 366) and making the rear wall incline sharply forwards to project the heat on to the feet of those seated round the fire, whereas with fires of the earlier type feet were almost always in a cold draught. The inclining of the fireback also narrows the flue and makes for slower burning. These arrangements are essentially those recommended several decades ago by Dr Pidgin Teale which have come in everywhere, so that one can doubtless regard the improved fire-place as a lasting attainment of the English house.

In another type of fire-place the flue is closed and is regulated by a throttle at the top of the fire-place opening. In yet another type, the Eagle range, doors can partly or gradually close the opening. A grate known as 'Nautilus' and Barnard's 'Victoria' fire-place achieve a more satisfactory rate of fuel-consumption by yet other means. To eliminate the draught which is always drawn through the room towards the fire-place, air from outside is conducted to

ensuring that the interior is smooth, and one that is common today, is to insert square glazed clay pipes that exactly fit the cross-section of the flue. The cross-section of an English flue measures 23×36 cm. ($1 \times 1\frac{1}{2}$ bricks). One may assume that a section of one brick square would be ample, but the aforementioned size, or its equivalent round section of 30.5 cm. diameter, has been statutory since the law touching chimney-sweeps of 1840. Smaller flues are built in Scotland; flues are built one brick thick and lined with glazed clay pipes of round section, a construction that may be warmly recommended. Every English fire-place has its own flue and it is considered quite inadmissible to run two flueways into the same flue (a practice that does, indeed, lead to severe inconveniences). In England, as everywhere, smoking chimneys are a public nuisance. Wherever one looks at a roof one sees a cowl or other device for increasing the draught on almost every chimney-pot. There are experts who specialise in stopping fire-places smoking. But the only means available would seem to be to fit one of these caps. There are many different contrivances to prevent smoking in the construction of the chimney itself.

It is generally recognised that the utilisation of fuel for heating in a fire-place is the lowest imaginable. A mere 14% of the heat effect benefits the room, all the rest of the heat flies out through the chimney. With the passage of time, the hearth has become narrower and the heat less. With the old Elizabethan fire-place, which was a tall, wide recess with the fire burning on its floor, one could still believe that a fair heat was given out. When wood gave place to coal (which it began to do at the turn of the seventeenth century), the two iron fire-dogs which supported the burning logs were replaced by a basket-grate that held the glowing coals together. This form of grate, also known as a dog-grate, is still frequently used today; it is true that at the beginning it still stood in a spacious recess, the brick or stone walls of which surrounded the fire, were warmed by it and so radiated their warmth into the room like a stove; but as time passed the recess became ever narrower, presumably because the draught was poor. The dog-

365 Fire-place in which draught is conducted from sides and from below (well fire)

Parts of the fire-place. The grate

Of the three parts of the fire-place from the point of view of which its artistic development may be considered – the grate, the chimney-piece and the fire-place recess – the form of the grate changes least. The form of the more modern slow-combustion grate is fixed and barely susceptible of artistic development. Only the dog-grate and the basket-grate, both of which are also still in common use, admit of artistic possibilities. The dog-grate, so named after the projecting vertical metal pieces resembling fire-dogs, is a relic of the old andirons which supported the logs in earlier times (Fig. 370). Nowadays they are made all in one with the grate. These vertical pieces are the object of often extremely meticulous artistic treatment and are often very prominent, as in Fig. 108, where they terminate in polychrome bunches of flowers. The head at least is nearly always of some considerable size and is an elaborate example of the metal-worker's art. When the dogs stand at some distance from the actual grate the fire-irons are likely to be leant against

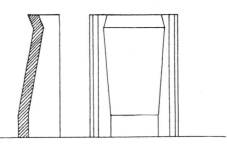

366–368 Above: Shaped fireback made of baked clay (*Chamotte*), cross-section, view and plan. Below: Grate with sunk fire and draught conducted from sides and from below (well fire, dotted lines indicate channels through which the draught is conducted)

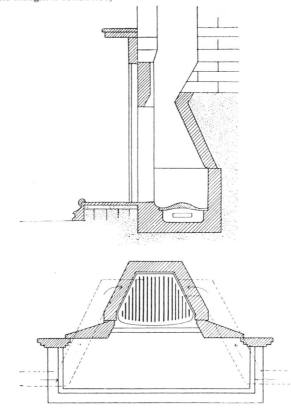

the fire by means of a pipe running under the floor of the room to the hearth itself. Finally a fire-place known as a 'Well Fire'[28] has had a fairly swift rise to popularity; here the fire burns in a grate at floor-height or below, while the actual hearth is raised some 10 cm. above the floor of the grate. The up-draught, which can be regulated, enters at the side or at the front of the fender; the air passes through the warmed channel that leads under the hearth to the fire and issues on to the grate fairly far back, with the result that it arrives at a very high temperature and the fuel is more thoroughly consumed (Figs. 365, 367, 368).

Screen for regulating the draught

As all these devices have reduced the draught, it is also necessary to have special provision for increasing it when necessary, e.g. when lighting the fire or when the wind is in an unfavourable quarter. This is done by means of a screen set in the top third of the opening that turns on a hinge at its upper edge and can be turned outwards or closed to, by a handle, as desired. An even more effective device is a sliding plate that is pushed vertically downwards to close the opening to the height of the burning fire. When the opening is closed in this way, all the air that would otherwise stream through the whole opening and up the chimney is directed on to the fire itself, with very invigorating results. A sheet of glass inserted into the top quarter or third of a chimney-piece will usually prove an effective remedy for a smoking chimney.

[28] Bowes' Patent Well Fire. The name has been chosen because the fire burns in a sunk hearth.

369 The White House, Helensburgh, nr Glasgow. By M. H. Baillie Scott. (See also Figs. 239–241 and 323). Dining-room

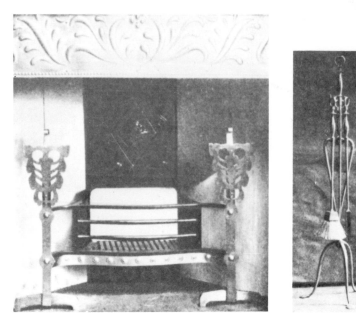

370 The White House. Fire-place, dog grate
371 Fire-irons in polished steel by George Walton

372 House at Weybridge, Surrey. Designed by George Walton. (See also Fig. 339). Fire-place

the bar that links them. Basket-grates occur in an immense variety of forms. They are sometimes placed high, sometimes lower. They are nearly always surmounted by a funnel-shaped hood; originally intended to increase the draught, this has become a favourite artistic motif in the hands of certain architects (see Figs. 369, 372, 374). It is usually made of beaten copper and is sometimes almost the principal motif of the entire fire-place. The fire-back is sometimes faced as of old with a cast-iron plate decorated in relief (Fig. 370).

The chimney-piece

The variations in the surround of the actual hearth are endless. As we have seen, tiles are nowadays the first choice as a surround for the hearth itself because they have the required ability to give out a steady heat, though metal (hammered copper or brass) is often used as well. The ordinary ready-made form of fire-place that can be bought in the shops usually consists simply of a short panel sloping towards the jambs and made nowadays entirely of tiles. Plain tiles are preferred in this position, although there are quantities of the decorated variety on the English market, the shrill patterns of which often disfigure not only the fire-place but the whole room. Morris too liked boldly decorated tiles; the patterns are often greenish-blue or red with a metallic iridescence. Since the colours go well together, the effect is not unpleasant, although not always desirable. Old Dutch tiles are sometimes used and collectors have managed to bring together old Persian examples in sufficient numbers and matching colours to adorn their fire-places. Popular though this practice was in the 1860s and 1870s, the ordinary monochrome tiles with their much quieter and more harmonious effect are preferred today. Pale green or red long-shaped tiles look best. Moreover, the shops sell these tile panels ready set in cement, which greatly reduces the labour of installing the fire-place. In many cases the actual hearth is situated in a stone or plain brick wall (Fig. 369), especially when the fire-place is in a recess. Or the fire-place may be in a recess, of which the semi-circular stone or brick-faced arch forms the simple transition to the wall.

The ordinary fire-place, however, almost always has a chimney-piece of a clearly architectonic character that forms a transition to the wall of the room. It is made of stone or wood and either terminates in a cornice at breast-height or extends to the ceiling in the old way. Norman Shaw has produced two splendid examples of more ambitious chimney-pieces in the picture-galleries at Dawpool (Fig. 373) and Cragside. At Dawpool the stone superstructure rises through two storeys, on each of which is a little chamber with windows from which one can look out; at Cragside the whole of the upper wall is covered with finely composed relief decoration. Ernest George for the most part adheres strictly to the Elizabethan manner but is fond of carrying his chimney-pieces right up to the ceiling. Among younger architects Lethaby has made a speciality of keeping the surrounds of his fire-place perfectly plain but uses the most costly varieties of marble with curious veining to give an interest to the fire-place (see Figs. 63, 64). Edgar Wood likes chimney-pieces of great dressed stone slabs with figural sculpture (Figs. 99–101). Chimney-pieces have also been made of terracotta, witness the splendid example in the law-courts in Birmingham[29] by Aston Webb and Ingress Bell. Indeed, the variety of ways in which more recent English art treats these features is inexhaustible.

[29] Published in the writer's *Die englische Baukunst der Gegenwart*.

No less varied than the solid chimney-pieces are the wooden ones, usually painted white, that are used in cheaper houses. The lower part of the structure consists of plain jambs, while the mantelshelf – these can also be purchased separately – is a fanciful confection of some kind, composed of mirrors, little cabinets, shelves, etc. One sees every kind of combination, not all in the best of taste. Shops supply these surrounds and mantels ready-made at moderate prices; their catalogues contain hundreds of different kinds. Yet the catalogues of John P. White of Bedford (see p. 117) are probably the only ones in which one will find artistically satisfying or really pleasing articles. White has enlisted the services of prominent artists to design chimney-pieces, an enormously praiseworthy service which should be widely followed. Figs. 375–377 illustrate some of the artist-designed chimney-pieces sold by White. The commonest form of wooden chimney-piece seen in English houses nowadays has a central mirror and little shelves to either side. Instead of one continuous cornice-shelf, some chimney-pieces consist of two, one above the other, forming little shelves on which to stand objects or to display bibelots. Not infrequently one finds a small glass-fronted cabinet instead of a mirror in the centre of the shelf, or there may be a long narrow mirror in the centre and two tall, narrow glass-fronted cabinets at the sides. A popular arrangement is to combine book-shelves with the fire-place so that they

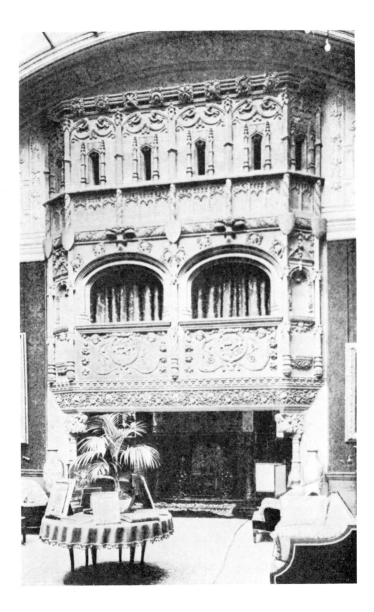

373 Dawpool, Cheshire. By R. Norman Shaw.
(See also Figs. 34, 35, 161.) Fire-place in the picture gallery.
374 Brockhampton Park, Gloucestershire. By Atkinson.
(See also Fig. 132.) Fire-place in the hall

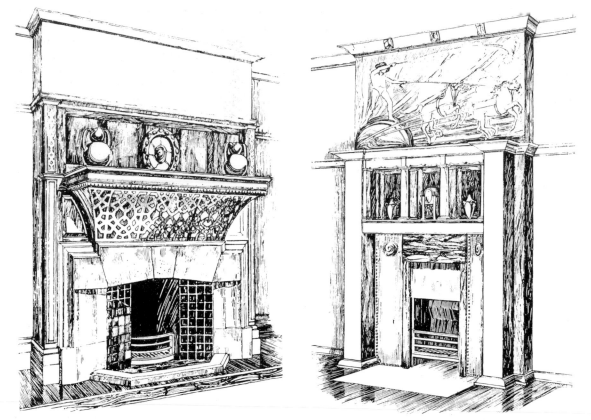

375, 376   Designs for fire-places by C. H. B. Quennell
supplied by John P. White in Bedford

377   Design for a fire-place by C. H. B. Quennell
supplied by John P. White in Bedford

378   Fire-place surround with seat

occupy the lower part of the surround on either side (Fig. 380).
When sitting in front of the fire to read, it is pleasant to have one's
favourite books to hand. The whole design of this chimney-piece
aims at intimacy, at making the fire-place snug, at forming a world
in little in which one can feel as much at ease as possible as one
basks in the glow of a warming fire.

Metal, especially cast-iron, chimney-pieces were also made, in
addition to those of wood and stone, and a few years ago the
Coalbrook Dale Co. commissioned designs from artists of note.
Those of Ashbee were the most successful (Fig. 381). These fire-
places were meant to be painted and so to make their impact
through colour; polished metal ornament appears at certain
points. Voysey too has designed iron fire-places (Fig. 379) for
Longden & Co., a firm that deserves great credit for its artistic
fire-places. Iron fire-places are best suited to smaller bedrooms,
spare bedrooms etc. They make too cold and unwelcoming an
impression in more pretentious surroundings and in reception-
rooms, etc.

Fenders

A number of accessories, which have become essential parts, go
to make the complete fire-place. The most important of these is
the fender, which is meant to protect the surrounding carpet and
wooden floor from leaping sparks. The fender is not very old,
indeed it hardly existed before the eighteenth century, for there
was no need for it before the introduction of coal fires. Nowadays
it usually consists of a low metal enclosure some 10–20 cm. high;
the sides may be pierced or may take the form of a small
balustrade or a brass rod on spherical cornerpieces or some other
metal decoration. Sometimes, as in clubrooms or the like, the
fender takes the form of a balustrade of the appropriate height
and is upholstered in leather to make a seat (Fig. 378). In
nurseries it always encloses the hearth completely to a height of

90 cm. Recently the fender has been omitted altogether from better reception-rooms and replaced by a marble kerb projecting some 10 cm. Or the kerb may be made of glazed bricks (Fig. 377), especially when the floor immediately in front of the fire is similarly covered, an arrangement that is popular today. A high grate will necessitate special protection against flying sparks. This is provided by a smallish wire-mesh guard that is either hung on the grate itself or, in the form of a small triple-leaved guard, is stood in front of it.

Fire-irons

The set of fire-irons or fire-brasses – poker, shovel and tongs – must be described as an integral part of the fire-place (Figs. 386–388). They are a permanent feature of every English fire-place and are made of brass or iron. They were originally used for the definite purpose of tending the fire, but they have now become more or less lifeless ornaments and are left unused to keep them bright and shining. This applies to the shovel at least and usually the tongs, for which substitutes for actual use are kept out of sight in the coal-scuttle or elsewhere. The three implements, the tongs on one side, the poker and shovel on the other, either lean against the fender in front of the fire or against special supports, called fire-dogs, inside the fender (see Fig. 382). So that they shall not slide out of place and become untidy, which can happen all too easily when the fire is being tended, a piece of metal resembling a paper-weight is laid in the middle between them. Thus in the average English house the small space inside the fender is almost entirely taken up with useless implements. It need hardly be said that fire-places that have been designed by artists do not have these accessories or have them in a better form. Useless implements, the shovel and tongs, are omitted entirely or are hung on the wall beside the fire-place or on a special stand (Fig. 371), but in this case they are meant for use. Besides these implements there is sometimes also a brush, with which ash may be brushed under the grate, and bellows; these two implements are not usually regarded as decoration but are essential for the extremely fastidious care that the English bestow on the fire. The coal-scuttle stands beside the fire and can

take any number of different forms; nowadays it is sometimes tub-shaped (Fig. 384) and made of bright metal (copper), though a black lacquered box with a hinged lid used to be the normal thing. One more article completes the equipment of the fire-place: it is as well to have a fire-screen to enable those sitting in front of the fire to shield themselves from the direct heat if they so wish. Standing or folding screens of many different sorts are used for the purpose. Standing screens are used in English houses altogether more than in the continental, because of the draughts. Sometimes too a small protective cloth is hung from a rod projecting from the mantelpiece, which merely shields the face of someone sitting by the fire. But it hardly adds to the beauty of the fire-place. Finally, another accessory that is often seen is a small brass stand on which the teapot is placed, so that it just reaches the height of the fire (Fig. 385).

The fire-place recess

The feature that first made the fire-place the most prominent artistic motif of the room in modern art was the spatial design of its immediate surroundings. As we have already said (pp. 16, 88), the old rustic motif of the ingle-nook was revived and with the adoption of the fire-place recess the modern room gained an incomparable centre of attraction. A fire-place recess must be lit, which means that it must be situated either on or near an outside wall. Fire-place recesses are sometimes sited on inside walls but then, of course, they have no special lighting (Fig. 372). The wall opens into the recess in all sorts of ways, either with a large arch, as in Figs. 372, 389, or simply with a rectangular opening under the frieze of the room, as in Fig. 369. The recess may be rectangular, polygonal or round; it usually forms a little room on its own, the walls and floor of which are either solid (e.g. built entirely of brick) or faced with wood or may continue the decoration of the room. The floor is always level with the floor of the room, as is the case with all recesses in English rooms. There will always be seats along the sides; they are usually made of wood and fixed to the wall. Certain architects, such as George Walton (Fig. 372) and Mackintosh (Fig. 113), like to make the fire-place itself a sort of seating-place by raising the hearth to

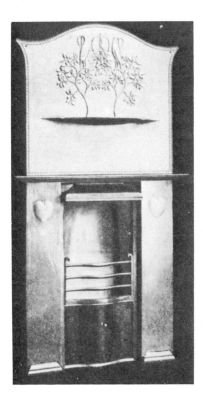

379–381 Left: Cast-iron fire-place by C. F. A. Voysey.
Above left: Wooden fire-place surround by John P. White in Bedford.
Above right: Cast-iron fire-place by C. R. Ashbee

382 House at Dunblane, Scotland. By George Walton.
(See also Figs. 341, 358.) Fire-place in the hall

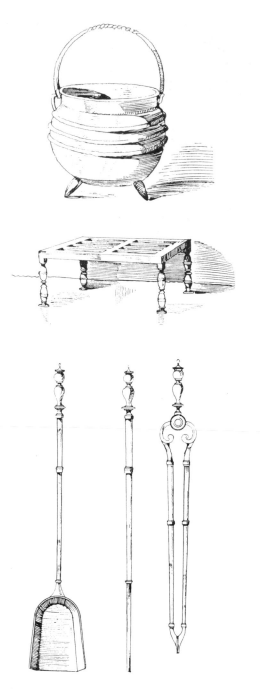

384–388 Cast-iron coal-scuttle. Small brass trivet for standing teapot in front of fire. The customary set of fire-irons (shovel, poker, tongs)

383 House in Birmingham. By W. A. Harvey. Fire-place with 'cosy corner'

chair-height and providing seating on either side. The notion of making the area round the fire extremely comfortable has finally led architects to put in something like an ingle-nook when the fire-place is not in a recess. This entails surrounding it with fixed projecting wooden walls as in Fig. 377. Other means, in particular low partition walls are used to enclose the fire-place and make what is known in England today as a 'cosy corner' (Figs. 382, 383). This device is particularly welcome when the door is very near the fire-place, making the fire-place extremely draughty (Fig. 383). But in general fire-place corners of this sort are among the most popular features in the English house of today. If some architects even tend to overdo the notion (in some houses every fire-place has its recess), the frivolous affectations of the ingle-nooks that are supplied ready-made from shops almost turn them into caricatures.

Other means of heating

Means of heating other than the genuine old fire-place have so far not become established in the English house. There are whole series of stoves suited as far as possible to the form of the fire-place, but in fact one sees them only in catalogues and one can scrutinise a hundred English houses without finding one of these objects. They may be said to be non-existent. Nor has the gas-fire really taken root in the English house. It is true that here and there, especially in the houses of the small men, the philistines, one sees imitation coal or log fires, constructed of clay and asbestos and made to glow by gas-flames designed to simulate the magic of the fire in the hearth; but cultivated Englishmen with their sound good sense rightly resist this substitute. Imitation fire-places have as yet gained no ground in England. If we

389 Design for a fire-place by C. H. B. Quennell
supplied by John P. White in Bedford

introduce them in Germany we must not forget that this contrivance is in no sense of the word a fire-place but only a caricature of one. An honest gas-fire is quite unexceptionable in itself, but why make it simulate an open fire-place?

Fire-places covered up in summer

The fire-place creates certain difficulties in the few summer months during which rooms are not heated. As soon as the outside air becomes warmer than the interior of the room it sends a sooty smell down the chimney into the room. Moreover, an unused fire-place is scarcely a cheerful sight. Various devices have been tried in an effort to surmount this obstacle but none has proved satisfactory. One can overcome the difficulty to some extent simply by placing paper that matches the colour of the walls of the room behind the front of the grate. If the structure of the fire-place permits, one can close the whole opening with a mirror during the summer; in doing this it is advisable to make sure that the sooty opening is hidden from sight rather than allow a conspicuous arrangement to draw attention to the fact that the fire-place is not in use.

2. Doors and windows

Doors few and small

The influence of the modern movement in art on the doors of the English house has been in the main a restrictive one; not only are doors considerably fewer in the modern house than in the house of sixty years ago but they are also smaller. Handsome two-leaved doors were as popular in English houses of earlier times as they are in the average German house. In England too not only were all the rooms linked by the widest possible doors but dummy doors were created to preserve symmetry. Those times have gone. We have already discussed the view that led to the abandonment of communicating doors (p. 27f.). The reduction in the size of those doors that remained was simply the result of

the sounder ideas about purpose and beauty that were emerging. Doors nowadays no longer stand out as architectonic motifs, they simply fulfil their purpose and are made no larger than is necessary. It is extremely rare to find doors wider than 91 cm. (3 ft.) clear in an English house. In smaller houses doorways are sometimes so narrow that our average continental pieces of furniture would not go through. Two-leaved doors are no longer found at all in new houses and our continental sliding doors which can be opened to throw two rooms into one are virtually unknown. When wide openings of this kind do occur, sliding doors are not used but sections of the door are made to fold together.

Door furniture: finger-plates and door-knobs

There are two characteristic features of door furniture that perhaps deserve mention: at the point at which the hand grasps the door to open it, all doors have a protective plate, and in place of our handle, a round or oval knob is always used. The finger-plate is well worth copying. It is placed above or below the knob, or sometimes half above and half below. Or it may embrace the lock furniture and, if it does so, is of considerable size (Fig. 391). It is usually made of brass, occasionally of copper or aluminium and in better interiors even of silver. The finger-plate is the object of special workmanship, embossing or other decorative work being used (Fig. 390). Finger-plates are often also pierced but this has its disadvantages, since dirt settles in the voids during cleaning. The fact that they have to be cleaned is in any case the weakness of finger-plates; it is virtually inevitable that the part of the door immediately surrounding the plate, i.e. the painted or polished door will be touched and, in time, damaged. This is why porcelain or glass are used instead of metal, but this expedient is unsatisfactory, for the plates appear to be in some way an alien material on the door. Wooden plates are often used in older houses. But brass plates are by far the commonest nowadays. Since the plates are merely fixed to the door by two or four small nails they can easily be removed for more thorough cleaning.

It is difficult to find any justification for the English habit of using a knob rather than a lever to open the door. Turning a knob is the most unsuitable way of exerting pressure on a spring, especially when, as is usually the case, it is small and slippery. Whereas a German maid with both hands full can still press down the door-handle with her elbow, her English counterpart has to lay whatever she is carrying on the floor before she can open the door. Knobs are used everywhere in England to open and close locks. Bolts also have them and they often look exactly

390, 391 Brass repoussé finger-plates for doors (Birmingham Guild of Handicraft). Combined lock and finger-plate. By Edgar Wood

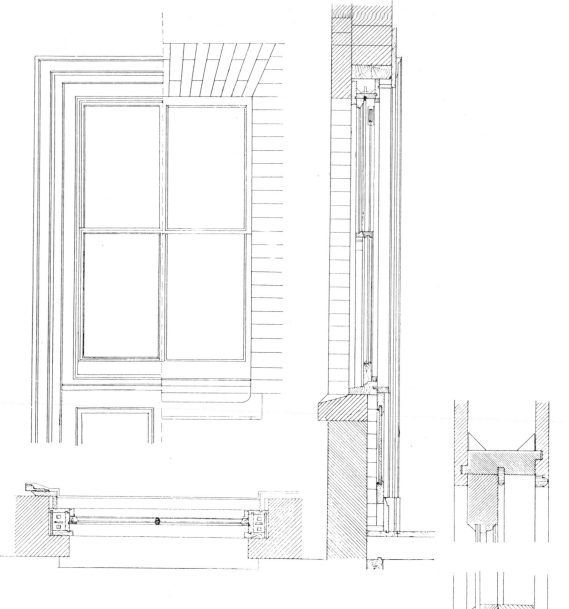

392–396 Above: Typical English sash-window: view, plan and cross-section. Details of construction in plan and cross-section. Bottom left: Cross-section of casing containing weights and inner window-frame. Right, bottom to top: Cross-section of lower transom of inner light and lower horizontal of casing. Above right: Cross-section through central meeting-point of inner and outer lights and cross-section of upper transom of outer light and upper horizontal of casing

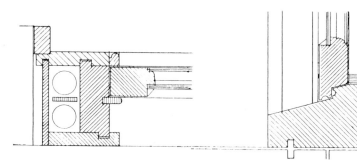

like a turning lock, to the embarrassment of the unversed who try to open a door. Shop entrances are the only doors in England that have handles of the German sort.

No threshold

One peculiarity of the English door is that it has no threshold. There is not even a suggestion of a threshold, the floor-boards simply run straight through. This undoubtedly has advantages in that there is nothing to hinder traffic through the door. But since the proximity of the carpet always necessitates hanging the door slightly above floor-level, there is always a gap of 1–2 cm. under the door. This gap is the principal source of draughts in English rooms. Various means of closing the gap have been tried, including fixing a trailing rubber draught-excluder. However, no one has yet tried to introduce the continental threshold.

Knockers

Everywhere in England there are knockers on the front-doors of houses. A knocker was once the only means by which a caller could make his presence known; but nowadays the bell has in fact rendered it superfluous. Callers knock and ring or simply ring when it would seem too familiar to knock. But the postman always uses the knocker to announce his visit as he pushes the post through the letter-box into the house. With a little practice one can judge the importance of his delivery by the way in which he knocks: for printed matter one will simply hear a curt, disdainful fall of the knocker, a loud knock will signify a letter, and registered post and telegrams, for which the door must be opened, will be heralded by two loud knocks. The English door-knocker is usually of the simplest kind; it is very rarely the object of outstanding artistic treatment.

The wood of the doors

Oak doors are preferably left untreated, as is the woodwork of the whole English interior. Otherwise there is a great fondness for painting doors white or, less often, green or another plain colour. Doors are no longer painted in imitation of wood. And the designers of the modern movement very rarely use the mahogany doors that were once so popular. Where walls are panelled up to a fair height in wood, doors are usually on such a scale that they do not in any way stand out as doors and are recognisable as such only by their furniture (see Fig. 329). They then simply form part of the flat pattern that is the aim of English panelling.

Outside doors of houses are often made of teak. One is struck by the very vivid greens or reds in which the doors of many English houses are painted. Another English peculiarity is the linen curtain that is hung over the front-door in summer, an everyday sight on hot summer days in the London suburbs. The curtain is meant to shade first the front-door and then the interior of the hall from becoming too hot and also to enable the door to be opened to the through-draught while preventing passers-by from seeing into the house.

Many varieties of window

There is a far greater variety of windows in the English house than of doors. Indeed, three entirely different types of window appear side by side, which perhaps makes it richer in this respect than the house of any other country. The three types are the fixed leaded window, the casement-window like ours and the sash-window that slides up and down.

The sash-window. Its advantages

The sash-window is by far the commonest. It came to England with the Dutch influence at the turn of the seventeenth century and was adopted in such numbers that it widely replaced the leaded windows that had been the norm until then. It has been in general use since the eighteenth century and in the nineteenth century it became the universal window of the English house. Its justification probably lies largely in the fact that it is easy to handle and can provide any degree of ventilation very simply. A crack can be opened at top or bottom or both and much or little air let in according to the size of the crack, or a very thorough airing can be given by opening the top or bottom half of the window to its full extent. In short, it offers the ideal solution to the problem of regulating airing. It can be opened by a light movement of the hand at any time and despite wind or weather the window will remain in the position into which it has been put. Considering the importance of fresh air in the English house (see p. 67) one can easily understand why the English value the sash-window so highly. There is a little fillet at the bottom edge of the lower sash, through which a constant, very gentle stream of air may enter (Fig. 396); it also prevents air from entering at the bottom when the lower sash is slightly raised while allowing a small crack to open in the centre of the window through which rain cannot enter. A further considerable advantage of the sash-window is that the open lights of the window take up no space and are in nobody's way.

Disadvantages

But these advantages carry their own disadvantages, the chief of which is that the windows do not shut tightly. To enable the windows to slide up and down there must be play, which is the opposite of close-fitting. In particular the point at which the two halves meet in the closed position is not airtight. Another disadvantage is that the windows are difficult to clean when open because the lights mask one another whenever they are raised. The only way of cleaning them properly is to take a ladder to the exteriors from outside the house. This may have something to do with the fact that in England windows are not cleaned by the servants of the house but by special window-cleaners who call at regular intervals, usually every four weeks. (The dirty windows that one sees so often in England may arise out of this arrangement, for the household has no means of removing any dirt that may appear between visits.) Another serious disadvantage of sash-windows is that they rattle in the wind, due to the play that must be allowed to enable them to slide. Moreover, the rather complicated mechanism by which they are hung can easily go wrong, the cords break and the weights get entangled, damages that only a joiner can repair since the jamb has to be removed before the frame can be reached. More recently, with the growth of concern for the demands of hygiene, there have been objections to the cased frame for the weights, for dirt can accumulate and vermin live there. And finally sash-windows are widely criticised on aesthetic grounds because the lights of the two halves of the window do not lie in one plane. But all these disadvantages have so far done little to reduce their prevalence in England.

Construction of the sash-window

An English sash-window consists of two halves divided horizontally, each half sliding up and down independently. To enable them to do this, each is balanced by means of two cords attached to weights of the exact weight of the lights which pass over pulleys immediately under the lining inside the frame. They naturally move up and down in two planes, one behind the other. The two sliding surfaces are enclosed on the outsides by a moulding and separated from one another by an inset strip of hardwood. Since this strip separates the planes of the two halves of the window, the point of contact of the two central frames that come together when closed is staggered to make the joint airtight (Fig. 396). A fastening in the form of a sprung revolving bolt (Fig. 397) holds the two halves of the window in the closed position. The staggering of the point of contact is a good way of preventing the bolt from being opened from outside with a knife-blade. Figs. 392–396 illustrate the details of the construction of the English sash-window. For the window to work well it is essential that the frames be firmly jointed and made of good wood, for the cords to be made of the best quality hemp, for the weights not to touch the ground, because they would become unhooked, and for the cased frames containing the two weights to be separated by an inserted strip of wood. The weights are made of cast-iron and are in normal circumstances

397 Sprung revolving bolt for fastening the two halves of a sash-window

398 Metal-framed window with catch and stay

round. But if windows are very heavy and larger weights are needed to balance them, the weights will be made of lead and will probably be rectangular in order to utilise the space in the cased frames. Heavy windows always have two handles on the lower frame for lifting, while the top one has a contraption for pulling it down with two cords, which, however, can usually only be handled successfully by the initiated. Sash-windows in general cease to be desirable beyond a certain size, for whereas up to that point they are easy to handle the situation then becomes reversed.

All kinds of attempts have been made during recent decades to overcome the deficiences of the sash-window, in particular to simplify the cleaning of the outsides of the lights. When an outside ladder is not used for cleaning, the window-cleaner nowadays usually starts from inside the room and sits on the window-sill, from which he still cannot reach every part of both halves. The many accidents that have occurred as a result of this practice have led to the invention of devices that enable the window to be opened inwards. This is done either by hingeing the whole window, including the two cased frames for the weights; or by considerably changing the original construction so that the two halves of the window have a hinged movement as well as the sliding one. This latter form of improved sash-window has been successfully introduced by the N.A.P. Window company. Although this window is not yet in daily use, it is probably always used nowadays by clients who seek the best workmanship and are advised by good architects. But it would not appear to equal Stumpf's improved sash-window in Germany, the chief advantage of which is its virtually air-tight closure.

The casement-window

As regards wood-framed windows other than sash-windows, very little use has been made of our casement-window. It is always felt to be un-English and is used only in the form of a French window, opening on to a balcony, a garden terrace, etc. The objections to our window are that the leaves project into the room when open and it is difficult to regulate ventilation.

The fixed leaded window. Metal windows

By contrast, during the past fifty years with the boom in house-building, the old fixed leaded window has become the favourite in English houses. Only certain lights of these windows are made to open, the main area being immovably fixed in a stone or wooden frame.

When the jambs are made of stone, the leaded panes are inserted from outside and secured with special putty, but when the jambs are wooden, they are simply nailed from the outside on to the strips of lead. Those lights that are meant to be opened rest in specially inset iron, steel or bronze frames; they themselves, in similar frames, fit closely into these. This type of metal window has been developed to great perfection in England. Since these are windows that belong in the main to houses built by good architects and in which good workmanship has been a prime condition, much care and attention has gone into the development of good constructions. These metal windows are manufactured by a mere handful of firms, of which the best known are George Wragge in Manchester and Henry Hope in Birmingham. Each firm has its frame with its own cross-section with which it attempts to make its windows as air-tight and water-tight as possible. Different cross-sections are used according to the prevailing weather. Most of the windows open outwards because an outside closure is more water-tight than an inside one. They may open on either a vertical or a horizontal axis. High window lights usually open horizontally because they are manipulated by a pull or by a mechanism worked by turning a handle. Another popular arrangement is for the lights to turn on a central axis as this facilitates cleaning the outside. These lights are closed in the old way by a handle, which, by means of a spring or an inclined plane also closes the light tightly against the fixed frame. Better appointed houses have a bolt at top and bottom similar to our lever or espagnolette locks. There are always plenty of devices for securing the window when open; the simplest and most effective would seem to be the one that can be used both as a kind of catch and as a stay: one unhitches it, pushes the window open with it and presses it down on to a pin which fits into one of the holes designed for the purpose. All the fittings on these rolled metal frames are made of bronze. House-owners are usually perfectly satisfied with these windows, which are the only ones known to the English building industry that will close really tightly. Price alone prevents them from being used more generally.

Coloured glass

The use of coloured glass was a natural accompaniment to the leaded lights employed nowadays in most houses with any claim to an artistic interior. Like all romantic motifs, coloured glass was particularly popular the time of the new movement in English decoration, i.e. under Morris. If the new English art of coloured glass, which is naturally used very largely for churches, already goes in for lighter colours than ours on the continent, the principle of transparency is still extremely strictly observed in the coloured glass that has been used in domestic architecture. Coloured lights are put into halls and other prominent spots, such as front-doors, ends of passages, etc. It always has to be a special occasion that permits the use of this means of decoration. The older school tended rather to follow church glass in its style of decoration. But younger artists have at last broken away and have evolved a style of treating glass which no longer has anything to do with ecclesiastical forms. Walter Crane, Selwyn Image, Brangwyn (Fig. 400) and others have produced excellent designs for domestic windows. Selwyn Image (Fig. 399) in particular has managed to bring an entirely new spirit into his ornament of dense leafage that is totally modern and personal in its effect. Oscar Paterson in Glasgow produces some of the most original designs for glass. He transposes fairy-tales, landscapes and city-scapes into glass, the leading of which always follows the contours of the design. Despite decidedly realistic leanings, he still adheres to a delicate style that takes account of the limits of the medium and purpose (Fig. 401). The new Glasgow School (p. 51f.) as a whole has looked at glass through entirely new eyes and has developed it to a high degree of artistic perfection. Mackintosh and George Walton have produced superb results. They have created an art of domestic decorative glass that on the whole aims at charm of line rather than of colour, the pieces usually being colourless and held together by vigorous and imaginative lines of lead, with only small touches of colour at scattered points. The effect of these is therefore more attractive, almost suggesting precious stones, while the original purpose of the window as dispenser of light remains unchanged. Even when leaded windows are not treated in any particular decorative way, the leading provides an opportunity of suggesting a monochrome pattern, a frieze or border.

In general, however, the English are perfectly satisfied with simple rectangular or lozenge-shaped panes, indeed it is unusual to find any other motif in reception-rooms. It could all too easily lead to the fancifulness and over-elaboration so much disliked by sober English taste and would be peremptorily rejected by the English house-owner, like any other extravaganza or any obtrusive element in the decoration of his living-rooms.

Means of darkening windows

Means of darkening windows are almost as important an element in the furnishing of a house as the windows themselves. Curtains are important decorative features, the actual means of excluding light or safety-devices on windows, such as blinds and shutters, are important interior fittings. The English still adhere widely to the old traditional shutters that fold back against the jambs and these – provided that the walls are thick and the jambs deep enough – form the best protection imaginable. But even when the jambs are not deep, a means of utilising the space is often found by constructing the surround in such a way that it projects into the room and may at the same time create space for a comfortable

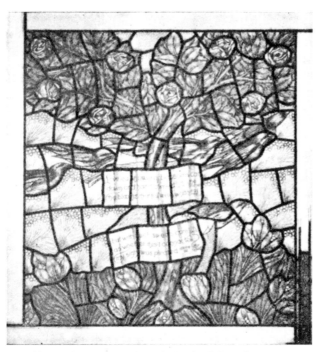

399   Design for a stained-glass window by Selwyn Image

400   Design for a stained-glass window by Frank Brangwyn

401   Stained-glass window by Oscar Paterson in Glasgow (The Knight Sintram from Fouqué's tales)

window-seat. In the way of external shutters, one still occasionally finds the type that were in use until the eighteenth century and that open sideways and have movable slats. One is struck by the fact, however, that, compared with German houses, windows in English houses go virtually unprotected. It is surprising how little concerned people in England are to secure their houses against burglary. Even in isolated houses in the country one will often find that no precautions whatever are taken to secure the windows and so the majority of houses are entirely without shutters either inside or out. The Venetian blinds which we like so much are seldom seen in England. Where there are blinds, this type may be replaced by external adjustable ones made of striped linen that project obliquely and fold back into boxes on the window lintels. England has developed something of an industry in these, now modern, adjustable blinds, which come in a great variety of forms, many of them attractive.

Roller-blinds

Light may also be excluded by interior roller-blinds. Our usual type with the endless cord has been totally abandoned in England in favour of an automatic spring-device which enables the blind to be pulled down to the desired point by means of a cord attached to the centre of the lower edge. The action of pulling down the blind locks a spring that allows the blind to jerk up again when the same cord is pulled with a slight forward tug. These roller-blinds are used universally in England and are found in every house; they wear excellently and the mechanism is so well designed that it never goes wrong. Roller-blinds are certainly extremely useful contrivances but they have a certain unalterable air of impoverishment and are totally lacking in artistic quality. They are not decorated in any way and when fully rolled up they are barely visible. Made of very dark, strong material, they can shut out almost all the light from bedrooms etc. that have no shutters.

Curtains

The English movement in art has by its influence greatly simplified the old form of interior window-hanging. The curtain-fitter who hung a curtain with elaborate folds from under a richly carved canopy of precious material and submitted a bill that accounted for a substantial part of the total cost of furnishing the room has disappeared from the newer English house. The carved canopy has been replaced by a simple brass rod, from which two curtains that can actually be drawn hang on rings in natural folds. Lace curtains still survive, but only in the houses of the old-fashioned and people who cannot bring themselves to part with the old knick-knacks. As regards curtains proper there is a marked tendency to choose lighter materials in place of the heavy, costly stuffs, the velvets and brocades of earlier days – to such an extent, indeed, that the favourite material is now chintz, which is also used generally to make covers for furniture. The brass rod from which the curtains hang is nowadays of only medium thickness (2–3 cm.), whereas formerly it was very thick, a relic of the great mahogany rods of the Victorian age that measured up to 10 cm. It rests on absolutely plain brass brackets and terminates at both ends in plain knobs. Short curtains made all in one piece (so-called lambrequins) are no longer used; people nowadays are not afraid to see the gap between the two curtains that is exposed to view when they are drawn back.

Short blinds

But besides the heavy curtains, English windows have smaller ones hung against the actual lights which they call short blinds. Often, as, for example, in round bays with continuous strips of window, from which main curtains are automatically precluded, they are the only curtains. They will then be made of thicker material so that they really shut out the light and there will be a series of smaller curtains for the upper lights, as for the lower. In other cases, especially in the normal type of town house, short blinds are only used for the lower lights and are made of thin muslin. Here their purpose is to prevent the room, or at least the lower part of it from being seen by passers-by, but without excluding the light. There is an extraordinarily plentiful choice of these filmy, soft materials suited to this purpose. The introduction of muslin was a result of the strong Indian influences that made themselves felt during the first half of the nineteenth century. They are produced in the most delightful patterns and form a particularly attractive branch of English textile-weaving. Because it enlisted the services of the modern movement in art, this industry has risen to such a high artistic level that it has become a model for the whole world.

The *Stores* [curtains] of which we are so fond are unknown in England, nor is the name English. The word, which we use for curtain, comes from the French and means in France the little roller-blinds on carriage-windows.

C. General comments on modern English furniture and other fittings

English attitude towards modern art

Anyone who comes to England with the idea of finding unmistakably modern arts and crafts penetrating to all levels of the population is in for one of those disappointments that have become almost typical for the fourteen-day visitors to London who make these journeys of enquiry into arts and crafts. The number of houses in London furnished in a 'modern' style is infinitesimal; there is an almost total absence of shops devoted to the new handicrafts in the way that certain firms in Berlin and Paris are. Hotels, clubs and private houses, which the foreigner usually sees, are equally silent on the subject of the hoped-for new art. And yet it would be wrong to draw over-hasty conclusions from this. Unheard-of modernity, the modernity that upset people because it was in direct opposition to the familiar, had its day in the 1860s and 1870s, when Morris confronted public taste with his materials, a few architects with their brick buildings and Burne-Jones and Whistler with their paintings. Those were the days of sensation and strife, when the patient shook their heads and the impatient condemned. But those things that were the butts of all this criticism have become our dear familiars, they no longer strike us; of course they are good, who can doubt it today? There have been few new sensations since then, at least in England itself. Only a handful of northern artists, such as Baillie-Scott and the Scots (see p. 47f.) have passed from the new path of those days to an even newer one to the accompaniment of the same head-shaking, the same condemnation, this time not on the part of the public only but also of those who had themselves followed the path formerly regarded as new. Such is the age-old way of all artistic development. Little has ever been seen of the Scots in England, least of all in London. But the London movement has not advanced beyond the point at which Morris left it in 1896. It is easy to forget that the London movement must be considered a piece of history; and one must also be clear about the fact that it was after all no more than an artists' movement addressed to a small circle. But it it impossible to discover during a short stay in London how far this circle has widened in the course of years, to what extent any part of its thinking has been transplanted unnoticed to a wider public. Most of the people mainly concerned do not live in London at all, but somewhere in the country. Even there their houses are not on the road but are hidden behind hedges and bushes, and on country roads one can pass by hundreds of them without so much as noticing them. Correct judgment can only be reached after longer experience.

Misunderstandings about modern English art

The drift of this judgment must then be that the circle of those who truly and from inmost conviction incline towards a clarified understanding of art is relatively large in England, that sounder ideas on art have gained considerable ground, that Ruskin's reassessment of artistic values has also spread to wider circles, that the average level of taste is higher in England than in the continental countries. This judgment is particularly apposite when one considers the sureness with which the well-made, simple article is preferred to cheap trash. How far removed we are in this particular point from the English average! And this very liking for what is simple, genuine and unobtrusively well-made is the best part of the influence that the new departure in the domestic arts of some fifty years ago has demonstrably exerted. If we bear this in mind we shall immediately recognise the difference between present-day English taste and what we on the continent have for the past fifteen years called modern art. In the first place modern art on the continent became embroiled in a superabundance of all sorts of decorative bombast that is in direct opposition to the English attitude. It looked like an irony of fate that the so-called modern art of the continent was supposed to stand on the shoulders of English art, almost to have grown out of it. Indeed, the remarkable fact was that the so-called 'English style', which figured for a time in the catalogues of furniture and interior decorating shops and of which they displayed samples in their windows, had never existed in England. It is almost incomprehensible that the belief could have grown up on the continent around the turn of the century that modern English furniture was irregular, its structure a picturesque distortion, that it had all sorts of extra pieces, excrescences and fancy accessories. This is partly explained by the fact that there were at the time a few shops that actually made this kind of fancy furniture to feed the voracious continent, for it is the only customer for such pieces. But the real explanation must surely be that continental buyers wanted these flights of fancy and saw and imagined them where they did not exist. A youthful design in *The Studio*, a single piece of furniture made for the continent, worked like the germs of a disease that attack a predisposed organism and immediately wreak wide-spread havoc. This is what happened during the period of the lack of understanding of Englishness that probably reached its climax around the year 1900. As continental taste has consolidated, the mania for outlandish abnormalities has also disappeared and given place to a calmer and juster assessment of English art.

The three types of modern furniture.
1: The revival of eighteenth-century furniture

As regards that section of modern English furniture that can in any sense be considered as works of art, three types can be distinguished: revived eighteenth-century-type furniture, the furniture of the Arts and Crafts movement and the furniture of several independent artists who cannot actually be accounted members of this group. In addition, of course, certain sections of the aristocracy obtain their furniture from Paris, as they have done in all ages and in every country. And in the little suburban houses of the lower middle classes one still finds the shabby splendours of nineteenth-century art in their second flowering, the same that still dominate the average German room. Apart from these types, imitation eighteenth-century furniture accounts for by far the largest part of present-day demand. Sheraton reigns once more in drawing-room and bedroom, Chippendale chairs in the dining-room. Large factories, each employing hundreds of workers, devote all their effort to the production of this furniture, furniture shops are full of new copies of Sheraton and Chippendale, for these are the pieces that the English public most desires. All the techniques of the late eighteenth century – inlay, satin-wood veneer, painting on wood – have been recovered. The old furniture pattern-books of the eighteenth century provide manufacturers with an inexhaustible fund of motifs for furniture-making that is so rich and varied that modern furniture cannot absorb it all. For, as we have already remarked, in certain directions the life of English society in the eighteenth century has reached a high level of culture that we today have scarcely equalled. The furniture of that period is still perfectly adequate to the needs of the modern English house.

In general these copies of old pieces do not in any sense aim at archaeological truth, parts that would nowadays appear markedly un-modern are altered, turned and carved features are omitted; in short, the middle-class, modern simplification once performed by the cabinet-makers of the eighteenth century on Louis XVI furniture has been carried a good step further. Furniture such as cabinets and cupboards follow the tradition of Sheraton and Hepplewhite; chairs tend rather to be modelled on Chippendale, whose chairs were in the main more weighty and comfortable-looking than those of his successors and therefore suit modern taste better. In view of the high degree of accomplishment of English eighteenth-century furniture, which lies equally in its good taste and the genuine middle-class culture it reflects, no one is likely to find fault with the revival of this art, indeed, one would like to wish England good fortune in continuing her old tradition. Sadly, however, a strong anti-quarian tendency has made itself felt recently and those who affect it have turned their attentions also to the whimsical forms of earlier days, the chinoiseries and Gothick imitations of the eighteenth century. Numerous workshops are now busy copying old pieces and copying them in such a way that the public is deceived about their origins, that is to say, they use artificial means of ageing. The connoisseur will be aware of what has gone on. Only the public at large, especially buyers in continental countries, to whom the fakers' activity is primarily addressed, all too easily assume these pieces to be genuine and purchase them at prices three and four times above their true value.

2. Arts and Crafts furniture

The new trends in furniture-making begun by the modern Arts and Crafts movement under Morris continue today mainly in the pieces displayed at the Arts and Crafts Exhibitions. Morris was actually not a tectonic artist but a designer of flat pattern. Least of all did he feel at home in designing furniture, which he left entirely to others, principally Philip Webb. Webb was extremely catholic in his choice of means: he used Gothic and Renaissance forms, such materials as oak and mahogany, his treatments included polished and natural wood, inlay and painted ornament. He always aimed for simplicity. But Morris furniture does not shun echoes of historical art; and it always retains a certain degree of refinement. In the following generation the situation changed. Artists insisted on wood being left untreated, revived primitive rustic forms, always – often rather osten-tatiously – allowed the construction to show and had little time for comfort and refined forms of life. Behind all this lay the belief that they must begin at the beginning if they were to get away from the corrupt state of culture that the nineteenth century had produced. The only room in the house to which the so-called artistic aspirations of the period had not extended was the kitchen. So they returned to kitchen furniture: kitchen chairs provided the ideas for the new forms of seat, kitchen cupboards for cupboards. The only difference between these new pieces and real kitchen furniture was that the former were some ten times more expensive because they had been produced, economically speaking, under the conditions of works of art. They have been shown at the Arts and Crafts Exhibitions in London for the past fifteen years with every pretence to being works of art, not only because the prices are those of works of art but also because, in addition to the name of the 'designer', that of every single craftsman involved in making the piece is listed in the catalogue. Is there any wonder that the public are scornful of such demonstrations?

The average piece of furniture of the London Arts and Crafts movement today – of which the chief representative in the field of furniture is Sidney H. Barnsley – is primitive to excess. It would be an anachronism to call it modern, it is reactionary. These people are so deeply involved in the ideal of handicraft that they have ears for no other. And since there are no large personalities who possess that something more that goes to make a true work of art, the ideal of handicraft naked and unadorned fully satisfies the demands of the artist-craftsmen of London. The curse, however, that weighs upon their furniture is its lack of economic viability. Thus the furniture is the very branch of the work of the London Arts and Crafts that is bound to disappoint. We look for modern art, that is, for pieces that fully meet our modern requirements, and we find roughly jointed kitchen cupboards for which we are expected to pay as many pounds sterling as they are worth in thalers.

In his furniture too C. F. A. Voysey is an exception among the members of the London group. Like the others he too designs almost exclusively in untreated oak, he too is plain to the point of being primitive, he too forces the construction on the attention. But beyond the construction, his furniture has higher artistic qualities, his pieces have style and a personal idiom. And above all, they are designed as elements in the concept of the interior (see Figs. 402, 403, 416, and 78–80). Artists of the same circle who have, like Voysey, produced furniture of a notably high standard include Edgar Wood (see Figs. 404 and 99–102), W. J. Neatby, Charles Spooner, Ambrose Heal junior and the Bromsgrove Guild of Handicraft; while that inspired artist Henry Wilson and the excellent designer C. H. B. Quennell far outshine the rest of the group and produce work of high artistic sensibility.

3. Other artist-designed furniture

In actual fact Voysey's, Quennell's and Wilson's furniture belongs to the third group of modern English furniture, that designed by independent artists. All the modern interior designers go their own way, each has an individual style which makes it impossible to confuse his furniture with that of any other artist. Baillie-Scott knows how to imbue his primitive forms with a high degree of refinement and poetry by colouring his pieces in almost joyful tones (see Figs. 405, 406). A subtle artist, George Walton combines lucid construction with elegance to an unusual degree; he has no wish to cast a shadow on the aspirations to modernity of a society that, despite all, is basically refined and offers it pieces that are both well made and unquestionably pleasing (see Figs. 407, 339, 341, 358 and 118, 119). Charles Rennie Mackintosh and his Glasgow circle are the most pronouncedly individual artists of a modern age (see Figs. 410, 111, 113). They do, however, address themselves to initiates, to whom the lofty, rather mystical spirit of their art – which nonetheless has the effect of a lovely fairy-tale world – has been revealed. No artist who moves in spheres far above the ordinary and the every-day is ever understood immediately and may even be ridiculed or attacked. It has ever been the privilege of the masses to oppose new artistic ideas. Mackintosh's art is in very truth what Shakespeare calls caviar to the general. But he was the first in England consistently to pursue and achieve the aim towards which the whole of the newer Arts and Crafts movement was pressing, the strictly artistic unity of the interior.

Tasteful commercial furniture

Neither the furniture of the Arts and Crafts group nor artist-designed furniture will be found in houses other than those whose owners have wanted an artistically distinguished interior. And there are none too many houses of this kind in England. Yet the general level of domestic furniture is relatively very high. England is the one country in which one can nowadays find in furniture shops a selection of furniture that, while it cannot pretend to be great art, yet meets all the requirements of good taste, and at extremely reasonable prices. There are whole series of English shops that specialise in simple and tasteful furniture for middle-class houses and provides the comparatively large percentage of the English population that is already enlightened in matters of taste with the opportunity of purchasing not only decent furniture but also good and tasteful materials, carpets, curtains and fire-places – in short, all that is needed to furnish a house. It is true that we too in Germany now have a number of shops specialising in arts and crafts, in which we can buy all kinds of good and beautiful things to furnish the interiors of our houses. But apart from these shops, the German of educated taste still finds it difficult enough to furnish his home, because of our shop-keepers' lack of appreciation of good, simple articles. The Englishman is spared this trouble, he can find what he needs in any average shop. These in the end are fruits of the new Arts and Crafts movement which should not be under-estimated. Indeed, one can have no hesitation in seeing this rise in the general level that is reflected in the very improvement in the stock of the commercial interior-decorating shop as the most valuable outcome of the aspirations of our Arts and Crafts movement.

The most striking development recently has been the improvement in good, tasteful bedroom furniture. Great credit in this connection must go to the furniture shop of Heal & Sons, who have introduced simple, well-proportioned and yet reasonably priced furniture designed for the firm by artists. There are also numerous extremely pleasant forms of chairs of various types on the market, also chests-of-drawers, sideboards, book-shelves, tables and furniture for men's studies. One can see that everywhere the attempt is at least being made to produce well-made and modestly decent furniture. We shall cite examples as we consider the furnishing of individual rooms.

Special features of English furniture. The wood and its treatment

One can enumerate several external qualities in which English furniture differs from the furniture of other peoples, especially those of the continent. First there is the marked English fondness for mahogany. Even the furniture in workmen's cottages is made of mahogany, which is not regarded as anything special in England. Prices of furniture in oak, walnut and mahogany are usually the same. Walnut is very little used today; it is unfashionable. As we have said, oak is the favourite wood of the

Arts and Crafts people, who, indeed, leave it entirely unstained and untreated. But the light colour of this furniture makes it very vulnerable to dirt, which quickly begins to show at points where it is handled. Furniture in so-called fumed oak is very popular in the wider market. The slightly darkened colour of this furniture is produced by exposing the piece, after construction, for some time to the fumes of ammonia. Softer woods, such as birch, are also used but are always stained or painted. There was a craze for green-stained wood, but that has passed. The difficulty is that the green stain is not light-resistant and so turns brownish in time, or fades entirely on surfaces exposed to light. Ash is the best and favourite wood for stained furniture. Of painted furniture, white pieces for bedrooms are commonest. Good furniture is painted with extreme care, as is white-painted panelling (see p. 167). This form of painting is known as japanning, a word that has survived from the eighteenth century, when the first attempts at imitating fine Japanese lacquer were made. A glossy finish is avoided in white-painted furniture by rubbing down the surface until it is softly matt. Mahogany furniture usually takes a high French polish. But, largely as a result of Morris's continued protests, there has been a certain cooling recently and people now want matt surfaces. Mahogany furniture is produced with an entirely matt stain which is very effective. Wholly untreated mahogany has been used occasionally and it is always a great surprise to see the handsome yellowish-red of the wood.

Among the finer colonial woods, satin-wood is being widely used again, as in the eighteenth century. This wood is almost exclusively employed as a veneer; there are only a few parts, such as slender table legs etc., for which solid satin-wood is used. Other expensive woods are used merely as inlays, which have become common again as a result of the fashion for the Sheraton style. Alternating with natural woods, inlays may be made also of ivory, tin and all kinds of brightly coloured woods. Besides the strip borders of the Sheraton style and other ornament, a chequer-board-like border pattern has recently become popular,

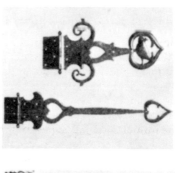

408
Fittings by C. F. A. Voysey

409
Fittings by Edgar Wood

407 'Japanned' furniture by George Walton

indeed has almost become the fashion for a certain class of furniture (Fig. 404).

Technique

An important difference between English and continental furniture is that English furniture of all kinds is made of solid wood. Generally speaking, veneers are unknown, nor are drawers, etc. made of lighter and cheaper wood. The drawers of a mahogany piece, for example, are always made of mahogany throughout (there is a distinction here between the modern Sheraton-style furniture and the original in which drawers were always made of oak), those of an oak piece of oak and of an ash piece of ash. Ply-wood is practically unknown in England, even in the best work; the small fluctuation of temperature between the seasons and the constant level of humidity do not, as with us, necessitate the use of this expedient to counteract the shrinkage and cracking of the wood. To this extent, English cabinet-making is still at a somewhat primitive stage.

Although the best work is executed with nothing like the care to which we have become accustomed in Germany today, the standard of the great volume of average work is far higher than with us. Not even in cheap furniture-shops will one find real catch-penny stuff, for even the small man and the workman know that it is uneconomical to buy rubbish. It is precisely in the furniture intended for the workman's cottage that one is struck by the solidity of the wood, the good quality of the leather coverings and the general sterling worth, especially when one considers the cheapness of the goods.

Fittings

Another point in which English furniture is superior is in the quality of locks and fittings. Even in ordinary commercial furniture one can rely on the locks being solid and made to last; and all the fittings will be of a standard that must seem almost perfect to a modern continental observer. Cast and pressed rubbish is not to be found in England. A large choice of key-plates, handles for cupboard-doors, fittings for drawers and all the different parts of fittings is available on the market. A small point worth mentioning in this connection is that English cupboard-doors always have a special opening device (usually a ring or similar handle) to spare the key. If the key is used to open the door etc. it will damage the lock by the continual strain on its elements.

410 Pair of small drawing-room cupboards by C. R. Mackintosh

Lightness and small size of the pieces of furniture

The general appearance of modern English furniture is distinguished not only by its quietness and its air of being well-made, but also by its lightness and the ease with which it can be moved, qualities which contrast with the ponderous appearance of the Victorian furniture and which it has acquired only in recent decades with the revival of eighteenth-century furniture styles. The influence of Japan (see p. 157) that prevailed for some time also contributed greatly to the development of this trend. All pieces, except, perhaps, large bedroom wardrobes are lightly constructed and easy to move. There are no vast sideboards such as we have; these are small edifices in themselves and can only be moved to their appointed positions through wide doors and abnormally wide staircases. The very openings and passage-ways in English houses are unsuited to such pieces. Moreover, apart from the dining-table, there is not a single large table in an English house today. All have been replaced by little occasional tables. Nor are our huge sofas anywhere to be seen: their place has been taken by small, free-standing sofas, which should actually be thought of simply as double chairs. A German is much struck by the fact that the English have nothing in their reception-rooms in the way of a day-bed, on which to recline at full length. Only in the bedroom and the smoking-room will one see the piece of furniture for this purpose that we call a *chaise longue*.

English furniture is on the whole much plainer than our modern German furniture. Its positive aim is delicacy and daintiness, a reaction against the ubiquitous heaviness and massiveness of the Victorian era, which all too often degenerated into clumsiness. This daintiness is seen in mouldings, cornices and in the treatment of surfaces, which are also a complete contrast to the obtrusive architectural furniture of fifty years ago. Cornices are not prominent, mouldings between frames and infills have almost entirely disappeared and the surface of infills is flat. Younger designers even prefer to make frames and infills flush, but this fashion is senseless, because it is contrary to the nature of joinery. Like the old daintiness, the old principle of folding to save space has also been revived, particularly in the case of tables. The tables found in English houses in addition to the dining-table all have a folding leaf, so that when the table is not in use it occupies about one-third of its normal space.

Reasons

The desire to save space is connected with the unusual way in which the English room is utilised, dominated as it is by the fire-place. The rallying-point is the fire-place, which means that there is a comparatively small space along the wall of the room, into which many people have to crowd. A large table like our sofa-table, or a large day-bed, would not fit in. Furniture must not be fixed, it must be easy to move, since the idea is to be able to change its position in relation to the fire-place at will. It would perhaps not be entirely wrong to explain the whole development of English furniture in the light of the peculiar nature of the English fire-place – itself determined by the climate – in which case this would be an example of how climatic influences may extend even to the design of furniture.

Built-in furniture

From the moment when the house began again to be built from inside to outside, furniture began more and more to be replaced and built-in furniture of the wall-cupboard type came into its own again. As has already been noted, bedrooms were now generally provided with built-in wardrobes and there were built-in sideboard recesses in dining-rooms and built-in book-cases in libraries. One of the aims of the really perfectly appointed room is clearly that the cupboards, etc. shall be built in. Mass-produced movable furniture scattered about the room, an accumulation of all sorts of small objects, obviously cannot improve the artistic effect of a room. How splendid it would be if all our needs could be met by built-in furniture and we could have almost empty rooms! They would give the inmate a feeling of distance, freedom, exaltation, instead of making him feel hemmed-in, restricted, choked, as our present-day rooms packed full of furniture do. Admittedly the man in the street is far from feeling this urge for freedom. On the contrary, people draw a succession of bits and pieces into their rooms until they are so completely surrounded that they deprive themselves of the last remaining shred of free movement and, more importantly, of spiritual freedom. These false beliefs have gone so far that people feel uncomfortable unless they are smothered in a clutter of furniture. The discreet and subtly planned, almost entirely empty room of the Japanese house gives a valuable pointer here. If we wish to reform our homes, we shall have to begin by throwing out all our useless household utensils and decorations.

Lighting appliances

Having discussed the furniture, the most important of the appointments of the interior, we shall devote a few words at least to certain other elements of the English house, starting with lighting appliances. Electric light is becoming more and more general and one may assume that for the future electric lighting appliances, already the commonest, will be the only ones worth considering. Even remote houses in the country now have electric light, each one having its own little generating machine. For the smaller house not yet connected to the electricity supply, there is admittedly little to be done at present, except to use the old oil-lamps or candles. There is widespread dislike of gas-lighting in England, where nobody is prepared to use gas-lights anywhere except in halls and domestic offices for fear of the dirt caused by soot and recognition of the danger to health that arises from piping gas into the room.

It is worth stressing at this point that England was in a position to demand artistic qualities of her lighting appliances much earlier than the continent because her considerably older modern movement in art had from the first included metal-work in its purview. More specifically, as early as the 1880s, the architect W. A. S. Benson was the first to solve the problem of design in metal in the more modern spirit when he created the lamps that were later to have a revolutionary effect on all our metalware. Benson was the first to develop his design directly out of the purpose and the character of the metal as material (see Figs. 411–414). Form was paramount to him. He abandoned ornament at a time when, generally speaking, even the new movement was fond of ornament. In so doing he opened up new ground. It is probably typical of the English dislike of gas that he worked relatively little for gas-lighting. But when electric light appeared on the scene, he saw his true field open before him. If one looks at electric lamps as a whole, one can see how much further the artistic means of the time had developed already, in a way that does not apply to gas-lamps; for as the problems posed by electric lighting arose, so the right forms were found in the shortest possible time. Benson was the leading spirit in electric lighting-appliances in England, on the continent he was the fruitful instigator. He developed not only the most pleasing lines and forms but also many surprising ideas about lighting. Thus he was the first to illumine dining-room tables with light reflected from a shiny metal surface while keeping the actual source of

411–413   Lamps by W. A. S. Benson

illumination hidden. This eliminates all traces of unpleasant dazzle and lights the table with a soft, gentle, extremely agreeable glow. Benson it was who first produced the combined table-lamp and wall-lamp which has since been copied everywhere. This is artistically excellent inasmuch as it appears entirely natural whether it is used as bracket, in which case it is simply hung on a nail, or as a table-lamp (Fig. 411). When electric light came in, a number of metal-workers besides Benson addressed themselves to the new problem and Nelson and Edith Dawson, Rathbone, the Birmingham Guild of Handicraft, Ashbee and the Bromsgrove Guild of Applied Art all produced excellent lighting appliances, all of which were distinguished by absence of ornament, form derived purely from the character of the metal, beauty of line and lightness and elegance of design. It must be said, however, that England has not maintained her former position of distinction in this field. The importance of her pioneering work is mainly historical.

Lamp-shades

England introduced a strange adjunct to the light-appliance in the form of the material shade. It has been popular in England for many decades and most graceful forms have been evolved. Silk lamp-shades were first used on the standard-lamps that stand free in a room and are the height of a man – lamps that were once an English speciality and have since come into general use on the continent – and later came to be used on table-lamps and even on candles. It is taken for granted in England that every candle that appears in a reception-room, but especially those that decorate the dining-table, shall have its little shade. Short candles are used nowadays on dining-tables, to keep flames below eye-level. The little shades screen them completely and project all the light down on to the table and the set places. These little silk shades are supported by wires attached to the sides of a clamp that holds the candle. As the candle burns down, the clamp has to be pushed down from time to time. In order to avoid this tiresome procedure, casings for the candles have been devised, with fixed shades; the candle stands on a spiral spring and is continually pressed up towards the opening above, through which the flame appears, so that the flame remains constantly at the same level.

English lamp-shades differ from the American mosaic-glass shades in that they are always made of silk. Shades for tall standard-lamps are fairly ample and richly adorned with flounces. Liberty's soft silks are excellently suited to them. Shades of table-lamps of all kinds and of pendant lamps are always made of silk. Shades are indispensable for the pendant

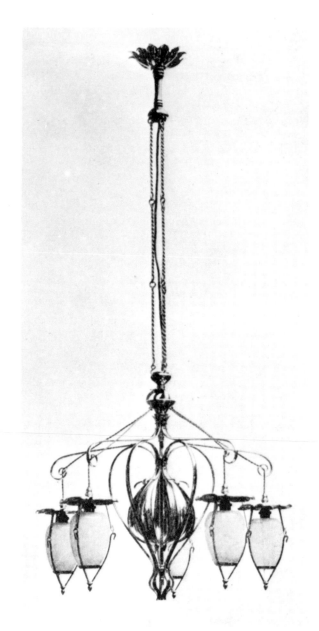

414   Chandelier by W. A. S. Benson

lamps that light the dining table and the six that illuminate the billiard table, whether they be oil, gas or electric.

Other metalware

Just as England was the first to find the right form for metal lighting-appliances, so metal has long been used there in an exemplary manner for small domestic articles. The concisely constructed, undecorated brassware simply composed of rods, that has now reached Germany, has been established in England for decades. Thus for many years there have been wash-stands with brass legs in English bathrooms, stands for sticks and umbrellas in English halls; cakes are handed at tea on brass stands like *étagères*; there are brass stands of the right height on which to rest tea-pots to keep warm at the fire (Fig. 385), etc. In table-ware too, as in tea and coffee sets, trays etc. English metalwork has attained a high level of technical and artistic perfection; these undecorated pieces, the design of which relies simply on the development of the form of the vessel, have become models of modern metalwork, which embody modern ideas of art in the best sense.

Casings for radiators

Metalwork has been most successfully adapted to casings for radiators. In place of the ordinary wooden, pedestal-like, oil-painted coverings with pierced metal fronts, in houses designed by good architects one sees simple brass casings with a metal plate at the top, and at the side either a series of simple round or rectangular rods, or some kind of interlace pattern of flat brass bands. Artistically these are extremely satisfying in that they have the same metallic character as the radiator.

Pictures as decoration

A word must be said about pictures as wall decorations, at least in so far as they are hung on walls, since this is one of the most important aspects of interior decoration. Pictures are objects that are placed ready-made in the hands of the designer of the interior, except when the collector and designer are one and the same person. It cannot be denied that accumulations of pictures on walls that take no account whatever of the appearance of the interior are among the greatest of all enemies of the idea of the room. In its colour-values an oil-painting is a complete, self-contained work. But a room is expected to have artistic unity, to which every element is subordinated. There are therefore only two possible ways of achieving a good effect: either the design of the interior must be based on the picture in question, or the choice of the picture must be governed by the artistic plan to be realised in the room. Any other procedure will lead to inartistic results, no matter if the pictures be supreme works of art. The designer is therefore in an extremely awkward position in any room that is supposed to house any appreciable number of pictures. The problem that faces him is inartistic in itself and insoluble. The only course open to him is to look upon the room as a store-room with no possible claim to artistic quality. The corollary to this is that it is up to the interior designer to enter an objection against the common practice of over-decorating the walls with pictures. Indeed, even if he reduces the number of pictures, the designer will still not find his ideal in the movable incidental painting, but in the picture that fits in to the room, that is intended for the room, the purest form of which is the wall painting.

Differentiation according to the character of the room

Considering the mass-production of oil-paintings into which modern art has drifted and the accumulated riches in English hands, it was inevitable that large numbers of pictures should find their way into English houses. By the eighteenth century walls were already covered with them, as a glance at a Hogarth print will show. Indeed, the architects of the eighteenth century, led by Robert Adam, attempted to adapt the picture organically to the wall by making the divisions of the wall surround the pictures like frames. Many surviving interiors of the period exemplify this practice and give yet another ground for admiration of the sureness of the artistic sensibility of the time. All this was lost in the nineteenth century. When the new movement in house-building began, leading architects felt obliged in many instances to build special store-rooms, i.e. picture-galleries, on to the houses to accommodate the overflow of pictures and thus partially relieve the rooms (see p. 90). Recent designers have tried to distribute the pictures that remain in the rooms in an appropriate and artistic way. Pictures are few, one or two to each wall, and they are also made to harmonise to some degree with the decoration of the room. Oil-paintings are separated from water-colours and water-colours from prints.

We may also note that original paintings only are found in English rooms. Engravings and prints of all kinds, including photographic reproductions, belong in English opinion to halls, passages and staircases. It is one of the surprises in store for the visitor to England to find water-colours in the drawing-room of even the smallest suburban house and is a sign of the widespread prosperity of the country. The English in general have a special affection for water-colours, an affection that is growing with their increasing fondness for light-coloured interiors. It is almost as though the overcast English sky were too dark for oil-paintings, just as it has been responsible for the progressive lightening of English coloured-glass windows. It is an old English idea to hang oil-paintings, especially family portraits, in the dining-room; the hall too, if it is large and roomy, is a place for oil-paintings. But water-colours are hung in the drawing-room and in the bedrooms; and original drawings, uniformly framed and hung in rows, are also to be found in bedrooms. The habit of separating the types of wall decoration according to the character of the room is certainly a step forward in the process of suiting the picture to the decoration. The choice of uniform, simple frames that harmonise with the room represents a further step. Yet the aim ought everywhere to be to limit the number of pictures. One often hears the Japanese practice of hanging one single picture in the appointed position, the key position in the room, cited as the ideal way of using pictures. Were we to vary this one picture and also follow the further Japanese example of locking all the other ornaments and bric-à-brac besides the superfluous pictures into the store-room, bringing them out only to be enjoyed occasionally, we should already have done a very great deal for our modern interior.

The hanging of pictures. The picture-rail

In recent decades in England there have been most remarkable improvements in the hanging of pictures that have now become general and have already been copied outside England. Since the 1870s and 1880s iron rods with rings, like slender curtain-rods for hanging pictures, have been run round rooms below the cornice in the familiar manner of picture-galleries. And this is undoubtedly the best way of hanging heavy oil-paintings. But it was soon found that lighter pictures could equally well hang from an ordinary rail. A wooden picture-rail is now a permanent feature of every English wall. It will be found at different points according to the division of the wall. On walls that are papered all over, it is placed immediately below the frieze. It consists of an ordinary wooden rail, usually with a moulding, and is fastened to the wall with dowel-pins (Fig. 415). The rail has a groove at the top to take a kind of brass hook made specially for the purpose, from which the picture is hung. These hooks enable the picture to be moved with the greatest of ease; and another advantage of the rail is that it does away with the need to make nail-holes in the wall. With these hooks one can therefore hang the picture in any position on the wall, according to choice. Pictures can be hung in this way so easily that there is no need to drive in nails even where one would otherwise expect a propensity for doing so and a picture-rail would be a real blessing in flats in Germany with their changing population. When one thinks of the trouble

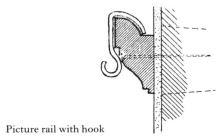

415   Picture rail with hook

involved in driving picture-hooks into a solid wall and the amount of damage that it does, it almost amazes one that such a simple substitute has not been thought of long ago.

In England pictures are often hung from two hooks instead of one, so that the cords drop parallel to one another. Pictures often tilt slightly forward as they hang, which only makes sense, of course, when they are hung above eye-level. With the normal division of the usually very low wall into frieze and lower zone, the picture-rail is usually placed on the dividing-line between the two areas, thus only slightly above eye-level. The pictures are hung on twisted metal wires specially made for the purpose, which have the advantage that they can be much thinner than string or cord capable of carrying the same weight. If two pictures are to hang vertically one above the other, the wires for the lower picture simply pass under the upper one.

Framing

The favourite type of frame is quite flat; solid oak ones can be had in all widths at very moderate prices. Indeed, the cheapness of the frames, which can be bought everywhere, either ready cut or ordered to measure, is surprising. The oak will either be left untreated or will be stained or painted to suit the colour-scheme of the room. All the frames in one room are always kept as uniform as possible.

By ancient custom, water-colours are framed in a sunk gold mount, never in white or coloured mounts, which are thought to detract from the colours of the drawing. But recently it has become equally common to frame them without any paper mount. It is customary nowadays to omit the paper mount altogether when framing photographs, prints and engravings and to bring the frame up to the edge of the printed surface. The reason for doing so is that there is a reluctance to introduce the white patch of the paper border into what may otherwise be a nicely balanced colour-scheme.

At this point it should be stressed that the fancy frames that

416   House in Bidston Road, Birkenhead. By C. F. A. Voysey. Furniture in hall

circulate on the continent and are nicknamed 'English frames', in which the motifs of the picture are repeated on the frame or the frame itself has some kind of bizarre contour, are entirely unknown in England. One could travel the length and breadth of the country without finding a single example of such a frame. The English have, quite correctly, always held that a picture-frame should be no more than a quiet outer delimitation of the picture-surface and a transition to the wall and that it is therefore inappropriate to make it the object of any special emotional outpourings. It is certainly wrong to use adventurous forms of any kind to give a frame the character of an entity in itself. The fancy frames, some of which nowadays even have plastic motifs reflecting the subject of the painting are examples of a degeneration in taste into which only an extremely low-grade outlook on art could fall. They have no connection with England, which, say what one will, is outstanding for three things in particular in its more recent notions of art: a good attitude, rationality and an unclouded eye for what is fitting.

The furnishing of individual residential rooms

1. The hall

Different sorts of hall

Of all the rooms in the English house, the hall is the one that we are accustomed to think of as the most English. No room in recent decades has been found as suggestive abroad as the English hall. It has not mattered that, as we have already seen (p. 90), the programme of the hall is very different in different houses and is generally really rather indeterminate. It has been in the main its sentimental qualities that have been valued and imitated. Not only is the hall a centre of great memories of a proud past, but the particular form of the hall, which is the outcome of its position in the ground-plan and of the elaboration of a romantic chain of thought, weaves a special magic round this room. This applies almost exclusively to the medieval-looking hall, which was revived in the nineteenth century after Palladianism had been forced to yield to more indigenous forces.

But besides the hall with its medieval overtones there are also vestibules of continental type, especially in town houses. And even in country-houses the hall is not infrequently merely a rather small anteroom. Leading out of the anteroom and communicating with the rooms one will often find a broad passage-way that has some of the impressive qualities of the hall. In the little run-of-the-mill house there is often merely a small, narrow passage out of which the stairs rise steeply.

The hall comfortably furnished

But whatever the form of the hall, the English always try to make it more than a mere anteroom, believing that it should create a homely impression. It represents one of the most attractive assets of the English house. One steps out of wild nature straight into a warm, friendly atmosphere. Even as one crosses the threshold one is surrounded by a sense of comforting hospitality and open-armed welcome. This sense results from the cosy furnishing of the room, a faint echo of which is apparent in our own small suburban houses.

Even in small houses halls always have a fire-place. Halls are furnished and their floors are carpeted. Wood-panelling is the favourite treatment for walls, indeed it is considered the ideal decoration for the hall of an English house. To preserve its comfortable air in all circumstances, the hall is not permitted to rise through two storeys, unless it covers so large an area that this would seem desirable. Many serious mistakes are made on the continent in this respect. An exiguous hall is raised through two storeys, producing the effect of a well-shaft and striking those who enter as cold and cheerless.

The English like beamed ceilings in their halls. The hall is sometimes the first, or the only, room to have its walls treated monumentally with either a painted frieze or tapestry-hangings, as in Morris's Stanmore Hall (see Figs. 319, 320). Stained glass is the obvious choice for hall windows and is sought after, wherever circumstances allow. The floor may be composed of squares of coloured marble or other stone flags, or – the current favourite – of a hard wood. All-over carpeting is avoided, doubtless because visitors enter the hall in wet clothes in rainy weather. But there is always a deep-piled, warm rug in the centre and a thick one in front of the fire, though an animal-skin is often substituted here. A piece of coconut matting is recessed into the floor immediately inside the front-door.

In large country-houses, where owners want their halls to resemble the medieval hall, the ceiling takes the form of a timbered roof (Fig. 425); the walls will be of unwhitewashed stone above wood-panelling, it will be lit by tall windows and a wide carved wooden staircase occasionally rises against one wall. In town houses the large staircase well is comfortably furnished as a hall. Where space is limited, the hall takes the form of a wide

417 House at Edgbaston, nr Birmingham. By W. H. Bidlake. (See also Figs. 235, 236, 356) Hall

418 House at Edgbaston. Hall

419 Windyhill, Kilmacolm, nr Glasgow. By C. R. Mackintosh. (See also Figs. 109, 110, 328) Hall

420 The White House, Helensburgh, nr Glasgow. By M. H. Baillie Scott. (See also Figs. 239–241, 323, 369, 370) Hall

421 Hinton House, Ayr, Scotland. By James A. Morris. (See also Fig. 142) Hall

422 Hall settle of carved oak

423 Norney, Godalming, Surrey. By C. F. A. Voysey. (See Figs. 190, 191) Hall

424 Norney. Hall. View towards staircase

passage-way, as in Fig. 419. It is often transformed into a comfortable central room of the house, which may be expected to be elegantly furnished with seats, bay windows and shelves, as in Figs 417, 418. The staircase well does not lead out of the hall nearly as often as we continentals imagine. But where it does do so, architects are reluctant to expose the whole flight to view and permit only the first few steps to be seen (Figs. 418, 420). It will be appropriate in town houses for the staircase to lead out of the hall, for here it ascends to the drawing-room on the first floor. In the long, low country-house it is concealed, largely because it leads only to the bedrooms, which are considered to be private.

Furnishing

The furnishing of the hall varies widely, according to the purpose it serves. There are certain pieces of furniture, however, that reappear in every kind of hall. These include a heavy hall-table and a settle. They are still sometimes modelled on the corresponding pieces of the Elizabethan period; old English round gate-legged tables are very popular as hall-tables (Figs. 417, 421). The hall-table is used mainly as a place on which to lay all sorts of portable belongings, especially out-door clothes, which the English servant carefully folds and lays on the hall-table, hat and gloves on top, stick or umbrella to the side. This is the usual routine for short visits, when the caller does not go to the adjacent cloakroom. A table on which to lay belongings will always stand to one side of the hall, so that in large halls there will be room for another table in the centre or in front of the fire. In front of the fire one will often find two comfortable chairs upholstered in leather for waiting guests. Close to the front-door will be seats for messengers and the like and for servants on duty in the hall. In smaller halls there will merely be several wooden chairs and a wooden settle. The chairs and settle are usually heavy in appearance. This is taken for granted in the hall; they are mostly copied from early English rustic chairs. Besides one or two chairs, the ubiquitous feature of the smallest halls is the hall-stand, consisting of a small cupboard with a drawer (for brush and comb), a mirror, clothes-hooks and an umbrella-stand, all combined in one piece of furniture. There will naturally be no hall-stand if there is a cloakroom immediately adjoining the hall, but it will be found to be a permanent feature in all the smaller and many older medium-sized town houses. Everywhere in England one will find long brass racks on brackets instead of hooks on which to hang hats.

The hall is also considered the proper place for heavy cupboards, coffers, etc. All hall furniture is heavy in appearance and made of hard wood, preferably oak or mahogany. It was fashionable for a time to furnish the hall in old English carved oak; this furniture (Fig. 422) is being produced again in large quantities for the purpose. The never-failing finishing-touch to the furnishing of the hall is the tall longcase clock of ancient memory; one of these, usually an antique, is found in the hall of every English house. Like the clock, the ancient lighting appliance, the pendant lantern, has survived from the old days. In the course of decades it has held many and various types of lighting. Finally, no English hall is complete without its gong, which is beaten to summon the family to meals.

The hall-living-room

In those houses in which the hall has assumed the character of a real living-room, it will naturally be furnished accordingly. It will be similar in character to the drawing-room, though it will never have the light appearance of that room. Halls of this sort always house a grand piano for music-making and sometimes a billiard-table. In this case the hall tends to become the

425 Country-house for E. P. Barlow. By C. J. Harold Cooper. Hall

comfortable all-purpose room of the house, in which each member of the family can follow his favourite pursuit and spend his time as he likes. Baillie Scott has created an ideal room of this kind at Blackwell on Lake Windermere (Figs. 321, 106). A gallery, which usually develops naturally out of the staircase-landing, is a popular addition to this type of hall. The gallery at Blackwell has been made into a charming little room with two windows; elsewhere it takes the form of a passage-way (Fig. 420) commanding a view over the whole hall. Here we have a re-emergence of the romantic element that has attached to the hall throughout the centuries up to the present day; the hall today is primarily intended to be a room to delight the heart and eye. To all who traverse it, it offers an impression of beauty, it bids welcome to those who enter, to those who linger in it it gives a feeling of space and, as an all-purpose room, a sense of freedom and informality. This is why in many a country-house to this day the hall is the favourite room of all.

2. The dining-room and the laid table

Changed appearance of the modern dining-room. English tradition of serving food

By long tradition the English dining-room is serious and dignified in character, its colour-scheme rather dark than light, its furniture heavy and made of polished mahogany; it has a Turkish carpet on the floor and oil-paintings, preferably family portraits, in heavy gilt frames, on the walls. But in recent times a more joyful atmosphere has entered this room also. Here too the decoration is becoming ever lighter; furniture modelled on that of the Chippendale and Sheraton period has become light and pleasing; the heavy curtains in dark material have given way to curtains of a lighter and brighter material. The room has developed in a decidedly happy direction, 'cheerfulness' is now the goal, whereas in the mid-nineteenth century the desired impression could be described as 'massive' and 'substantial'. This was all part of the general development of the outlook on life and the social circumstances that we have already described. The laid table, the focal point of the room, has become as refined as the decoration. It is no longer customary for the cloth to be removed after the meal and for the men to settle down to a hearty evening's drinking once the ladies have retired to the drawing-room. In the same way the whole arrangement of the dinner-table has become more agreeable, more attractive, more feminine, and similarly the whole character of the dining-room had become more refined.

The meal in England, especially the large main meal at about seven o'clock in the evening, is more than a mere appeasement of hunger. From the very fact that the members of the household regularly meet for dinner in evening dress (see p. 86), the whole act of eating assumes the character of a cheerful festival. Not that anything special is expected of the food and drink itself. Both are extremely plain and simple at the present-day English table, indeed we would think them decidedly modest. The food lacks the charm of having been artistically prepared and drink is so much a secondary consideration nowadays that understanding of it has almost been lost. But the act of taking nourishment is sublimated by a pleasing presentation of what is offered. And this is where England can take credit for having created a fine tradition which has become the model for the world at large.

Furnishing of the room

This tradition is reflected in the very furnishing of the room, though perhaps even more in the way in which the table is set. As regards the treatment of the room, the popular wood-panelling has become almost typical of the dining-room, as of the English house as a whole. It extends to a good height in order to give the room an air of warmth and cosiness. The wood is usually left in its natural state, but for the dining-room too the appeal of white-painted wood-work is growing. Wherever possible, the side-board will be built in to the panelling of one of the narrow sides of the room, a very convenient device that eliminates any projecting piece of furniture that might impede circulation. Wood-panelling is liked on the ceiling as well as the wall. A thick carpet covers the floor to enable the servants to move noiselessly. A wall-painting will sometimes adorn the frieze in the dining-room, as in Lord Carlisle's house, where the painting is by Burne-Jones (see Figs. 10, 11). Walls are also often hung with tapestries.

A handsome, inviting fire-place, if possible in a bay, would seem to be essential to a well-designed dining-room (see p. 88). An adequate ventilating system that will continuously and effec-

tively remove the smell of food is held to be of the greatest importance. The room will be lit in the evenings by lights that are either hung so low and are so completely shaded that they throw their whole light on to the table in such a way that those seated there cannot see the light itself, or that provide only a soft, reflected glow (see p. 200).

Furniture. Dining-table

The furniture of the dining-room comprises a very broad dining-table, a set of chairs, a side-board, a few pieces on which dishes may be set down and a couple of comfortable armchairs by the fire. It is exceptional to find a couch in the dining-room; couches are only seen in smaller houses where the dining-room combines the purposes of the living-room. The dining-table in the average English house is nearly always a telescope table (Fig. 430). Its construction is based on a discovery made in the first quarter of the nineteenth century, since when it has slowly been supplanting, and has now entirely superseded, the draw table that was in general use until then. On the long axis below the table-top there is a screw-thread which is operated by a handle at one end of the table and increases the length of the table by the length of its frame. The table-top parts in the centre and the gap is filled by extra leaves. If the shaft of the screw itself is female and can receive another screw, the table can be extended to three times its length, but then it will require one or two central legs. The telescope table has the advantage over the draw table that the length can be varied at will and that the legs remain at the corners, where they disturb nobody, whereas with the draw table they are in the centre of the long side, where they are often in the way. One disadvantage is that the extra leaves have to be stored somewhere when not in use.

An English dining-table is always of some considerable width. It will hardly ever measure less than 1.22 m. (4 ft.) and will often run to as much as 1.68 m. (5 ft. 6 ins.), the average width of a largish dining-table will be 1.37 m. (4 ft. 6 ins.). All the tables are extremely solid and massively built and are therefore expensive. They are lower than those to which we are used; the English find it convenient to eat at a low table. One sometimes finds a round table in place of a rectangular one; just recently, in fact, as we have already noted (p. 87), it has become fashionable to eat at round tables. This means that if the party is larger than usual

426   Dawpool, Cheshire. By R. Norman Shaw. (See also Figs. 34, 35, 161, 373) Dining-room

427 Small house in Scotland. By Rome L. Guthrie. Simple dining-room

428 Small house in Scotland. Another view of dining-room

there is no alternative to eating at separate tables, though this seriously impairs the cohesion of the company. When closed, the telescope table is often round. Round tables are particularly convenient when the table-top simply rests on a central column since it has no legs to get in the way. Morris and the artists of the new movement had no liking for the telescope table and in their interiors contented themselves with ordinary tables without any lengthening mechanism except simple drop-leaves. Several square tables that can be pushed up together as occasion demand will often be provided.

Chairs

English dining-room chairs attract our attention because they all have normal backs like other chairs. Remarkable though it may seem to us, no one in England has so far championed the idea that a dining-room chair should have a very low back to facilitate serving at table. In fact one often sees extremely high-backed chairs (Figs. 431, 432). This may well be explained by the fact that visitors in England are never handed large boards with several dishes or even whole roast joints. The man of the house

429 Shiplake Court, Henley-on-Thames. By E. George and Peto. Dining-room

serves the meat, vegetables are handed in small dishes. Chippendale chairs are nowadays the favourites for dining-rooms and are always upholstered in morocco leather. The chairs are sold in sets of eight, twelve or twenty and there are always two armchairs to a set. The armchairs match the ordinary ones but are slightly wider and have wooden arms. They are meant for the narrow ends of the table and are used by the man and woman of the house, who always sit at the two narrow ends. It might be considered uncivil that the more comfortable chairs are not given to the guests. But the reason for the practice lies in the entrenched English view that the armchair is the proper seat for the chairman or man at the head of the company.

Plain rush seats rather than leather-covered ones are found quite often. They are really only endurable when a loose cushion is laid on them. Squabs are often provided for the ladies' feet at table, though they are used less frequently than they used to be. Those dining-room chairs that are not in daily use stand in a row along the dining-room wall. The two upholstered chairs by the fire are the usual easy-chairs that are characteristic of drawing-rooms and especially of smoking-rooms. They are leather-covered, as is the sofa that is found in smaller establishments.

The sideboard

The sideboard, for us the largest and most expensive piece of furniture in the dining-room, is less important and much smaller in England. The reason for this is that in the English house there is a room, the pantry (pp. 100, 134), that relieves the sideboard of some of its burden. It houses all the utensils that we keep in the sideboard: silver, crockery, glass are all kept in the pantry. There are usually merely a few drawers in the sideboard for the most important utensils in daily use at the table and a lockable cupboard for drinks (since many English servants are fond of the bottle, it has become a standing rule that all spirituous drink shall be carefully locked away). A sideboard has no upper part; at most there are a few small shelves, which serve little practical purpose. One still often sees a mirror on the back wall of the kind that was general in the Victorian period. The essential significance of the English sideboard is still that it is a table from which food is served. Yet at every-day meals, the joint is carved at the table, by the man of the house, who serves his fellow-diners in turn, using the warmed plates in front of him. Later on his wife will see to the serving of puddings and sweets. To serve in this way would cause

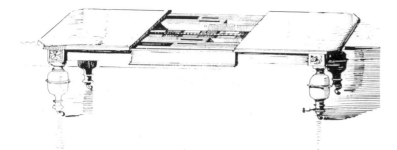

430 Telescope table

431, 432 English dining-room chairs with leather seats

too great a delay when the company is large and would also be difficult on festive occasions when every seat is occupied, so the butler carves the meat at the sideboard when the company exceeds a certain number. To bring food in from outside in portions as in hotels would be irreconcilable with English notions of domesticity. The whole joint is carried from the kitchen to the dining-room and set down on the sideboard. This custom explains why the serving-room (pp. 86, 101), an important room in our houses, is almost always non-existent in the English house.

In recent years the fine, graceful form of the Sheraton sideboard has become extremely popular once more. All the old pieces that have remained unused for decades and have, perhaps, been in store have come into their own again and now adorn the dining-rooms of the best houses. New furniture using the forms of these old pieces is being manufactured in quantity, for only so can the demand for these sideboards be satisfied and today they are still unquestionably the ones most commonly found in the English house.

Besides the Sheraton sideboard, there are a number of new forms that depend rather on the continental type of sideboard-cupboard, i.e. a closed chest-like piece of furniture at the bottom, with an upper part containing a cupboard or a set of shelves one above the other, or a combination of both. As we have already remarked, this form bears a greater resemblance to the English kitchen dresser than to the traditional dining-room sideboard. No distinct form has yet been evolved for this new kind of sideboard-cupboard. But, wherever it appears, it is small and graceful and again in this form cannot be compared with the wooden edifices of our sideboards (Figs. 433, 434).

Other furniture

To relieve the pressure on the sideboard and especially as a surface on which to lay dishes, plates etc. there exists a smaller, breast-high piece consisting merely of a frame of three shelves one above the other held by four supports at the corners and known as a dinner-waggon (Fig. 435). It stands on casters and was, no doubt, once meant to be used to wheel food round, like the similar piece used in hotels today. But it is no longer used for this purpose; it stands in a corner and often, indeed, has no casters, which makes its name entirely inappropriate. There is often a smaller cupboard in the dining-room, which used to be called a chiffonier and which also serves simply to relieve the pressure on the sideboard. Anyway there will always be two sideboards in large dining-rooms; in earlier days they used always to be made in pairs for large establishments. One still very often finds the wine-cooler of ancient memory standing under the sideboard or in its central open part, although the cooling of drinks is conspicuous by its absence in England. White wine, beer and champagne – all are drunk warm.

Another almost indispensable piece of dining-room furniture is a large folding screen that is supposed to protect those seated at table from the worst inconveniences of draught. They often occur in the Chinese or Japanese form, though independent forms of this necessary piece of furniture have been developed on the same principle. The leaves of the screen are either covered in leather, or carry painted decoration, or else the top parts are glazed.

Table manners

Just as to English eyes the central attraction of the dining-room is the laid table, so the art of setting it has been most lovingly

433 New style of sideboard

434 Sideboard with shelves above

cultivated in England. And not only that, eating, even sitting, at table have been developed to a fine art and are subject to strict conditions. Every deviation from the rule – could one even imagine this happening in England – is judged severely. Correct behaviour at table or 'table manners' is one of the most important branches of the upbringing of children. These strict manners and orderliness in eating, which the English learn from earliest childhood, together with precepts for behaviour in other situations in life, is one of the explanations of the complete composure which characterises the Englishman everywhere and which, even in his day, Goethe found so striking in the young Englishmen visiting Weimar. It is entirely erroneous to conclude from these strict precepts, as some do, that there is lack of intellectual freedom. By regulating the small superficialities of life, so that they are taken for granted and performed without fuss, they in fact contribute to the freedom and true comfort of life. Freedom does not lie in lawlessness. It is true that the rules of eating have not developed logically but often amount simply to

arbitrary or contradictory fashions. Thus, to cite one small example, there is a contradiction between the universal form of our soup-spoons and the custom of taking soup not from the tip but from the side of the spoon. Custom and the form of the utensil do not correspond in this instance; if current custom were to be followed, the stem would have to be removed from its present position and soldered to the long side of the bowl. But despite all fashions strict table-manners are in place. They are simply a social compromise and therefore of great value, because they undoubtedly sublimate the act of eating, in which so much depends upon purely emotional values, and help to bridge the gulf between mere feeding and an easy deportment at table. It is recognised everywhere that an unconstrained demeanour at table is of great importance not only spiritually but also purely physically – in other words, that good table manners aid health.

The laid table

Good table manners in England begin with the laying of the

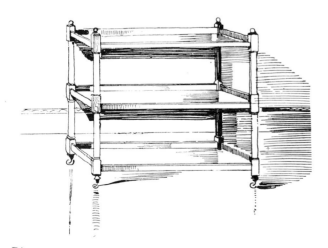

435 Dinner-waggon

436 Leather-covered fireside chair

table. There is always something extremely clean and pleasant and even joyful and festive about the appearance of a laid table. Working people even eat at tables with white cloths and in the smallest houses, before she sits down to table, the solitary maid of all work transforms the kitchen table into a dining-table by spreading a white cloth over it. The practice in German beer-houses of eating at a bare oak table, or at best a table on which a red and white checked cotton cloth has been spread, with tooth-pick holder and match-box stand as the sole decoration, is the quintessence of barbarity to an Englishman. But with the good food that the German table generally provides, why not ease as well? Besides spreading a white cloth over their tables, however, the English decorate them daily with flowers. It is taken for granted that the dining-table must have flowers; there is a great demand for flowers and they are sold cheaply throughout the year, so that this luxury implies no economic extravagance. But where, nevertheless, there are no flowers, as, for example, at the workman's table and that of the maid-servant, there will be a pot-plant instead. One finds quantities of flowers artistically arranged on a well-laid table. Tall centre-pieces are, however, avoided for the same reason that table lights are kept low: so that those seated at the table can all see one another. Flowers are placed in low silver or crystal bowls and are held upright by lead bands or tubes or wire-netting. The flower bowls stand on a runner and grouped round them at regular intervals are a number of smaller vases containing single specimens or little arrangements in which the flowers stand gracefully. Often the runner will be edged with loosely laid greenery or a chain of flowers. If not of the same kind, the flowers will all be of the same colour; the colour is repeated in the runner (if it is embroidered in colours) and reappears again in the little shades that are provided, as we have seen, to keep the light of the candle-flames out of the diners' eyes.

To make the table still more decorative, the fruit is set out beforehand. Dried foods to be eaten at the end of the meal, such as chocolates, salted almonds, figs and dates are placed in position from the beginning, each in its little silver dish, not forgetting the dainty little forks with which one helps oneself. Fruit and dessert are no longer handed round in those tall fancy stands topped by a bunch of flowers, which must then pointlessly go the rounds with it. Fruit is piled simply into bowls with a few leaves here and there. Grapes are always accompanied by grape-scissors with which each diner cuts off as much fruit as he wants; there is always a melon-knife with a melon. Apart from fruit and dessert, nothing is set on the table by way of decoration, least of all compotes and cooked dishes. There would be a feeling that they would be exposed to the comings and goings of the servants, which might perhaps make them less appetising. With the sole exception of champagne, wine comes to the dining-room not in bottles but in crystal decanters that are filled outside and placed at either end of the table. Wine is poured by servants, who offer sherry with the soup, followed by red or white wine or champagne, and port-wine with the dessert. Port glasses are not placed on the table until the end of the meal. Somewhere on the table there will be one or two carafes of water with glasses for those annually increasing numbers of people who do not drink wine.

The table is laid as follows. In the centre of each place lies a simply folded napkin, with a bread-roll on it. There are no plates at the places, for unwarmed plates would be useless and it would be inconvenient and pointless to put the soup-plates on them. To the left of the napkin lie two forks and a fish-fork, to the right two knives, a fish-knife and a soup-spoon, across the top lie a spoon and fork, these are the size of children's spoons and forks in Germany but are in England the normal utensils for puddings. At the right-hand top corner stand whatever wine-glasses are required. Very small containers holding salt and pepper stand either at each place or centrally between each two places. There is always a tiny spoon for each salt-cellar so that no one is put into the embarrassing position of having to dig his knife into the salt. Any other implements for use during the meal will be specially laid beside each place at the proper time. These will include fruit knife and fork (not knife only), a knife for cheese, a finger-bowl, which will be brought in, half-filled with water, resting on the fruit plate, and all the knives, forks and spoons for other foods. One further point: a thick wool cover will be spread over the table under every table-cloth, not merely to protect the table-top but also to eliminate as much noise as possible and to soften the hard feel of the table.

Serving at table

As we have said, at dinner-parties nowadays all dishes are set down on the sideboard and served from there. With a number of dishes this is now beginning to be done in ordinary life as well, so that in many houses it is only the joint and the pudding, and perhaps the soup as well and whole fish, that are placed on the table to be served by the man of the house and his wife. The relatively new habit of serving the food on a plate to the diner at his place in fact contradicts the traditional English belief that all dishes should be served from the table. The new practice, known as *diner à la russe*, has been introduced here and there, especially in towns, and its justification is that it saves time and formalities. It is a sign of the infiltration of continental practices, which are breaking through the old native English customs at a few points and are expressed, for example, in the fairly recent adoption (see p. 135) of blocks of flats in towns.

Just as the table is laid with the utmost meticulousness and neatness, so the service at table is most punctilious, precise – and noiseless as well. In houses where no butler is kept, the maid is chosen largely for her ability to serve well at table and to lay the table well.

It is part of good service at table that the person serving should look well and should be scrupulously clean and tidy in external appearance. The English maid's uniform, with the simple black dress and the little white cap with long streaming white ribbons, the neat apron and starched collar and cuffs is in itself a cultural heritage as refined as the beautifully laid table that the maid arranges and at which she serves.

Guests at dinner

An important point about the English table is that the preparations we have described are not made simply for visitors but also for daily use. The only difference that the appearance of guests makes is that a few extra places are laid. An Englishman is therefore always in the position of being able to ask one or more casual visitors to stay on to a meal and so to extend his hospitality in the true manner – and the manner most pleasing to both sides – of sparing his guest the feeling that he is upsetting the household. This is the case with English invitations in general. Few people are invited so that they do not seriously extend the limits of the household. The guests for their part come with no particular culinary expectations but rather for the sake of sociability towards their host. How different from the resplendent banquets so dear to us, for which the household is turned upside down! All the guests are aware of the fact, not only from the ostentatious special arrangements but also from the enormous discrepancy between the host's ordinary way of life and the one he assumes for sociability's sake. The fact that it is customary for the guests to help to pay for the host's servants by tipping them is in keeping with the cultural level that this betokens. These tips sometimes even play a part in the contractual agreements between employers and servants. A candid host ought to consider it an insult to his house that his servants are paid by his guests. Instead, this deplorable custom receives further encouragement from the members of the family, who refrain from conducting their guests to the door themselves so as not to interrupt the giving of tips. These are small but highly indicative signs that we are still deficient in domestic culture. There is no sign of such improprieties in the extremely advanced English ideas about life in the house. English sentiment in this respect is entirely natural and sincere.

Hospitality is one of the most precious assets of domestic life, but only when it is extended honestly, with good intent and impartially, and nowhere will one meet it in better and purer form than in the English house.

3. The drawing-room

Character of the drawing-room

Although it is the focal point of domestic life in the English house, the average drawing-room is artistically the least satisfying of the rooms. It suffers in general from having too many odds and ends packed into it and the deliberate informality all too often degenerates into confusion. Actually the province of the lady of the house (see p. 83), it bears the marks of her preferences: lightness, mobility and elegance, but usually combined with caprice and that love of frippery and knick-knacks by the thousand that characterises the modern English society woman. It has the least style of all the rooms.

The drawing-room combines within itself the purposes of reception-room, music-room and communal living-room. It is in actual fact the room in which one chats, plays and idles. The different purposes necessitate different arrangements but all boil down to creating comforts that make it agreeable to linger there. The lightness and in a certain sense the superficiality of the

present-day English social intercourse that goes on in the drawing-room precludes seriousness in the decoration and content of the room. The trend throughout is towards prettiness, casualness, lightness, a feminine character. The Victorian drawing-room with its plush furniture, on the backs of which were spread the antimacassars, beribboned in blue, with red plush frames on the walls and a tasselled plush cover over the mantelpiece, has been transformed into a room that is light in mood throughout, with light, graceful furniture – which is after all a clear improvement on the earlier room. Yet the many whatnots and shelves are still packed full of useless odds and ends and on tables and screens there are often many dozens of framed and unframed photographs.

Treatment of walls and ceilings

Treatment of walls and ceiling in this room aims at producing a pleasant, graceful effect. If walls are panelled in wood they will be painted white, as will any visible beams. Or else the walls may be covered with a light-coloured material in a white frame; the frieze will carry a delicate relief pattern that is faintly echoed in the plain white ceiling. Between the frieze and the lower zone of the wall there will often be a shallow shelf on which decorative plates and other bibelots are displayed. If a stucco ceiling has been chosen, the stucco will be quite flat and the motifs widely spaced. Morris decorated various drawing-rooms where ceilings and friezes were painted all over with his own characteristic delicately coloured flower-patterns executed by hand. Another favourite covering for drawing-room walls is silk. The silk is stretched either in white painted architectonically designed frames or over the whole surface of the wall. The continental type of parquet has become almost the rule for floors, with outstandingly beautiful and valuable rugs laid here and there at important points. Yet the old form of all-over carpeting is still very popular. A plain-coloured under-felt is often chosen and precious small rugs laid on top. Japanese rush matting makes a fine, clean surface and is very often chosen as an underlay. The drawing-room fire-place tends not to be in a bay, because during afternoon visits quite a large company may need to cluster round the fire. Artificial lighting must definitely be designed to illuminate the whole room with an even light: the best way of doing this is to hang many small lamps from the ceiling at regular intervals.

437　The architect's house, London. By W. A. S. Benson. Drawing-room

438　House in Glasgow. By C. R. Mackintosh. Drawing-room

439   House in Glasgow. By Ernest A. Taylor. Drawing-room

440   House in Glasgow. Another view of drawing-room

It is the drawing-room that in many houses continues to reflect a liking for French decoration. One sees completely French *salons* – French both in the treatment of the walls and in the furniture – and all firms of decorators are specially equipped to furnish drawing-rooms in the French taste. Even the designers of ordinary commercial furniture strive to offer a few reminiscences of French taste, though artistically speaking this is surely anything but an advantage, since the result is bound to be of doubtful value.

Drawing-room furniture

The furniture of the drawing-room altogether comprises a variety of pieces, which, from the artistic point of view, must be considered dangerous and makes it almost impossible to achieve a unified effect. The ordinary drawing-room suite of seats, comprising a sofa, two upholstered armchairs, two very low chairs and four other chairs without arms, is seen as the most essential item. The ordinary small round drawing-room table and a series of other even smaller tables are also considered indispensable and a china-cabinet and piano will be almost universal additions. Other normal pieces of furniture include a corner table with or without a back and upper structure, a lady's desk, another china-cabinet, one or more low book-shelves, a series of fancy chairs, little tables for all sorts of special purposes, cupboards that hang, corner-cupboards, semi-circular wall-tables and, not to be forgotten, a mantelpiece that in this context is often a movable piece of furniture.

Mantelpieces

Admittedly it is only in the more ordinary houses that one will find a mantelpiece that has been bought in a shop. It usually consists of a mirror, with little shelves one above the other on either side for displaying small ornaments. There are often also two little cabinets on either side or, again, the mirror itself may be in a cupboard-like structure. In the better houses one will always find that the mantelpiece is a built-in fixture. Here again the guiding principle will always be to create as much room as possible for small ornaments. Thus there will almost invariably be many shelves, or shelves combined with china-cabinets. Built-in cupboards, mainly intended for books, are often found immediately adjoining and on either side of the fire-place. One occasionally sees a mantelpiece framing a painting or piece of wall decoration.

Upholstered chairs, etc.

The most substantial pieces of furniture in the drawing-room are the comfortable upholstered chairs and other seating. Admittedly, those soft-cheeked monstrosities upholstered all over, which fit the human body at rest in a really refined manner and seem to be made for contemplation and day-dreaming, were perhaps developed in club-rooms rather than in drawing-rooms, yet there are always a pair of them in a well-furnished drawing-room. They are, of course, of doubtful value in this context since they can scarcely be used on social occasions, for no one likes to adopt the unceremonious posture of the body that they demand; but for unusable chairs they take up a great deal of space. This is doubtless why one sees them more rarely in newer establishments, where they are more commonly replacd by smaller, compacter armchairs. These exist in every imaginable form: small with low arms, magisterial with high arms, rectangular and rounded, fully and partly upholstered. One often finds that the armchairs in one room are all of different kinds so that everyone can choose the one that appeals to him most. The seats of most English armchairs are extraordinarily low, often no higher than 30 cm., which startles the newcomer as he sits down. The

441, 442 Chesterfield and armchair

444, 445 Sofa and upholstered armchair for drawing-room, Sheraton style

English have a most strange liking for low seats of this kind. They find them cosy because they are conducive to intimate chats. The open fire may also have contributed to their popularity since one is closer to the fire when seated in a very low chair than in a high one. In addition to the low armchairs, two very low armless chairs are permanent features of the English drawing-room; known as occasional chairs, they are extremely popular. The sofa that completes the ordinary suite of upholstered chairs comes in a great variety of forms; but it is always small and elegant and seats three people at most; it is positively not meant for reclining. The commonest type of sofa is the one known as a settee, a small long-shaped upholstered seat for two. A Chesterfield is a small sofa thickly and softly upholstered all over, with a very broad top edge on which to rest the elbow (Fig. 442). The most pleasing are the sofas known as Queen Anne (Fig. 446) and Sheraton (Fig. 444), both of which have armchairs to match. The pleasing thing about these pieces – in which the edges of the wooden frames are sometimes left exposed – is that the shape remains clearly recognisable and that all the contours are not lost in the sausage-like formlessness of upholstered furniture. Another piece that was very popular in the eighteenth century and that often reappears nowadays is a settee with a wooden back that is simply an extension of two or three chair backs. We have already remarked (p. 195) that all eighteenth-century forms of seating have recently been making their second triumphal entry into the English drawing-room, in particular the elegant chairs in the style of Sheraton and Hepplewhite.

Chintz covers

The covers of upholstered furniture are no longer made of velvet or plush but at best of a patterned woollen material. But chintz covers have recently become even commoner than wool. Chintz was originally used only for loose covers during the period when a house was uninhabited. Such covers are particularly necessary in London where the smoke from coal with which the air is

perpetually laden quickly begrimes unwashable materials. As a result of conditions in London, it soon became customary to keep the chintz covers on for daily use. To keep them looking pleasant they were now made of good, washable cotton and Morris's beautiful hand-printed chintzes became particularly popular for this purpose. Owners of these, however, found themselves possessed of such good material and especially such magnificent colours that they had no wish to uncover the original material again. The next step, to abandon the woollen material altogether, followed automatically. Once upholstered furniture had been covered with chintz, the same material began to be chosen for curtains. Thus the whole drawing-room has gradually been transformed into a room decorated in chintz. And one can hardly say that this has been a change for the worse. The clean chintz covers and matching curtains give the room an air of freshness, healthfulness and fragrance. One feels the same confidence in it as in a freshly made bed. And it is interesting to note here again that hygiene is nowadays everywhere preferred to the sump-tuousness and cosiness of the old style. Our whole culture aspires to the healthful and our aesthetic sensibility in all spheres, but especially in that of house-building, will soon conform so closely that the concepts of health and beauty may become identical.

The matching chintzes throughout give the room great homogeneity, for all the cushions in the room, all the squabs on window-seats, corner chairs and other things will be covered with the same material, so providing a means of pulling the muddled elements of the drawing-room together to create an artistic effect.

Fancy chairs

Several of the fancy chairs in the drawing-room (Figs. 450–455) are extremely comfortable and pleasing in shape. This is true in particular of a type of low-backed unupholstered armchair,

443 Comfortable upholstered drawing-room armchair

446 'Queen Anne' sofa

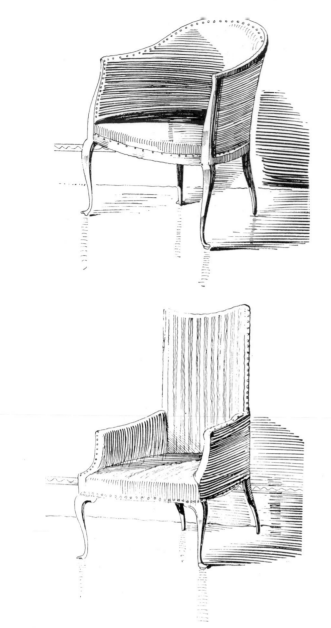

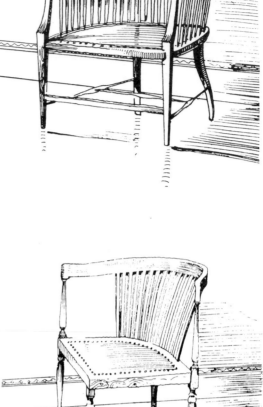

447, 448   Incidental armchairs for drawing-room

450, 451   Wooden drawing-room chairs

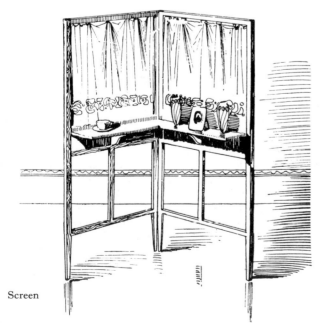

449   Screen

which may perhaps be counted among the best examples of modern furniture to have been developed in England (Fig. 450). One type of chair has a low, round back attached diagonally and is known as a corner chair (Fig. 451). The rocking-chairs of the American house are almost unknown in England.

Corner-seats and window-seats

A corner-seat, known as a 'cosy corner', has become one of the favourite spots in the English drawing-room (see p. 187f.). No opportunity is lost of creating such a spot whenever there is a suitable corner in the room, especially when the seat can be close beside the fire. It is best if a corner seat closely follows the decoration of the wall. In its simplest form it can be made of a long low wooden seat with a shelf above it and a hanging between the two; loose, flat, long cushions will be laid on the seat, usually with a number of down cushions – of which there are already many, almost too many, on sofas and chairs in the English drawing-room. Unfixed corner-seats can, of course, also be bought ready-made in shops (Fig. 456); but these usually lack the desired simplicity and naturalness; the manufacturers,

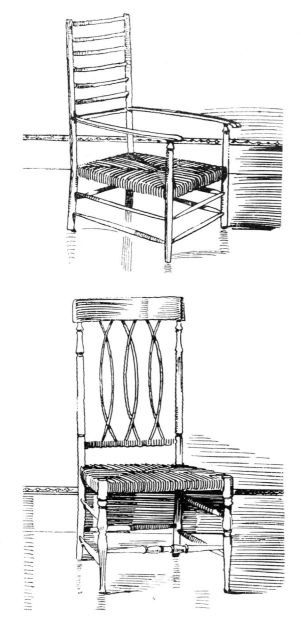

452, 453   Incidental wooden chairs with rush seats

454, 455   Incidental wooden chairs

feeling that they have to follow public taste, pile on all kinds of decorative accessories. Ready-made corner-seats often have a motley array of little cupboards and fancy shelves above the seat-back which good taste would omit. Window-seats are as popular as corner-seats. The drawing-room usually looks on to a terrace with flowers or has a bay opening towards a favourite view (see p. 187). Window-seats are welcome in both cases. A low window-seat covered with a loose squab is the simplest form.

Drawing-room tables

After the seats, tables play the next most important part in the drawing-room. They are no less numerous and varied than the forms of seating. But the most striking point is that only small occasional tables are allowed. The sofa-table of ancient memory has disappeared from the modern drawing-room, despite the fact that fifty years ago it was almost as much at home there as in the German parlour. This means that the room in fact has no fixed central point. Its only central point is an open space in front of the fire, into which chairs are moved when needed (see p. 199). The little sofa usually stands by the fire at right-angles to the

chimney-breast and forms the starting-point for the arrangement of the furniture round the fire-place. Like the chairs, it always stands free in the room, which means that it must be fully backed. Fireside tables are unwanted and would only be in the way. They are only needed in the drawing-room at tea-time and perhaps to receive the little cups in which coffee is served in the dining-room after meals. Having first moved one of the little tables near to the fire for the purpose, the maid serving afternoon-tea sets down a large tray (made of silver or wood and always provided with two handles), on which all the tea-things are stacked. The lady of the house pours tea for each person straight from the tray that is left on the table. Cakes and bread and butter are handed round on a cake-stand, usually by a man who springs to the hostess's aid. Special tea-tables also exist; these have little flaps on each side forming shelves for cakes and cups; those of poorer quality are made of bamboo. But they are not essential, tea is served on any sort of table, often even on a folding stand which the maid brings in with the tray and places anywhere in the room.

215

456 'Cosy corner' seat with panels and cupboards above

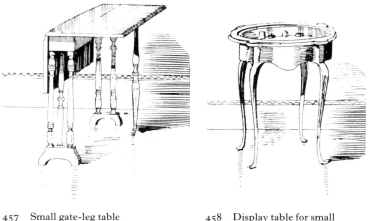

457 Small gate-leg table

458 Display table for small objects of value

The small round or octagonal drawing-room table (Fig. 459) should be regarded as a relic of the former sofa-table. Accordingly, its position among the tables is a somewhat dominant one. The table-top is seldom more than 70 cm. in diameter, its legs are usually slightly curved, while unusual upward-arching brackets rise from the lower part of the legs to support a central shelf. None of the drawing-room tables, this one included, is ever covered by a cloth. Its main use is as somewhere to lay books or to stand vases of flowers and framed photographs. All the other tables are folding tables with two drop-leaves to lengthen the top into a rectangle, circle or oval or

some fancy shape; a particular small form is known today as a Sutherland table (Figs. 457, 460). The flaps are supported either, in the manner of the little eighteenth-century tables, on a bracket that swings out or, in the manner of the old rustic gate-leg table, on a leg that swings out. But the tables are always small and elegant with very slender little spindle-legs. In this respect there has been a total return to the late eighteenth century; not only have the drop-leaf tables of the period been copied in large numbers but the surviving old pieces are also the most highly treasured pieces of furniture in the modern drawing-room. Eighteenth-century games-tables, the green baize-covered leaves of which fold together (they sometimes fold like an envelope, in which case the table is called an envelope table (Fig. 462)) have also come into their own again, as have the semi-circular tables that stand against a wall and may be placed two together to form one whole circular table, the four little nesting tables and the display table for small objects of value (see Fig. 458). Another piece of furniture that commonly stands in the drawing-room, a lady's writing-table, usually follows eighteenth-century models. As it is only used for writing the occasional letter, it usually takes the form of a small, long-shaped table with a very capacious drawer for writing-materials (Fig. 461). Sometimes, however, there may be shelves, pigeon-holes or something of the kind above the table-top.

Drawing-room cabinets

The real centre of attraction and the largest piece of furniture in the English drawing-room is the china-cabinet. It comes in all shapes and sizes but usually ends up as a fantastic combination of china-cabinet and open shelves. The most satisfying are the closed china-cabinets standing either on legs of medium height (Figs. 463–465) or on very low feet and reaching only to breast-height (Fig. 466). The inside of the cabinets is often lined with pale-coloured plush. As their name implies, these cabinets are filled with valuable porcelain; during the last decades in particular, the fashion for collecting blue-and-white Chinese porcelain and decorating the house with it has attracted whole ship-loads to England and filled every English drawing-room with this ware (p. 161). Only the really valuable pieces are kept in the china-cabinet; apart from these, the same ware often decorates the mantelpiece and all the cornice-shelves. Like the china-cabinets, of which there are usually two in larger rooms, corner cupboards, when they appear, whether they stand or hang, are usually broken-up, fantastic and therefore restless in design. The purpose alone of the drawing-room book-cases, which are usually so-called dwarf book-cases, i.e. they are no higher than chair-backs (see Fig. 471) suggests a more restful form and they therefore make an agreeable change from most of the drawing-room furniture.

Piano

Last of all the necessities in the drawing-room is the piano. But a grand is considered the only piano of good quality in England; an upright or 'cottage' piano smacks either of impermanence or impoverishment. In view of the fact that the English are probably the most unmusical race in the world the presence of a grand piano in every house is slightly surprising. Dilettantism is in its element in England and even among the educated there is a lack of critical judgment of quality in music that would be impossible in any other country. But despite the absence of discrimination in musical matters, love of music is deep and general among the English.

Pianos of German manufacture, especially those of Blüthner and Bechstein, have now entirely outrivalled those of the old-

459   Typical drawing-room table

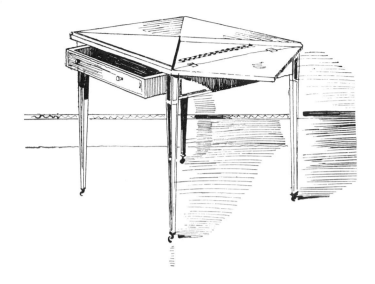

462   Card-table

460   Gate-leg table

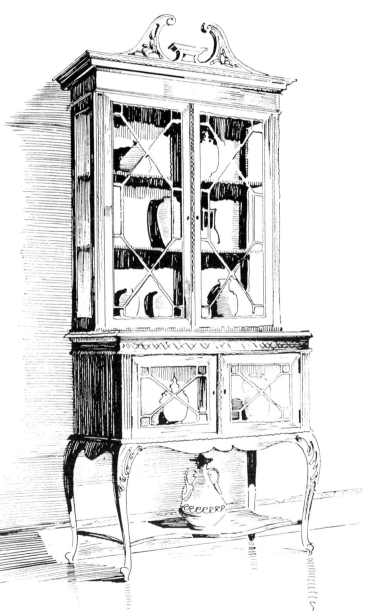

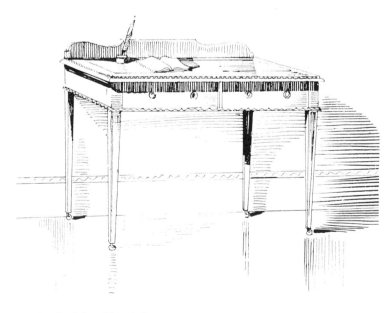

461   Lady's writing desk

463   Typical drawing-room cabinet

464 Drawing-room cabinet (in Jacobean style)

established English firm of Broadwood. But these instruments are all sold to England in rosewood instead of the black polish that is in general use with us. In England too during the past thirty years there have been all kinds of attempts to give the piano an artistic form. All the artists who design furniture have tried their hands at pianos. There have been a number of successful solutions, among the best being those of Morris, who decorated the casings of his pianos with inlay or gesso, and Burne-Jones (see Fig. 15). But most of the other attempts, especially those of the London Arts and Crafts group, suffer from their rustic character. The mistake has been to consider a casing put together like a barn-door suitable to a delicate mechanism like that of the modern piano. The most successful attempts so far to improve the form of the casing are those modelled on the Sheraton tradition (even Morris essentially followed this trend). The very thick single legs are replaced by elegant pairs of legs joined at the base. The English piano-stool usually has an upholstered seat, the base of which is adapted to contain music. One often also sees a long seat suitable for duet-playing. The appearance of this type of seat usually goes excellently with the piano and complements it far better than the types of chair in general use in Germany. The music cabinet that accompanies the piano takes the form of a small, slender, plain cupboard with little compartments that pull out.

Other furniture and ornamental pieces

In addition to these main pieces of furniture, the drawing-room contains a whole series of other small pieces that are considered more or less essential. One of these is the clock that stands on the mantelpiece and is usually of the encased and simple form of the Empire period. The tall brass standard-lamp (p. 200) comes into its own where there is no electric light. In particular, however, the screen is a permanent feature; here too it varies widely in form but is usually rather lighter in character than that in the dining-room. It is often covered in silk and has provision for fastening photographs to it. Or else there are little flaps half-way up that fold forward and form shelves for small ornaments (Fig.

465 Glass cabinet for the drawing-room

466 Glass cabinet for the drawing-room

449). Valuable old French screens are often used and, indeed, the drawing-room is regarded altogether as the proper place to have and to display old furniture, art-cabinets, fine little decorative cabinets, wood or metal-work coffers, in short, all the precious pieces in the house. But it is considered essential that these pieces too should be elegant in character and also really valuable. The aim is to make the room the jewel-casket of the house, in both content and form. The only pictures to be hung are of real artistic value and only choice collector's pieces are displayed. Besides the riches passed down from generation to generation in English families, middle-class houses also contain valuable, or at least very interesting, art-treasures, which are used to decorate the drawing-room. In very many houses the drawing-room has become almost a museum of valuable old furniture and art-treasures. We have already remarked that the room is often filled to overflowing in the process. The English have not yet accustomed themselves to the principle that it is better to lock valuable possessions away than to overload rooms with them. Well-to-do families should have an 'art-cabinet', from which the only pieces ever brought out should be those that really serve to decorate the room, without detracting from its appearance as an artistic area.

Even in the form of pieces of old furniture, so the English believe, the character of the room must always express the fact that it is the woman's realm. If the whole furnishing of the modern English house is in itself the opposite of massive and four-square, lightness and charm have become obligatory here. The English drawing-room is nothing if not 'dainty'.

4. The library

Character of the room

The character of the library differs in detail according to whether it is in a small or a large house, i.e. according to whether it is primarily a smoking-room and den for the man of the house or the room in which he works (see p. 87). But it always bears a certain solid, manly stamp. If in this respect it forms an agreeable contrast to the drawing-room, there is yet a feeling in many English libraries, especially those of the great houses, of some chilliness and desolation due to the fact that the room is very little used. The library is part of the programme of the English house and there are also valuable books that have been passed down from generation to generation and have to be housed. But the modern generation perhaps spends less time surrounded by its books than did its forebears. Those who possess most books are often the very ones who are least willing to bother with them: they prefer riding, hunting and travelling. The libraries reflect this clearly by giving the feeling that always strikes one on entering unused rooms. In smaller houses the library is the smoking-room and therefore less unfriendly; but seldom can one observe that a literary spirit really reigns in this room, that the book-cases are opened, that someone writes at the desk and sits reading in the comfortable leather chairs by the fire.

Culture of the book. The art of the book

The English house is immensely rich in books; this is one of the most striking characteristics that can be observed in England. Although he has not enjoyed a specifically scholarly education, the Englishman buys quantities of books, has them expensively bound and houses them in well-made book-cases. Most of his books, of course, fall into the category of *belles-lettres*. It is taken absolutely for granted that every good house will contain good editions of the principal English authors ancient and modern. The old books will usually have been inherited and the new ones will naturally be purchased as they appear. But important works of scholarship also find their way into good private houses. Many English noblemen still have some sense of responsibility for the intellectual values of the nation and feel bound to acquire certain important works for their libraries, whatever the subject. Price seldom enters into it. On the contrary, one can assume that a book that is offered for sale at a high price is more likely to find buyers than the ordinary mediocre book. This is provided, of course, that the book is finely produced. Books in particular in England have always maintained certain high technical and artistic standards, even during the period when artistic handicrafts were in decline; the tradition of the decently printed, well-produced book has virtually never been broken since the arts of the book attained a degree of excellence in the eighteenth century. Walpole, the Neo-Gothic writer, was the reformer in matters of typography then, just as Morris was to be a hundred years later. Thanks to Morris, England became the source of those great changes in book-production that have now ripened and borne such excellent fruit in Germany too. Morris's refinements in the printing of books consisted in making the page a powerful self-contained image. His principal successor was Charles Ricketts who continued to produce books of the highest artistic quality, first in association with Lucien Pissarro and later with Heaton; Cobden-Sanderson has recently been producing books that appear to outclass anything that has been done before in the way of noble refinement. So great is the appeal of the books of all these artists and a whole series of others that those wishing to obtain copies must subscribe in advance. By the day following publication they are often worth three times the original price.

Bindings

Like printing, book-binding has always been of a very high order in England. The public has been satisfied only with the best materials and the best workmanship. Leather spines and hand-blocked lettering were taken for granted at a time when Goethe was allowing the collected edition of his own works to be issued

467 Typical library bookcase

468 Cragside, Northumberland. By R. Norman Shaw.
(See also Figs. 24–26) Library

469 Stoneleigh, Kelvinside, Glasgow. By H. E. Clifford.
(See also Figs. 264, 270–271) Library

in paper wrappers, in which state it has remained to this day. The purchaser of an octavo book is quite prepared to pay from 5M to 15 M* to have it bound. And when in more recent decades small flaws began to appear in the leather, Parliament did not hesitate to set up a scientific commission to enquire into every phase of the present-day preparation and treatment of leather in order to discover the causes of the flaws. The memorandum issued by this commission is now a reliable guide to the selection and tanning of the best leather. Interest in bindings in particular has in fact increased recently. Classes for book-binders have been inaugurated at all the art-schools, in which the best kind of book-binding, technically and artistically speaking, is taught by competent professionals. In particular the old style of hand-tooling leather bindings has been eagerly revived.

Furnishing the library

A people so attentive to books and their exteriors must also furnish the rooms in which the books are to be housed to a high standard. And we find, indeed, that the English library is well and solidly furnished with dignity and good taste. The ideal library, as the English see it, must always have its four walls, or at least three of them, lined with built-in book-cases. They are so arranged that lower cupboards measuring from 30 to 40 cm. in depth surround the room to the height of the dado, while glass-fronted shelves measuring some 20 cm. in depth rest on them. The lower cupboards are for portfolios, prints and folio volumes, the upper ones for octavos. The book-cupboards project some 15–20 cm. and there are very often small extra leaves under their tops which can be pulled out and on which one can consult or read a book. The cupboards have a variety of fittings according to the type of material to be accommodated. There may be drawers, trays that are open at the front or straightforward shelves. Where open shelves replace the glass-fronted cupboards there is always a narrow strip of leather that hangs down and covers the empty space between the rows of books and the shelves above and keeps out some of the dust (Fig. 471). This device would be worth imitating. Whether glass-fronted or not the shelves are always movable: a toothed fillet is attached to back and front of the cheek of the book-case, little pegs are pushed in and the shelf rests on them. No new invention that has sought to better this simple and

very old device has so far met with much success. The built-in book-cases are often very tall and one has to use the library-steps provided for the purpose to reach the top shelves. When book-cases occupy one or two walls only, the wood-panelling is continued on the others. The favourite woods for libraries are mahogany and oak. When there are fewer books to be accommodated and those few are ordinary-sized, the lower cupboard will probably be omitted altogether and the shelves will begin at the bottom and finish moderately low (Fig. 468). Or there will be book-cases all round the room but extending only half-way up the walls, an arrangement that is preferable to the previous one. In both cases a fair expanse of the upper part of the wall will remain unoccupied and can well be used to hang oil-paintings. Like that of the dining-room, the library ceiling will be serious and dignified in character, whether it has beams or stucco decoration of simple design or is plainly painted or papered. A thick carpet covers the floor so that readers or those absorbed in study shall be as little disturbed as possible by the sound of footsteps.

470 Clencot, Gloucestershire. By E. George and Peto. (See also Figs. 54, 55)
Library

*English equivalent 5s. and 15s. at the time. [DS]

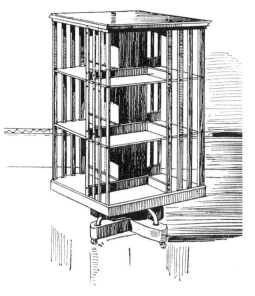

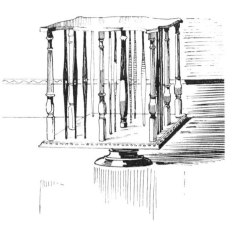

471   Dwarf bookcase

472, 473   Revolving book-stands, the smaller one for use on a desk

474, 475   Library armchairs

476, 477   Leather-covered upholstered
armchairs for the smoking room

Book-cases

Where there are no fixed book-shelves, there will be book-cases constructed essentially on the same principle as the built-in book-cases that we have described. The old form of book-case, of which there are so many examples in Chippendale's furniture pattern-book, has survived until the present day. In their simple appearance these book-cases are the direct successors to the furniture of the eighteenth century (Fig. 467); the lower section is usually break-fronted while the glazed upper part is flat. The panes of glass are still separated in the old manner by extraordinarily slender, finely proportioned cross-bars. Book-cases usually measure 1.83 m. (6 ft.) in height. Naturally, however, there are also narrower and, indeed, also lower book-cases which have no lower cupboards; there are also combined writing-tables and book-shelves in a great variety of forms.

Tables

Other furniture in the library includes one or more large central tables on which books, portfolios, etc. can be laid and opened and a desk for the man of the house. The desk is nearly always of the type that we nowadays call a *Diplomatentisch*, although one does see desks with drawers, etc. above. The central tables are strongly built, absolutely simple large tables with numerous drawers. They and the desk are always covered by thick, firm leather that is stuck down and provides a splendid surface on which to work. The very practical but rather clumsy American roll-top desks have not taken root in private houses in England; they look too 'office-like'. A revolving book-stand of a kind that has recently become familiar in Germany (Fig. 472) often stands beside the desk. It is a piece of furniture that has proved very agreeable in use as a stand for reference-books, but must be very solidly made if it is not to develop a wobble.

Chairs

Wooden armchairs are the favourite form of seating in libraries and the old English rustic types have been copied with good results (Figs. 474, 475). There has also been some American influence in chairs. But the very comfortable American desk-chairs with their revolving and tipping seats are seldom seen; these again smack too much of the office. Somewhere near the fire there are usually a few comfortable leather-covered armchairs like those found in clubs (Figs. 476, 477).

Smoking-room furniture

When the library is used mainly as a smoking-room and the man's den there will be no lack of other comfortable seating, possibly a sofa, with a smoker's table, containers for cigars, etc. The ideal will then be the altogether cosier atmosphere of the 'gentleman's den' (p. 89), which is equipped only for intimate conversation over a smoke and a drink and for which, therefore, comfortable seating and a cosy plan are the aims from the outset. Here and in the smoking-room proper, if there is one, the fire-place will again be made the centre of the room and the men will cluster round it as the women do in the drawing-room. But here in the smoking-room the character is definitely that of a club-room: the furniture will comprise large leather-covered lounge-chairs, little smoker's tables, a table in the centre for newspapers and periodicals and a few leather-covered sofas, while the room will be decorated in warm, comfortable tones. Nothing adds so much to this character as tall wood-panelling. The best and certainly the best-equipped smoking-rooms will be found in hotels and clubs. Artistically speaking the best are those created by Charles Rennie Mackintosh for Miss Cranston's tea-rooms in Glasgow.

5. The billiard room and the other residential rooms

Billiard-room

The billiard-room (for its layout see p. 89) rather resembles the smoking-room in treatment as a den generally speaking meant only for the male members of the household and their friends. Here again high wood-panelling is really the obvious treatment for the walls; for the rest, its appearance will be kept as plain as possible. Seats, possibly with backs upholstered in leather, must be ranged all round the room on a raised platform and these in themselves lend the room a certain unified restfulness. An ingle-nook provides a comfortable corner for non-players – and is particularly appropriate in this room where the whole space round the table is taken up by the players. The billiard-table itself virtually completes the furniture of the room. In each case in which architects have been involved in furnishing a billiard-room, they have designed the table specially in order to avoid the ordinary ready-made tables. The problem does not present the same difficulties as the similar one of producing an artistically good design for a piano (see p. 216) and the solutions that have been found, especially those illustrated in Figs. 478, 101, may be considered extremely satisfactory. Electricity solves the earlier difficult question of artificial light for the billiard-table with perfect ease: six or eight lamps suspended from the ceiling are hung low and screened with opaque shades. Here again the silk shades with frills at the bottom that are so generally used in England are the favourites and are the best-looking of all lampshades (see Fig. 160). The floor of the billiard-room is always a good wooden one. Only the circuit round the table is covered by a wide runner. One occasionally sees linoleum used but, as we have said, it is really employed only for domestic offices and subsidiary rooms.

478 Stoneleigh, Kelvinside, Glasgow. By H. E. Clifford.
(See also Figs. 264, 270–271, 469) Billiard-room

Other rooms

There is nothing notably distinctive about the appearance of the other reception-rooms in the house. Where breakfast-rooms exist they are merely smaller and simpler versions of the dining-room. The furniture will be simpler: chairs, for example, will have rush seats instead of leather ones, the thick woollen carpet will be replaced by a more modest one and there will be a small sideboard instead of a large one.

Similarly the morning-room will be a simplified drawing-room, except that there will be no piano, nor will there be any little fancy chairs and small tables, for these are used only by afternoon visitors. There are, however, a few pieces for real work, including a capacious desk for the lady of the house and a table for books and so forth. The layout of the room is far simpler than that of the drawing-room.

The boudoir (see p. 88) has to serve many purposes. When it is situated among the reception-rooms it is often a particularly delicately, elegantly and consistently designed little gem of a room, for the furnishing of which owners will often follow French models. But if it is next to the bedroom and is a little private room for the lady of the house, in which no outsider ever sets foot, simplicity will be the keynote, however delicate and feminine the furnishings. The main piece of furniture will be a desk at which the lady will work; and book-cases, comfortable chairs and a sofa on which she can recline will complete the furnishing.

The room in which the man sees to business will be an absolutely simple and plain office-room with a desk, cabinets for papers and books and a large table in the middle. It forms a direct link with the better rooms of the working part of the house, i.e. the steward's, butler's and housekeeper's rooms, about the furnishing of which we have already said all that is necessary (see p. 100f).

The bedroom and ancillary rooms

1. The master-bedroom

Considerations of hygiene in the furnishing

Of all the rooms in the house the bedroom has undergone the most sweeping changes during the past hundred years. For the bedroom was the prime goal of the movement towards more hygienic living that, as we have several times remarked, has of recent years been the most powerful influence on the English dwelling. And this is understandable, for as regards time, the bedroom is the most used room in the house, the room in which we spend a good third of our life's span. So great is the preoccupation with questions of hygiene in the English bedroom that certain apostles of the cult go so far as to forbid window-curtains; they would rather see bare windows than be surrounded by so many metres of dust-trapping material. Wallpaper too is often avoided and, where walls are not panelled, they are plainly painted. Wood-panelled walls are nearly always painted white, the colour of immaculate cleanliness, because they show the minutest speck of dirt, thus reminding one to remove it. Floors nowadays are required to be made of good boards or wood-blocks and may be left uncarpeted; small rugs that can be shaken out every day are merely laid at scattered points: by the bed, the clothes cupboard and the fire-place. Because, as we have already seen, it puts many people in mind of the office, linoleum is very seldom used. All-over carpeting is still the commonest form of floor-covering, though, as we have said, it is no longer considered up-to-date and only survives because people are used to it.

The question of the ventilation of the bedroom is usually solved by sleeping with the windows partly open. Indeed, this is done throughout the year, only the amount of the opening varies between winter and summer. It has already been shown that sash-windows are ideal for adjusting the ventilation in this way (see p. 191).

Comfortable appearance

Despite these notions of hygiene, the bedroom is expected to look comfortable and snug. After all, in smaller and medium-sized houses it is the room in which the woman spends several hours in the morning writing letters, to which, if she has no boudoir, she sometimes retires in the afternoon and to which, in particular, she repairs several times a day to attend to her elaborate toilet. The aim is therefore to combine hygiene with comfort, care is taken over the choice of colours of materials, pleasing shapes for furniture, the form of the fire-place. This desire for an air of friendliness and comfort is responsible for, among other things, the fairly new fashion for once more abandoning metal bedsteads in favour of wooden ones. The introduction of the much-loved ingle-nook into the bedroom is another reflection of the desire to be comfortably ensconced in the bedroom. Washable cotton or silk are the only choices for curtain-materials – the call for curtain-less windows has so far found little response. The lower parts of the bedroom windows are always covered by the little short curtains discussed earlier (p. 194); they give a sense of privacy while dressing, etc., even when there is nothing opposite to overlook the room.

Built-in wardrobes

Built-in cupboards form a major element in the treatment of walls and are the most characteristic feature of the modern English bedroom (Fig. 481). They consist of sections of wall of the depth of cupboards and embrace every piece of furniture that is otherwise found in a bedroom. Built-in cupboards have become so popular during the past twenty years that it would be hard to find a newish bedroom without them. The writings of the architect R. W. Edis may have been to some extent responsible for their general acceptance; these appeared during the 1880s and recommended built-in cupboards very strongly, mainly on grounds of hygiene, as a means of avoiding dust-traps on and underneath wardrobes. But he did not omit to indicate that the cupboards must really extend upwards to the ceiling. For if they are made to terminate at a lesser height, one will be left with the same surfaces upon which dust will collect as with movable cupboards; and if the space above the cupboards is closed in and left unused by bringing the cornice forward to meet the cupboard wall a happy hunting-ground for rats and mice is created.

Built-in cupboards in the English bedroom often occupy a large part of the available wall-space, not infrequently two or three complete walls. On mature reflection one may conclude that this is excessive and may have an adverse rather than a beneficial effect on hygiene. For the cupboards are full of dresses, hats, underclothes and boots. The only way of airing the contents is to take them out, but this is seldom done, since it involves a considerable amount of work. To sleep in the midst of these crammed cupboards is like sleeping in a warehouse – assuming the best of cases, i.e. that all the things are new and unworn. Hygienically speaking it would be far better to keep only the

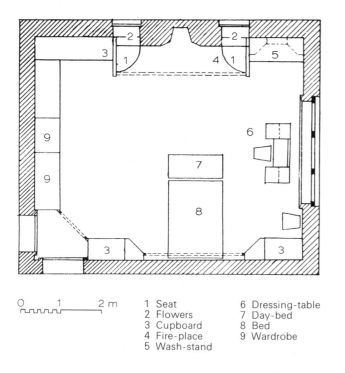

0   1   2 m

1 Seat	6 Dressing-table
2 Flowers	7 Day-bed
3 Cupboard	8 Bed
4 Fire-place	9 Wardrobe
5 Wash-stand	

479   Bedroom with built-in cupboards. Plan

480 Windyhill, Kilmacolm, nr Glasgow. By C. R. Mackintosh.
(See also Figs. 109, 110, 328, 419) Bedroom

482 Stoneleigh. Typical arrangement of furniture round the fire-place in a bedroom

most essential clothing in the room itself and all the rest in a clothes-closet that can be aired, that is, a clothes-cupboard enlarged to the size of a room with a window to the outer air. Another extremely questionable phenomenon of the ubiquitous built-in cupboard type is the wash-stand in a recess. It is contrary to the purpose of a wash-stand to build it into a recess, and all the more so if the walls of the recess are wooden. One needs elbow-room for washing and should not have to remind oneself anxiously not to make a single splash. The right kind of wash-stand is not built-in and, like the stand itself, its surround is of a kind that will not be harmed when splashed with water. All these considerations lead one to the conclusion that built-in furniture is often used to an exaggerated extent nowadays. Fig. 479 shows the plan of a bedroom in which there are far too many built-in fixtures. Almost everyone entrusts the furnishing of a bedroom of this kind to a shop, many of which execute the order with little thought, when it might very well be a worthy subject for an interior designer.

Advantages

Built-in cupboards have many advantages in themselves and are certainly to be recommended so long as they do not overstep acceptable limits. Built-in furniture in any form represents an advance on free-standing pieces since it saves a great deal of space and can be made to suit individual requirements far better than the movable, ready-made piece. Artistically it has the great advantage that it keeps the room free and empty, so creating an impression of spaciousness and size. These built-in fixtures should replace furniture in private houses on a much larger scale than they have done hitherto. For the one objection that can be raised against them, that one cannot take built-in furniture away with one, applies to rented accommodation and not to private houses. But even in flats some of the cumbersome household effects could very well be made superfluous by suitable wall-cupboards. The extra rent that this would involve would still represent a great saving to the renting public if it meant that it

481 Stoneleigh, Kelvinside, Glasgow. By H. E. Clifford.
(See also Figs. 264, 270–271, 469, 478) Bedroom

483 Stoneleigh. Typical bedroom with built-in cupboards
(from Liberty's catalogue)

225

484 Wooden bedstead

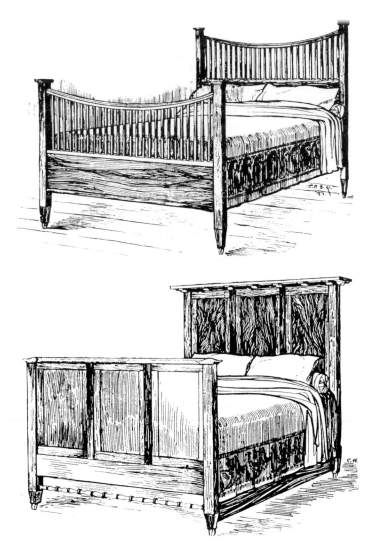

486, 487 Wooden bedsteads for double beds (Heal & Sons)

could dispense with some of its cupboards. The more detailed make-up of the built-in cupboards in the bedroom will best be explained as similar to that of the movable cupboards, which we shall discuss and which they have only recently begun to replace.

The bed

The most important piece of furniture in the bedroom is the bed, in the reform of which England has set the standard for the whole world. Metal bedsteads were introduced to replace wooden ones after the Great Exhibition of 1851. It is said that vermin were such a serious nuisance in London at the time that metal bedsteads were immediately recognised as the best remedy and became widely popular. The bed that had been in universal use in England until then was the traditional double four-poster. The old generation had their own views on the question of sleeping behind drawn curtains that shut out the air, views that we find surprising. Samuel Pepys in his *Diary* describes as one of his most painful experiences how, during the terrible days of the Fire of London in September 1666, when his house was threatened and he was obliged to seek shelter in that of a friend, he had to sleep in a bed without curtains. Nobody in the past had the slightest idea that it was unhealthy to sleep in the little enclosed space. Not only was the old four-poster sealed off by curtains at night, but the bedstead itself was entirely sealed. In earliest times the bedstead was filled with straw; later, the floor of the bed consisted simply of long planks of hard wood, which also had some degree of elasticity, on which a paillasse was laid. Spring-mattresses did not reach England from the continent until fairly late. But more recently England moved ahead again with the introduction of wire-mesh mattresses, which, during the past decades, have become enormously popular far beyond English shores.

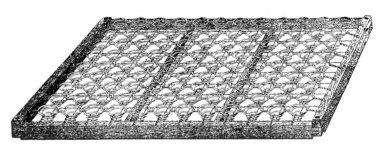

485 Spring-mattress (Heal & Sons)

The mattress

Largely because of its advantage to health but also because of its cheapness, the wire-mesh mattress became acclimatised quickly. But it must be said that in England it is far from being looked upon as a good bed and is used only in cheaper and more ordinary beds. One is therefore surprised to find that it has been introduced into otherwise good hotels in Germany, which pride themselves expressly on their 'English' beds. Their drawback is that the weight of the recumbent body causes them to sag in the middle like a hammock, so that the sleeper is put into an uncomfortable position. This can be partially counteracted by tightening the mattress but the elasticity slackens again in time and the trouble begins again. In the simplest iron beds the wire mattress is fixed to the bedstead. These bedsteads can be bought in England for as little as 15–20 M and a further 10 M for a woollen mattress will buy a poor man a comfortable and hygienic bed. The better wire mattresses are stretched on strong wooden frames.

A spring-matress is naturally considered a preferable type of elastic mattress in England too. It is the only one that provides complete comfort because the weight of the body does not affect the whole extent of the mattress but is taken by separate springs at each point. In place of the old mattress, once ubiquitous in Germany, with its upper surface covered by a layer of horse-hair or wool, we now use mattresses in which the whole base of springs is exposed – and again the change has been entirely for reasons of hygiene. The springs are held firm by a wire grid that links them together at the top (Fig. 485). These mattresses are nowadays considered the best in England; they are found in all good beds and come in various types; the commonest is a French one that is sold under the name of *sommier élastique portatif*. It has a removable drill cover and is hinged to fold in the middle. Apart from this, the German stuffed mattress (always referred to as 'the best German mattress') is still considered the best and is also the most expensive. Thus, together with German music and German beer, it is one of the few German products that really arouse respect in the English heart.

Other accessories

A woollen or horse-hair mattress some 10–25 cm. in thickness is always laid on top of the under-mattress. The wide difference in quality between wool and horse-hair means that the merits of these mattresses vary greatly and their prices differ accordingly. Fillings are often like those of the French, consisting of a central layer of horse-hair, encased in wool, yet the commonest mattresses are pure horse-hair. Spring-mattresses and horse-hair mattresses in England always have loose covers to protect them from dust. Another peculiarly English practice is to hang a removable white flounce from the long side to hide the bottom part of the bedstead. Sheets on English beds never hang down at the sides but are always tucked in on both sides of the horse-hair mattress so that it is entirely enclosed. To complete the bed there is a horse-hair bolster of the same width as the mattress which lies at the head of the bed and serves as a base for the pillow (which is always rather small). Wedge-shaped pillows of the continental type are often found in hotels but hardly ever in private houses. The English use only white woollen blankets to cover themselves and these are washed regularly at fairly long intervals. The advantage of woollen blankets as covers is that the number may be varied with the seasons, apart from the fact that they are washable, which is the prime consideration. Feather-beds and quilts are considered unhealthy because they make the sleeper too warm and cannot be washed. Cushions filled with very fine down have begun to be introduced recently to cover the foot of the bed, though more usually these take the form of a fine and very light quilted eiderdown the same size as our quilts but laid loosely on the bed over the top counterpane. This counterpane, in fact the top cover of the whole bed, is made of light material, preferably white, or often of chintz the colour of the covers of the furniture and the curtains (Fig. 483) and is edged with a flounce. It is never removed when the bed is in use for it would expose the blankets which are enclosed by a sheet underneath and this counterpane on top.

With the sole exception of the inside of the horse-hair mattress everything on the modern English bed is accessible and can always be kept clean. This idea has been uppermost in the whole transformation that the bed has undergone in England during the past fifty years. Any inaccessible part is detested. One encounters this notion everywhere in the English house, but it applies with special force to the bed which is rightly considered to be of prime importance in matters of health.

Metal bedsteads

There are two types of metal bedstead: one the type that is in general use, which is slightly higher at the head and lower at the foot and which is surprisingly known as a 'French bedstead' (see Fig. 483) and the other the form known as an 'Italian bedstead', with a very high head from which project two brackets to support a hanging. The Italian form is fast going out of use and must in any case be regarded as a transition from the old four-poster to the uncurtained bed. For it is difficult to understand what purpose is served by the relics of curtains at the extreme head of the bed; in order to protect the head from draughts the curtain would have to extend at least half-way down the length of the bed. Both types of bedstead are made either entirely of iron or entirely of brass or in a combination of iron and brass. The price depends mainly on how much brass is used. The most expensive brass bedsteads are usually artistically the most questionable, for they are smothered in hideous factory-made ornament, the brass parts are usually of a totally senseless thickness and their aesthetic effect is therefore devoid of beauty. The most bearable are in any case the absolutely simple bedsteads made of flat brass rods of moderate thickness, which are obviously machine-made (see Fig. 483). Now that the English custom whereby married couples share a conjugal bed is occasionally abandoned, pairs of bedsteads are being made that embody the idiotic idea that the head and foot of each bed shall rise towards the central dividing-line, which means that each bed is asymmetrical. Thus the old double bed with the central ornament now makes its appearance chopped into two. This is another interesting example of the usual process of an innovation coming into being tectonically via the old forms.

The form of the wooden bedsteads which are now coming back into use and replacing the old metal ones is further confirmation of this principle. The ends were at first formed of rods like those of the metal beds (Figs. 484, 486), whereas a closed panel is the obvious choice for wood (Fig. 487). The means of connecting the head and foot of the wooden bedsteads has also been taken over just as it stood from the metal ones. Iron sockets with vertical openings to the front are screwed to both ends and iron connecting side-bars are slotted into them just as in metal bedsteads. Wooden side-pieces are avoided because the result would be the old frame that had been abandoned on grounds of hygiene. Thus, as far as structure goes, these wooden bedsteads are in fact the old metal ones, except that the ends have been replaced by wooden ends.

The introduction of twin beds to replace the old double beds has meant that the beds have to be pulled apart every day before they can be made. To avoid damaging the floor-covering, flat iron rails on which the castors of the beds run have been devised. When not in use, the ends of the rails that protrude on both sides fold upwards at right-angles.

The wardrobe

The next most important pieces of furniture in the bedroom are the cupboards for dresses and underclothes. During the nineteenth century fairly capacious cupboards had developed out of the smaller chests-of-drawers and cupboards of the eighteenth century; these large pieces are now typical of those English bedrooms that do not yet have built-in cupboards. These cupboards have been much imitated on the continent. But the point about them that has usually been overlooked is that the clothes cupboard in three sections is meant to hold the woman's clothes, for, to the English, she alone has the prerogative of dressing in the bedroom (p. 91 f.). The man always has a separate dressing-room, where he has a cupboard that is arranged differently from the woman's. A third of the Englishwoman's clothes-cupboard is arranged for hanging, while part of the other two-thirds contains compartments for underclothes and hats and part open-fronted pull-out shelves and drawers. Of women's clothes only skirts are hung on hangers and go into the hanging

488 Lady's wardrobe

489 Wardrobe with three doors (Heal & Sons)

part of the cupboard, all the rest are laid flat, like men's clothes. The hanging part is usually, therefore, rather short, the total length also being reduced by a very deep drawer at the bottom (Fig. 488). These cupboards are seldom less than 1.83 m. (6 ft.) long and are fairly deep (at least 50 cm.) because the clothes-hangers must hang crosswise in the hanging section. The central door has a large bevelled mirror and the central section usually projects. The earlier simple form with three large doors at the front (Fig. 489) is often replaced nowadays by more picturesque forms, so that one-third is partly drawered and partly entirely open compartments and shelves (Figs. 488, 490). Smaller cupboards in two parts have been introduced: half of these contains hanging space and the other half pull-out compartments. And finally, two-thirds of the cupboard is sometimes meant for hanging, in which case it is usually anticipated that there will be another chest of drawers for underclothes or at least that the dressing-table will have capacious drawers at the bottom.

Wash-stand

The woman has a wash-stand and a dressing-table in the bedroom for her toilet; these pieces always form a pair in England and their form shows that they belong together (Figs. 493, 494). Since only the woman uses the wash-stand, it need not be double-sized as it is in Germany. The top and back of the wash-stand are usually made of marble, though this is sometimes replaced by tiles for both parts. From the practical point of view, however, tiles do not make the perfect top that marble makes, if only because a wooden border has to be left. Only when this is replaced by a metal border does a tiled top become acceptable. The lower part of the wash-stand varies considerably; sometimes it contains only one or two drawers with a shelf for boots at the very bottom; or there may be a little cupboard for chamber-pots, or it may have a closed cupboard with two doors for boots, or it may stand on two pedestals with doors that close, like a desk. Sunk wash-basins are rare; much more commonly the wash-basin, soap-dish and perhaps a larger sponge-dish and a holder

490 Wardrobe with two compartments

Built-in wash-basins with hot and cold water laid on, for which there is at the moment a real craze on the continent and which are considered the acme of comfort, are no longer fitted in rooms used for living or sleeping in England.

Dressing-table

No English bedroom is without a dressing-table; it is thought essential even in a maid's room. It stands in front of the window where the light is good. The back-view of the tall mirror inside the bedroom window is a familiar sight to anyone looking at a house from the street. This back view is, of course, not made to be looked at; if it were, it would at least have to be treated in the same way as the front of the piece. An even better way of getting over the problem would be to construct the dressing-table in one with the window: a mirror should be set into the central light of a three-light window, from which the daylight is in any case excluded by the mirror, the window-sill should be made a little deeper and drawers fitted to right and left in the surrounding wall-space. If the room has a bay window, the dressing-table will stand in the bay, but not so near to the outside wall as it otherwise would. This is an ideal position for a dressing-table, for, as she dresses, the user can at the same time enjoy the outlook to left and right (provided that there are no other bay windows on the same façade, in which case she could be overlooked from the other bays). The dressing-table consists of a table with drawers and a mirror above (Fig. 493). The mirror is always made to tilt and sometimes on both sides below it there are small compartments for jewellery. The lower part of the piece may be a complete chest of drawers, but this is unpractical since it makes it difficult to get near to the mirror. The best form is constructed like a man's desk, i.e. the lower part is open in the centre. The two sections on either side still provide enough room for drawers. The form in which the mirror extends down to floor-level is rare in England. The woman uses the dressing-table only for doing her hair and there is a large mirror in the wardrobe or a long standing mirror for full-length dressing (Fig. 491). A device using movable mirrors that pivot on a central axis and enable the dresser to see her head in profile is also rarely seen. On the dressing-table will be a good set of brushes and combs, which are very important to the Englishwoman. One sees sets made of ivory, tortoise-shell and silver; the most pleasing forms in silver are probably the

for tooth-brushes comprise the normal set of loose pieces for the wash-stand, with the addition of a porcelain pail and often a porcelain foot-bath. This ware has been white hitherto, often with painted decoration, but fine, colour-glazed forms have been introduced; they are quite without ornament and depend for their charm on pleasing contours and an interesting colour (Fig. 492). The basin and jug are very large. To the English way of thinking, every wash-stand should be accompanied by a towel-horse on which two hand-towels are held apart as they hang and so have room to dry. Towels dry much more slowly in the damp English air than they do with us.

492 Wash-basin and jug

493, 494 Typical dressing table and wash-stand (Maple & Co.)

496–500 Bedroom furniture in oak (Heal & Sons)

absolutely plain ones. The individual pieces of the set lie neatly arranged on a long-shaped tray of their own material. Candlesticks, bowls, bottles, boxes and caskets also form part of these sets. The top of the dressing-table is usually made of wood and is covered by an elegant little cloth. The greatest importance is attached to the appearance of the dressing-table in England; it must always be complete and immaculate, if only because the bedroom is sometimes used as a cloakroom for the ladies, in which case the guests will use the dressing-table (see p. 94).

Chairs and bedside cupboards

Two or three chairs, usually light in character and too small and unsuitable for real use complete the furniture of the bedroom. An English bedroom no longer necessarily contains a bedside table. These do not form part of a bedroom suite nowadays and are only made to order. This shows that on the one hand the habit, or rather the bad habit, of reading in bed is little known in England; on the other that the bathroom and lavatory that always adjoin the bedroom have already had the effect of relieving it of some of its uses.

495 Inexpensive bedroom furniture (Bartholomew & Fletcher)

Good taste in bedroom furniture

Ordinary suites of bedroom furniture, consisting of a wardrobe, wash-stand, dressing-table and several chairs, have recently appeared on the market in extremely acceptable, sometimes surprisingly good, designs (Figs. 493–506). Forms are simple and pleasingly proportioned and the absence of ornament is most welcome. The most popular bedroom furniture is made of oak (Figs. 496–500), sometimes stained dark with ammonia fumes; but mahogany furniture, once again using the forms of the Sheraton period (Figs. 502–506), also enjoys great popularity. For a time green-stained bedroom furniture was all the rage. White-painted soft-wood furniture is also obtainable but is chosen mainly for cheaper furnishing schemes. Since wooden bedsteads have been re-introduced, it will be necessary to include a bed to match the forms of the other furniture.

Make-up of the built-in cupboard

Since the built-in bedroom cupboard is intended to combine within itself all the purposes that would otherwise be served by a wardrobe, including, perhaps, a chest of drawers for under-clothes, a wash-stand and sometimes a wardrobe with a full-length mirror, it contains a mixture of hanging space, drawers, pull-out shelves, boot-racks, hat-cupboards and shelves for underwear. The relative proportions of the individual compart-ments depend on immediate requirements. Besides the closed compartments, there are often a few open, niche-like areas, which may perhaps be shut off by little curtains, in which to keep lighter articles; and possibly also a few book-shelves. Little additions of this kind are desirable also because they make for variety in what can easily become the monotonous and heavy effect of the fronts of the cupboards. For the aim in the bedroom is not severity and solidity but cheerful, friendly comfort.

Other articles

The furniture that we have already examined as part of the ready-made suites is considered insufficient to make a bedroom

501 Wickerwork basket for soiled linen

502–506 Mahogany bedroom furniture (Story & Co.)

cosy and comfortable. The main extras required are a sofa and one or two comfortable armchairs. The armchairs are sometimes quite tall and enclosed on both sides like a beach-chair, to give complete protection from draught to the occupant sitting by the fire. The sofa stands at the foot of the bed or beds. Since the head of the bed is always against the wall with the foot jutting out into the room (see Fig. 162 for the position of the furniture in the bedroom), the sofa occupies the very position in front of the fire that is desired (Fig. 482).

The fire-place itself is often comfortably arranged, where possible with seats. With built-in cupboards it will not be difficult to provide these – if the bedroom does not already have an ingle-nook, which designers always try to provide in master-bedrooms nowadays.

Besides all this furniture there will be a small table for books, papers, etc. We have already seen (p. 92) that the lady of the house often has her desk in the bedroom. The sofa at the foot of the bed sometimes has a chest below it for the washing, dresses, etc. Soiled linen is otherwise thrown into a large wickerwork basket about twice the size of a waste-paper basket and is removed by the servants daily (Fig. 501).

Finally the bedroom will contain a series of small articles commonly believed to make a room cosy and comfortable; they include wall-cupboards (particularly useful in this context for medicines, etc.), book-shelves, shelves for vases, photographs etc., not forgetting pictures: framed drawings and water-colours are preferred, though prints are just about admissible. They must, however, be light and amiable in character.

The English bedroom is always expected to look light and cheerful. The whole room breathes a healthy freshness. It is evocative of freshly laundered white linen, to which an aura of sunshine in the open air still clings.

2. The dressing-room

The man's clothes-cupboard

As we have seen (p. 92), there is always a dressing-room for the man attached to the master-bedroom in the English house. It contains all the furniture in which the man's clothes and underclothes are kept, as well as a wash-stand, a dressing-table and a few chairs. Traditionally a man's clothes-cupboard in England consists of a piece of furniture with drawers and pull-out shelves, for a man's clothes are all laid flat when put away. Coats and waistcoats are usually folded; to lay trousers flat the bottoms are put together with all four seams lying exactly one above the other, so that the creases at back and front always remain the same. Clothes keep their shape better if laid flat instead of being hung up, though naturally one must see that creases do not arise from the actual folding. When lying folded, clothes are more or less in a state of rest, whereas, when hung, their own weight causes changes, e.g. vertical creases down the fronts of coats.

One cannot broach this subject without drawing attention to its comic side, which is that the whole male world on the continent today has artificial pressed creases ironed into its trousers in imitation of an English custom that is merely the natural result of the practice of laying clothes flat. Thus we have one more example of the imitation of a purely superficial phenomenon! Folding trousers will produce creases without pressing, provided that the same pair of trousers is not worn continuously. An Englishman always has a whole series of suits in use and changes frequently for different occasions and times of day. A modern Englishman requires a special suit for every occasion, occupation and time of day, each one appropriate to the purpose and varying conditions; thus a different suit is worn for chores about the house in the morning, for the business of the day and for the main meal; different again are the outfits for games, cycling, travelling, visiting; different suits are worn in town and

507　Tallboy for the man's dressing room

508　Typical clothes cupboard for the man's dressing room

country; this thinking has ousted the old popular idea of an every-day suit and another for Sundays in all classes of the English population. Obviously it has radically increased numbers of suits.

Each suit lies on one of the shelves that occupy the major part of the man's clothes-cupboard (Fig. 508). This usually consists of a lower section containing drawers for underclothes, ties, etc. and an upper section with two doors: when these are opened suits are exposed to view. Men's clothes cupboards may contain a small hanging section, but this is exceptional. There is space for shoes either in the wash-stand or on a special shelf that resembles a low book-shelf, the front of which is closed by either a curtain or a door. The familiar wooden trees are always kept in boots that are not in use. These are of great benefit to footwear, which not only keep their shape better because of them, but also last longer because the leather is prevented from collapsing. A dressing-room often contains in addition a tallboy like the one in Fig. 507.

Other articles. Washing and sleeping kept separate

Wash-stand and dressing-table are both similar to those in the bedroom, but the dressing-table is extremely simple. There is often a small shaving-table as well. There may be no wash-stand at all if the bathroom communicates directly with the dressing-room. In this case it is assumed that the man will do his washing when he takes his morning bath. Bathroom and dressing-room cannot be combined into one room because the damp that comes from the bath would damage both the clothes that are kept in the dressing-room and the wooden furniture. The English always go into the bathroom to wash. And the direction in which the bedroom department of our dwellings will develop will undoubtedly be towards the total removal of the processes of bodily cleansing and other more objectionable matters to rooms specially designed for the purpose. Not until this happens shall we be able to speak of a bedroom that meets the highest standards of cleanliness and general culture, of a room that is used purely for repose and from which all processes in the slightest degree suggestive of uncleanness are rigorously banished.

3. The nurseries

Day and night-nurseries

The arrangement and furnishing of the nurseries reflect the care that is devoted in the English house to the upbringing of children. As we have seen (p. 93f.), the children's department is separate from the rest of the house. Above all else the children enjoy a full measure of peace and their little – but to them so important – daily lives are not disturbed by the activities of the grown-ups. At the appointed hour, usually between tea-time and dinner, they make their appearance before their parents, where they feel and behave like visitors and are treated with the consideration due to visitors. The children's world consists of two rooms, one for the day-time and one for the night. It is considered quite inadmissible for children to spend the day in the room in which they have slept, because both rooms must have every opportunity to air. They eat, play and are dressed in the day-nursery.

Decoration

Both rooms are genuinely equipped for children, they are simple and solid, though not without beauty. The walls will be brightly painted or papered with a 'nursery wallpaper'. There are many of these to choose from; they depict animals, birds, figures from fairy-tales (Fig. 515), Noah's arks; all carry primitive designs that children can understand, in bright colours. All the artists who design wallpapers have done attractive papers for children: Voysey has been particularly successful in this field. A few furnishing firms, Story & Co. in London in particular, have recently taken up nursery decoration with enthusiasm; they showed two nurseries at an exhibition (Figs. 509, 510) that aroused great interest among the public and went much of the way towards starting a movement to transform the already neat and pretty nursery into one of unmistakable beauty. They commissioned the celebrated draughtsmen Cecil Aldin and John Hassall to do the decoration. Most of the designs by these artists, who are famed far beyond England's shores for their delightful illustrations to children's books, consisted of friezes of animals

509   Day nursery by Aldin and Hassall (Story & Co.)

510   Night nursery by Aldin and Hassall (Story & Co.)

and similar subjects, which stood out with redoubled charm from the otherwise undecorated walls. They are printed in simple colours and can be bought in the shops (Figs 516, 517) Wood-panelling is naturally best for nursery walls, even if it extends only to the height of the cornice. In the absence of panelling a washable paint is selected. Only above the cornice is it appropriate for the wall to be decorated with papers. The wall-to-wall floor-covering will be of linoleum or cork. The only rug will usually be a washable one like a very thick rough bath towel in front of the fire. These hearth-rugs also come with special patterns for children; Voysey has designed several with scenes from fairy-tales that nourish the childish imagination.

Fire-place

An English room of any kind, but most especially an English nursery, is unimaginable without a fire-place. The fire that glows is the glowing life of the room. Not only does it warm the nursery but also takes the chill off underclothes and other garments. No garment is ever put on a child that has not previously been exposed to the drying glow of the fire, a necessary precaution in the prevailing dampness. The nursery fire-place is of a special kind, combining an open fire with a device for boiling or keeping water hot and is often indeed equipped with a hot-water storage tank, from which hot water can always be drawn (see Fig. 167). The nurse can boil the water for her tea at this fire, but any other cooking at the nursery fire is out of the question; even milk is not warmed at the fire but on a small gas-ring or spirit-lamp. Since children are immensely interested in fires, the nursery fire must be doubly securely enclosed; and a large nursery fender, a guard of table-height made of brass mesh or wire-netting (see Fig. 509) is used for the purpose. Clothes are also hung on the fender to air.

Furniture in the day-nursery

The furniture in the day-nursery comprises a cupboard for underclothes and other garments, a breast-high toy-cupboard, with a book-shelf on top for picture-books (every English child has dozens of these), a play-table, a dining-table and various chairs. The play-table is low, but the dining-table is of normal height, is laid in the usual way and even has a vase of flowers in the centre. Children are supposed to become accustomed to orderliness and good behaviour at table at an early age and a correct table would seem to be the best means to that end. To compensate for differences in height, they have high-legged

chairs, the highest falling to the smallest child (Fig. 513). In this connection the practical American chairs have fairly successfully ousted the earlier English ones. We have already noted (p. 71) that meals are prepared separately in the main kitchen for the nursery and its staff. Special nursery table-ware marked with an N or decorated with a design suitable for children (animals, geese, little trees, etc.) is also always used. A maid brings all the dishes to the door, where the nurse takes them from her and serves them on the dishes that always remain in the nursery and so are washed up there as well. But clothes-washing in either day or night-nursery is strictly forbidden. Besides the articles already mentioned, the day-nursery contains a few comfortable armchairs and a chair that the English nanny finds indispensable: it has very short legs, the seat slopes backwards and she reckons that without it she could never lull an infant to sleep (Fig. 514). The infant will sleep in a cradle with muslin curtains in the day-nursery. The English hold that no child's perambulator should ever be brought into the room.

Furniture in the night-nursery

The nurse's bed and the children's beds are in the night-nursery. If there are many occupants it is important that the room shall be large enough. The nurse expects it to be furnished with the articles due to the upper servants in the house, i.e. a dressing-table as well as a wash-stand and a sizeable clothes-cupboard. The children's beds will be made either of metal or wood but are enclosed by railings all round and constructed so that the long sides can be lowered easily. Care is taken in the case of wooden bedsteads to see that there are no sharp or spiky parts. For the rest, the night-nursery contains nothing that distinguishes it appreciably from bedrooms in general.

Pictures in the nurseries

In addition to the fixed wall decorations, movable pictures play a large part in nurseries. A number of English artists deserve credit for having painted pictures suitable for children's nurseries, by far the most important being again Cecil Aldin and John Hassall. But even before them, good artists, especially Heywood Sumner, had painted excellent nursery pictures, though they were possibly a little too serious and pious for the youngsters. Aldin's and Hassall's paintings are not guilty of these sins. Children find their gaiety and exuberance quite fascinating and they can, furthermore, be considered almost model wall-decorations with

511   Chair for the nursery

512   Nursery wash-stand for the nanny

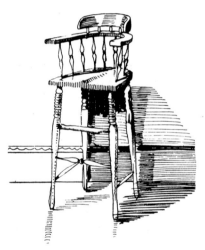

513   High chair for small children

514   Nursing chair for the nanny

515   Nursery wallpaper with fairy-tale characters

516, 517   Friezes of fairy-tale characters by John Hassall

their simple treatment of contour and colour. The best known are a series of paintings by Cecil Aldin of hunting and sporting subjects (*The Fallowfield Hunt, Mated, Revoke, The Whip, The Huntsman*, etc.). These are paintings of delightful freshness and liveliness of vision, in the same general tone of brilliant humour in which Randolph Caldecott in England was so influential that he caused a complete revolution in the illustration of children's books. The sentimental figures of children that used to be set before the young do not interest them half as much as these entertaining tales from the grown-up world, in which they are quick to discover the comedy and the felicities.

The nursery window-sill will be lined with flowers and plants in pots, in which children, guided by their nurses towards an understanding of them, are quick to take an interest. The care of children in England is a field that has been fully thought out, a highly evolved cultural development in which England is far ahead of the continent. It is pursued with a confidence and absence of fuss that is taken for granted and which is the characteristic trait of the entire English household. The most

234

surprising aspect of this regulated nursery upbringing is that it inculcates good habits and strength and freedom of will simultaneously. English children behave like perfect 'ladies and gentlemen' without forfeiting one iota of their childish freshness, naïveté and gaiety. More one cannot expect of education in earliest youth.

4. The bathroom

Development

Although the bathroom has long been of exceptional importance in eastern cultures, it is the most recent addition to the accommodation of our northern houses. England has led all the continental countries in developing the bathroom. The presence of a bathroom was taken for granted in England at a time when it was still an exception in the German house. The smallest houses in England have bathrooms nowadays and, though they contain very few rooms, none of the new workmen's cottages lacks a bathroom as an integral part of the dwelling. Because a general demand for bathrooms developed earlier in England, all the installations and parts connected with them were invented and developed there too. One might almost say that this was a cultural problem that was solved in England in the nineteenth century. Until recently the sanitary installations in the house represented an area over which England ruled supreme and all other countries were dependent upon her. Hand in hand with the general introduction of the bath at an early date went the general introduction of a hot-water system into the house (see p. 163). Without this, of course, a perfect bath is unthinkable, since it is the only means of installing a bath without irksome devices for heating the water. With the disappearance of the geyser we have seen the last of a piece of bathroom furniture that was difficult to use, sometimes dangerous and always unwelcome and the bathroom will become more hygienic, spacious and pleasanter in general appearance. Before reaching the bath, the hot-water pipes form a towel-rail similar in shape to an ordinary wooden towel-horse (p. 229; Fig. 519), a simple device, thanks to which dry bath-towels are always available and the room is maintained at an agreeable temperature.

Wall and ceiling

A hard surface for walls and floors is important in the furnishing of the bathroom. In the simplest bathrooms the walls are painted with a paint that is impervious to water; a better finish is

519 Towel-rail

obtained with hard polished plaster or with tiles; marble facing gives the best finish of all (Figs. 518, 520). The great affection for wood-panelling has meant that this has occasionally found its way into the bathroom, where it is usually highly polished. The floor is usually solid, covered with tiles or mosaic or, in the best bathrooms, marble slabs. There will be a gully-hole in the centre of the floor. Mats are laid at certain points; there is rarely a carpet. The floor may also be of polished hardwood. A bathroom ceiling is often smooth and slightly arched, so that any condensation can run down the sides.

Furnishing

A well-equipped bathroom will contain a bath, shower-bath, wash-basin, hip-bath, bidet, heated towel-rail, mirror, clothes-hooks, a shelf for towels and a receptacle for used towels. As we have seen (p. 93), a lavatory is practically never found in an English bathroom; indeed it is considered downright inadmissible to have one there. When, nevertheless, it is found, so unusual an arrangement will have been due to a particular wish on the part of the owner or some other circumstance. One must hasten to add that it is easy to assume from dipping into English catalogues that baths and lavatories are combined in one room. But we saw on another occasion how deceptive catalogues in general are. The compiler of the catalogue wishes to sell his goods and endeavours to show all that he can supply. Every firm

518 Bathroom from Shanks & Co., Barrhead

520 Bathroom furniture from Shanks & Co., Barrhead

that installs baths has lavatories as well and it is only natural that they should recommend installing as many of their articles as possible in the bathroom. The same applies to the hip-bath and bidet, which are not very often found in bathrooms, though they always appear in the specimen bathrooms in catalogues. In any case the proper place for the bidet is the water-closet rather than the bathroom. But in a house of any standing at all it is desirable and, indeed, essential to have one there and one may take it as certain that a later culture will regard it as an inescapable necessity in the water-closet.

The bath

Porcelain baths are the most popular and have entirely replaced most others. Copper still appears here and there; enamelled cast-iron is frequently used in cheaper bathrooms; but zinc is very unusual in England. In good bathrooms in the past the bath used regularly to be encased in wood; but the custom has now ceased entirely and all parts are expected to be accessible for cleaning purposes. A bath that is sunk into the floor, an institution that has no advantages of any kind other than purely romantic ones, is virtually unknown in England. The bath stands free on feet high enough to allow the floor beneath it to be washed daily; or else it is fixed to the floor and side-wall. Recently fixed baths have begun also to be relegated to corners. The attached wooden rim that was generally used in the past is disappearing today and to compensate for its absence the natural rim is made really comfortable. Suspended seats that made for greater convenience when bathing are sometimes seen. Metal holders for soap and sponges are also hung on the rim of the bath (Fig. 524); or else a bridge-like rack for the same purpose is laid across the foot.

The shower

The shower may be attached to the bath or separate from it. According to present ideas, shower and bath are best separated. In this case the shower will stand in a corner of the room; it is specially constructed of water-pipes (see Figs. 518, 520), from which a shower-bath sprays the bather standing therein from all sides at the height of the trunk, while another shower sprays the head from above. There is often a further attachment that sprays

521   Bath with shower-screen above

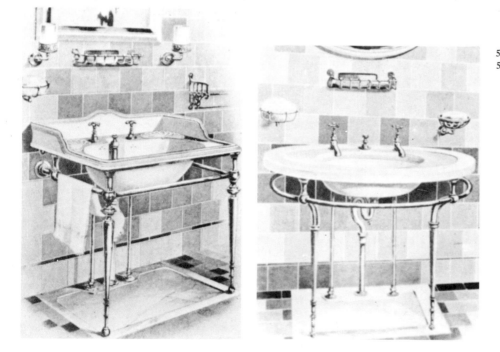

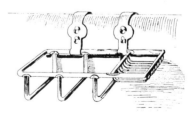

522   Basin fixed to wall on nickle-plated legs (Shanks & Co.)
523   Free-standing basin on chrome legs (Shanks & Co.)

524   Soap-dish for bath

236

from below. The whole structure stands on a flat marble or porcelain basin with a gully-hole in the centre. The whole apparatus is always enclosed within a water-proof curtain. One still often sees a shower and douche of the kind that was common in the past, where the apparatus is fixed to the head of the bath (Fig. 521). Here the curtain is usually replaced by a water-tight, half-cylindrical zinc surround. Since certain difficulties have always been involved in joining bath and superstructure, the vertical element is attached quite separately by screwing the four uprights to the flange of the bath.

Fixed wash-basins

England has developed a great many excellent forms of fixed wash-basin with hot and cold water laid on. Whereas the tipping basin was in general use in the past, fixed basins are now preferred, largely because certain parts of the tipping basin were inaccessible and therefore vulnerable to dirt. The modern basins either rest on brackets or stand on metal legs (Fig. 522) with one side against the wall, or else are wholly detached and stand on metal legs, which is considered the best arrangement since it does away with inaccessible parts (Fig. 523). If a hip-bath and bidet are built-in, they too stand free in the room. All the metal parts (legs, brackets etc.) are of either untreated or nickel-plated brass, taps and on-and-off devices are made of nickel-plated or silver-plated bronze. Space does not permit of a more detailed examination of the mechanism of these parts, for the subject has become almost a science in itself; but the English fittings are celebrated everywhere and form the foundation of the better installation businesses all over the world. The continuing development of this field in England is in the hands of a few influential manufacturers, who are ceaselessly engaged in trying to perfect bathroom furniture. Pre-eminent among them are the firms of Shanks at Barrhead and Doulton in London, whose catalogues are the best guide to the present state of development of the bathroom.

Other articles of furniture

A tendency to avoid wood altogether can be observed in all the articles of furniture in the present-day bathroom. The mirror has a metal frame; screwed into the wall behind the wash-basin are a sponge-rack, soap-dish, holders for glasses and one for brush and comb all made of elegant round metal bars (Figs. 522, 523). Even the receptacle for used hand-towels is made of brass bars.

The style of the bathroom

When this principle is followed, a distinguished style – artistic in the best sense of the word – is created in the bathroom; and if ornamental accessories, which always destroy the general appearance of a bathroom, are really kept out, a truly modern character will be achieved. It is so genuine and will endure because it has developed strictly logically and ignores sentimental or studied atmospheric qualities. A modern bathroom of this kind is like a piece of scientific apparatus, in which technique of a high intellectual order rules, and if any 'art' were dragged in it would merely have a disturbing effect. Form which has evolved exclusively out of purpose is in itself so ingenious and expressive that it brings an aesthetic satisfaction that differs not at all from artistic enjoyment. We have here an entirely new art that requires no propaganda to win it acceptance, an art based on actual modern conditions and modern achievements that perhaps one day, when all the fashions that parade as modern movements in art have passed away, will be regarded as the most eloquent expression of our age.

Absence of luxury

So that while the English bathroom, at its best, is interesting enough even from artistic points of view, there are disappointments in store for the visitor to England who expects really luxurious bath installations like those demanded by well-to-do house-owners on the continent. Large chambers with domed ceilings, opulent colour-schemes on walls and floors, a marble bath sunk into the centre of the floor and billowing cushions in the recesses are conspicuous by their absence in England. The bathroom is always the simple, plain room dictated by need. Everything is of the best, but the room is fundamentally modest and unpretentious. It is alien to the nature of an Englishman of standing to envelope himself in luxury; it is a role that would be painful to him, for he is a man of sensibility and his simple character would make it quite impossible for him to maintain the posture of a *nouveau riche* of imperial Rome or even of an eighteenth-century French aristocrat strutting on stilts above the heads of ordinary humanity. Everything nowadays moves on the same level and the level is a simple one. Not that self-confidence and pride are lacking in England. But a strong sense of justice keeps them within limits that makes any desire to overstep the bounds of convention unseemly.

Remarks in conclusion

To those with an intimate knowledge of England, this peculiarity of the English character, though little understood outside England, is one of the deepest causes of the phenomenon of the modern English house. There is no display or sign of high living, no outward showmanship or magnificence, no luxury or opulence. The greatest possible solidity and comfort are thought essential, pomp and circumstance are emphatically rejected. Dislike of pomp is often so extreme as to amount to a denial of art. Modern opinion would avoid even that which is so commonly dubbed 'architecture', i.e. the proliferation of articulating and decorative forms.

Everything must be plain, no matter if it be formless, and if the Englishman has always felt a special affection for the rustic, a wave of sentiment that idolises it has arisen today. There is still much of the peasant in every Englishman, although in England, of course, the peasant as a class has practically disappeared from the scene. But the natural, unaffected intelligence, the generous dose of common-sense, that we find in the Englishman, his fondness for his native place with its fields and ploughed land, his love of fresh air and open country – all this shows that some of the best qualities of the country-dweller have persisted in him. In no country in the world has so strong a sense of the natural and the rural been passed down to modern times as in the land of the greatest traditional wealth. Having advanced to a peak of cultural refinement thanks to resources that have been flowing in for centuries, England proves also that great influxes of wealth need not necessarily emasculate a people and corrupt their morals, as one historical dogma maintains.

Naturalness makes up the best part of the Englishman's character. And we see this character in its present-day form reflected in the English house more truly and clearly, perhaps, than in any other manifestation of English culture.

Index

This index contains the names of artists, craftsmen, architects and their buildings examined by Hermann Muthesius in *Das englische Haus*. It consists of two sections. The first is an index of names; the architects' names being followed by a list of their buildings described and reproduced in this book. The second section lists the buildings, under their names for country-houses, under places for other houses. In the case of named buildings in towns and villages cross-references also refer the reader to the appropriate place names.

Names

Buildings

Abbeystead, nr Lancaster, by John Douglas (*c.* 1880) for Lord Sefton 33; Fig. 47

Abergele, Wales, Kinmel Park by W. E. Nesfield (1866) 20, 22

Adcote, Shropshire, by R. N. Shaw (1875) 27, 90, 100; Figs. 32, 33

Albert Hall Mansions by R. N. Shaw, *see* London

Alderbrook by R. N. Shaw, *see* Cranleigh

Alliance Assurance House by R. N. Shaw, *see* London

Avon Tyrell, nr Salisbury, Hampshire, by W. R. Lethaby for Lord Manners 114, 176; Figs. 59–64

Ayr, Scotland, Hinton House by J. A. Morris Figs. 142, 421

Balcombe Place, Sussex, by G. C. Horsley Figs. 71, 72

The Barn by E. S. Prior, *see* Exmouth

Barrow Court, Cheshire, by J. Douglas 33, 102; Fig. 159

Batsford, Gloucestershire, by E. George 36

Bedford, house nr, by C. E. Mallows and Grocock Fig. 201

Bedford Park, nr London, garden suburb by R. N. Shaw (*c.*1880) 30–32, 58, 75, 108, 124, 148, 160; Figs. 37–45

Belgaum by W. Crane, *see* Woking

Bexley Heath, nr London, The Red House by P. Webb (1859) for William Morris 17, 124; Figs. 5–9

Bickley, Kent, stables by E. Newton Fig. 173

Birkenhead, Bidston Road, house by C. F. A. Voysey Fig. 416

Birmingham, house by W. A. Harvey Fig. 383

Birmingham, Law-courts by A. Webb and I. Bell 185

Blackhill by C. R. Mackintosh, *see* Helensburgh

Blackwell on Lake Windermere, Westmorland, by M. H. Baillie Scott 49, 130, 174, 175, 205; Figs. 103–108, 321

Bournville, nr Birmingham, workmen's village by R. Heaton for G. Cadbury 58, 60; Figs. 136–138

Brahan by Bedford and Kitson, *see* Perth

Brickwall, Sussex, garden Fig. 208

Brigland, Kinross-shire, Scotland, by R. S. Lorimer Fig. 143

Broadleys on Lake Windermere, Westmorland, by C. F. A. Voysey 42; Figs. 73–80

Brockhampton Park, Gloucestershire, by Atkinson Figs. 132, 374

Bromley, nr London, house by R. N. Shaw (1863) 24

Bryanston, Dorset, by R. N. Shaw (1895) 27; Fig. 36

Buchan Hill, Sussex, by E. George 36

Bullers Wood, by E. Newton, *see* Chislehurst

Cavenham Hall, Suffolk, by A. N. Prentice 79, 86, 89, 100, 101; Figs. 146–149, 174

Chesters, nr Newcastle, by R. N. Shaw (1890) 27

Chislehurst, nr London, Bullers Wood by E. Newton 39

Clencot, Gloucestershire, by E. George (*c.*1885) 36; Figs. 54, 55, 470

Cliff Towers, Devon, by C. Harrison Townsend 41

The Close by W. H. Brierley, *see* Northallerton

Clouds, nr Salisbury, Hampshire, by P. Webb 19; Figs. 12, 13

Cloverly Hall, Shropshire, by W. E. Nesfield (1864) 20, 100, 101; Figs. 150–152

Cobham, Surrey, house by M. H. Baillie Scott 129; Figs. 237, 238

Cold Ash, nr Newbury, Berkshire, by L. Stokes 45; Fig. 90

Combe Abbey, nr Coventry, enlargement by W. E. Nesfield (1859) 20

Compton, Surrey, Prior's Field by C. F. A. Voysey Figs. 180, 247–250, 326

Cragside, Northumberland, by R. N. Shaw (1870) for Lord Armstrong 24, 90, 175, 185; Figs. 24–26, 468

Cranleigh, Surrey, Alderbrook by R. N. Shaw 129; Figs. 229, 230

Cromer, Norfolk, Overstrand Hall by E. L. Lutyens Figs. 221, 222

Dawpool, Cheshire, by R. N. Shaw (*c.* 1880) for T. H. Ismay 27, 90, 91, 185; Figs. 34, 35, 161, 373, 426

Dickhurst, nr Haslemere, Surrey, by C. Harrison Townsend 41, 131; Figs. 226, 227

Dunblane, Scotland, house by G. Walton Figs. 341, 358, 382

Dunley Hill, Surrey, by E. George 36

Duntreath, nr Glasgow, by S. Mitchell & Wilson 62; Fig. 141

Earlshall, Fifeshire, Scotland, restoration by R. S. Lorimer 62, 118; Figs. 197–199

Eaton Hall, nr Eccleston, Cheshire, the Duke of Westminster's estate, cheese-diary by J. Douglas 32, 102; Fig. 46

Edgbaston, nr Birmingham, Garth House by W. H. Bidlake 55

Edgbaston, nr Birmingham, house by W. H. Bidlake 129; Figs. 235, 236, 356, 417, 418

Edgerton, nr Huddersfield, Yorkshire, house by E. Wood 46; Figs. 95–102

Edgeworth Manor, Gloucestershire, by E. George 36

Edinburgh, small houses in Colinton, by R. S. Lorimer 62

Elstree, nr London, The Leys by G. Walton 53; Figs. 115–119

Esher, Surrey, The Gables by Seth Smith 129; Figs. 242, 243

Eventide by W. Cave, *see* Woking

Exmouth, Devon, The Barn by E. S. Prior 129, 132; Figs. 244–246

Fernley by A. Marshall, *see* Nottingham

Fifield, Oxfordshire, house by T. E. Collcutt (1894) 36; Fig. 58

Filey, Yorkshire, North Cliff by W. H. Brierley Figs. 200, 214

Fives Court by C. Brewer, *see* Pinner

Flagstaff Hill, Colwyn-Bay, Denbigh, plan of garden by T. H. Mawson Fig. 182

Flete Lodge by J. D. Sedding, *see* Holbeton

Forest Row, Sussex, Pressridge, garden design by T. H. Mawson Fig. 196

Four Oaks, nr Birmingham, the architect's house, by W. H. Bidlake 55; Fig. 322

Four Oaks nr Birmingham, house by W. R. Lethaby Fig. 350

Four Oaks, nr Birmingham, Yates House by W. H. Bidlake Figs. 127–131

The Gables by Seth Smith, *see* Esher

Gallop's Homestead, Sussex, by C. H. B. Quennell 133; Figs. 256–258

Garth House by W. H. Bidlake, *see* Edgbaston

Gerrards Cross, nr London, Maltman's Green, house by W. A. S. Benson Figs. 86, 259

GLASGOW:

The architects' flat, by C. R. Mackintosh and Margaret Macdonald-Mackintosh 52; Figs. 111, 112

House by C.R. Mackintosh Fig. 438

House by E. A. Taylor Figs. 439, 440

Kelvinside, Stoneleigh by H. E. Clifford Figs. 264, 270, 271, 469, 478, 481–483

Miss Cranston's tea-rooms, smoking-rooms designed by C. R. Mackintosh 222

Godalming, Surrey, Norney by C. F. A. Voysey Figs. 190, 191, 423, 424

Greenock, nr Glasgow, home for sailors by E. L. Lutyens Fig. 126